Contents

W9-AUO-583

Map of Book 2[*]

In Unit	FUNCTIONS AND SKILLS Students will learn to	NOTIONS, TOPICS AND SITUATIONS Students will learn to talk about
1	Make introductions; ask for and give information; describe people; listen for specific information.	Themselves and their interests, people's appearance and behaviour.
2	Make commentaries; express doubt and certainty; take part in simple discussions.	Appearance of things; beliefs.
3	Narrate; express past time relations.	Accidents; basic office situations.
4	Describe; compare.	Similarities and differences; people's appearance.
5	Ask for things without knowing the exact word; make and reply to suggestions, requests and offers.	Shopping; household goods; clothes.
6	Predict; speak on the phone; negotiate.	Probability; certainty; the future; appointments.
7	Ask for and give information.	People's experiences and habits; national and local news; duration; changes.
8	Improve scan reading skills; link written texts; explain reasons for a choice; make reverse-charge phone calls.	Travelling to and in Britain and the US; holidays.
9	Ask for and give information; narrate; apologise and accept apologies; make excuses; link written texts.	Emergencies; causation; blame and responsibility.
10	Predict; deduce; describe processes; give instructions.	Conditions and probability; superstitions; cooking.
REVISION 11	Use what they have learnt in different ways.	Employment; they will revise vocabulary.
12	Ask for explanations; describe processes; express doubt and certainty.	Manufacturing and other processes; causes of past events.
13	Ask for and give directions; describe; define.	Landscapes; towns; houses; objects.
14	Ask about and express preferences; connect written text; express agreement and disagreement.	Relatives; family life.
15	Express wants, hopes and intentions; ask for favours; agree to requests; thank and reply to thanks.	Jobs; leisure activities.
16	Express opinions; negotiate.	Personal expenditure; budgets; quantity.
17	Narrate; ask for and give information; link written texts.	Time relations; habits.
18	Express opinions; report; use dictionaries when reading.	History; scientific discoveries; probability.
19	Make small talk: greet; welcome; ask for and give opinions; ask for repetition; take leave.	Job routines; food; entertainment.
20	Give instructions; give opinions; suggest; persuade; warn.	Housework; plans; the notion of orientation; personal problems.
21	Express preferences, opinion and obligation; complain.	Electrical appliances; breakdowns in common possessions.
REVISION 22	Use what they have learnt in different ways.	No new topics.
23	Give information; express positive and negative emotions; ask for and give advice.	Emotions; moods; personal relationships.
24	Express degrees of formality; ask for and give permission.	Authority; government; plans.
25	Ask for and give information; express likes and dislikes; negotiate; suggest.	Art and music.
26	Express notions of classification and deduction; paraphrase.	Animals and man; household objects.
27	Express possibilities; ask for and give information; hypothesize; describe.	Changes in people and things.
28	Express opinions and hypotheses; complain; ask for and give details.	Illness and health.
29	Express wishes; report states of knowledge.	Intelligence and memory.
30	Ask for and express opinions; ask for and give information.	Work; job routines.
31	Enquire formally; give directions; explain; request.	Means of transport; travel by car.
REVISION 32	Use what they have learnt in different ways.	No new topics.

[*]This 'map' of the course should be translated into students' language where possible.

VOCABULARY: Students will learn about 1,000 common words and expressions during the course.

GRAMMAR	PHONOLOGY
Students will learn or revise these grammar points	**Students will study these aspects of pronunciation**
Simple present; *be* and *have*; *have got*; adverbs of degree; *like . . . ing*, no article for general meaning.	Hearing unstressed syllables in rapid speech.
Present progressive; contrast between simple present and present progressive.	/ɪ/ and /iː/; pronunciations of *th*.
Regular and irregular past tenses; past progressive; *when*- and *while*-clauses; ellipsis.	Hearing final consonants; pronunciations of the letter *a*.
Comparative and superlative of adjectives; *than* and *as*; relative clauses with *who*; *do* as pro-verb; compound adjectives.	Decoding rapid speech; stress, rhythm and linking.
At a + shop; *a thing with a . . .*; *a thing for . . . ing*; modal verbs; infinitive with and without *to*.	Rhythm and stress; /eɪ/ versus /e/; spellings of /eɪ/.
May; *will*; *going to*; present progressive as future; prepositions of time.	/əʊ/; 'dark' l; stress and rhythm.
Present perfect simple; present perfect progressive; non-progressive verbs; *since*; *for*; *used to*.	Letter *e* stressed and unstressed at the beginning of words.
Can for possibility; *may* and *will*; linking devices for writing.	/ʃ/ and /tʃ/; rising and falling intonation.
Present perfect and its contrast with simple past; *there has been*; *make* + object + adjective or infinitive; past progressive.	/θ/ and /ð/; decoding conversational expressions spoken at speed.
If-clauses in open conditions; *if* vs *when*; imperatives; present tense as future in subordinate clauses; *when* and *until*.	/ɪ/; pronunciations of the letter *a*.
General revision.	Fluency practice.
Simple present passive; past passive; present and past participles; question forms.	Hearing /ə/; /h/; decoding rapid speech.
Imperatives; *there is/are*; *feel/smell* + adjective; relative pronouns and their omission; preposition at end of clause.	Decoding rapid speech; /iː/, /ɪ/ and /aɪ/; pronunciations of the letter *i*.
Would rather; *should*.	Linking with /r/, /j/, and /w/; sentence stress.
Want, *would like*, and *would love*; *want* + object + infinitive; *hope/going/try to*; *I/We wondered if* + past.	/əʊ/; decoding rapid speech.
Must and *can*; quantifiers; *will* for proposals; *too/enough to . . .*	Linking, liaison and assimilation.
Time clauses with *as soon as, before, after, until*; *still, yet, already*; *such* and *so*; past perfect.	/ɒ/, /ɔː/, /əʊ/ and their spellings; decoding rapid speech.
Reported speech; *used to*; word order in reported questions; modals; *likely*; *say* and *tell*.	Rhythm; initial consonant clusters beginning with *s*.
Question-tags; prepositions in questions; *so/neither (do I)*.	Intonation of question tags; fluency practice.
Infinitive of purpose; *by . . . ing*; *had better*; negative imperatives; hypothetical conditions; *ought to*; *Let's*; *Why don't*.	Consonant clusters with *ex*, final consonant clusters.
Should; phrasal verbs; present tenses; simple past; *won't = refuses to*.	Spellings of final /ə/; decoding fast speech.
General revision.	Exceptions to general rules about spelling/pronunciation links; fluency practice.
Let + object + infinitive; questions with *who* as subject and object.	/ə/; initial consonant clusters.
Simple present active and passive; *who* and *which* relative clauses; *must, have to, will have to*; emphatic imperatives.	Strong and weak forms of *must*.
Quantifiers; word formation; passives, and passive questions with final prepositions; interrogative *which* and *what*.	Pronunciations of *r*; intonation.
Although; relative clauses; articles; *a . . . one*.	Stress for emphasis, weak and strong forms.
Get-structures; past conditional.	Unstressed initial /ə/ and /ɪ/.
Verbs with two objects; relative *who* and *that*; frequency adverbs; reported commands.	Linking.
Wish + past tense.	Word stress.
Adverbs of manner with past participles; *have to*.	Pronunciations of the letter *u*; pronunciations of *au* and *ou*.
Deixis (*come/go, here/there, this/that*); modals of obligation.	/ə/ in unstressed syllables; /θ/ and /ð/.
General revision.	Fluency practice.

Introduction

The nature and purpose of the book

This is Book 2 of *The Cambridge English Course*, a four-level course designed for adult students who are learning English for general practical or cultural purposes. The material for each level consists of a Student's Book, a Teacher's Book with interleaved Student's Book, a Practice Book, and a set of Class Cassettes. There is also an optional Student's Cassette, containing some of the material from the Class Cassette for use at home; and a Test Book providing tests for use after each third of the book.

Book 2 is for elementary and lower intermediate students. They will have had perhaps 100 hours' classwork before Book 2 and will be able to use English to achieve a certain number of simple practical aims. Classes at this level are often composed of students from a variety of backgrounds: some will have followed *The Cambridge English Course* Book 1, or another good beginner's book; some may have learnt from inadequate beginner's course material, or learnt informally, or learnt some time ago. Students may have gaps in their knowledge of one or another area of English, or may have half-remembered knowledge. Book 2 is designed to accommodate a mixed-background class, and the first third of the book revises all important structures from the beginner's level; vocabulary revision also plays an important part throughout the Student's Book and Practice Book.

Student's Book 2 contains about 100 hours' classwork for an 'average' group (though of course the time taken to work through it will depend on many things: the students' mother tongue, the way their classes are organised, where they are studying, whether they use the Practice Book, how strong their motivation is, their previous learning experience of English, and various other factors). Used as suggested, the book will take students up to a point where they can understand and produce English well enough to handle a variety of everyday situations and topics with relative ease (a level somewhat above 'Threshold' in the Council of Europe's terminology).

***The Cambridge English Course* Book 2 is** different in some ways from most lower intermediate courses. For example, its organisation is not simply 'structural' or 'functional', but 'multi-syllabus': it is based on a combination of eight different syllabus-inventories. There is very considerable variety of lesson design and activity types; students often participate actively in choosing exactly what language they will learn; great importance is given to the systematic teaching of vocabulary; dictionary use is an integral part of the course; some reading and listening material is deliberately pitched well above the productive level of the learners; recordings of natural unscripted English form the basis of some listening exercises; pronunciation work is integrated into the lessons throughout the book, and includes linking of spelling and pronunciation. These differences stem from the principles which have guided us in writing the book, which include respect for the learner as an adult, with an individual learning style and adequate communication skills in his or her mother tongue; and respect for the language, which is complex and not susceptible of being mapped out realistically by means of a single syllabus. A more detailed description of the principles underlying the design of the course is given in the Introduction to Teacher's Book 1.

Organisation of the course

The course consists of 32 units, each divided into two lessons. Each lesson (which takes up two pages of the Student's Book) contains adequate material for a class of around an hour and a half with learners of average ability, so a unit will take roughly three hours of class time. In some cases spending 100 hours on the course may not be practical; for teachers in this situation the Teacher's Book contains suggestions about which activities to leave out of each lesson in order to save time, while ensuring that the main language items are learnt. In some cases teachers may choose to save time by leaving out lessons which are less relevant to their students' needs.

Each unit is organised around a thematic, functional, or notional area – for example 'Families', 'Small talk', or 'Causes and origins'. In choosing the subjects of the units, we have tried for a balance between those dealing with the students' own lives and those concerned with the 'outside world'. Some fiction is introduced, and language material is presented with the aid of fictional characters and dialogues where this suits the purposes of the lesson. However, there is not a standard 'cast of characters' or story-line running through the students' book. Much of the work is based on non-fictional material; for some of the activities imaginative input comes from the students themselves.

A revision unit and a detailed Revision Test occur after each third of the course, and can be used to see how effectively students have assimilated new material. These are in addition to the revision of basic language items undertaken in the first ten units of the Student's Book, and the revision of new items in the Practice Book. The Tests are in the Test Book, as well as in the Teacher's Book (where answers are provided for quick marking).

The Student's Book contains presentation material (introducing and demonstrating new language) and exercises. For some of the exercises, the teacher will have to make use of cassette recordings, or material in the Teacher's Book. At the end of the Student's Book there are Summaries of each unit, containing lists of the structures and vocabulary which students are expected to learn.

The Practice Book is intended for individual follow-up and revision work at home or in the classroom. It will make a great deal of difference to the students' learning if they can do at least some of the Practice Book work after each lesson.

The Teacher's Book provides detailed step-by-step guides to each lesson. These are intended particularly as a support for less experienced teachers, and for teachers who have little time to prepare. More experienced teachers, and teachers with ample time available, will probably prefer to approach the lessons in their own way, but they may find it useful to look over the Teacher's Book before each lesson. Note that some lessons cannot be done without the Teacher's Book. An introductory section in the instructions to each lesson lists the new language items introduced (structures, words and expressions, and phonology), mentions any special materials that may need to be prepared, and gives notes on language points that may present problems.

The cassettes contain recordings of presentation material, prompts for practice activities, listening exercises, pronunciation exercises, and some practice examples. Much of the material can be demonstrated directly by the teacher if preferred, but the cassettes are desirable for dialogue material and essential for most listening exercises.

Recorded material is indicated in the Teacher's Book by three symbols. The symbol 📼 shows that the exercise cannot easily be done without the recorded material; the symbol 📼 means that the material is recorded for the teacher's convenience, but can simply be read out in class if desired. The symbol Ⓐ indicates that the recording is authentic (unscripted speech of native speakers who are unaware of language teaching principles).

Using the book: general notes

Some students may be unfamiliar with the approach used in this course. If your students have not followed Book 1 of *The Cambridge English Course*, you may want to tell them before beginning Book 2 that it is likely to be different from other language teaching textbooks that they have had, and to explain briefly why and how it is different.

Monolingual classes will require some extra work on the teacher's part for the most effective use of this course. Designed to be used with students from a range of first-language backgrounds, the book cannot deal exhaustively with the special problems which English presents to the speakers of specific languages. Occasional mention will be made, in the *Language notes* at the beginning of lesson instructions, of a particular difficulty for speakers of one language or language group, but the remarks are usually more general. Teachers will therefore need to supplement the book with occasional information and practice on important first-language-specific problems.

A British model of the language is used throughout, but attention is sometimes drawn to important differences between this and other varieties of English; you will notice American, Commonwealth, and regional British accents in some of the listening exercises. While some elements of British culture appear, care has been taken to avoid parochialism. We have also tried to avoid a picture of Britain as a middle-aged (or youthful) white middle-class society of married couples with 2.4 children per family.

Grammar is more prominent in this course than in some single-syllabus, functionally-oriented courses. Most of the grammar is presented and taught in a communicative framework, but we have not hesitated to devote special exercises to questions of grammatical form where this seems necessary. Such exercises will inevitably look less attractive than others which are more directly communicative, but they are an important part of the course.

The vocabulary inventory for this book is based on a 'core' list of around 950 of the most common and useful words to be learnt at this level. These are carefully presented and practised, and listed in the language Summaries at the back of the Student's Book.

Notional lessons play a part in the book: these lessons, based on common concepts or 'notions', such as movement, distance, speed, or grief, will enable students to express essential ideas. Lessons of this kind are necessarily largely concerned with vocabulary teaching, and the lack of new structural or functional language items may make some teachers and students uncomfortable. But unless students can make appropriate and fluent use of the words and expressions that are needed to refer to common concepts, they will not be able to speak English, however much time they have spent on structures and communicative functions.

Presentation devices vary greatly from one lesson to the next: there is no one standardised format. Students may be taught vocabulary through a prose text, a dialogue or a labelled illustration; they may discover words and expressions by pooling their collective knowledge, by asking the teacher, or by looking up words in a dictionary; in some cases the 'model sentences' may be sentences of the students' own construction. This is not only for the sake of variety; different learning styles and personal interests require different approaches, and not all language items can be best demonstrated in the same way.

Pronunciation exercises are a regular feature of the book. Students need both to understand spoken English, and to speak comprehensibly; the book gives systematic training in these two aspects of phonology. Important areas dealt with in listening and production exercises include: hearing stress, remembering how words are stressed, identifying unstressed vowels and weak forms of words; identifying and producing linking devices between words; the regular relationships between spelling and pronunciation; intonation; certain vowel and consonant problems. We suggest that in all of these exercises, it is comprehension and comprehensibility, rather than perfection, that should be the goals of teacher and learners.

Learning to listen to spoken English, a major source of difficulty for many students, comprises training both in 'perception' (decoding sounds into words) and 'interpretation' (making sense of the words they hear). Interpretation exercises include practice with authentic recordings, to develop the skills that will help students manage to understand the English they hear outside the classroom.

Extensive reading and listening are important features of the course. Some of this material is authentic (not produced for language-teaching purposes); some is adapted or specially written. You may have to work very hard at the beginning to keep students from trying to understand every word. It is important that they realise that they need only understand some parts of the text – those that are necessary for the task they have been given. Note that, although the students' comprehension skills are often deliberately stretched, learners are never required to perform tasks that are beyond their capabilities. If properly guided, students will get into the habit of coping with material that is beyond their level (as they will have to do in 'real-life' situations in English), so that they can learn strategies for getting maximum useful information from this type of input.

Preview is often provided for important language items: you will find casual occurrences of new words in exercise instructions, sample sentences, listening exercises or reading texts. Students should learn not to worry about items of this kind, which will be dealt with in more detail later in the course.

Bilingual dictionaries are required for some of the exercises in the course: encourage students to buy suitable dictionaries (not pocket editions), and advise them on their choice if possible. In the early stages, you may want to help students in order to ensure that they are making effective use of their dictionaries. Show them, if necessary, how the entries are organised and what kinds of information they can provide. Make sure students understand that words have different translations in different contexts, and that they can only discover meanings with a dictionary if they learn to select the appropriate translation from among the several that are offered. As students work with dictionaries, they will become more skilled in autonomous work outside the classroom.

Interaction patterns vary from one exercise to the next. Many of the exercises require students to work in pairs or groups, which may be new for some students and teachers; but this sort of work greatly increases the quantity of practice that takes place in the classroom, and it is not difficult to accustom students to working efficiently in this way. (With adolescents, who can be difficult to control, it may be necessary to start in a small way with very short pieces of pair work, and gradually build up to more ambitious activities.) Mistakes may occur, but mistakes are an inevitable part of the learning process, and the more serious ones will disappear as time goes on. Some exercises, designed to sharpen 'survival skills', actually encourage the students to put fluency before accuracy.

Tolerance of error is a subject worth thinking about even outside the framework of group activities. It is obviously one of the teacher's rôles to let students know when they have made mistakes, so that they can adjust their map of what English is like and get closer to producing standard language. But individual students may be learning English for different reasons, and have different strategies for achieving the degree of fluency they desire. Some will aim for a high level of correctness; others will be satisfied with relatively faulty English. Provided students communicate effectively, they should not be given a sense of failure because they make mistakes.

Revision of newly-taught items has been built into the course in a cyclical fashion, so that the various language items, once taught, recur from time to time. This is not done in any mathematically regular way, but organised pragmatically so that each item comes up in various natural contexts. The Practice Book also includes systematic revision exercises, and students who use it will have a much more solid foundation in the basics of English. A revision unit comes at the end of each third of the book, and is followed by a Revision Test (in the Test Book; answers in the Teacher's Book). This gives students a chance to look over what they have learnt and consolidate their knowledge. They should be given plenty of time to prepare for the tests, if possible.

Practice Book work is of three kinds: extra practice in points arising in each lesson; revision of points that have come earlier; extensive reading material, with exercises to develop reading skills (these also contain 'preview' structures and vocabulary). Students' learning will be much more efficient if they do some of the Practice Book exercises after each class session. Note that few students will have the time to finish all the activities. This is deliberate: we have tried to provide enough material so that teachers can choose what is most appropriate for their students, assign remedial work for students who have problems, and give extra exercises to keen students who want to do more. Answers are given in the back of the Practice Book for some exercises, such as crosswords and general-knowledge questions; but no key is given for exercises where the teacher can easily see what the answers are.

The language Summaries in the back of the Student's Book contain the grammatical points in each lesson, and a selection of vocabulary to be learnt. These Summaries are not simply an appendix, but an essential part of the course. It is very important that teachers go through the Summary with the students at the end of each unit, to help them to focus on the material from the unit that they are expected to learn. Learning can be enjoyable, and we hope that much of the learning that students do with this book will be so; but a certain amount of work is necessary in order to learn a language at an appreciable rate. The Summaries represent the minimum that students are expected to learn in order to continue with the course, and they will have to spend some time with the Summaries between classes. We have included phonetic transcriptions for the vocabulary lists, on the principle that those teachers and students who want to use them can, and those who do not can ignore them. The transcription system used is that found in the *Longman Dictionary of Contemporary English,* with one or two minor modifications. We have marked primary stress only.

Knowing where you are and what you have achieved so far is not so easy in a multi-syllabus course as in a course with a simpler structure. The 'Map of Book 2', after the Contents page in the beginning of the Teacher's Book and Student's Book, gives an overview of how the different syllabuses progress from unit to unit. It would be a good idea to translate this Map into the students' own language where this is possible, so that they can have an accurate idea of how each lesson is moving them towards defined language goals.

Teachers should adapt and supplement the course, where they feel that it is not perfectly suited to their particular situation. Their experience and instinct will tell them what is right for their students, and for themselves as teachers. No textbook can meet all the needs of one group of individuals, and classes work in such different circumstances that the role of the book cannot possibly be the same in each case. Where time

allows, it would be very beneficial to encourage supplementary reading, perhaps with a circulating class library of simplified readers.

Please write to us with comments, suggestions, and criticisms on your experience with the book. *The Cambridge English Course* has been extensively piloted before publication, and all of the lessons have been tried out successfully in a variety of teaching situations. Nevertheless, improvements are still possible, and we would be delighted to hear from any teachers who would like to write to us. Letters can be sent to us c/o Cambridge University Press (English Language Teaching), The Edinburgh Building, Shaftesbury Road, Cambridge CB2 2RU, Great Britain.

Michael Swan   Catherine Walter   March 1985

Unit 1

People

A Tell me about yourself

1 Listen to the conversations and practise the sentences.
Introduce yourself to some other students. Find out their names and where they come from.
Then introduce some students to each other.

Unit 1: Lesson A

Students learn the expressions used in introductions; they revise the language used for giving and eliciting personal information.
Principal structures: revision of simple present tense verb forms.
Words and expressions to learn: *kind* (= sort); *spare time; football match; classical music; answer* (noun); *work* (noun); *introduce; interest* (verb); *travel; find out; go out; cheerful; glad; whereabouts; so much; I'd like to introduce...; May I introduce myself?; I'm glad to meet you; Nice to see you again; I didn't catch your name; What nationality are you?; What kind of...?*

Methodology and class dynamics

This lesson and the next one give students a chance to 'break the ice' and to get to know each other (and you). At the same time, you have the chance to watch a new class in action, and to see where their main strengths and weaknesses lie. The class will start getting used (if they are not already) to the methods used in the course; it will help if you can explain the reasons for any exercises which students find unfamiliar or confusing. If students are not used to working in pairs or small groups, this kind of activity may need to be introduced gradually, starting with very short and simple exercises so as to build up confidence.

If your students already know each other well, you will need to adapt some of the exercises slightly (see suggestions below).

Names

It is usually easier (and more friendly) to use first names, but note that students from certain cultures may find it strange or even offensive to use first names to strangers. Some students (for instance Japanese) may find it particularly difficult to address a teacher in this way, because of the seeming lack of respect involved. You may wish to tell students something about British and American attitudes in this area.

Note: revision

Structures: This lesson gives you an opportunity to see whether your students already have a good grasp of present tense verb forms and certain other basic structures. Weak students will find suitable grammar revision work in the Practice Book exercises for this and the next few lessons.

Vocabulary: Words taught in Book 1 of this course have not been listed as items to learn in the Teacher's Book (see 'contents box' above) or in the Student's Book Language Summaries. Students who have not used Book 1 may need to learn other high-priority vocabulary as it comes up. They will find this listed separately in the revision sections of the Language Summaries.

For a general note on the way revision is handled in the course, see *Introduction*, on page VIII.

If you are short of time

Exercise 7 can be dropped if necessary.

1 Introductions

- Start by introducing yourself and finding out the students' names
- Then play the recording, while students listen with their books closed.
- See if they can remember any of the expressions.
- Play the recording again (books open this time).
- Explain any difficulties (for instance, the difference between *How do you do?* and *How are you?*). Practise the pronunciation of the sentences, paying special attention to intonation and rhythm.
- Get students to introduce themselves to their neighbours or (even better) to go round the class introducing themselves to several other people. Join in yourself.
- Then get students to practise introducing people to each other (using the expressions they have learnt).
- If students already have some fluency, this can develop into a more general conversation involving questions about nationality, occupation and so on.
- Finish by making sure that students know *first name, Christian name, surname, Mr, Mrs, Miss, Ms.*

Alternative to Exercise 1

- If your students already know each other well, this exercise can be done using false names.
- Ask students to get into groups of four or five. In each group, they should give each other new names.
- When they have done this, tell students to introduce themselves to people from other groups, and to introduce members of their groups to other people, using the expressions they have practised.

2 Matching questions and answers

● This and the next two exercises test/revise a variety of elementary structures, and help to prepare students for Exercises 4–7.

● You may prefer students to work individually at first, so that you can see who has difficulty with interrogative structures and basic vocabulary.

● Let them ask you about words that they don't understand, or tell them to use their dictionaries where necessary.

● When they have matched up the questions and answers, let them compare notes with other students. Then go over the answers with them, explaining any problems.

● (Note that the Practice Book exercises for this lesson include work on interrogative and negative structures and third-person -s. If your students have serious problems with elementary grammar, you may like to go over these exercises in class after finishing the other work.)

Answers to Exercise 2
1c 2k 3i 4b 5f 6n 7a 8l 9e 10h 11j 12d
13m 14g (10g is also possible.)

3 What are the questions?

● This can be done orally (books closed): read out the answers in turn and let students try to decide what the questions are. Or get students to do the exercise in groups (books open).

Answers to Exercise 3
Various solutions are possible. For example:
1. What's your name?
2. Where are you from?
3. What do you do?
4. How old are you?
5. How tall are you?
6. Have you got any brothers or sisters?
7. Are you married?
8. Where do you live?
9. Why are you learning English?
10. Can you speak German?
11. What do you do in the evenings?
12. Do you like pop concerts?
13. How often do you go dancing?

4 Making up questions

● Make sure students understand that they are preparing questions for a real interview activity (Exercises 5 and 6). If they know each other well, they should avoid preparing questions to which they already know the answers.

● Encourage students to use bilingual dictionaries, and to ask you and other students for help, using the expressions shown in the Student's Book. (Explain these and practise the pronunciation if necessary.)

● When students have prepared their questions, look over them to check that they are reasonably correct and comprehensible.

5 Interviewing the teacher

● Try to give the students some genuine and interesting personal information about yourself. This will encourage them to feel that English is a real vehicle of communication and not just a classroom subject.

6 Interviewing other students

● If possible, make sure students work with partners whom they don't know well. Each student in the pair should interview the other.

● Teach the expression *I'd rather not answer*, for use if somebody finds a question embarrassing.

● With fluent, confident students the exercise may go on for a long time; with a less experienced class it may last no more than two or three minutes.

● You may want to give some sort of 'change-over' signal at half-time.

● If you have an odd number of students, put three good speakers in one group.

● In a multilingual class, try to ensure that partners do not have a language in common.

7 Reporting

● Before starting the exercise, ask everybody to tell you something they have found out about their partner. This will give you a chance to check on the correct use of third-person forms.

● Then get pairs to move into groups of four (you may have one or two larger groups).

● Each student should tell the new people in the group about his or her partner.

8 Introducing the Language Summary

● Show students the Summary section at the back of the Student's Book (pages 134–155).

● Explain that the Summary shows them what structures and vocabulary have come up in each lesson.

● Tell them that if they want to learn English properly they must memorise the important new words and learn the grammar. The purpose of the Summary is to help them to do this.

● For a note on ways of learning vocabulary, see *Introduction*, page VII, *Presentation devices*.

● For a note on the phonetic transcriptions, see *Introduction*, page IX, *The language Summaries*.

Practice Book
● The Practice Book is an important part of the course. It contains essential consolidation and revision work. (See *Introduction* page VIII.)

● Tell students which exercises you would like them to do; you may wish to go over the exercise instructions in class to make sure that students understand what to do.

● If you have plenty of time, some Practice Book exercises can be done in class.

WHEREABOUTS IN INDIA?

RECEPTION

5th International *TBA* C

3 Here are some answers. What are the questions?

1. Carlos Peña.
2. Venezuela.
3. I'm an engineer.
4. Twenty-five.
5. One metre seventy-eight.
6. Two brothers and a sister.
7. No, I'm not.
8. In a small flat in Caracas.
9. I need to read it for my work.
10. No, but I can speak a little French.
11. I watch TV or I go out with friends.
12. No, I don't, but I like dancing.
13. About twice a week.

2 Match the questions and the answers.

1. What nationality are you?
2. Do you do any sport?
3. What kind of music do you like?
4. What kind of books do you read?
5. Are you shy?
6. Can you play the piano?
7. What do you like doing in your spare time?
8. Why are you learning English?
9. Where do you live?
10. Do you like watching football matches?
11. What does your father look like?
12. What's your mother like?
13. Have you got any brothers or sisters?
14. How do you feel about snakes?

a. Knitting and reading.
b. Mostly novels; sometimes history books.
c. Austrian.
d. She's very calm and cheerful.
e. In a small town near Vienna.
f. No, I'm fairly self-confident.
g. They don't interest me.
h. I prefer playing games to watching them.
i. Classical music.
j. He's tall and fair.
k. Yes, long-distance running.
l. I'd like to travel more, and I think it's a useful language.
m. Yes, two sisters.
n. Yes, but not very well.

4 Write some more questions to ask people in the class. You can ask the teacher for help, like this:

'How do you say marié?' 'Married.'
'What's the English for Leichtathletik?' 'Athletics.'
'How do you pronounce "archaeology"?'
'How do you spell ....?'
'What does "hobby" mean?'
'Is this correct: "............"?'

5 Interview the teacher. Find out as much as possible about him/her.

6 Work in pairs. Interview your partner and find out as much as possible about him/her.

7 Work in groups of four. Tell the other two students about your partner from Exercise 6.

8 Study the Summary on page 134.

B Married with two children

JOBS: nurse; secretary; policewoman; printer's reader; works with racehorses; part-time.

BUILD: slim; heavily built.

CLOTHES: shirt; blouse; sweater; T-shirt; trousers; jeans; skirt; ear-ring; olive green; striped; short-sleeved.

1 Copy the table. Then listen to the descriptions of the five people and fill in the details. Here are some of the words and expressions you will hear.

NAME	Keith	Sue	John	Alexandra	Jane
AGE					
MARRIED?					
CHILDREN?					
JOB					
HEIGHT					
HAIR					
BUILD					
CLOTHES					

2 Can you put the right names with the photos?

A

B

C

D

E

Unit 1: Lesson B

Students practise talking about people's appearance and behaviour; they work on recordings of authentic speech.
Principal structures: simple present tense; *be* and *have*; *have got*; position of adverbs of degree; *like...ing*; no article with nouns used in a general sense.
Words and expressions to learn: *nurse; secretary; policewoman; T-shirt; ear-ring; history; newspaper; thriller; chocolate; wear; mend; part-time; slim; striped; least; I don't mind.*
Phonology: perceiving unstressed syllables in rapid speech.

Language notes and possible problems

1. Authentic listening material Students who have used Book 1 of *The Cambridge English Course* will already be experienced in working with recordings of natural unscripted speech. Other students may not have done this kind of work before, and could find it difficult at first. Exercise 3 provides an easy introduction to work on authentic recordings. You should make sure that students understand clearly in advance what is expected of them. Most important: *they do not have to understand every word they hear* (just as they will not understand every word if they listen to natural English speech outside the classroom). Their job is simply to listen selectively so as to understand the key information which is required for the task they have been given.

You will probably want to play authentic recordings more than once, so that students can get used to the sound of the language and pick out all the information they need. However, it is not usually advisable to 'go through' the recording intensively, writing up the whole text and explaining every word. This takes up time which could more usefully be spent on other things: the authentic recordings are designed for listening training, not for intensive vocabulary and structure work.

2. Be and have Speakers of some languages may tend to use *have* instead of *be* in certain expressions. Look out for mistakes like **I have 25 years*; **I have cold*; **I have hungry*. Exercise 7 helps with this.

3. Have got In informal English (especially British English), the normal present-tense forms of *have* (when used to talk about possession, physical characteristics and similar ideas) are *I've got, you've got* etc. Students may not be familiar with these forms, and may find them confusing.

4. Articles Students should note the use of *a/an* in sentences which identify people's professions (e.g. *She's a secretary*). You may also need to remind them that we do not use *the* before an uncountable or plural noun used in a general sense (e.g. *I like dogs; I can't stand chocolate*). This point is practised in Exercise 8.

5. Word order Students may be inclined to put adverbs of degree and frequency between a verb and its object or complement (e.g. **I like very much skiing; *I have often bad dreams*). The position of adverbs of degree is practised in Exercise 8; frequency adverbs are revised in the Practice Book.

If you are short of time
Drop Exercise 7 if this point is not a serious problem for your students; drop Exercise 8 or give it for homework.

1 Listening to descriptions

- Tell students to copy the table, leaving plenty of room to write in the information.
- Explain the vocabulary in the box (or let students look up the words in their dictionaries).
- Play the recording once right through without stopping.
- Ask students if they can fill in any of the spaces in the table.
- Play the recording again, while students take notes. Stop after each description for a minute or two so that students can enter their answers in the table.
- Play the recording one more time without stopping.
- Let students compare notes in pairs or small groups; then give them the answers.

Answers to Exercise 1
KEITH is 37; married; has got two children (a boy and a girl); is a printer's reader; is very tall; has got light brown hair; is quite slim; is wearing white trousers and a blue striped T-shirt; wears an ear-ring. (You may wish to comment on the difference between *is wearing* and *wears*.)
SUE is 33; married; has got two children (a boy and a girl); is a part-time nurse; is not very tall; blonde; slim; is wearing olive green trousers and shirt.
JOHN is 41; married; has got two children (a boy and a girl); works with racehorses; is very short; has got dark brown hair; is slim; is wearing black trousers and a blue short-sleeved shirt.
ALEXANDRA is 17; not married; has no children; wants to be a policewoman; is not very tall; has got red hair; is rather heavily built; is wearing a brown and white sweater and blue jeans.
JANE is 37; married; has got two children (a boy and a girl); is a part-time secretary; is not very tall; dark-haired; slim; is wearing a grey skirt and a white blouse.

Tapescript for Exercise 1: see page 178

2 Names and photos
- From left to right, the photos are of John, Alexandra, Sue, Keith and Jane.

3 Authentic listening: interviews 🔲 Ⓐ

- Go over the questions and vocabulary list, and clear up any difficulties.
- Tell students that they must try to note down the answers to the questions as they listen.
- Make sure they realise that they do not need to understand every word of the interviews.
- Play the recording without stopping.
- If necessary, play it a second time. (In a weak class, you may need to pause after each interview for students to finish making notes, but try to avoid this if possible.)
- Let students compare notes in pairs or groups, and then go over the answers with them.

Answers to Exercise 3
1. 7.30 to 4.15 (with a 45-minute lunch break).
2. Not very often.
3. By car.
4. Reading.
5. Sixteen.
6. Yes.
7. 'Just a little'.
8. No.
9. *The Express*.
10. Twenty.
11. Science fiction.
12. Keith and Jane.

Tapescript for Exercise 3: see page 178

4 Students' reactions

- Students should have reactions to at least some of the people they have heard. Encourage them to say whatever they feel; help with vocabulary and structures if necessary.
- This exercise may work best if students exchange their reactions in pairs or small groups before talking in front of the whole class.

5 How many words? 🔲

- This exercise gives students practice in separating out the 'stream of speech' and perceiving unstressed syllables (which are sometimes pronounced so quickly that students may not hear them).
- Play the recording, stopping after each sentence. Ask students first of all just to say how many words they hear, and then to try to decide what the words are.
- Play the sentences a second time if necessary.

Tapescript for Exercise 5
1. Tell me about your job, Keith. (6)
2. What sort of hours of work do you have? (9)
3. I start at seven thirty in the morning. (8)
4. I cycle from here to Didcot Station. (7)
5. Well, I'm quite interested in antiques. (7)
6. Do you go to church? (5)
7. A girl who is eight, and a boy who's seven. (11)
8. How do you get to work? (6)
9. It's only half an hour morning and afternoon. (9)

6 Descriptions: observation game

- Go over the examples with the students. Make sure they understand the reason for the present progressive in *He/she is wearing...*, and the use of *got* with *have* (see *Language notes*).
- Demonstrate the exercise with a volunteer.

- Then get students to do the exercise, either taking each pair in turn, or (in a large class) letting students work simultaneously and talk to each other (*You're wearing...*).
- (This exercise, and the following *Optional activity*, are adapted from *Drama Techniques in Language Learning* by Maley and Duff, Cambridge University Press.)

Optional activity   Observation game

- Get two teams of students (six to eight in each team) to stand facing each other about ten feet apart. Tell the students that they have three minutes to observe the opposite team without speaking. Each student must try to memorise the appearance of all the people opposite – clothes, appearance and position.
- Separate the teams. If possible, put one team outside the classroom or in another room. One person in each team acts as secretary; with everybody's help, he or she writes down everything the team can remember.
- Tell each team to make as many changes to their appearance as possible, exchanging glasses, jewellery and articles of clothing.
- Tell teams to come back and stand opposite each other again, but to line up *in a different order*.
- Students now speak in turn. Each student tries to get one thing put right. He/she might say, for instance:
  Juan, go and stand next to Fritz. Alice, that's Rosita's watch. Yasuko, where's your scarf? Brigitte, you've got Olga's shoes on.
  Put a few examples on the board (using these structures) to help students make their sentences.
- If possible, students should get the opposite team back in the original order, dressed as before.

7 Is or has?

- This revision exercise is only necessary for students who confuse *be* and *have*.
- It can be done individually or round the class.

8 Likes and dislikes; adverbs of degree

- Go over the vocabulary and explain any difficulties.
- Put your own list of preferences on the board, and then ask the students to make their lists.
- When they are ready, let them walk round comparing their lists, trying to find somebody who has exactly the same order.
- Next, go over the five sentence patterns and point out the word order (see *Language note 5*).
- Ask students to try to complete the blanks with three sentences for each pattern. Help with vocabulary if necessary.

9 Summary

- Remind students to look at the Summary on page 134 and learn the new material.

Practice Book
- Tell students which exercises you want them to do for homework. Make sure they understand what is required.

3 Now listen to the recording of the five people talking. Try to note down the answers to the following questions.

1. What hours does Keith work?
2. How often does he go to church?
3. How does Sue get to work?
4. What does she like doing?
5. How old is John's daughter?
6. Does John like gardening?
7. How much does he say he drinks?
8. Does Alexandra read history books?
9. What newspaper does she read?
10. How many hours a week does Jane work?
11. What does Jane not like reading?
12. Two of the five people are married to each other. Which two?

Before you start, make sure you understand these words and expressions.

> antiques   cycling   darning socks   decorating
> history   historical novel   mending   philosophy
> science fiction   thriller
> Dick Francis (a popular thriller writer)
>
> Newspapers: *The Express*   *The Sun*
> *The Times*   *The Sunday Times*   *The Telegraph*

4 How do you feel about each of the five people? Do you find them interesting or not? Intelligent or not? Shy or self-confident? Do you like or dislike them? Which one would you most like to meet? Which one would you least like to meet?

5 Pronunciation. Listen to the recording. How many words do you hear in each sentence? What are they? (Contractions like *I'm* count as two words.)

6 Work in pairs. Look at your partner carefully for one minute. Then close your eyes (or turn your back) and say what he or she looks like, and what he or she is wearing. Useful structures: *He/she has got...*
He/she is wearing... Examples:

'*He's got dark brown hair.*'
'*She's wearing a light green blouse and black trousers.*'

7 *Is or has?*

1. She's 37.
2. What's he done?
3. It's late.
4. He's 1m 85 tall.
5. She's got blue eyes.
6. He's wearing a dark suit.
7. She's hungry.
8. He's cold.
9. She's gone to London.
10. He's married.
11. What colour's your new car?
12. She's tired.

8 Do you like or dislike these things? Write them in order of preference. Then see if anybody else in the class has put them in the same order.

> maths   dancing   dogs   snakes   babies
> cooking   shopping   chocolate

Now complete the table.

I very much like ....
....
....

I quite like ....
....
....

I don't mind ....
....
....

I don't much like ....
....
....

I can't stand ....
....
....

9 Study the Summary on page 134.

Unit 2

Other worlds

A There's a strange light in the sky

1 Look at the pictures and listen to the commentary.
There are some differences. What are they?

2 How well can you remember the
commentary? Complete the commentator's
sentences.

1. 'Everybody .... up.'
2. 'The light .... from a
   strange machine.'
3. 'A door .... in the top.'
4. 'A strange thing .... out.'
5. 'They .... green suits.'
6. 'Now they .... across the
   field.'
7. 'He .... him over to the
   spaceship.'
8. 'He .... him inside.'
9. 'I .... down to have a word
   with our visitors.'
10. 'It .... out a gun.'
11. 'It .... it at me.'

3 Pronunciation. Listen to each word, and
say whether you think it comes in the
commentary or not. Examples:

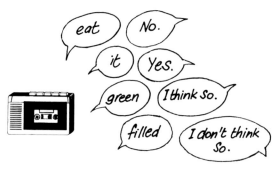

Unit 2: Lesson A

Students learn to make commentaries.
Principal structures: revision of present progressive tense.
Words and expressions to learn: *light* (noun); *sky; machine; suit; field; visitor; gun; strange; round.*
Phonology: /iː/ and /ɪ/.

Language notes and possible problems

1. Present progressive (present continuous) In this lesson, students revise the use of the present progressive to say what is happening at the moment of speaking. The Practice Book has exercises on the formation of questions and negatives, and on the spelling of *-ing* forms, for students who need extra work on this.

2. Non-progressive verbs You may want to point out that some verbs (e.g. *think, believe, wonder, see*) are not generally used in progressive forms in certain of their meanings, even to talk about things that are going on at the moment of speaking. Examples in the lesson: *I wonder* (in Exercise 1); *I think so* (Exercise 3).

3. Commentaries Both the present progressive and the simple present are used in commentaries. The progressive is used for longer actions; the simple tense is used for brief actions which take less time to happen than to describe.

4. Pronunciation Exercises 3 and 4 are only necessary for students who have a problem distinguishing between /iː/ (as in *eat*) and /ɪ/ (as in *it*), and for whom pronunciation is an important priority.

Optional extra materials
Cards for mime exercise (see the *Optional activities*).

1 Finding differences

• Give students a few minutes to look at the first cartoon strip.
• Then tell them that they will hear somebody talking about what is happening, but that he makes mistakes – there are some differences.
• Students do not have to understand every word in the text, but they must find the differences and make a note of them.
• Play the recording without stopping; students should jot down quick notes of the differences.
• Play the recording again so that students can complete their notes.
• Let them discuss their answers together; tell them any points they haven't noticed.

Answers to Exercise 1
The score is *England* 8, *Spain* 1.
The flying saucer is *square*.
The door is in the *side* of the saucer.
The things have *four* arms and *four* eyes.
They are wearing *red* suits.
Two of them take hold of Evans, not one.
The thing is holding the gun in its top *right* hand.

Tapescript for Exercise 1
... a beautiful afternoon here at Wembley, with the score at Spain 8, England 1. Campbell to Evans, to Murchison; Murchison on to Barker – and Gonzalez intercepts. Very

good play there by Gonzalez, by Gonzalez... That's funny. There's a very strange light in the sky. A strange red light. Everybody's looking up. And I think – I think I can see – yes, the light's coming from a strange machine. Not an aeroplane – it's round, and very big – very big indeed. It's coming down very low now, and – yes – it's landing. This is amazing. Now a door's opening in the top, and a strange thing is getting out. And another. And another. Three strange things are getting out. They're wearing green suits, and they've got – just a moment – yes, six arms and three eyes. Now they're walking across the field towards the centre. And now – one of them has taken hold of Evans, the England striker – yes, he's pulling him over to the spaceship. He's taking him inside. I must find out what's going on. I'm going down to have a word with our visitors. ... Excuse me, sir, er, madam, er, sir – I'm Brian Carter of BBC radio news. I wonder if I might ask you a few questions. Oh – it's taking out a gun. It's holding it up in its left hand – its top left hand – it's pointing it at me – Aaaaaaaaaaaaaaaargh!

2 Present progressive forms

• The purpose of this exercise is to refresh students' memories of the present progressive tense.
• Ask for the first answer. If students have difficulty, write it on the board and remind them how the tense is formed (*I am* etc. + ... *ing*).
• Get students to work out some of the other answers individually; then let them compare notes in groups before giving them the answers.
• Check that students understand that the present progressive can be used to talk about things that are going on around the moment of speaking, but not usually to talk about permanent states or repeated actions. The two present tenses will be contrasted in the next lesson.

Answers to Exercise 2
1. 's (or is) looking   2. 's/is coming   3. 's/is opening
4. 's/is getting   5. 're/are wearing   6. 're/are walking
7. 's/is pulling   8. 's/is taking   9. 'm/am going
10. 's/is taking   11. 's/is pointing

3 Pronunciation: /iː/ and /ɪ/
• Say the words or play the recording.

The words are:
eat (*NO*)   ship (*YES, in 'spaceship'*)   field (*YES*)
grin (*NO*)   it (*YES*)   sheep (*NO*)   field (*YES*)
green (*YES*)   eat (*NO*)   sheep (*NO*)   filled (*NO*)
green (*YES*)

• If students find this difficult, spend plenty of time on Exercise 4 (perhaps coming back to it several times during the course). If they find it very easy, drop Exercise 4.

4 Pronunciation (continued)

- Play the first part of the recording (or say the words), and ask students whether they hear words from column A or column B.

The words are:

eat   green   ship   field   it   green   sheep   filled   eat
grin   sheep   filled

- As a variant, you can ask students to write down what they think they hear.
- Now play the next part of the recording, and ask students whether the words in each group are the same or different. (Make sure students say *the same* and not *same*.)
- When there are three words in a group, ask which one (if any) is different – the first, second or third.

The words are:

eat, eat   eat, it   green, grin   filled, filled   ship, sheep
field, field   eat, it, eat   green, green, grin
ship, ship, sheep   filled, filled, filled

- Now get students to practise saying the words in the two lists. (These are recorded.) Note that the difference between /iː/ and /ɪ/ is not simply one of length – a long /ɪ/ doesn't sound like /iː/, and a short /iː/ is not at all the same as /ɪ/.
- Ask students if they can think of other words containing /iː/ or /ɪ/. You may like to mention *women* (/ˈwɪmɪn/), *minute* (/ˈmɪnɪt/) and *business* (/ˈbɪznɪs/).
- If students have trouble pronouncing /ɪ/, get them to relax their lip and jaw muscles, and to move their tongues down and back from /iː/ towards /ɪ/, pronouncing the sound without too much energy.
- You may like to get students to try giving each other 'A or B' and 'same or different' tests.

Pronunciation follow-up

- Remember that pronunciation training is useless unless it is followed up regularly. While working on the next few units, remind students from time to time of how /ɪ/ is pronounced, and (without overdoing it) pay a little extra attention to their pronunciation of words that contain this vowel (such as *if*).
- Note that the techniques used here can be adapted to practise any vowel or consonant distinction – you simply need to make up your own list of minimal pairs and proceed as in Exercise 4.

5 Students' commentaries

- Tell students to look at the second set of pictures.
- Get them to say something about what is happening in each one. Make sure they use the present progressive tense.
- Then tell students to work in groups, preparing commentaries like the one in Exercise 1. They should incorporate some factual mistakes – if possible, mistakes that they hope the other students will not notice.
- Help with vocabulary if necessary.
- When students are ready, get one person from each group to read out the group's commentary, while the rest of the class listen *with their books closed*.
- The listeners must try to pick out the mistakes, relying on their memory of the cartoon strip.

Optional activity   'Blind students'

- If you want more practice on the present progressive, it can be done as follows:
- Students sit in pairs, one facing the front and one with his/her back to you.
- Do a series of slow actions (for instance, stand up slowly, walk up and down, stop and look at one of the students, look out of the window, draw something on the board, . . .).
- The students who can see you have to tell their 'blind' partners what you are doing.
- The 'blind' students can then practise past tenses by trying to remember what you did.

Optional activity   Mime

- Prepare cards of two kinds.
- One set has the names of activities on the cards (e.g. *playing cards, singing, talking, shopping, watching football, playing football, taking a baby for a walk, waiting for somebody*).
- The other cards have one of these sentences: *It's raining. It's snowing. It's hailing. It's foggy. It's windy. The sun's shining.*
- Students work in groups. Each group in turn draws two cards and has to mime the activity, while at the same time showing what the weather is like.
- The other students watch and try to guess. (For example: *You're playing football. It's raining.*)

6 Summary

- Remind students to look at the Summary and learn the new material.

Practice Book

- Tell students which exercises you want them to do for homework. Make sure they understand what is required.

Unit 2: Lesson B

Students talk about beliefs, doubt and certainty. They learn some of the language of discussion.
Principal structures: simple present and present progressive tenses in contrast.
Words and expressions to learn: *death; a god; the future; an experience; belief; reason; expression; nonsense; rubbish; guess; choose; explain; definitely* (*not*)*; yes and no.*
Phonology: /iː/ and /ɪ/; pronunciations of *th*.

Language notes and possible problems

1. *Believe* You may wish to point out the difference between *to believe somebody* (= believe what he/she says) and *to believe in somebody/something* (= to believe that he/she/it exists).

2. *Agree* Look out for the common mistake **I am agree.*

3. Present tenses The exact rules for the use of the simple present and present progressive are of course quite complicated. It is probably best to teach very simple 'rules of thumb' at this stage; suggested formulae are given in Exercise 5.

4. Pronunciation of *th* Students may pronounce unvoiced and voiced *th* (/θ/ and /ð/) as /s/ and /z/, /t/ and /d/, or /f/ and /v/, depending on their mother tongue and the position of the sound in the word. Exercises 3 and 7–9 will help to correct this.

If you are short of time

With a weak class, drop Exercise 4; if your students' grammar is good, drop Exercises 5 and 6, or give Exercise 6 for homework.

1 Beliefs

● Go through the questions explaining any difficulties. (*UFOs* = unidentified flying objects.)
● Then put students in pairs. Ask them to write down their own answers, and also the answers they think their partners will probably give.
● When they are ready, let them compare notes with their partners and find out if their guesses were accurate.

2 Listening for gist

● This speaker has a northern (Newcastle) accent, but speaks slowly and clearly. Students will not understand every word, but they should not have much difficulty in deciding what his opinions are.
● Play the recording once through without stopping. Then play it again, pausing after each section so that students can write down their answers.
● Play it once more, and then let them compare notes with each other before checking the answers.
● Unless you have plenty of time to spare, it is probably not worth going right through the recording explaining everything.

Answers to Exercise 2

UFOs: *?* ('*I wouldn't say yes and I wouldn't say no.*')
Life on other worlds: ✓ ('*There's got to be... Yes.*')
Reincarnation: ✗
Life after death: ✓ ('*I've got to believe in that a little bit... There's got to be something there.*')
Horoscopes: ✗
Ghosts: ✓ ('*Definitely.*')

Tapescript for Exercise 2

UFOs. Er, well. That's a thing I haven't seen, so – I don't know. It could be, it can't be – it's – UFOs – I'm not – I wouldn't – I wouldn't say yes and I wouldn't say no about it.

Life on other worlds. Got to be, really. Other worlds – there's got to be life on them, there's life on this one, why not on others? You know, it's, I don't know. Yeah, I would say, life on other worlds, yes.

Reincarnation. No. I wouldn't like to give a reason. I just (You just don't think... that once somebody has lived, their soul can come back in another person.) No, I can't see that. I mean, a person is a person and that's it, you know – I couldn't see that.

Life after death. I suppose I've got to believe in that a little bit. What is life after death? Not coming back as reincarnation, although there's got to be something there.

Horoscopes. No. You can pick up two papers and they'll tell you different things. You can't believe in them anyway.

Ghosts. Definitely.

3 Pronunciation

● If students have difficulty with the difference between /iː/ and /ɪ/, get them to practise the first two lists of words.
● Then say or play the two lists of shorter words and expressions with *th* and let students practise them.
● Show them how to make *th* (with the tip of the tongue touching the bottom of the top teeth).
● Then practise the longer expressions, paying attention to the rhythm:

   I 'think that there 'may be in'telligent 'life...
   I 'think that we can 'learn 'things from 'dreams.

● Note the weak forms of the unstressed words *that* (/ðət/), *there* (/ðə/), *can* (/kn/) and *from* (/frəm/).

4 Discussion

- Explain and practise the expressions listed. Put students in groups of four or five and let them talk for as long as they find it easy.
- Help with vocabulary where necessary, but don't try to supervise all the discussions, and avoid making corrections unless it is absolutely essential.

5 The two present tenses

- Students have already revised the simple present and present progressive tenses. Here they see them in contrast.
- Get them to try to explain the difference in meaning between the two tenses (in their own language if this is feasible).
- An easy 'rule of thumb':

The **simple present** is used to talk about 'general time': permanent states and repeated actions.

The **present progressive** is used to talk about more temporary situations and actions which are going on at or around the present moment. (The use of the present progressive to talk about the future will be revised in Unit 6.)

6 Discrimination exercise

- This can be done as a 'whole-class' exercise, with students discussing the right answer to each question and clarifying their understanding of the rules as they do so.

7 Ear-training: /θ/ and /ð/

- Here students listen for the difference between:
  /θ/ and /s/ or /t/
  /ð/ and /z/ or /d/
- They must simply write S if the two words they hear are the same, and D if they are different.
- You may want to play the recording more than once.

Tapescript and answers to Exercise 7
1. thumb, thumb (*S*)
2. sink, think (*D*)
3. path, pass (*D*)
4. sheath, sheet (*D*)
5. thin, thin (*S*)
6. thanks, thanks (*S*)
7. they, day (*D*)
8. doze, those (*D*)
9. bathe, bathe (*S*)
10. there, there (*S*)

8 Ear-training (continued)

- Students continue practising discrimination of *th* sounds.
- Ask them to copy the list of words.
- Play the recording right through once.
- Then play it again, stopping after each item while students circle the word they think they heard.
- Play the recording one more time and let them compare notes with their neighbours; then check the answers.

Tapescript for Exercise 8
1. mouth 2. thin 3. taught 4. thanks 5. dare
6. bays 7. they

9 Pronouncing /θ/ and /ð/

- Before beginning the exercise, get the students to practise saying the words with *th* after you.

10 Summary

- Remind students to look at the Summary and learn the new material.

Practice Book

- Tell students which exercises you want them to do for homework. Make sure they understand what is required.

4 Discussion. Work in groups of four or five. Talk about your answers to Exercise 1. Did you have more or fewer 'yes' answers than the others? Try to give reasons for some of your beliefs. Ask the teacher for help with vocabulary if necessary.

Useful expressions:
I agree with you.
I don't agree.
I think you're right.
Definitely.

Definitely not.
Yes and no.
Nonsense!
Rubbish!

Language Study

5 Grammar revision. Compare these pairs of sentences.

They're walking across the field.
They usually walk to work.

The light's coming from a strange machine.
Our light comes from the sun.

What are you drinking?
Do you ever drink beer?

What is the difference between *they are walking* and *they walk*; *it is coming* and *it comes*; *are you drinking* and *do you drink*?

6 Choose the correct verb forms.

1. He *is smoking / smokes* 20 cigarettes a day.
2. What *are you looking / do you look* at?
3. 'Excuse me. *Are you speaking / Do you speak* French?' 'No, but I *'m speaking / speak* a little Spanish.'
4. 'Come and have a drink.' 'I'm sorry, I can't just now. I *'m working / work.'*
5. 'Why *are you driving / do you drive* so fast?' 'Because we're late.'
6. I *'m going / go* dancing every Friday night.
7. '*Do you often travel / 'Are you often travelling* abroad?' 'Four or five times a year.'
8. *Do you spell / Are you spelling* your name with one *n* or two?
9. 'What *are you thinking / do you think* about?' 'I'm not going to tell you.'
10. Water *is boiling / boils* at 100° Centigrade.
11. Can I turn off the TV? You *aren't watching / don't watch* it.

7 The same or different? You will hear ten pairs of words. If the two words in a pair are the same, write 'S'. If they are different, write 'D'.

8 Pronunciation. Can you hear a *th?*
Circle the words you hear.

1. mouth / mouse
2. thin / sin
3. thought / taught
4. thanks / tanks
5. there / dare
6. bathe / bays
7. they / day

9 Test other students. Say one of the words from Exercise 8. The other students have to say *Yes* if they hear a *th.*

10 Study the Summary on page 135–136.

The past

A A true story

1 Listen to the recording without looking at the text, and see how much of the story you can understand.

2 Read the text and fill in the gaps with words from the boxes.

ESCAPE FROM THE JUNGLE
(This is a true story.)

On Christmas Eve 1971 Juliana Koepke, a seventeen-year-old German girl, ... Lima by air with her mother. They .... on their way to Pucallpa, another town in Peru, to spend Christmas with Juliana's father. Forty-five minutes later the plane .... up in a storm, and Juliana .... 3,000 metres, strapped in her seat. She was not killed when the seat .... the ground (perhaps because trees broke her fall), but she .... all night unconscious.

The next morning Juliana .... for pieces of the plane, and .... for her mother. Nobody answered, and she .... nothing except a small plastic bag of sweets.

Juliana's collar bone was broken, one knee was badly hurt and she had deep cuts on her arms and legs. She had no shoes; her glasses were broken (so she could not .... snakes or spiders, for example); and she was wearing only a very short dress, which was badly torn. But she decided to try to .... out of the jungle, because she .... that if she stayed there she would die.

So Juliana .... to walk. She did not .... anything to eat, and as the days went by she got weaker and weaker. She was also in bad trouble from insect bites. She .... helicopters, but could not see them above the trees, and of course they could not see her. One day she .... three seats and .... that they had dead bodies in them, but she did not recognise the people.

After four days she .... to a river. She saw caimans and piranhas, but she .... that they do not usually attack people. So Juliana walked and .... down the river for another five days. At last she .... to a hut. Nobody was there, but the next afternoon, four men arrived. They .... her to a doctor in the next village.

Juliana .... afterwards that there were at least three other people who were not killed in the crash. But she was the only one who .... out of the jungle. It took her ten days.

Put the correct forms of these verbs into the gaps marked .

be   break   call   fall
find   hit   leave   lie   look

Put the correct forms of these verbs into the gaps marked .

find   find   get   hear
know   see   see   start

Put the correct forms of these verbs into the gaps marked .

come   come   get
know   learn   swim   take

sweets   snake   spider   piranha   caiman   hut   helicopter

14

Unit 3: Lesson A

Students work on the language of past narrative.
Principal structures: revision of regular and irregular past verb forms.
Words and expressions to learn: *Christmas; Christmas Eve; storm; bag; sweets; bone; knee; cut (noun); helicopter; call; hit; stay; recognise; deep; above; afterwards.*
Phonology: perceiving final consonants.

Language notes and possible problems

1. Irregular verbs In this lesson, students concentrate on revising irregular past tenses. Past participles will be revised later. (There is also frequent revision of irregular verbs in the Practice Book.)

2. Past tenses A common mistake is to use the past tense instead of the infinitive after *did*. (For example **She did not saw*; **Did you saw?*) Exercise 4 deals with this, and there is further work on the point in the Practice Book, if this is needed.

3. Pronunciation of *-ed* If your students are aiming at a very high standard of pronunciation, you may wish to work on the different pronunciations of the past ending *-ed*:
a. after a voiced sound: /d/ (e.g. *called*)
b. after an unvoiced sound: /t/ (e.g. *looked*)
c. after /t/ or /d/: /ɪd/ (e.g. *started*)

4. Pronunciation: final consonants Some students have difficulty distinguishing final consonants and consonant clusters (particularly if their language has a simpler syllable structure than English). This can lead to grammar problems, since they may not hear the difference between, for example, *stop, stops* and *stopped*. Exercise 6 will help with this.

5. Spelling The Summary (page 136) contains revision notes on the spelling of regular past tenses.

6. Level This is a more difficult lesson than those in Units 1 and 2. The text work is quite demanding, and weak students may not be able to get through all of it. Note, however, that there is no need for students to understand every word of the text.

If you are short of time

Leave some of Exercise 2 for homework, or drop Exercise 7. Drop Exercise 3. Drop Exercise 6 if the point is not difficult for your students.

1 Listening for gist

● Get the students to close their books. Make sure they understand the title *Escape from the jungle*. You may also want to pre-teach *by air* and *plane*, if you are not sure that everybody knows them.
● Play the recording once through without stopping. Students will not of course understand everything, but this does not matter. Ask them to tell you anything they can remember, from any part of the story. Don't be too perfectionist – the main thing at this stage is that the students should say *something*.
● Play the recording again, and see if students can recall the story in a more organised form.

2 The text; irregular verbs

● Let students open their books, and give them a few minutes to read over the text and look at the illustrations.
● Let them use dictionaries, or ask about difficult words, within reason, but encourage them to guess the meanings of new words from the context and the illustrations.
● Then get them to do the first part of the exercise. They should write down in order the verb forms which belong in the gaps coloured blue.
● When students are ready, let them compare notes in pairs or groups, and then check the answers with them.
● The second and third parts of the exercise can be done in the same way, or (for the sake of variety) by whole-class discussion.
● If time is short, leave some of this for homework.

Answers to Exercise 2
1. left were broke fell hit lay looked called found
2. see get knew started find heard found saw
3. came knew swam came took learnt (*or* learned) got

14

3 Recall

- Ask students to close their books again.
- Play the recording, or say the sentences. After each sentence, students should write S (if the sentence corresponds to the text) or D (if it doesn't).
- Let them compare notes with their neighbours, and then go over the answers with them.

Tapescript and answers to Exercise 3
1. Juliana left Lima by air on Christmas Eve. (S)
2. Juliana fell 5,000 metres when the plane broke up. (D)
3. She lay unconscious all day. (D)
4. She had no shoes or glasses. (S)
5. She had a broken bone. (S)
6. She found some fruit to eat. (D)
7. After walking for four days, she came to a river. (S)
8. The river was very cold. (D)
9. Juliana walked and swam down the river for five days. (S)
10. At last, she came to a hut with four men in. (D)

4 Grammar: past tenses

- The purpose of this exercise is simply to ensure that students have no trouble making past tense questions.
- It is probably best to ask students to write the answers individually, so that you can spot anybody who has a problem.

5 Students' questions

- Give students a few minutes to prepare their questions. Go round helping where necessary, and check that there are no serious mistakes.
- Before students start asking their questions, practise the 'first-aid' sentences illustrated (*Sorry, could you say that again?* etc.).

6 Pronunciation

- Tell students to write down the words.
- Then play the recording, pausing after each sentence so that students can circle the word they think they hear.
- Let them compare notes and then check their answers.

Tapescript for Exercise 6
1. She worked in a jeweller's.
2. It rained almost every day.
3. It's starting early.
4. There's something wrong with it.
5. It smelt strange.
6. It stops quite often.
7. There was no sound.
8. We tried to help them.
9. She puts food out for the birds.
10. My car's using a lot of oil.

7 Conversation

- Before starting the exercise, ask students to think for a minute or two, to try to remember a bad day in their lives. When they are ready, tell them to work in groups and tell each other about the experience in question.
- You may like to start the ball rolling by telling them a very simple story about an experience of your own.
- This is a fluency exercise, so it is best to let students talk freely without correcting them. If you join one of the groups, choose a confident group which will not be intimidated by your presence.

8 Summary

- Remind students to look over the Summary and learn the new material.

Practice Book
- Tell students which exercises you want them to do.

15

5 Prepare five questions about the text.
Example:

'When did Juliana leave Lima?'

When you are ready, work with another
student. Close your book. Ask your questions,
and answer your partner's.
If you have problems understanding each
other, use these sentences to help you.

'Sorry, could you say that again?'
'I'm sorry, I don't understand.'
'What do you mean?'

If you can't answer a question, say:

'Sorry, I don't know.'
'I'm afraid I can't remember.'

6 Pronunciation. Copy these words. Then
listen to the recording and circle the words you
hear.

1. works / worked
2. rains / rained
3. starting / started
4. There's / There was
5. smells / smelt
6. stops / stopped
7. There's / There was
8. try / tried
9. puts / put
10. using / uses

3 Can you remember what you read? Close
your book, listen to the recording, and write 'S'
('the same') or 'D' ('different') for each
sentence.

4 Put in the correct forms.

1. How did Juliana *leave / left* Lima?
2. She *leave / left* by air.
3. How far did Juliana *fall / fell*?
4. She *fall / fell* 3,000 metres.
5. What did Juliana *look / looked* for?
6. She *look / looked* for pieces of the plane.

7 Work in groups of five or
six. Tell other students about
a bad day in your life.

8 Study the Summary on
page 136.

B Did you have a good day?

1 Listen to the conversation with your book closed. Who did Lorna talk to during the day?

GEORGE: Hello, darling. Did you have a good day?

LORNA: Not bad. The usual sort of thing. Meetings, phone calls, letters. You know.

GEORGE: Did you see anybody interesting?

LORNA: Well, Chris came into the office this morning. We had a long talk.

GEORGE: Oh, yes? What about?

LORNA: Oh, this and that. Things. You know.

GEORGE: I see.

LORNA: And then Janet turned up. As usual. Just when I was trying to finish some work.

GEORGE: So what did you do?

LORNA: Had lunch with her.

GEORGE: Where did you go? Somewhere nice?

LORNA: No. Just the pub round the corner. A pie and a pint, you know. Then in the afternoon there was a budget meeting. It went on for hours.

GEORGE: Sounds like a boring day. Did anything interesting happen?

LORNA: Don't think so, not really. Can't remember. Oh, yes, one thing. Something rather strange.

GEORGE: What?

LORNA: Well, it was this evening. I was getting ready to come home. And the phone rang. So I picked it up. And there was this man.

GEORGE: Who?

LORNA: Well, I don't know. He wouldn't say who he was. But he asked me to have lunch with him tomorrow.

GEORGE: What?

LORNA: Yes. He said he wanted to talk to me. About something very important.

GEORGE: So what did you say?

LORNA: Well, I said yes, of course. How was your day?

2 Look at this sentence.

Had lunch with her.

Lorna leaves out the pronoun *I*. Can you find any more sentences where Lorna leaves out words?

3 Now listen again to George's side of the conversation with your book closed. Can you remember the beginnings of Lorna's answers?

Unit 3: Lesson B

Students learn more about expressing past time relations.

Structures: past progressive; *when*- and *while*-clauses; introduction to ellipsis.

Words and expressions to learn: *darling; meeting; talk (noun); phone call; memory; turn up; go on; get ready; rather; together; you know; I see; as usual; round the corner; sound like; not really; I can't remember.*

Phonology: pronunciations of the letter *a*.

Language notes and possible problems

1. Past progressive tense The past progressive (or 'past continuous') is often used to show the 'background' for past events – to say what was going on at the time when something happened. The past progressive is used for the longer 'background' action; the simple past is used for the shorter action which came in the middle, or interrupted what was going on. (See diagram in Student's Book.)

2. Conjunctions *When* and *while* are often used in sentences with the past progressive. Note that the *when/while*-clause can come either at the beginning or at the end of the sentence.

> I found some old letters **when/while I was cleaning up the attic.**
>
> **When/While I was cleaning up the attic,** I found some old letters.

Note also that *when* can introduce either a simple past or a past progressive.

> They met **when** she was studying in Berlin.
>
> **When** they met, she was studying in Berlin.

The rules determining the exact choice of structure and conjunction are complex, and it is not necessary for students to learn them at this stage.

3. Conversational syntax The dialogue contains some examples of structures which are more common in speech than in writing.

a. Ellipsis Subject pronouns are often left out in speech when they can be understood from the context. Examples: *Had lunch with her. Sounds like a boring day. Can't remember.*

b. Separation of clauses In writing, it is unusual to separate subordinate or coordinate clauses from the rest of the sentence they belong to. In speech, this often happens. Examples: *And there was this man. But he asked me to have lunch... Just when I was trying to finish some work.*

4. Somebody, anybody etc. You may wish to remind students of the difference between *somebody* and *anybody, something* and *anything.* Note also the structure *somebody interesting; something important:* this may be difficult for some students.

5. Have You may wish to point out the uses of *have* in the dialogue (*have a good day; have a talk; have lunch*).

6. Reported speech Reported speech is previewed here. It will be studied systematically later in the course.

If you are short of time

Drop Exercises 2 and 3 (but look over the text of the dialogue before doing Exercise 4). Exercise 6 can also be dropped.

1 Presentation

- Play the conversation while students listen with their books closed. Stop the recording before Lorna's last answer and see if students can guess what she says.
- Ask if students can remember the people Lorna talked to (Chris, Janet, people at a meeting, a man on the phone). See what else they can remember.
- Play the conversation again while students follow in their books.
- Explain any points which are preventing students from understanding the gist of the conversation. It is not necessary to deal with every point in the dialogue unless you particularly want to.

2 Ellipsis

- Students do not need to be able to make sentences like these, but they should be familiar with the structure so that they can understand them easily.
- Other examples: *Sounds like a boring day; Don't think so; Can't remember.*

3 Recall

- Tell students to close their books again.
- Play the conversation once more, stopping before Lorna's answers. See how well the students can predict what she is going to say.

4 Pronunciation 🔊

• This exercise helps students to see which vowels are usually represented by the letter *a*, and what kinds of words have which vowel sounds (in standard southern British English).
• See if students can remember how to pronounce the words in the four groups.
• Help them to see the patterns (/ɑ:/ before *r* and often before *f*, *th* and *s*; /eɪ/ in the combinations *ai* and *ay*, and also before *consonant + e*; /ɔ:/ in *all*, *alk* and *aw*; /æ/ in most other cases).
• Get students to apply these rules by sorting out the list of words and putting them into the right groups.
• Then look over the 'special pronunciations'.
• The pronunciation rules given here have exceptions, of course. Note also that they are only valid for standard southern British English. Many educated speakers from other parts of Britain use /æ/, not /ɑ:/, in *after*, *rather*, *ask*, *glass*, *bath*, *half*, *past* and similar words. This also happens in American English.
• The exercise is recorded in a southern British, a northern British and an American version, for purposes of comparison.

Answers to Exercise 4
(Standard southern British pronunciation)

Group 1 (/æ/)	Group 2 (/ɑ:/)	Group 3 (/eɪ/)	Group 4 (/ɔ:/)
black	hard	wait	law
hat	glass	hate	ball
happy	start	late	fall
stand	car	make	awful
	bath	paid	all
	arm	rain	walk
	part	may	
	half		
	past		

5 Use of tenses

• Talk the students through the diagram. (See *Language notes* for a simple version of the rule.)
• The exercise can be done by class discussion, but you may like to ask students to do the last few questions individually, to make sure that everybody has grasped the point.
• There is further work on this point in the Practice Book.

6 Preparation for improvisation

• Explain that students have to take on an imaginary personality for the purposes of this exercise.
• Get them to spend ten minutes deciding what their occupations are and how they spent their day.
• Go round helping where necessary.

7 Improvisation

• Ask students to get into pairs.
• First of all, they should decide what their relationship is (flatmates, husband and wife, . . .)
• Then ask two good students to begin. They should imagine that one of them is coming home after work (the other has already arrived home).
• They must improvise a conversation in which they exchange all the information they have prepared.

• Make sure they use the simple past and past progressive tenses where appropriate, as well as plenty of words and expressions from the dialogue.
• When they have finished, ask everybody to start improvising in pairs. They should go through the conversation several times until they are fluent.
• If there is time, ask some of the pairs to perform their improvisations for the class, or for other pairs or groups. You may like to tape-record or video-record the performances.

Optional activity   'Talk yourself out of this'
• A woman rang her husband at the office, and was told he was in an important meeting.
• So she switched on the TV to watch the Wimbledon tennis finals.
• During the match, the camera showed a close-up of the crowd. There was her husband, sitting watching the match and talking to a beautiful woman.
• When he came home, she asked him for an explanation.
• Students should work in groups. Their task is to decide what the husband said.
• (Note: if you or your students feel the situation is too much of a cliché, you can reverse the sex-roles, making it a man who rings his wife at the office, etc.)

8 Personalisation

• Put students in groups of four or so.
• Give them a minute or two to choose what they want to talk about. Help with vocabulary if necessary.
• Then tell them to start talking.
• If necessary, remind them not to use the present perfect for past narrative.
• When everybody has spoken, ask each group to choose *one* of the narratives for the whole class to hear.

Optional activity   Remembering two accounts
• Ask two students to prepare accounts of what they did yesterday.
• They should make their accounts as similar as possible (for instance, by both saying what they had for breakfast, what they listened to on the radio, . . .).
• They give their accounts to the class in turn.
• Then the other students see if they can recall both accounts without getting mixed up.

Optional activity   Who is lying?
• Two students prepare accounts of what they did yesterday: one true, the other completely untrue.
• They tell their stories in turn, making them sound equally plausible. The class decide who is lying.

9 Summary

• Remind students to look over the Summary and learn the new material.

Practice Book
• Tell students which exercises you want them to do.

4 Pronunciation: the letter *a*. Can you pronounce these words?

1. bad   had   happen   rang   man   (/æ/)
2. darling   afternoon   rather   ask   glass   (/ɑ:/)
3. came   strange   day   say   train (/eɪ/)
4. call   talk   saw   (/ɔ:/)

Put these words in group 1, 2, 3 or 4.

wait   hate   hard   glass   start   law   car
bath   late   ball   black   make   paid   arm
rain   fall   hat   part   happy   half   past
awful   may   all   stand   walk

Special pronunciations:

what   wasn't   want   watch   swan   (/ɒ/)
many   any   again   says   said   ate   (/e/)
about   America   England   umbrella   (/ə/)

5 Grammar: simple past and past progressive. Study the examples.

> *Just when I* **was trying** *to finish some work*
> ―――――――――――――――――――――
> *Janet*
> **turned** *up.*
>
> *I* **was getting** *ready to come home*
> ―――――――――――――――――――――
> *and the*
> *phone* **rang**.

Now put the correct verb forms into the sentences.

1. Andrew .... when I was getting ready to go out. (*arrive*)
2. The phone rang while I .... a bath. (*have*)
3. I first met my wife when I .... in Berlin. (*study*)
4. When I looked out of the window, it .... (*rain*)
5. I stopped because the car .... a funny noise. (*make*)
6. Where were you going when I .... you yesterday? (*see*)
7. When I was cleaning the house, I .... some old love letters. (*find*)
8. The accident .... while we .... into Copenhagen. (*happen*; *drive*)
9. I .... all my money when I .... from Istanbul to Athens. (*lose*; *travel*)
10. When I .... her, she .... reading. (*see*; *sit*)
11. The lights all .... while we .... supper. (*go out*; *have*)
12. When I .... the train, I .... my ticket onto the railway line. (*get off*; *drop*)

6 Imagine that it is six o'clock in the evening. You have just arrived home after an interesting day. What did you do? Make up answers to the following questions (ask the teacher for help if necessary).

What is your job?
How did you spend the morning?
Where did you have lunch? What did you have?
How did you spend the afternoon?
What places did you go to? Why?
You saw somebody interesting during the day.
Who? When did you meet? ('*When I was ... ing.*') What did you talk about? What did you do together?
Something interesting or strange happened during the day. What? When did it happen? ('*When I was ... ing.*')

7 Work in pairs. You and your partner are members of the same family, or husband and wife, or flatmates or roommates in college. Talk about how you both spent your day (using the ideas from Exercise 6). Useful expressions:

Did you have a good day?
Did you see anybody interesting?
What about?
You know.
I see.
as usual
So what did you do?
Where did you go?
What did you say?
What happened then?
Did anything interesting happen?
Not really.
(It) sounds like a boring/interesting day.

8 Work in groups. Tell the group what you did yesterday; or tell them about your last holiday; or about a journey that you made once; or about your earliest memory.

9 Study the Summary on page 137.

Comparisons

A Things are different

1 Look at the pictures. How many differences can you find between them?
Example: *'The fridge is bigger in picture B.'*

A

2 Revision. *-er* or *more*?

Examples: tall ....*taller*....

important *more important*....

old   interesting   beautiful   long   short
difficult   small   easy   cheap   expensive

-est or *most*?

Examples: tall .....*tallest*.....

important *most important*.....

fast   heavy   surprising   cheerful   boring
nice   young   light   intelligent   hard

3 Copy the table. Then listen and fill in the gaps.

	A	B	C	D	E	F
Number of wheels	4					
How many people does it carry?						1
Top speed (in kph)						
Weight (in kilos)						
Price (in pounds)						

18

Unit 4: Lesson A

Students practise talking about similarities and differences.
Principal structures: revision of comparative and superlative adjectives; modification of comparatives; sentence structures used in comparisons; *as* and *than*.
Words and expressions to learn: *difference; wheel; vehicle; ship; lorry; pram; horse; bird; piano; violin; trumpet; cottage; intelligence; free time; top speed.*
Phonology: decoding rapid speech.

Language notes and possible problems

1. Comparatives and superlatives There are introductory revision exercises on the forms at the beginning of the lesson; further revision work on the forms and meanings will be found in the Practice Book. Note that the rules given (in the teaching notes for Exercise 2 and in the Practice Book) are somewhat simplified; there are exceptions.

2. As and *than* Some students may confuse these words. They should do Exercise 3 in the Practice Book.

3. Modification of comparatives Make sure students realise that *very* cannot be used to modify comparatives. Exercise 7 has examples of *much* and *far* with comparatives.

If you are short of time

Exercise 9 can be dropped; Exercise 5 can be done for homework.

1 Comparing pictures

- This can be done as a whole-class discussion.
- Let students use any suitable structures (not just comparative clauses).
- Write their sentences on the board: see how many comparisons they can make. (There are ten differences altogether.)

Answers to Exercise 1

In picture B: the fridge is bigger; the table is higher; there are more chairs; there are fewer cupboards; the switch is lower; the cooker is wider; the sink is smaller; the clock shows a different time; there are more plants on the window-ledge; there are fewer cups on the table. (Answers can of course be expressed in different ways.)

2 Comparatives and superlatives

- Ask students to write the first few answers, and check whether they know all the rules.
- If necessary, remind them of the basic facts:
- short (one-syllable) adjectives form comparatives and superlatives with *-er* and *-est*.
- long adjectives (with three or more syllables) form comparatives and superlatives with *more* and *most*.
- two-syllable words ending in *-y* have *-ier*, *-iest*.
- most other two-syllable words have *more*, *most*.
- Do the rest of the exercise orally or in writing.
- See the Practice Book for further revision work.

3 Listening for specific information 📼

- This exercise helps students to realise that they do not need to understand every word they hear in order to interpret a spoken message.
- Go over the table with them, making sure they understand the various questions.
- Tell them to copy the table.
- Play the recording, pausing at suitable moments (but not after every sentence) while students fill in the answers.
- You will probably want to play each section more than once, but don't make it too easy – the purpose of the exercise is to accustom students to real-life listening.
- When they have completed the table as well as they can, let them compare notes in groups and then complete the table on the blackboard.
- Don't tell the students every word that was said – this is not the point of the exercise.
- You may want to follow up with further practice in understanding numbers, if students have found this difficult.

Tapescript and answers to Exercise 3

	A	B	C	D	E	F
Number of wheels	4	4	2	6	10	2
How many people does it carry?	1–2	4	1–2	72	100	1
Top speed (in kph)	6	160	224	110	2,160	25
Weight (in kilos)	15	695	236	9,000	175,000	13.5
Price (in pounds)	72	5,000	1,700	65,000	?	140

A. It's got four wheels, and usually carries one person, but it can carry two. Its top speed is around six kilometres an hour, and it weighs about 15 kilos. It costs £72.
B. This vehicle costs about £5,000. It can go at up to 160kph, and can carry four people in comfort. It weighs 695 kilos when it's empty. There are four wheels.
C. These two-wheeled vehicles are very popular with teenagers. They are fast, but much less safe than vehicles A or B. This model has a maximum speed of 224kph, and weighs 236 kilos. It can carry one or two people, and costs £1,700.
D. This vehicle, which costs £65,000, is commonly used for public transport. It has two decks, or floors, and can carry 72 people when full. Its maximum speed is 110 kilometres an hour, but it doesn't usually go faster than 80. It has six wheels, and weighs 9,000 kilos.
E. This vehicle was built by two countries working in collaboration. It travels at 2,160kph – faster than sound – carrying a maximum load of 100 people. When it is fully loaded with passengers and fuel, it weighs 175,000 kilograms. It has ten wheels. Each of these vehicles cost hundreds of millions of pounds to produce – it is impossible to say exactly how much.
F. 'How many wheels?'
  'Two.'
  'What does it weigh?'
  'Thirteen and a half kilos.'
  'How much does it cost?'
  '£140.'
  'How many people can it carry?'
  'Just one.'
  'Top speed?'
  'It depends. For most people, perhaps about 25kph.'

18

4 Drawing conclusions

- Students shouldn't find it too difficult to guess what the vehicles are.
- A is a pram, B is a car, C is a motorbike, D is a double-decker bus, E is an airliner (Concorde), and F is a bicycle.
- Some of the data given are of course approximate (a bicycle doesn't really have a maximum speed, for instance). If students want to argue about the accuracy of the answers given, so much the better (provided they argue in English).

5 Superlatives

- This exercise gives practice in using superlatives.
- Students can work individually and then compare notes.
- (If they get stuck on 8, point out that the sentences come in pairs of opposites.)
- Make sure they don't forget the definite article.
- If necessary, remind students of the difference between comparatives and superlatives.

Answers to Exercise 5
3. E (a plane) can carry the most people.
4. F (a bicycle) can carry the fewest people.
5. E is the fastest.
6. A (a pram) is the slowest.
7. F is the lightest.
8. E is the heaviest.
9. E is the most expensive.
10. A is the cheapest.

6 How many words?

- This is an important exercise. It gives students practice in recognising and separating out common words pronounced naturally in rapid speech.
- The pronunciation of words (particularly unstressed words) often changes a good deal under the influence of the sounds that come before and after. Students who have learnt only the pronunciations that words have alone or in deliberate speech may have great trouble understanding them in natural conversation.
- In this exercise, the focus is on the unstressed pronunciations of *as* (/əz/) and *than* (/ðən/).
- Ask students first of all just to say how many words they hear, and then to try to decide what they are.

Tapescript and answers to Exercise 6
1. Today's not as cold as yesterday (7)
2. She's older than he is. (6)
3. You're different from your photo. (6)
4. She goes to the same school as my brother. (9)
5. She's not nearly as tall as me. (8)
6. She's the nicest of the three girls. (8)
7. Her eyes are the same colour as yours. (8)
8. Both of us like dancing. (5)
9. Your house is much nicer than mine. (7)
10. There are a lot of words in this sentence. (9)

7 Comparatives in sentences

- Run over the list of structures and make sure students understand them all.
- The exercise can be done in pairs, in groups or as a whole-class activity.
- With a quick class it can be done orally without preparation, with students spontaneously saying their sentences as they work them out.
- A slower class may need time to prepare sentences.

8 Survey: preferences

- Begin by demonstrating yourself.
- Choose one of the groups of things and ask several students which of the things in the group they would prefer to have.
- If possible, get them to say why. Encourage the use of comparatives and superlatives.
- Then tell students to choose one of the groups, and to walk round the class asking about people's preferences.
- They should make a note of the answers and the reasons given.
- (If it is not feasible for students to walk round, tell them to ask as many people as they can without moving from their places.)

9 Reporting the survey

- Students can report either to the whole class or to groups, as you prefer.

Summary
- Remind students to study the Summary on page 137.

Practice Book
- Tell students which exercises you want them to do.

4 **What are A, B, C, D, E and F? Choose the correct vehicles.**

ship   plane   car   bus   lorry   tank   pram
train   motorbike   bicycle

5 Complete these sentences.

1. E has got ...*the most*... wheels.
2. C and F have got *the fewest* ...... wheels.
3. E can carry .... people.
4. F can carry .... people.
5. .... is the fastest.
6. A is the ....
7. .... is the lightest.
8. E ....
9. E .... expensive.
10. .... cheapest.

6 Listen to the recording. How many words do you hear in each sentence? (Contractions like *she's* count as two words.)

7 Look at the table and make some sentences (some true, some false). Ask other students if they are true or false. Use these structures:

...... has got more wheels than ....
...... hasn't got as many wheels as ....
...... can carry (far) more people than ....
...... can't carry (nearly) as many people
         as ....
...... is (much) faster/heavier than ....
...... costs (much) more than ....
...... doesn't cost (nearly) as much as ....
         (OR: ...... costs much less than ....)
...... has got the most/fewest ....
...... can carry the most/fewest ....
...... is the fastest/slowest/heaviest/etc.

8 Choose one of these groups of things. Ask other students which of the things in the group they would most like to have, and why. Ask as many people as possible, and write down the answers.

1. a dog   a cat   a horse   a bird
2. a Rolls Royce   a Citroen 2CV   a motorbike
   a bicycle
3. a piano   a guitar   a violin   a trumpet
4. a holiday in the mountains / by the sea /
   in London / in San Francisco
5. a flat   a cottage   a big house
6. more money   more intelligence
   more free time   more friends

9 Tell the class what you found out in Exercise 8. Example:

'*I asked about Group 1. Most people would prefer a bird, because it doesn't eat as much as the others.*'
(OR: '*... it eats less than the others.*')

B People are different

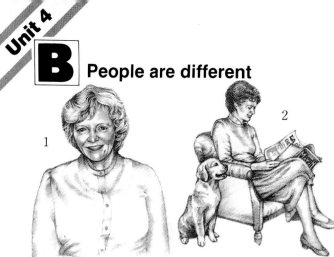

1 Look at pictures 1–6 and the descriptions. Can you put the right name with each picture?

ANN is a dark-haired woman who is rather shy.
LESLIE is a young doctor who plays tennis.
SUSAN is a fair-haired woman who speaks French.
PAT is a company director who eats too much.
KATE is a fair-haired woman who does not smoke.
CAROL is a dark-haired woman who likes animals.

2 Now look at pictures 7–12. Make up names and descriptions for the people in them. (Use *who* in your sentences.) Then see if other students can put your names with the right pictures.

3 Go round the class, and see how many of these people you can find in five minutes. Write down their names when you find them. Prepare your questions first. Examples:

'Do you like fish?'
'When were you born?'

FIND:
somebody who doesn't like fish.
somebody who was born in June.
somebody who has been to New York.
somebody who likes maths.
somebody who believes in horoscopes.
somebody who can't swim.
somebody who has got a cold.
somebody who hates pop music.
somebody who often has bad dreams.
somebody who has got a headache.
somebody who is very shy.
somebody who is not shy at all.

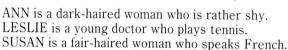

Unit 4: Lesson B

Students practise the language used for describing and comparing.

Principal structures: comparative structures; relative clauses with *who*; *both* and *neither* in sentences; compound adjectives like *dark-haired*; *do* as pro-verb; *was/were born*; *like . . . ing*.

Words and expressions to learn: *fish*; *maths*; *company director*; *pop music*; *interest* (noun); *party*; *computer*; *hate*; *dark-haired*; *fair-haired*; *similar*; *left/right-handed*; *broad-shouldered*; *neither*; *quite*; *I would rather not answer*.

Phonology: stress, rhythm and linking.

Language notes and possible problems

1. Both   Note the word order with *both*. It can go in the same position as frequency adverbs – that is to say:
a. before a one-word verb (*We both play . . .*).
b. after auxiliary verbs and *be* (*We are both shy*; *We were both born in September*).
Note also the structure *both of us/you/them* (and *neither of us/you/them*).
The structure with *both* as a determiner (as in *both the children*) will be studied later.

2. Relative clauses   Clauses with *who* and *that* were studied in Book 1. Here students revise clauses with *who*.

3. Do   Students may not be familiar with the use of *do* as a pro-verb (*She sings better than I **do***; *He plays football, but I **don't***).

4. Born   Look out for mistakes like **My sister and I are both born in September*.

5. Rather   Note the two meanings of *rather*: in *rather shy* (Exercise 5) it is an adverb of degree (like *quite*, but 'stronger'); in *I would rather not answer* (Exercise 8) it means 'preferably'.

If you are short of time
Exercise 6 can be done for homework.

---

1 Relative clauses: matching exercise
● This exercise can be done individually at first. After a few minutes, let students compare notes in groups.
● Help with vocabulary if necessary, or let students use dictionaries.

Answers to Exercise 1
1. Kate   2. Ann   3. Pat   4. Carol   5. Leslie   6. Susan
Note: 2 could apparently be either Carol or Ann; but 4 can only be Carol (because Ann is shy); so 2 must be Ann.

2 Relative clauses: practice
● Students should try to make up sets of descriptions like those in Exercise 1. (This activity works well if done in groups of three or four.)
● Get them to write down their descriptions; make sure they use relative clauses with *who*.
● When students are ready, they should exchange papers and try to work out who is who.

3 Find somebody who . . .
● Make sure students understand the vocabulary in the various descriptions, and know how to form the appropriate questions.
● Give them five minutes to go round asking their questions, and then see who has collected most names.
● This is a noisy activity (like all walk-round exercises), but this does not matter at all provided the students are speaking English.
● The list of descriptions can of course be adapted to suit the interests and personalities of the people in the class.
● (The idea for this exercise came from Mario Rinvolucri.)

4 Listening to comparisons

- This is part of the same conversation which was used for the recording in Lesson 1B.
- Here, Keith and John went out of the room, and the others were asked to describe and compare them from memory.
- Explain the situation to the students; then run over the sentences and explain any difficulties. (They may be able to decide about two or three of the sentences from their memory of Lesson 1B.)
- Tell them to write the numbers 1–9 on a piece of paper.
- Then play the recording, while they listen and write *T* or *F* against the numbers of the sentences.
- Play the recording again if necessary.
- Let the students compare notes in groups before you give them the answers.

Answers to Exercise 4
1. T   2. T   3. F   4. F   5. F   6. T   7. F   8. T
9. F? (he is wearing dark socks)

Tapescript for Exercise 4: see page 179

5 Stress, rhythm and linking

- Play or say the sentences, and get the students to imitate them as well as they can.
- Start by making sure they put the stresses in the right places.
- Then work on rhythm, getting the students to say the stressed syllables more slowly than the unstressed syllables.
- Note that many of the unstressed words and syllables are pronounced with /ə/ (for instance *and, as, than, but, are, from*).
- Note also the pronunciation of *different* (two syllables only: /ˈdɪfrənt/) and *interested* (three syllables only: /ˈɪntrəstɪd/).
- Finally, pay attention to linking words together smoothly (particularly where the second or third word in a phrase begins with a vowel).
- After the first few sentences, get students to try to say the sentences *before* they hear them, and then play the recording so that they can check their pronunciation.
- Note that the structures in this exercise will be used in Exercise 8.

6 Compound adjectives with *-ed*

- This is an easy exercise, which can be done in class or for homework as you prefer.

Optional activity: informal talk
- Talk for a few minutes to the class about yourself and a friend or relation – the similarities and differences between you. You don't need to ask 'comprehension questions': they don't add anything to the exercise.

7 Predicting differences

- You may like to begin by demonstrating the exercise yourself with a good student.
- Try to make sure that students work with partners that they do not know very well. (They may have to change places.)

- Walk round helping with vocabulary and structures, but don't try to control the discussions too closely.

8 Similarities and differences

- Once again, you may like to start things off by demonstrating with a good student.
- When students have established five things that they have in common and five differences, they should write down what they have found out, using the comparative structures they have learnt (Exercise 5 has numerous examples).
- They may need help with the position of the word *both* (see *Language notes*).
- If you want to give the students some extra speaking practice, they can change partners and tell other people what they have just found out.

Optional activity: grouping people
- A volunteer divides the class into groups according to the similarities and differences between the students.
- The volunteer does not tell the other students on what basis he or she is dividing them. They have to work out what the people in each group have in common (for instance hair colour, jobs, personality).
- As the volunteer divides the students, he or she should put each group in a different part of the room. This provides an opportunity for revision of prepositions (*Go and stand by the door/under the picture/near the blackboard/*etc.).
- When students have managed to guess how they were divided, another volunteer takes a turn.
- Help with vocabulary and structures if necessary.

Summary
- Remind students to study the Summary and learn the new material.

Practice Book
- Tell students which exercises you want them to do.

21

4 Listen to the recording, and decide whether the following sentences are true or false.

1. Keith is much taller than John.
2. Keith and John are both slim.
3. They both like gardening.
4. Keith's hair is darker than John's.
5. Keith has some sort of dressing in his hair.
6. John's face is thinner than Keith's.
7. Keith is wearing a black striped T-shirt.
8. John is wearing black shoes.
9. John is wearing black socks.

5 Pronunciation. Say these sentences. Pay attention to stress, rhythm and linking.

1. My **bro**ther and **I** are **ve**ry **dif**ferent.
2. He's **not near**ly as **old** as **me**.
3. He's **much tall**er than **me**.
4. His **in**terests are **dif**ferent from **mine**.
5. He **looks like** our **fa**ther, but **I look** like our **mo**ther.
6. He **likes** foot**ball**, but **I don't**.
7. He en**joys par**ties **much more** than **I do**.
8. He's **in**terested in com**pu**ters, but **I'm** not.
9. My **sis**ter and **I** are **quite si**milar.
10. We **both have fair hair**, and we are **both left-hand**ed.
11. Her **eyes** are the **same** colour as **mine**.
12. We **both play** the piano.
13. She **sings bet**ter than **I do**.
14. We were **both born** in Sep**tem**ber.
15. She **likes tra**velling, but **I don't**.
16. **Both** of us **play ten**nis.
17. **Nei**ther of us can **swim**.
18. She is a **bit tall**er than **me**.
19. We are **both ra**ther **shy**, and we **both like li**ving alone.

"Got any S shirts?"

6 A person with dark hair is *dark-haired*. Somebody who writes with his or her left hand is *left-handed*. What are the adjectives for these people?

1. a person with brown hair
2. somebody with blue eyes
3. a person who has broad shoulders
4. people who write with their right hands
5. a person with a thin face
6. somebody with long legs

Now say these in another way.

1. a blue-eyed girl
   '*a girl with blue eyes*'
2. a brown-haired man
   '*a man . . .*'
3. a left-handed child
   '*a child who . . .*'
4. a fat-faced person
   '*somebody who has . . .*'
5. a dark-eyed woman
   '*. . .*'
6. a long-sleeved pullover
   '*. . . with . . .*'

7 Work with a student that you don't know very well. Write down three ways in which you think you are different from your partner, and three ways in which you think you are similar. Then exchange your papers and discuss what you wrote. Were you right?

8 Now find out more about your partner. Try to find at least five things that you have in common, and at least five differences, and write them down. Use some of the language from Exercise 5; ask your teacher for words you don't know.
Useful expressions:

'*Do you mind if I ask you a personal question?*'
'*No, that's all right.*'

'*How old are you?*'
'*I would rather not answer.*'

21

Asking and offering

A Have you got some stuff for cleaning windows?

1 Vocabulary revision. Where do you buy these things?

meat bread vegetables sugar shoes
soap books clothes writing paper petrol
stamps aspirin films

Example:

'You buy sugar at a grocer's or at a supermarket.'

2 Look at the conversations and try to fill in some of the gaps. Then listen to the recording and write the complete conversations.

1. 'Good afternoon.'
   'Hello. .... a shampoo for
      dry hair.'
   'Large, medium or ....?'
   '..................... the small bottle?'
   '76p.'
   '..................... two bottles, please.'

2. '.....................?'
   'Yes, ...'

3. 'Can I help you?'
   '..................... I'm being served.'

4. '.....................?'
   '..................... a child's tricycle.'
   'Yes. .... the child?'

5. '..................... a pint of milk, please?'
   'Yes, of course.....................
      ....?'
   'No, ..., thanks.
      ....?'
   '24p.'

6. 'Hello, Sid. .... any
      flashbulbs?'
   'I'm afraid not, Fred. ....
      some in next week. Can you look in on
      Monday?'
   '..................... be away on Monday,
      but I'll call in on Tuesday.'
   'OK. ....'
   'Bye, Sid.'

7. '..................... a dishwasher.'
   '............. .... make?'
   '..................... Kleenwash XJ126?'
   'Yes, we have. It's a very good machine.'
   '..................... guarantee?'
   'Five years, madam.'
   '..................... deliver?'
   'Yes, we do, sir. Up to 20 miles.'
   'How much is it?'
   '....................., plus VAT.'

Unit 5: Lesson A

Students revise and extend their knowledge of the language of shopping; they learn to ask for things without knowing the exact word.
Principal structures: *at a grocer's/butcher's etc.; a thing with a hole/handle; a thing / some stuff for ...ing.*
Words and expressions to learn: *soap; stamp; film (for a camera); tool; stuff; liquid; powder; material; hole; wood; guarantee; make (noun); cut; deliver; round; Can I look round?; I'm being served; I'm looking for...; that's all; I'm afraid not; Anything else?*
Phonology: rhythm and stress.

Note: timing
This lesson includes a dramatisation activity (Exercise 6). It is advisable to do this if at all possible, but note that it will be necessary to allow extra time – perhaps as much as an hour on top of the normal lesson period.

Optional extra materials
A set of pictures for practising 'paraphrase strategies' (see instructions to Exercise 5).

If you are short of time
Drop Exercise 6.

1 Vocabulary revision
● Check that the students know the words in the list; teach any new words.
● Help them to practise the pronunciation; make sure they only pronounce three syllables in *vegetables* (/ˈvedʒ·tə·blz/).
● Then divide the class into groups and let them pool their knowledge to try and decide where each of the things is bought. (They can use their dictionaries.)
● Supply any words that students cannot work out for themselves; make sure they learn the normal words that are used for these shops in modern English, as dictionaries sometimes contain words (such as *shoemaker*) which are no longer in general use.

An appropriate set of answers might be:
meat: butcher's
bread: baker's
vegetables: greengrocer's
sugar: grocer's
shoes: shoe shop
soap: chemist's
books: bookshop
clothes: clothes shop / dress shop / tailor's
writing paper: stationer's
petrol: petrol station / filling station / garage
stamps: post office
aspirins: chemist's
films: chemist's

● Of course, most of these things can also be bought elsewhere (in supermarkets or department stores, for instance).
● Students should note that stamps are normally sold only in post offices in Britain and the US.

● Note also that in modern English the *'s* in words like *butcher's, chemist's* is quite often dropped.
● If your students are in, or planning to go to, an English-speaking country, you may want to teach a more complete list of shop names.

2 Shop conversations
● This exercise has two purposes: to revise and present some of the expressions used in shopping, and to give students practice in understanding common expressions spoken at natural speed.
● You may not want to use all seven of the conversations.
● Put the students into groups of two or three and get them to try to fill in the gaps in the first conversation. (Note that a gap may correspond to an expression of several words.)
● When they have done what they can, play the recording through once.
● If they are still unable to fill in everything, play the recording again one or more times, with a pause after each sentence. But don't make the exercise too easy: the purpose is to 'stretch' students' listening ability so that they get used to understanding natural speech.
● Let them compare notes; then replay the conversation while you give them the answers.
● Deal with the other conversations in the same way.
● This may be a good opportunity to revise the difference between *some* and *any*.
● You may also need to explain the meaning of *VAT* (= Value Added Tax).

Tapescript for Exercise 2
1. 'Good afternoon.'
   'Hello. I'd like a shampoo for dry hair.'
   'Large, medium or small?'
   'How much is the small bottle?'
   '76p.'
   'I'll take two bottles, please.'
2. 'Can I look round?'
   'Yes, of course.'
3. 'Can I help you?'
   'It's all right, thanks. I'm being served.'
4. 'Can I help you?'
   'I'm looking for a child's tricycle.'
   'Yes. How old is the child?'
5. 'Could I have a pint of milk, please?'
   'Yes, of course. Here you are. Anything else?'
   'No, that's all, thanks. How much is that?'
   '24p.'
6. 'Hello, Sid. Have you got any flashbulbs?'
   'I'm afraid not, Fred. We'll have some in next week. Can you look in on Monday?'
   'I'm going to be away on Monday, but I'll call in on Tuesday.'
   'OK. See you then.'
   'Bye, Sid.'
7. 'We're looking for a dishwasher.'
   'Yes. What make?'
   'Have you got a Kleenwash XJ126?'
   'Yes, we have. It's a very good machine.'
   'How long is the guarantee?'
   'Five years, madam.'
   'And do you deliver?'
   'Yes, we do, sir. Up to 20 miles.'
   'How much is it?'
   'Two hundred and forty pounds, plus VAT.'

3 Rhythm and stress

● These expressions, or others like them, will be needed in Exercise 4, and students should make sure that they can pronounce them with a good rhythm and stress.

● Pay attention to the 'weak' pronunciation of *of* (/əv/) in *a pint of milk* and *Yes, of course*.

4 Dialogue practice

● Choose one or two of the dialogues from Exercise 2 for intensive practice.

● Go through the conversations again with the recording, explaining any difficult expressions and practising the pronunciation.

● Don't insist on students' pronouncing the sentences as fast as the speakers on the recording. They should learn to *understand* a fast colloquial pronunciation, but at this stage they should be satisfied if they can *speak* slowly and clearly with a good natural rhythm.

● Let them practise the dialogues in pairs; encourage them to learn them by heart if they can do this easily.

5 Paraphrase strategies

● The purpose of this lesson is *not* to teach vocabulary, but to help students to ask for things when they do not know the exact word for what they want.

● Look through the lists of 'useful words' and 'useful structures'. Make sure students understand these, and that they realise that *thing* is a 'blanket' term for countable nouns, while *stuff* replaces uncountables.

● (*Stuff* is a little slangy, and it may be better to use a more specific term such as *liquid*, *powder* etc. where possible.)

● When students have practised the words and expressions a little (pay attention to the pronunciation of *thing*), look through the example.

● Check whether students know common request structures (*I'd like...*; *Could I have...?*; *I'm looking for...*). Write them on the board.

● Then get individual students to try to ask the class for things whose names they don't know, using the expressions they have just learnt. (They can do this in groups if the class is large.)

● They can of course use any other ways of conveying meaning that they like, including mime, but they should include *some* language!

● The illustrations in the Student's Book can be used for this exercise, but it is even better if you prepare a set of pictures in advance (perhaps cut from magazines), and give them to individuals *without letting the others see them.*

● When a student asks for something, the rest of the class or group can try to draw the product or object he is describing, or name it in the mother tongue.

● After the exercise, students may want to know the names of some of the objects and substances they have been talking about. Try to persuade them not to spend too much time on learning these – they are not all very important words, and the purpose of the lesson is not to teach new vocabulary.

The objects illustrated are: an alarm clock, a bandage, washing powder, a shopping bag, a nail brush, a wallet, a cardboard box, a drill, window-cleaning liquid, a hoover, coloured ribbon, a hole punch, glue, crampons, a stapler, furniture polish, bubble-bath mixture, a foot pump.

6 Dramatisation

● This exercise will take up a good deal of time, and it will probably be necessary to allocate an extra period of 45–60 minutes.

● If time is short, you may prefer to drop the exercise, but if it is done it will prove to be a very effective aid to learning.

● The activity is relatively flexible as regards level. Weak students can prepare simple conversations with just one or two exchanges, while better students can work in groups of three or four to produce more elaborate sketches.

● You may wish to record the final sketches or film them on video: this can serve as a powerful incentive to students to practise what they have prepared.

● Give the groups a fair amount of time to prepare and practise their dramatisations, but set a time-limit of, say, 25–35 minutes.

● Students may want to write everything down; encourage them to work from brief notes or from memory if possible. Conversations that have been completely scripted usually sound unnatural.

● Don't let the students produce complicated material full of 'translationese': they should base what they say mainly on what they have learnt in the lesson.

● When all groups have prepared and practised their sketches, turn one end of the room into a 'shop'; let each group perform its sketch for the others.

● Start with a group that is likely to produce a successful performance, but don't take the best group first – this can discourage the others.

● Shy students will need to be pushed a bit, but are likely to enjoy the activity once they get going.

Summary

● Remind the students to study the Summary on page 138.

Practice Book

● Tell students which exercises you want them to do.

3 Rhythm and stress. Say these expressions.

Good **af**ter**noon**.
I'm **be**ing **served**.
a **pint** of **milk**
a **child's** **tri**cycle
Yes, we **have**.
Yes, of **course**.
Here you **are**.
I'm a**fraid** **not**.
the **small** **bott**le
How **much** is the **small** bottle?
How **much** is it?
How **old** is the **child**?
It's a **very** **good** ma**chine**.

4 Dialogue practice. Work with a partner and practise one or more of the conversations from Exercise 2.

5 Here are some ways to ask for things when you don't know the word.

Useful words:

a thing	stuff	square
a machine	liquid	round
a tool	powder	
	material	

Useful structures:
a thing **with** a hole / **with** a handle

a machine **for making** holes
a tool **for cutting** wood
a thing **for putting** pieces of paper together

some material **for making** curtains
some liquid **for cleaning** windows
some powder **for washing** clothes
some stuff **for killing** insects

Example:
A: *Excuse me. I don't speak English very well. What do you call the round glass in a camera?*
B: *The lens.*
A: *The lens. OK. I need some material for cleaning the lens.*
B: *A lens cleaner. Yes, we have ...*

Now look at the pictures and ask for one of the things illustrated.

6 Dramatisation. Work in pairs or groups of three. Prepare and practise conversations in shops. Use some of the expressions from Exercises 2 and 5.

23

B I haven't got anything to wear

1 Read the conversation and then listen to the recording. How many differences can you find?

JAN: Hello, Kate. What's the matter?

KATE: Hello, Jan. Oh, dear. I'm going out with Tony tonight, and I haven't got anything to wear.

JAN: What about your blue dress? That's lovely

KATE: That old thing? No. It makes me look like a sack of potatoes.

JAN: Well, why don't you borrow something of mine?

KATE: Could I really?

JAN: Yes, of course. Would you like to?

KATE: Well, I'd love to. If you really don't mind.

JAN: What about that green silk thing?

KATE: Green silk?

JAN: Yes, you know. The dress I wore to Andy's birthday party.

KATE: Oh, yes. I remember.

JAN: You'd look great in that.

KATE: Oooh!

JAN: And I'll lend you my new shoes to go with it.

KATE: My feet are bigger than yours.

JAN: I don't think they are, Kate. Anyway, try the shoes and see. What about a jacket? Have you got one that will do?

KATE: Not really.

JAN: Well. have one of mine.

KATE: Oh, Jan. I feel bad, borrowing all your things.

JAN: That's all right. What are friends for? I'll borrow something of yours one of these days.

KATE: Well, thanks a million, Jan. I'd better get moving. Tony's coming in half an hour.

JAN: OK. Wait a second. I'll go and get the dress. Shall I iron it for you?

KATE: Oh, Jan, ...

Unit 5: Lesson B

Students learn more about making and replying to suggestions, requests and offers.
Principal structures: modal verbs (*can, could, shall, will*); infinitive with and without *to*.
Words and expressions to learn: *silk; birthday party; change* (for £1); *to iron clothes; come round* (to visit); *have a look; give somebody a hand; put something back; wait a second; one of these days; Have you got the time?; in a hurry; That's very kind of you; I'm a stranger here myself.*
here myself.
Phonology: the difference between /eɪ/ and /e/; spellings of the sound /eɪ/.

Language notes and possible problems

1. Infinitives Some students may tend to use the *to*-infinitive after *can, could* and other modal verbs. (For example: **Can I to help you?*)

2. Vocabulary load The dialogue in Exercise 1 contains a large number of useful idiomatic expressions and conversational structures. Students can learn a selection of these (those listed in the Summary, plus any others which you or the students feel are especially important), but they should probably not try to learn all of them at this stage unless they find it easy to do so.

3. *Have got* Remind students about this structure, which is commonly used in present-tense sentences to talk about possession, especially in informal British English. (There are examples in Exercises 1 and 2.)

If you are short of time

Drop Exercises 3 and 4 if these are not essential for your students; drop Exercise 5 or give it for homework.

1 Dialogue: finding differences 📼

- Give students a few minutes to read through the dialogue. Explain important new words, but don't spend a lot of time on vocabulary at this stage.
- Tell students to close their books. Play the recording right through and ask students what differences they noticed.
- Let them listen again with their books open, and see if they can find some more differences.
- This can be done as a group task if you like.
- When the task is completed, you may want to spend a little more time on the text, pointing out useful words and structures. Note particularly:
  - Ways of making suggestions (*What about...? Why don't you...*).
  - The use of *to* instead of repeating a whole infinitive (*Would you like to? I'd love to*).
  - Revision of *have got*. (There is an exercise on this in the Practice Book.)

Tapescript and answers to Exercise 1
(Words which are different are in italics.)

ANN: Hello, Kate. What's the matter?
KATE: Hello, *Ann*. Oh, dear. I'm going out with *Tom this evening*, and I haven't got anything to wear.
ANN: What about your *red* dress? That's lovely.
KATE: That old thing? No. It makes me look like a sack of potatoes.
ANN: Well, why don't you *wear* something of mine?
KATE: Could I really?
ANN: Yes, of course. Would you like to?
KATE: Well, I'd love to. If you really don't mind.
ANN: What about that *blue* silk thing?
KATE: *Blue* silk?
ANN: Yes, you know. The dress I wore to Andy's *Christmas* party.
KATE: Oh, yes. I remember.
ANN: You'd look great in that.
KATE: *You're right. I would.*
ANN: And I'll lend you my new shoes to go with it.
KATE: My feet are *smaller* than yours.
ANN: I don't think they are, Kate. Anyway, try the shoes and see. What about a *belt*? Have you got one that will do?
KATE: Not really.
ANN: Well, have one of mine.
KATE: Oh, *Ann*. I feel bad, *taking* all your things.
ANN: That's all right. *We're friends, aren't we?* I'll borrow something of yours one of these days.
KATE: Well, thanks a *lot, Ann*. I'd better get moving. *Tom's* coming in *twenty minutes*.
ANN: OK. Wait a *minute*. I'll go and get the dress. Shall I iron it for you?
KATE: Oh, *Ann*, ...

2 Requests and offers

- This exercise revises common ways of making and replying to requests and offers, and also presents a number of useful conversational expressions.
- Note particularly the use of *can* and the more polite form *could* in requests; the use of *Shall I . . . ?* in offers, and the use of *I'll* when volunteering to do something.
- Make sure that students understand clearly the difference between *lend* and *borrow*.
- Give students a few minutes to try to match up the items on their own, and then let them continue in groups. Help with vocabulary if necessary.

Answers to Exercise 2
(Alternative answers are possible to some questions.)
1b   2e   3g   4i   5a   6l   7c   8f   9j   10d   11k   12h

3 Pronunciation: /eɪ/ and /e/

- This is a difficult distinction: students who do not have the sound /eɪ/ in their own language may pronounce it as a monophthong, so that, for example, *paper* sounds like *pepper*.
- Demonstrate the pronunciation of the pairs of words, and then play the recording, stopping after each word so that students can decide whether it is in list A or list B.
- Repeat the exercise if necessary, so that students get a clear sense of the difference between the two sounds.

The words recorded are: sale let get main pepper pen whale wet

- When students can hear the difference reasonably well, get them to practise saying the sound /eɪ/, first of all in isolation and at the ends of words like *say*, *may*, *way*.
- At the beginning of the vowel, the mouth should be relatively open, with the top and bottom teeth far enough apart for one to be able to get one's little finger between them. As the vowel is pronounced, the mouth closes and the tongue moves up to the position for /iː/.
- Finally, ask students to choose words from the two lists and say them. Other students must decide whether the words are from list A or list B.

4 Spellings of /eɪ/

- Point out that the four groups of words show typical spellings of the sound /eɪ/: *a* + consonant(s) + *e*; *ay*; *ai*; and in the ending *-ation*.
- Practise pronouncing them.
- Then ask students if they can add more words to any of the groups.

5 Infinitives

- This exercise will help students who confuse the two forms of the infinitive.
- It can be done as an individual, group or whole-class activity, as you prefer.
- After you have been through it, you may like to sum up the rules:
– Infinitive without *to* after modal verbs such as *will*, *can*, *shall*, after auxiliary *do*, and in the structure with *make* in Question 6.
– Infinitive with *to* in most other cases.

6 Borrowing

- Give students a minute or two to prepare their requests, and then ask them to borrow things from as many people as possible.
- Encourage them to ask and answer in different ways, so that they practise as much of the new language as they can.

At the end of the exercise, you can take the opportunity to practise the expression *give something back*.

7 Writing notes

- While students write their notes, you may like to walk round helping and checking that they are not making serious mistakes (but don't over-correct).
- When notes are ready, you can act as postman.

Summary

- Remind students to study the Summary on page 138.

Practice Book

- Tell students which exercises you want them to do.

2 Match the questions and answers.

1. Can you lend me some stamps?
2. Excuse me. Have you got the time?
3. Can I borrow your pen?
4. Could you help me for a few minutes?
5. Have you got a light?
6. Shall I post these letters for you?
7. Could I borrow your bicycle for half an hour?
8. Have you got change for £1?
9. Could I use your phone?
10. Would you like to play tennis this evening?
11. Excuse me. Can you tell me the way to the station?
12. I'll give you a hand with the cooking, shall I?

a. Sorry, I don't smoke.
b. I think so. How many do you need?
c. Sorry, I'm afraid I'm using it.
d. Sorry, I'm not free. My son's coming round.
e. Just after half past three.
f. Perhaps – I'll have a look. Yes, here you are.
g. OK. Can you put it back on my desk when you've finished with it?
h. That's very kind of you. Could you do the potatoes?
i. Well, I'm in a bit of a hurry.
j. Of course. It's over there on the table.
k. Sorry, I'm a stranger here myself.
l. Yes, please, if you don't mind.

3 Pronunciation. Which words do you hear?

A	B	A	B
sale	sell	paper	pepper
late	let	pain	pen
gate	get	whale	well
main	men	wait	wet

Now pronounce some of the words yourself. Ask other students which words they think you are saying.

4 Pronunciation and spelling. Say these words.

1. Kate   change   table   strange   make
2. day   way   play
3. wait   chain   fail
4. station   pronunciation

Can you think of any more words to put into groups 1, 2, 3 and 4?

5 Grammar. Infinitive with or without *to*?

1. I haven't got anything *to eat* / *eat*.
2. Why don't you *to take* / *take* a holiday?
3. I would like *to go* / *go* out tonight.
4. 'That's the doorbell.' 'I'll *to go* / *go*.'
5. Can you *to lend* / *lend* me some money?
6. That dress makes her *to look* / *look* funny.
7. I hope *to see* / *see* you again soon.
8. Shall I *to carry* / *carry* that bag for you?
9. What time do you have *to start* / *start* work in the mornings?
10. It's nice *to see* / *see* you again.

6 Ask other students if you can borrow things from them. Use questions and answers from Exercise 2.

7 Write two or more notes to other students. In your notes, you must ask somebody for something, offer something to somebody, or offer to do something for somebody. Answer the notes that you get. Use words and expressions from Exercises 1 and 2.

Dear Anne,
Could I borrow your bike this evening? Yours, Patricia

Dear Pat,
Of course you can, I'll give it to you after the lesson.
Anne

Dear Tony,
Shall I drive you to the airport on Saturday?
Love,
Alice

Dear Alice,
Thank you very much. That's very kind of you. My plane's at 11.30.
Love,
T.

The future

A Their children will have blue eyes

1 How much do you know about genetics? See if you can complete the sentences correctly. When you have finished, ask the teacher for the answers.

1. If both parents have got blue eyes, their children:
   - will certainly have blue eyes.
   - will probably have blue eyes.
   - may have blue eyes.

2. If both parents have got brown eyes, their children:
   - will certainly have brown eyes.
   - will probably have brown eyes.
   - may have brown eyes.

3. If one parent has got blue eyes and one has got brown eyes, their children:
   - will certainly have blue eyes.
   - will probably have blue eyes.
   - may have blue eyes or brown eyes.
   - will probably have brown eyes.
   - will certainly have brown eyes.

4. If a man (but not his wife) is colour-blind, their daughters:
   - will be colour-blind.
   - may be colour-blind.
   - will probably not be colour-blind.
   - will almost certainly not be colour-blind.

5. If a man (but not his wife) is colour-blind, their sons:
   - will certainly be colour-blind.
   - may be colour-blind.
   - will probably not be colour-blind.
   - will certainly not be colour-blind.

2 Look at the picture. The couple are going to have a baby. What do you think it will be like? Make sentences beginning *It will* ... or *It may* ..

3 Pronunciation. Say these words and expressions.

know   so   go   hope   don't   won't
I know   I hope   I won't
I don't know   I hope so   I won't go

Now say these words and expressions.

will   I'll   you'll   he'll   she'll
I'll tell   I'll think   you'll be
she'll have   it'll rain
I'll tell you tomorrow   I'll think about it
You'll be sorry   She'll have to go soon
Do you think it'll rain tonight?

Carol works in a computer firm. She is rather shy, and often gets depressed. She is not very interested in sport, but she likes playing tennis. She is very musical, and can play several instruments.

Lee is a bus driver. He is a very sociable, outgoing person, optimistic and cheerful. He likes sport, especially ball games. He is interested in science, and he is studying maths at night school. He is not at all musical.

26

Unit 6: Lesson A

Students practise talking about probability, certainty and the future.
Principal structures: *may, will* and *going to*.
Words and expressions to learn: *grandchild; ball games; science; firm; (musical) instrument; colour-blind; sociable; outgoing; optimistic; musical; may; several.*
Phonology: /əʊ/ (as in *go, won't*); 'dark l' (as in *I'll, will*).

Language notes and possible problems

1. Will and going to The rules for the use of these structures are complicated. As a rough guide:
– *Be going to* is used when we are talking about future events which already exist in the present in one way or another: they are already planned, or we can see that they are on their way. (For example, we say that a woman *is going to* have a baby if she *is* pregnant now.)
– *Will* is used when we are predicting the future, for instance by thinking, hoping or calculating. (For example, *If a couple have blue eyes, their child will have blue eyes.*)
Will can also be used when volunteering to do things. (E.g. *I'll lend you my new shoes.* See Lesson 5B.) For the use of the present progressive to talk about the future (e.g. *Anne's coming tomorrow*), see Lesson 6B.
2. Shall and will In modern English, *will* can be used in all persons as a future auxiliary. The use of *shall* in the first person is not taught at this stage. (For the use of *shall* in offers, see 5B.)
3. May Students should note that *may*, like other modal verbs, is followed by the infinitive without *to*. Point out that modal verbs have no *-s* in the third person singular.
4. Both Note the use of *both* in a noun phrase, often without an article. (*Both parents...*)
5. Pronunciation The phonology points in this lesson (/əʊ/ and 'dark l') are only important for students who are aiming at a high standard of pronunciation.

If you are short of time
Drop Exercise 3 if pronunciation is not a high priority; leave Exercise 8 for homework.

1 Will and may
● Make sure students understand this meaning of *may* (= 'will perhaps').
● Then get students to decide what they think the answers are (working individually at first, and then comparing notes in groups).
● When they are ready, tell them the answers.
● After finishing the exercise, you may like to point out the position of *certainly* and *probably* (after the auxiliary verb). Note also that *got* is not used with *have* in the infinitive (compare *both parents* **have got** *blue eyes* and *their children will certainly* **have** *blue eyes*).

Answers to Exercise 1
1. If both parents have got blue eyes, their children will certainly have blue eyes. (Blue is a 'recessive' characteristic: people only have blue eyes if they have no genes for other eye colours.)

2. If both parents have got brown eyes, their children will probably have brown eyes. (But the parents may also have genes for other eye colours, so their children are not certain to have brown eyes.)
3. If one parent has got blue eyes and one has got brown eyes, their children may have blue eyes or brown eyes, but most will probably have brown eyes. (Brown is 'dominant' and blue is 'recessive', so brown is somewhat more likely.)
4. If a man (but not his wife) is colour-blind, their daughters will almost certainly not be colour-blind. (Girls can only be colour-blind if they get colour-blind genes from both parents. This is very rare.)
5. If a man (but not his wife) is colour-blind, their sons will probably not be colour-blind. (Boys can only inherit colour-blindness from their mother; since it is rare, it is unlikely that both parents will carry the gene.)

2 What will the baby be like?
● This can be done by general class discussion.
● There are no right answers, of course; most of the students' sentences should begin *It may...* or *It will probably...*

3 Pronunciation: /əʊ/ and 'dark l'
● The standard British /əʊ/ is a difficult sound for most foreigners to make. It may also sound 'funny' to them, so that they may have a psychological resistance to making the sound.
● An easy way to learn to make it is to practise putting together the two sounds /ə/ (as in *father* or *about*) and /uː/ (as in *too*). Get students to say 'er-oo' a few times, and then tell them to put various consonants before the sound: 'ner-oo', 'ger-oo', 'ser-oo'. They should find themselves saying *no*, *go* and *so*.
● If students find the sound difficult, or are unwilling to make it, tell them that it is not very important for comprehensibility.
● 'Dark l' (the variety of *l* that comes at the end of a word) is also difficult for many students.
● An easy way to learn it is to start by saying /ʊ/ (as in *book*), and then to add *l* while continuing to pronounce /ʊ/. *Will, I'll* and *he'll* are almost like 'wi-ull', 'I-ull' and 'he-ull' pronounced rather quickly.
● Students who find this difficult should not worry too much about it: they will be understood even if they use the wrong kind of *l* at the ends of words.

4 Personalisation

- Look over the examples. You may wish to practise the pronunciation of *hope*, *don't* and *won't* again before going on.
- Give students a minute or two to think, and then ask for their sentences. Look out for the mistake *I think... won't...* (instead of *I don't think... will...*).
- Younger students may enjoy making insulting predictions about the appearance and/or personality of each other's children.

5 *Will be able to; will have to*

- Look through the substitution table, and explain that *be able to* acts as the infinitive of *can*.
- Ask volunteers to make some sentences from the table.
- When they have done this, get students to say more things about the future, using the same sentence structures.

Optional activity   Predicting

- If you want to give students extra practice in predicting with *will*, there are several possibilities.
1. Get them to say what they think tomorrow's weather will be like (if you are in a country with changeable weather). Write down their predictions; in the next lesson, see who was right.
2. Do the same with the results of football matches or other sporting events.
3. Organise an arm-wrestling tournament in the class; get students to say who they think will win out of each pair.

6 *Will* and *is going to*

- If you speak the students' language, the best thing is to explain the rule in their mother tongue.
- If this is not possible, let them use their dictionaries while they study the rule, and try to help with any difficulties.
- Exercises 7 and 8 should help to clarify the point.

7 What is going to happen?

- Obviously each picture can be described in various ways. Get students to think about them for a few minutes and then compare notes in groups. Finally, compare each group's answers.

Possible descriptions are:
1. The cars are going to crash.
2. The woman is going to open the door.
3. The man is going to cook something.
4. The woman is going to telephone.
5. The people are going to see a film.
6. The man is going to rob the bank.
7. The football is going to break the window.
8. It is going to rain.

8 *Will* or *going to*?

- This can be done by class discussion, with students trying to see the reason for the choice of structure in each case.
- You may like to get them to write one or two of the answers so that you can check up on the weaker students.

Answers to Exercise 8
(The dividing line between *will* and *going to* is not always very clear-cut, and in some cases both are possible, depending on the exact shade of meaning that is expressed. However, if students follow the rules in the Student's Book they will be quite safe. The answers given here are the ones that conform to these rules.)
1. going to   2. 'll   3. going to   4. going to   5. will
6. going to   7. going to   8. will

9 Personalisation: students' plans

- Encourage students to make sentences with *going to*, but don't reject sentences with *will* if these are correct according to the rules students have learnt.

Summary
- Remind students to study the Summary and learn the new material.

Practice Book
- Tell students which exercises you want them to do.

4 What will your children be like? (If you already have children, talk about your grandchildren. If you're not going to have children, talk about somebody else's children.) Use *will, won't, may. I (don't) think, I hope.* Examples:

'I hope my children will be good-looking.'
'My children may be musical.'
'I don't think my children will be tall.'
'My children certainly won't speak English.'

5 What sort of world will your great-grandchildren live in? Make some sentences.

6 The difference between *will* and *is going to.* Compare:

She **is going to** have a baby.
The baby **will** have blue eyes, and it **will** probably have fair hair.
She hopes it **will** be a girl.

Now study this rule. Use a dictionary to help you if necessary.

– We use *am/are/is going to* when we can already see the future in the present – when future actions are already planned, or are beginning to happen.
– We use *will* when we predict future actions by thinking, hoping, or calculating.

In 70 years, people (not) may will be able to have to go to the moon for the weekend. shop by computer. work. drive cars. travel where they like. speak Chinese. etc.

7 Look at the pictures and say what is going to happen.

8 *Will* or *going to*?

1. Look out! *We'll / We're going to* crash!
2. I hope one day *I'll / I'm going to* have more free time.
3. *Mary'll / Mary's going to* marry an old friend of mine in August.
4. I can't talk to you now. *We'll just / We're just going to* have lunch.
5. Perhaps in a few hundred years everybody *will / is going to* have an easy life.
6. 'What are your plans for this evening?'
   'I'll / I'm going to stay at home and watch TV.'
7. 'John's starting university in October.'
   'Oh, yes? *What will he / What's he going to* study?'
8. If you and your husband both have green eyes, your children *will probably / are probably going to* have green eyes too.

9 What are your plans for this evening / tomorrow / the weekend? Examples:

'This evening I'm going to stay in and wash my hair.'
'We're going to spend the weekend in the mountains.'

B How about Thursday?

1 **Here are the beginnings and ends of three conversations. Which beginning goes with which end?**

A

'Parkhurst 7298.'

'Hello. Paul?'

'Hello. Who's that?'

'This is Audrey. I wondered if you were free .... Tuesday.'

'It depends. What time?'

'............ the afternoon?'

'Yes, I could be. Why?'

'Well, my mother's coming down, and I'd like you to meet her. About half past four?'

B

'Hello, John. This is Angela. I'm trying to fix the Directors' meeting. Can you tell me what days you're free next week?'

'Well, let me see. Monday morning's OK. Tuesday. Not Wednesday, I'm going to Cardiff. Thursday afternoon. Friday's a bit difficult.'

'How about Thursday two fifteen?'

C

'Hello. I'd like to make an appointment to see Dr Gray.'

'Yes. What name is it, please?'

'Simon Graftey.'

'Yes. Three o'clock .... Monday, Mr Graftey?'

'Three o'clock's difficult. Could it be earlier?'

D

'Tuesday two fifteen. Let me look in my diary.'

'No, Thursday.'

'Oh, I'm sorry, I thought you said Tuesday. Thursday two fifteen. No, I'm sorry, I've got an appointment until three. Could we make it later? Say three fifteen?'

'Well, there's a lot to talk about. It'll take a couple of hours, at least.'

'Shall we say Monday morning, then?'

'Monday morning. All right. Nine o'clock?'

'Nine. I think that's all right. I'll ring you back and confirm.'

'All right. But ring .... five, could you?'

'I'll call you back .... about half an hour, Angela. All right?'

'Right you are. Bye, John.'

'Bye.'

E

'Two thirty?'

'No, I'm afraid I can't manage two thirty either. I'm seeing somebody .... two forty. Is two o'clock possible?'

'Yes, that's all right. Two o'clock .... Monday, then.'

'Thanks very much. Goodbye.'

'Goodbye.'

F

'That's difficult. You see, I'm playing tennis .... a quarter past. Then it'll take me a few minutes to shower and get changed.'

'What about later? Say, five?'

'Yes, OK. I'll come round .... five. Your place?'

'My place.'

'OK. See you then. Bye.'

'Bye.'

2 **Can you put these prepositions in the right places in the conversations?**

at	at	in	in	on	on
on	before	until			

Unit 6: Lesson B

Students learn more about making appointments, and revise the conventions for talking on the phone.
Principal structures: use of present progressive to refer to the future; revision of time prepositions.
Words and expressions to learn: *couple* (= two or so); *shower*; *diary*; *church*; *cake*; *wonder*; *fix* (= arrange); *manage*; *practise*; *get changed*; *confirm*; *it depends*; *let me see*; *I'll ring/call you back*; *say* (= I suggest); *not...either*; *my place*.
Phonology: stress and rhythm.

Language notes and possible problems
Present progressive with future meaning We often use present tenses to talk about future events which are already planned, arranged, or certain to happen. The use of *is going to* has already been revised. Here, students revise the future use of the present progressive (as in *My mother's coming down*; *I'm going to Cardiff*). This is particularly common with time expressions, or when it is clear exactly when something is happening. (See the dialogues in Exercise 1 for examples.)

Note that the simple present is rarely used to talk about the future, except in talking about timetables (e.g. *The train leaves at 4.13*).

If you are short of time
Drop Exercise 4 if your students find English stress and rhythm easy; drop Exercise 5.

---

1 **Beginnings and ends of conversations**
● This is an easy exercise: the purpose is simply to get students reading the conversations and thinking about what they mean.
● Get students to do the exercise individually and then compare notes.

2 **Prepositions of time**
● This exercise, too, can be done individually first of all, with students comparing notes in groups when they are ready.
● They should have little difficulty; if there are any problems, you may like to put the main rules up on the board:
– *at* with exact times
– *on* with days
– *in* with parts of days (*morning, afternoon* etc.)
– *in* to say how soon something will happen (e.g. *in half an hour*)
● Note that *at* is generally dropped in the expression (*At*) *what time?*

3 Language study

- Play the recording of the conversations.
- Then let students look through the texts for examples of the four listed structures.
- Encourage them to think about the use of the structures themselves, asking questions if necessary.
- Then give whatever explanations you feel are needed.
- Next, ask students to choose ten more items from the text to learn.
- When they have done this, let them compare notes and see if they have made the same choices as other students.
- Answer any questions they may have about their chosen items.

4 Stress and rhythm

- This exercise works well in groups of three or four.
- Get students to copy each sentence and mark where they think the stresses come.
- Then play the sentence and discuss the answer.
- Help students to see what kinds of word are stressed (nouns, verbs, adjectives and adverbs, but not usually pronouns, prepositions, articles or conjunctions, especially when they have one syllable). An auxiliary verb is not usually stressed if it is next to a main verb; in other positions, it may be stressed (e.g. **Can** you **tell** me . . .?).
- It is possible to identify several different degrees of stress. For the sake of simplicity, students are only asked here to distinguish between 'stressed' and 'unstressed' syllables.

Answers to Exercise 4
(Each sentence can of course be stressed in different ways to emphasise different ideas. Typical 'neutral' stress patterns are shown here.)
I **won**dered if you were **free** on **Tues**day.
In the **after**noon?
I'd **like** you to **meet** her.
I'm **try**ing to **fix** the Directors' **mee**ting.
Can you **tell** me **what days** you're **free**...
Friday's a **bit difficult.**
I'd **like** to **make** an ap**point**ment...
There's a **lot** to **talk about.**
It'll **take** a **couple** of **hours**...
I'll **call** you **back** in a**bout half** an **hour**...
I'm **play**ing **ten**nis un**til** a **quarter past.**

5 Practising the dialogues

- Get students to spend a few minutes practising one or more of the conversations in pairs.
- You may wish to play the recording to provide a model.

6 Diaries

- Get students to copy the diary pages, and to note the times and days when they plan to do their chosen activities.
- They should fill up most of their time (so that they only have three or four hours free).

7 Making arrangements

- Before starting the exercise, you may like to revise the various conventional expressions which we use when telephoning:
  Could I speak to . . . ?
  Speaking
  Who's that?
  This is . . .
  Can I take a message . . . ?
- Remind students that British people tend to answer the phone by giving their number. Note also the use of *that* to refer to the person at the 'other end', and *this* to refer to oneself, as in conversation A. (Americans use *this* for both.)
- Put students in pairs. The students in each pair should be some distance apart.
- One student in each pair (for instance the one on your left, or the one nearest you) must think of some activity that he or she wants to do with the other student at the weekend.
- Ask a good student to 'telephone' his or her partner and try to arrange something (or demonstrate with a good student yourself).
- When the conversation is finished, ask the class to suggest other expressions that could have been used.
- Then tell the other pairs to improvise in the same way, taking turns. (Or put them back to back and let them work simultaneously.)
- If time allows, get students to try their conversations two or three times, getting in more and more of the expressions that they listed in Exercise 3.

Summary

- Remind students to look over the Summary and learn the new material.

Practice Book

- Tell students which exercises you want them to do.

3 Listen to the conversations. Then look at the text and see how these words and structures are used. Ask your teacher for explanations if necessary.

1. Present progressive tense with future meaning (e.g. *My mother's coming down*).
2. *How about . . . ?* and *Shall we . . . ?* in suggestions.
3. *I'd like to . . .*
4. *I'll . . .* in promises.

Write down ten more useful words, expressions or structures to learn. Can you find any other students who have chosen the same expressions as you?

4 How many stresses? Where are they? Listen to the recording to check your answers.

I wondered if you were free on Tuesday. (3)
In the afternoon?
I'd like you to meet her.
I'm trying to fix the Directors' meeting.
Can you tell me what days you're free...
Friday's a bit difficult.
I'd like to make an appointment...
There's a lot to talk about.
It'll take a couple of hours...
I'll call you back in about half an hour...
I'm playing tennis until a quarter past.

5 Practise one of the conversations with another student.

6 Fill in your diary for Saturday and Sunday. Put in at least eight of the following activities (and any others that you want to add), but leave yourself some free time.

wash your hair   write to your mother
play tennis   buy a sweater   see a film
have a drink with a friend   go to a party
clean the kitchen   mend some clothes
practise the guitar   study English grammar
make a cake   do your ironing   wash the car
go to church   go and see your sister
do some gardening

7 'Telephone' another student. Try to arrange to do something together at the weekend.

Things that have happened

A Have you ever...?

1 Listen to the song. You will hear it twice. The second time, try to remember the words that have been left out.

2 Ask and answer questions beginning *Have you ever eaten / seen / climbed / met / been to / broken / ...?* etc. Example:

HAVE YOU EVER EATEN OCTOPUS?

NO, I NEVER HAVE.

YES. I EAT IT EVERY DAY.

NO, BUT I'VE EATEN SHARK.

YES, I ATE SOME LAST SUMMER.

YES, I'VE EATEN IT TWICE.

3 Match the words and the pictures. Then ask and answer questions beginning *Do you ever...?* or *When you were a child, did you ever...?* Examples:

'Do you ever go walking in the rain?'
'When you were a child, did you ever go camping?'

1. refuse to take medicine
2. stay up all night reading
3. dream of being someone else
4. take part in demonstrations
5. go out alone
6. want to be taller or shorter

Unit 7: Lesson A

Students learn ways of talking about people's experience and habits.

Principal structures: revision of present perfect simple tense; present, past and present perfect with *ever*; *I've been to ...*

Words and expressions to learn: *song*; *job*; *ankle*; *billion*; *boat*; *dollar*; *grammar*; *ice-cream*; *advertisement*; *climb*; *go camping*; *run away*; *fight*; *past* (adjective); *in hospital*; *recently*; *on one occasion*.

Language notes and possible problems

1. Present perfect tense The rules for the use of the present perfect are complicated. Here, students revise the use of the present perfect simple for *finished actions* in *unfinished time periods:* 'time up to now'.
Example: *I've eaten octopus twice (in my life)*.
At the same time, students are reminded that they cannot use the present perfect tense with adverbs or other expressions which refer to a *finished* time period. Look out for mistakes like **I have had a car accident last year*.

The present perfect progressive, and some other uses of the simple tense, are studied in Lesson 7B.

2. Past participles Some students may be unclear about the difference between simple past forms and past participles.

If you are short of time

Leave Exercise 9 for homework and drop Exercise 10.

1 Song

- The song is recorded twice – a complete version is followed by a gapped version.
- Play the complete version through once, while the students listen with their books closed.
- Ask what they have understood, and write on the board any words and phrases that they can recall.
- Play the complete version again, and see if students can recall any more.
- If they have found it easy to understand the song, go straight on to the gapped version. Play this once or twice, while students try to say or sing the words that go in the gaps.
- If this is too difficult, tell students that they can find the words of the song on page 156.
- Go through the text with them explaining any difficulties.
- Then tell them to close their books again, and try the gapped version.

2 Have you ever...?

- Look at the example question with the students. Make sure they understand the meaning of *ever* with the present perfect (= at any time in your life).
- Go over the answers and explain any difficulties.
- Point out that the answer *Yes, I ate some last summer* is in the simple past tense because there is an adverbial of finished time (*last summer*).
- Ask students if they can think of other examples of this sort of adverbial.

- Get a few students to ask others if they have ever eaten octopus; make sure the tenses in the answers are correct.
- Then get students to ask each other more questions beginning *Have you ever...?*
- You may wish to say a word about the use of *been* as a past participle of *go*, meaning *gone and come back*.

Optional activity Survey

- Ask each student to prepare a question beginning *Have you ever...?*
- Get everybody to stand up and walk round asking their questions and noting the answers.
- Then get students to report the results of their survey (e.g. *Seven people out of twelve have had piano lessons; Nobody has been to Australia*).
- (Note: this can also be done after Exercise 3.)

Optional activity Question-box

- Ask students to prepare at least two questions beginning *Have you ever...?*
- They must write their questions on separate pieces of paper, fold them up and put them in a box.
- The box is then passed round. Each student draws out a question, opens it, reads it aloud and answers.
- Tell students that they do not have to tell the truth if they don't want to. They can also reject one question, saying *I'd rather not answer* (put this on the board); but they are not allowed to reject two.
- When students have answered their questions, make sure they don't put them back in the box.
- (This activity can also be done after Exercise 3.)

3 Do you ever...? and Did you ever...?

- Give the students a minute or two to match the words and the pictures.
- Help with new vocabulary, and practise the pronunciation of the phrases.
- Then help them to practise the two example questions, paying attention to correct stress.
- Finally, get students to ask each other more questions in the simple present or simple past. They can use the phrases in the illustration or make up their own.
- This can be done in small groups, with each person asking the others at least two questions.

Optional activities

- If you have not already used the 'survey' or 'question-box' activity, these can be done now, using *Do/did you ever...?*

4 Use of tenses: working out the rules

- Give students a few minutes to discuss the question in groups. Let them speak their own language(s) if this is feasible.
- Then discuss the rules with the class.
- You may find a diagram helpful:

Have you ever...?

PAST_____NOW_____ FUTURE

Did you ever...? *Do you ever...?*

5 Use of tenses: discrimination exercise

- This will help students to see whether they have understood the rules correctly.
- Ask students to write some of the answers (so that you can check up on individuals); the others can be done orally round the class.
- Make sure students understand clearly the reason for the choice of tense in each case.
- In particular, they should realise:
1. that a present perfect tense is impossible with adverbials of finished time (questions 1, 2, 9, 12)
2. that the simple past cannot be used to talk about 'time up to now' (the other questions).

Answers to Exercise 5
1. did you ever run 2. had 3. Do you ever
4. Have you ever broken 5. have often dreamt
6. have travelled 7. I've never been 8. meet
9. didn't like 10. I've spoken 11. Have you ever
12. made

6 Listening for specific information

- Students hear native speakers talking about whether they have done certain things in their lives.
- First play the recording through while the students try to fill in the table.
- Then let them compare answers in small groups.
- Play the recording again if the students would like you to, and then check their answers.

Answers

	1	2	3	4
eating snails	✓	✓	✗	✓
going to America	✓	✓	✗	✗
spending more than a day in hospital	✓	✓	✓	✓
running a mile	✓	✗	✓	✓

- Then play the recording again, while students listen for the words in the list.
- Pause a few times, so that they can write down the words along with the verbs that go with them. (For answers, see tapescript.)
- Once the students have completed the task, you can move on to the next exercise – there is no need to spend time going over every word in the recording.

Tapescript for Exercise 6
1. Yeah, *I've quite often eaten* snails; I like them with garlic sauce. *I've been* to America *twice*. I've, er, certainly spent more than one day in hospital – I spent ten weeks in hospital once. And *I've, I've very often run* more than a mile, yeah.

2. I've eaten snails and enjoyed them. I lived in America for two years. Um, I spent more than one day in hospital when I had my children. Um, and *I've never run* more than a mile. (*Laughter*)

3. I don't think *I've ever eaten* snails, nearly sure I haven't. *I've never been* to America. *I have spent* more than one day in hospital, *recently*. And run more than a mile?
 – The pram race!
 – Yeah, I've run more than a mile. (*Laughter*)

4. Well, *I've eaten* snails *on one occasion*; quite enjoyed it. *I've never been* to America. *I have spent* more than one day in hospital *before now*. And *I have run* more than a mile, um, *quite, quite often*.

7 Preparing an interview

- Divide students into groups of three or four.
- Each group must write at least ten questions, and all the members of the group should write them down.
- Tell them they can use dictionaries; walk round the room to give any help that is needed.

8 Interviewing

- Each student finds a person from another group, and asks all the questions on his or her list.
- Get the students to note the answers (brief notes will do; complete sentences are unnecessary).

9 Writing

- Each student should select a part of the information learnt in the interview and write about it.
- Stress that you do not want a complete picture of the person's life, just six to eight sentences.
- Walk round and help, but don't correct errors (except serious tense mistakes) unless you are asked to. Make sure that students do not write their names or the names of the people they are writing about.

10 Listening and guessing

- When students are ready, collect up all the papers.
- Then read out the paragraphs, while students try to guess who is described in each one.
- Alternatively, you can number the papers and put them on the class notice board for students to read. Tell them to write down the numbers together with the names of the people they think are described.

Summary
- Remind students to study the Summary.

Practice Book
- Tell students which exercises you want them to do.

4 What are the differences between *Have you ever...?*, *Do you ever...?* and *Did you ever...?*

5 Choose the correct tense (present, present perfect or past).

1. When you were a child, *have you ever run / did you ever run* away from home?
2. My brother *has had / had* a fight with his neighbour last week.
3. *Do you ever / Did you ever* travel by boat?
4. *Have you ever broken / Did you ever break* your ankle?
5. I *have often dreamt / often dreamt* of having a billion dollars.
6. During the last three years, I *have travelled / travelled* about 100,000 miles.
7. 'Do you know Canada?' 'No, *I've never been / I never went* there.'
8. I've got a very interesting job, and I *meet / met* lots of famous people.
9. I *haven't liked / didn't like* grammar at school, but I'm very interested in it now.
10. *I've spoken / I spoke* to the President several times.
11. *Have you ever / Did you ever* put an advertisement in a newspaper?
12. When we were small, Mother *has made / made* us delicious ice-cream every Sunday.

6 Listen to some people talking about past experiences. For each experience put a ✓ if they have had it, and a ✗ if they have not.

	1	2	3	4
eating snails				
going to America				
spending more than a day in hospital				
running a mile				

Now listen again. Try to pick out these words, and write down the verbs that go with them.

quite often   twice   very often
never   ever   recently   on one occasion
before   now

7 In groups of three or four, make a list of ten or more questions that you can ask about someone's life, interests, work, etc. Examples:

'Where did you live when you were a child?'
'Can you talk about two happy times in your life?'
'Have you ever studied music?'

8 Find a person from another group. Ask the questions that you have prepared (and other questions, too, if you like). Note the answers.

9 Write some sentences (about eight), using some of the information from Exercise 8. Don't use the person's name in your sentences.

10 Pass your sentences to the teacher, who will read them to the class. The class has to guess who the sentences are about.

"Fifteen years we've commuted together on this train; fifteen years all we've ever said to each other has been 'Good Morning' – I'd just like you to know, I love you."

31

B Here is the news

1 Complete these sentences and write them out correctly. (You may need to put more than one word in a blank.) To get the information you need, look at the statistics and the background information on Fantasia, and listen to the news broadcast.

1. The population of Fantasia has *doubled / trebled / quadrupled* since 1900.
2. The population of San Fantastico *increased / decreased / has increased / has decreased* since 1900.
3. Fantasia used to be highly industrialised, but now has a mainly agricultural economy. True or false?
4. The Fantasians .... to have parliamentary elections every .... years. Since 1980, they *have / had / have had* parliamentary elections every .... years.
5. Mrs Rask *is / was / has been* President of Fantasia for .... years.
6. Fantasia has just .... a .... of Friendship and Protection with Outland.
7. Outland .... be a Fantasian colony. It *became / has become* independent in ....
8. .... of Outland and his wife have just arrived in Fantasia for a state visit.
9. President Rask and Mrs Martin *know / knew / have known* each other .... a long time.
10. They *first met / have first met* at the Olympic Games in 19.., where Mrs Rask *won / has won* a silver medal for the high jump.
11. Dr Rask .... just .... from a trip abroad.
12. He has been visiting Third World countries for the last .... weeks in his capacity as President of 'Families .... '.
13. The percentage of homeless people in Fantasia has *risen / fallen* considerably .... 1900.
14. Unemployment figures .... *improved / worsened* since 1950.
15. The percentage of women in paid employment has *risen / fallen* .... 1950.
16. A fire .... burning .... three days in Grand South Station.
17. It .... raining steadily .... the last .... weeks in Fantasia, and the river Fant .... burst its banks.
18. The heavy rains have ruined some crops, and .... prices in San Fantastico .... going up steadily for the last .... days. The Minister for Consumer Affairs .... announced that price controls on vegetables and fruit will come into effect ....

FANTASIA: SOME STATISTICS

ITEM	1900	1950	TODAY
Population	20m	35m	60m
Population of San Fantastico	1.2m	4.3m	3.6m
Average number of children per family	4.5	3.6	2
Working week (hours)	54	49	42
Paid holiday (weeks per year)	0	2	5
Size of army	500,000	200,000	50,000
Homeless	23%	17%	8%
Unemployment	20%	7%	17%
Women in paid employment	18%	23%	79%
Percentage of workforce in agriculture	84%	66%	19%
Contribution of agriculture to Gross National Product	78%	51%	8%
Contribution of industry to Gross National Product	11%	38%	83%
Foreign tourists per year	?	30,000	6m

FANTASIA AND OUTLAND: SOME BACKGROUND INFORMATION

Since the revolution in 1886, Fantasia has been a parliamentary democracy. There are two Houses of Parliament: elections to both used to be held every seven years, but since the Electoral Reform Act of 1980, elections have been held every four years. The president is elected separately by popular vote; the last presidential election was held three years ago. Mrs Kirsten Rask, the current president, is a distinguished physicist. She is also a former Olympic athlete who won a silver medal for the high jump in the 1960 Games.

Outland was formerly the Fantasian colony of South Wesk, but has become independent since the end of the War of Independence in 1954. Relations between the two countries have become more friendly since Mrs Rask's election, and Fantasia has just signed a 'Treaty of Friendship and Protection' with Outland. President Martin of Outland was at university with the Fantasian President's husband, Dr Erasmus Rask, and Mrs Martin and Mrs Rask have been friends since they met at the 19.. Olympics.

Unit 7: Lesson B

Students practise talking about news, about the duration of current states, and about changes.

Principal structures: more uses of the present perfect simple (including *have just*); present perfect progressive; non-progressive verbs; *since* and *for*; *used to*.

Words and expressions to learn: *election; economy; president; trip; percentage; unemployment; figures; minister; crops; fruit; silver; increase; sign; improve; average; abroad.*

Phonology: the letter *e* in stressed and unstressed syllables at the beginnings of words.

Language notes and possible problems

1. Level Exercise 1 may look difficult to students, but it is not unreasonably hard. Make it clear that they do not have to understand all the vocabulary in the texts or the news broadcast; they only have to grasp certain key words in order to complete the task. Some things (especially in the news broadcast) will not be completely clear. This does not matter: the exercise is designed to give students some 'real-life' exposure to natural-sounding language, with all its difficulties. Provided they stay calm and concentrate on the task which they are asked to do, they will be able to complete the exercise successfully.

2. Vocabulary Students are asked to learn a limited number of high-priority words. The lesson contains various other words connected with politics, economics or world affairs. These are listed separately in the Summary; encourage students to learn some of them as well if they have time.

3. Present perfect simple Students revise the use of this tense to give news (often with *just*) and to talk about changes. These uses follow the general rule that the present perfect is used (especially in British English) for past events which have a connection with the present or present importance. Remind students that the present perfect is not used with adverbs of finished time – there are several examples in the news broadcast.

4. Present perfect progressive This tense is used to talk about temporary states and actions which began in the past and have continued up to the present. One common use is to say how long something has been going on for (e.g. *rain...has been falling steadily for the past four weeks*). Some students may tend to use present tenses in this case (e.g. **I learn/am learning English since two years*).

5. *Since and for* Students may use *since* instead of *for* when talking about duration (in some languages the same word is used for both meanings). Look out for mistakes like **I am here since three days*. There is an exercise on this point in the Practice Book.

6. Non-progressive verbs Note that *know, have* and *be* do not have progressive forms in some of their meanings. So we say *How long have you known him?* (not **How long have you been knowing him?*); *I have had this car for three months* (not **I have been having...*); *I've been here all day* (not **I've been being ...*). Students may find this confusing.

7. *Used to...* Make sure students realise that *used to* has no present form. (To talk about present habits and

states, we just use the simple present tense.) Affirmatives and negatives are covered here; questions (*Did you use to...?*) will be practised in a later lesson. Note the pronunciation: /ˈjuːst tə/; not **/ˈjuːzd tə/.

If you are short of time
Divide the task in Exercise 1 so that each student only has six or nine questions to answer. If pronunciation is not important, drop Exercise 5.

---

1 Gathering information

- In this exercise, students focus on several structures (present perfect simple and progressive, *since* and *for*, *used to*) as they collect the information they need.
- Explain that students will find the information in the table of statistics, in the 'background information' text, or in the news broadcast.
- Tell them that they can use dictionaries or ask you for the meanings of difficult words if they wish.
- Do the first two questions with the class. Show them how the grammar problem in sentence 2 can be solved by looking carefully at the use of tenses in sentence 1.
- Then let them continue, working individually or in groups as you prefer. (If they work in groups they can save time by dividing up the questions between them, but note that earlier questions contain examples of the structures needed to answer later questions.)
- When students have done as much as they can by referring to the book, play the news broadcast. (The tapescript is on page 179.) This will provide the answers to the outstanding questions. (Students may need to listen more than once.)
- Finally, go over the answers with the class and give whatever grammar explanations you feel are necessary.
- A diagram may help to show how the present perfect progressive is used for an action or state continuing up to the present:

PAST ----|----|----|---- NOW -------FUTURE

It has been raining for four weeks

Answers to Exercise 1
1. trebled   2. has increased   3. false
4. used; seven; have had; four   5. has been; three
6. signed; treaty   7. used to; became; 1954
8. President Martin   9. have known; for
10. first met; 1960; won   11. has...returned
12. six; against Hunger   13. fallen; since
14. have worsened   15. risen; since   16. has been; for
17. has been; for; four; has
18. vegetable; have been; ten; has; next week

32

2 Comparing pictures

- This exercise gives practice in using *used to*; students also practise the use of the present perfect to talk about changes.
- Give the class a minute or two to look at the pictures.
- Look at the examples and explain any difficulties. Make sure students are clear about the use and pronunciation of *used to* (see *Language notes*).
- Ask students to suggest differences between the two pictures.
- Encourage them to express their answers with *used to* (affirmative or negative) or the present perfect. Help with vocabulary if necessary.

3 Present perfect and simple past

- This exercise helps students to understand the use of the present perfect to talk about duration up to the present.
- Ask students to think about the first question, write down their answers, and compare notes with other students.
- Then give them the answer and explain the reason for it.
- Treat the other questions in the same way.

Answers to Exercise 3
1. Yes. (The present perfect is not used with adverbs of finished time, so the 'six years' cannot be finished.)
2. No. (The use of the simple past shows that the 'three years' are a finished period.)
3. Sally. (The present perfect shows that the speaker is still working with Eric).
4. No. (The use of the simple past shows that 'at school' refers to a finished period.)
5. When it will end.
6. 'How long ago did your visit start?'

(**Grammatical note:** The present perfect progressive is possible in sentence 3, but we often prefer the simple tense when we talk about longer, more permanent states.)

4 Perfect, past and present

- This exercise should help students to get a clearer picture of the rules for the use of the present perfect progressive.
- It can be done in writing or by class discussion, as you prefer.

Answers to Exercise 4
1. have been writing (normal use of present perfect progressive)
2. am going (present progressive used for future)
3. have you been learning (normal use of present perfect progressive)
4. lived (simple past with adverbial of finished time)
5. have had (present perfect is needed to talk about duration up to the present; simple tense is used because *have* is a non-progressive verb when used to talk about possession)
6. have you known (same case as question 5)
7. have been (same case as 5 and 6)

5 Pronunciation: *e* in unstressed prefixes 🔘

- In standard British English when the letter *e* comes in an unstressed syllable at the beginning of a word, it is almost always pronounced /ɪ/.

- Go through the words with the students, helping them with the pronunciation, and getting them to decide how the *e* is pronounced.
- Then tell them to write the words in two groups (or do it yourself on the board), according to the pronunciation of *e*.
- Give students a minute or two to try to see the reason for the difference. Play the recording or say the words while they are thinking about it.
- If they can't work it out, ask them where the stress comes in each word.
- Practise the pronunciation.
- Ask if students can think of any more words that could be added to the two groups.

6 News bulletins

- If there is plenty of time available, each group can prepare a complete news broadcast which they can practise, tape-record or video-record, and play to the rest of the class.
- If you don't have time for this, get students to work in groups, preparing one short news item per group. They should of course use the structures (and if possible some of the vocabulary) which they have learnt from the lesson.
- When students are ready, ask a volunteer from each group to read out the group's news item.

Summary
- Remind students to look at the Summary and learn the new material.

Practice Book
- Tell students which exercises you want them to do.

2 Look at the two pictures. What differences can you see? Examples:

'There used to be a church to the right of the bridge.'
'People's clothes have changed.'
'People didn't use to travel by car.'

VIEW FROM WESK SQUARE AROUND 1890

VIEW FROM WESK SQUARE 1985

3 Grammar revision. Can you answer these questions?

1. A man says, 'I've been in France for six years'. Is he in France when he says this?
2. A woman says, 'I was in Japan for three years'. Is she in Japan when she says this?
3. Somebody says, 'I've worked with Eric for 30 years, and I worked with Sally for 25 years'. Which one does he still work with?
4. Somebody says, 'I did seven years' French at school'. Is he or she still at school?
5. You are in America. Somebody asks, 'How long are you here for?' Does the person want to know when your visit started, or when it will end?
6. What does 'How long have you been here for?' mean?

4 Grammar. Choose the correct form.

1. I *am writing / have been writing / wrote* letters for the last two hours.
2. I *am going / go / have been going* out with some friends tonight.
3. 'How long *are you learning / have you been learning* English?' 'Since last summer.'
4. When I was a child, we *have been living / have lived / lived* in a house by a river.
5. I *have had / have* this watch since my 18th birthday.
6. 'How long *have you known / do you know* Jessica?' 'We *have been / were* at school together 40 years ago.'
7. I *am / have been* ill for three days now. I think I'd better call the doctor.

5 Pronunciation. These words all have the letter *e* in the first syllable. In some of the words, *e* is pronounced /e/; in others, it is pronounced /ɪ/. Can you divide the words into two groups, according to the pronunciation of *e*? What is the reason for the difference?

become   depend
democracy   demonstration
economy   effèct   election
employment   end   every
held   medal   president
reform   relations   return
revolution   secretary
separate   seven   vegetable

6 Work in groups. Prepare a short news item, with information about what has happened recently in your country, in the world, in your class, or in Fantasia.

Know before you go

A Going to Britain

1 Look through the text to find the answers to these questions.

1. How can you write *fifty pence* in another way?
2. Where can you usually get a good inexpensive meal?
3. Where can you ask about an inexpensive place to stay?
4. Is all medical care for foreigners free in Britain?
5. Which is cheaper, travelling by train or travelling by coach?

Getting around   Trains are fairly good in Britain. If you are under 24 or over 65, or if you are travelling with a family, ask about 'railcards' for cheaper fares on the train. There are also coaches (long-distance buses) between some towns and cities; these are cheaper than trains. In towns and cities, there are usually buses, and in London there is also an underground. But the underground is not easy to use, so you should learn about it before you use it.

Writing home   Stamps can only be bought in post offices; but nearly every village (or part of a town) has a post office. Often it is inside a small shop.

Money   There are one hundred pence (100p) in a pound (£1). People sometimes say 'p' instead of 'pence'; for example, 'eighty p'. Not all banks change foreign money, but you can usually find at least one bank in each town that will do so.

Eating out   Restaurants are often expensive, and you cannot be sure the food will be good. But Indian and Chinese restaurants usually serve good meals at lower prices. Pubs sometimes do good inexpensive food. Fast food shops – fish and chip shops, hamburger shops – are cheap, but the food is not always very good.

Where to stay   Hotels are very expensive in Britain. A cheaper solution is a 'bed and breakfast' in someone's home. Information centres or tourist offices can help you to find these. There are also youth hostels and campsites in many places.

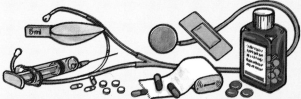

Medical care   If you get ill or have an accident while you are in Britain, and you must be treated before you return home, you can get free medical care. Your country may have an agreement with Britain for other medical care, too; ask at the British embassy or consulate before you leave. You may need a special paper from your country's national health service. If your country does not have an agreement with Britain, you may want to take out health insurance for the journey.

Unit 8: Lesson A

Students practise reading and writing skills while learning information about travelling in Britain.
Principal structures: *can* for possibility; revision of *may* and *will*; linking devices in paragraphs.
Words and expressions to learn: *campsite; fare; coach; distance; underground; accident; embassy; consulate; agreement; insurance; foreign; at least; free* (not paid for); *for example; also.*
Phonology: /ʃ/ and /tʃ/; hearing the difference between rising and falling intonation.

Language notes and possible problems

1. *You = one* *You* is used in the sense of 'one' in this unit. You may wish to point this out if there is not a parallel use in students' mother tongues.

2. *Can* for possibility Most languages have a structure which operates in the same way as *can* in English: to express both ability (*I can type*) and possibility (*Stamps can only be bought in post offices*). If your students speak a language that does *not* have a parallel structure, you may wish to do some extra work with them before doing Exercise 3. You will probably have to remind students that *can* is pronounced /kn/ in affirmative sentences when it is unstressed; and to listen for mistakes with *to* (for example, **You can to get...*).

3. The grammar of possibility is complex. As a rule, *can* is used for 'general' or 'theoretical' possibility (to talk about the sort of things that happen under various circumstances). To talk about the chances of something actually happening at a particular moment, we prefer to use *may* or *might*. Compare:
    People can do stupid things when they're in love.
    I'm afraid Mary may do something stupid.
In this lesson, students practise this use of *can* and revise the use of *may* to mean 'will perhaps'. You may not wish to make the distinction between the two concepts explicit at this stage.

4. Hearing intonation Students sometimes have trouble hearing intonation contours, especially falls: they tend to hear the high pitch that precedes a fall and do not hear the fall. Exercises 6 and 7 help with this.

If you are short of time

You can leave out Exercise 4, or Exercises 6 and 7, or get the students to do the second part of Exercise 5 for homework.

1 Scanning reading

● Explain to students that they are going to search a text for the answers to specific questions, and that they should not try to read or understand the whole text.
● Go over the questions with them to make sure they understand everything.
● Then get them to try to find the answers individually as quickly as they can.
● If students have trouble with unknown words, you can either let them use their dictionaries or get them to ask you (using correct English in their request). You may want to decline to give definitions for words which are not essential to understanding, telling the students that they are not important.
● When students finish, they should compare answers with the people sitting nearest, and the group should come to a consensus before checking with you.

2 /ʃ/ and /tʃ/

• Begin the exercise with recognition practice: write *sh* on one side of the board and *ch* on the other, pronouncing them as you do so.

• Call out words beginning or ending with one or the other (perhaps from the lists numbered 1 and 2). Students should raise the hand corresponding to the correct side of the board.

• Help the students pronounce the words in the numbered lists chorally after you or in the recording.

• Then go quickly round the class, letting each student pronounce one of the words in the unnumbered rows. You may want to point out that *tch* at the end of a word is pronounced in exactly the same way as *ch*.

• Finally, you may want to ask the students to volunteer any other words they know with *sh* or *ch* in them, or with the sounds /ʃ/ and /tʃ/. They may come up with exceptions like *school* and *sure*.

3 *Can* for possibility

• Go over the sample sentences with the students; you may want to ask them to tell you what the meaning of *can* is in these sentences.

• For the first question, get the students to work in groups of three or four. Then let the class pool answers.

• For the second question, students will have to work individually if they come from different places; the others will probably be interested to find out about each student's city/town/village/neighbourhood.

• If the students are all from the same place, this can be done in the same way as the first question.

• Alternatively, if students have some knowledge of other places, each can choose a place and make up five sentences about what you can do/can't do there. The other students listen to the five sentences and try to guess what the place is.

4 More scanning; *may* and *will*

• Let students work individually, as you walk round to give any help that is needed.

• Then get them to compare answers in small groups before checking with you.

• Exercise 1 in the Practice Book gives more work on *may*.

5 Writing practice

• The first part of this exercise gets students to focus on the linking words that hold written texts together.

• Ask students to look for the words in the text; some of them are used several times.

• The next part of the exercise can be handled in several ways:

1. If students are from different countries, have travelled a bit, or know about different countries: ask each one to choose a country, and then to write about one of the subjects from the opposite page.

2. Even if students are all from the same place and have little knowledge of other countries, you can distribute the subjects out to groups of two or three, getting more than one group to work on the same subject.

• In both cases, get students to exchange texts when they have finished (making it clear that you are not worrying about correct English for the moment). They can read them out, post them on the notice board for each other to read, or pass them from group to group.

• If students have written about different places, you can do a class survey: each student chooses one of the points from his or her paragraph, and finds out how things are in the other countries by asking all the other students (for example, *Can you buy stamps in a tobacconist's?*).

6 Intonation: preliminary exercise

• Play the examples numbered 1 to 4 while the students look at the words in their books with the intonation contours marked.

• Let students listen more than once to be sure they can hear the contours.

• Then play the second set of examples (5 to 8) so the students can decide if each one rises or falls at the end. (They all fall.)

• Play more than once if necessary.

• Check that everyone has understood before going on to the next exercise.

7 Intonation in conversation

• The conversation is recorded twice: once straight through and once with numbers and pauses.

• Let the students listen to the unpaused version first.

• Then get them to number lines 1 to 13 on a piece of paper, and to mark ↗ or ↘ according to whether the word or phrase goes up or down at the end.

• You may wish to play the recording twice or more.

• Then check the answers with the whole class.

• You may wish to get the students to repeat the sentences after the recording as a final stage.

Tapescript for Exercise 7

1. Hello? ↗
2. Hello, Annie. ↘
3. This is Bob. ↘
4. Hello, Bob. ↘
5. How are you? ↘
6. Fine, thanks. ↗
7. Listen, Annie. ↘
8. Are you still planning to go to London this summer? ↗
9. Yeah, we are. ↘
10. Why? ↘
11. Well, you don't need a place to stay, do you? ↗
12. My cousin has a small house in London, ↘
13. and she's looking for somebody to rent it to in July and August. ↘

Summary

• Remind students to look over the Summary and learn the new material.

Practice Book

• Tell students which exercises you want them to do.

2 Say these words after the teacher or the recording. Notice the difference in pronunciation between *sh* and *ch*.

1. should   shop   show
   British   wash   push
2. change   cheap   chip
   coach   teach   each

Now pronounce these words.

ship   shut   cheque   shower   cheers
switch   cash   fresh   watch   finish

3 Notice *can* in the text:

*. . . you **can** usually find at least one bank . . .*
*. . . tourist offices **can** help you to find these.*
*Stamps **can** only be bought in post offices; . . .*
*. . . you **cannot** be sure the food will be good.*
*. . . you **can** get free medical care.*

Now answer these questions.

1. What are seven things you can do in an airport?
   Example: '*You can have a meal.*'
2. What are five things you can and can't do in your city/town/village/neighbourhood?
   Examples: '*You can go swimming. You can't go skiing.*'

4 Look back at the text and decide whether *will* or *may* goes in each blank.

1. Not all banks in small towns in Britain .... change foreign money for you.
2. If you stay in a hotel in Britain, it .... be expensive.
3. Information centres .... have information about 'bed and breakfast'.
4. If 'bed and breakfast' is too expensive, there .... be a youth hostel nearby.
5. You .... have the choice between a train and a coach for travel from one city to another.
6. You .... only find stamps in post offices.
7. If you break your leg while on holiday in Britain, you .... not have to pay the hospital for treating it.

5 Look for these words in the text and notice how each one is used.

for example   but   these   also   it   and   so   too

Now choose one of the subjects from the opposite page (*Money, Where to stay*, etc.) and write about your own country or another country you know about. Try to use some of the words from the list. Then exchange papers with one or more students to read what they have written.

6 Listen.

1. Annie   Annie
2. Why?   Why?
3. in London   in London
4. July and August   July and August

Now listen again. Up ↗ or down ↘ ?

5. Annie
6. Why?
7. in London
8. July and August

B Going to the USA

1 What do you know about travelling in the USA? Try to answer these questions.

1. A penny is worth one cent ($0.01, or 1¢). How much are these coins worth: a nickel, a dime, a quarter?
2. Can you usually find a bank in a small American town that will change foreign money?
3. In what places are you likely to find campsites in the US?
3. Is it easy to tour the United States by train?
5. What is the cheapest way of touring the States?

2 Listen to the telephone conversation and write down the following information.

1. the telephone numbers
2. the name of the person phoning
3. the time the plane will land
4. the airline and flight number

Now listen again and see if you can remember some of what was said.

3 Work in threes. Imagine your wallet and passport have just been stolen in the airport in New York City. You were about to take a plane to Washington, and you still have your plane ticket and your traveller's cheques. Make some collect (reverse-charge) calls.

1. To your friend Pat in Washington. Ask him/her to come and pick you up at the airport when you arrive. (Pat's phone number: (202) 664–3572)
2. To your cousin Chris, who lives in Newark, New Jersey, to ask him/her to phone and cancel your American Express and Diner's Club credit cards – you don't have the numbers of the cards, but your parents do. Chris can phone them if there is a problem. (Chris's number: (201) 435–2090)
3. To Mr/Ms Bennett, who is expecting you in Boston tomorrow. You will have to stay in Washington to go to your embassy and get a new passport. (The Bennetts' number: (617) 975–4303)

4 Match the pictures and the phrases. Use your dictionary if you need to.

1. a passport
2. light clothes
3. a pickpocket
4. customs
5. a visa
6. traveller's cheques
7. medical insurance
8. immigration control
9. sunglasses

36

Unit 8: Lesson B

Students learn to make reverse-charge telephone calls and practise listening and speaking skills.
Principal structures: *should, will have to.*
Words and expressions to learn: (telephone) *operator; airline; wallet; passport; customs; pickpocket; competition; choice; pick up* (in a car); *cancel; go through customs; reverse-charge call* (British); *collect call* (American); *STD code / area code; immigration control.*

Language notes and possible problems
1. *Should* and *will have to* Students who have done Book 1 of *The Cambridge English Course* will be familiar with *should* for advice and *have to* for obligation, but you may need to give other students additional help. Since the students have recently revised *will, will have to* should not present a problem as a future form. The contrast between *must* and *have to* will be dealt with in a later unit.

2. 24-hour clock In the telephone conversation the young woman gives *19.46* as the time her plane will land. Note that while the 24-hour clock is in common use in plane and train timetables, this is the only situation in which you will hear times expressed this way in English.

If you are short of time
You can leave out Exercise 1 or Exercise 7.

1 Quiz
● Let the students try the questions; make sure they know that they can guess. You may have to help them with *worth, tour,* and *likely.*
● Once they have tried the quiz individually get them to compare answers in small groups before checking with you.

Correct answers
1. a nickel = five cents (5¢ or $0.05); a dime = 10¢; a quarter = 25¢.
2. Few banks in America change foreign money, even in big cities. (You should take traveller's cheques in dollars.)
3. A National Park is the only place in America where you stand a good chance of finding a campsite.
4. No. The American rail system is not very extensive.
5. On the buses that run between cities and towns. Some of the big national bus companies offer special tickets for tourists, at a flat rate for a given length of time.

2 Listening: phone conversation
● Ask students to get out a blank sheet of paper and write down the four items so they can be ready to note the answers when they hear them.
● Play the recording once without stopping. Students may want you to play it a second time to make sure of their answers before they check with you.

Answers: (0223) 103493 and (512) 442–9006; Joan Perry; 19.46; Pan Am flight 52.

● Then play the first part of the recording again (up until Helen answers), pausing after each of the operator's sentences.
● Ask the class to try and recall what Joan says each time.

● Do the same with the last part, but stop after Joan's sentences and ask the students to recall what her mother says.
● Explain any terms the students are still having difficulty with.

Tapescript for Exercise 2: see next page (page 37)

3 Improvisations
● Divide the class into groups of three. (One or two groups of four is all right.)
● Go through the situations in Exercise 3, making sure the students understand the vocabulary.
● In the groups, each student takes turns playing the caller, the operator, and the person who answers the phone. The person who is playing the operator can look at the book.
● Walk round to give any help that is needed.
● Students who finish early can change groups and begin again, or invent new reverse-charge calls.
● You may want to tape- or video-record some of the conversations if this is motivating for your students.

4 Vocabulary
● This exercise introduces and revises the vocabulary necessary for Exercise 5.
● Get the students to work in pairs trying to match the phrases with the pictures.
● They can use their dictionaries, or ask you about new words. If they do ask you, make sure they use correct forms (*What does x mean?*, etc.).
● Get each pair to compare its answers with another pair before checking with you.
● Point out that you *go through customs.*

5 *Should* and *will have to*

● Make sure the students understand where Florida is and what sort of climate it has; check that they understand why *should* is used in the first example and *will have to* in the second example.
● Then let them make sentences from the table, either as a whole-class activity or by writing sentences individually.
● They should be able to deduce what *watch out for* means, but help them if they don't.
● Exercise 2 in the Practice Book gives further practice on these points.

6 Reading: choosing a holiday

● Tell students that their task is to choose a holiday they would like to win in a competition, but that it is not necessary to read every word of every holiday description in order to make up their minds.
● Illustrate by saying that you love (or hate) sports, so you know that the holiday for you is (or is not) *White water magic*.
● Tell them they can use their dictionaries, but should only look up words they absolutely have to in order to understand the descriptions.
● Alternatively, let them tell you words they want to know the meanings of; only give them explanations for the words that are necessary for understanding (not *van* or *luscious*, for example).
● Walk round as they are working to give any help with the writing that is needed.

7 Fluency practice

● Get the students to stand up and walk around, if this is practical, or to talk to as many people as they can without moving from their seats.
● It would be a good idea to join in yourself.
● (The students should be using some of the ways of expressing the future that they worked on in Unit 6.)
● Each student tries to find at least one other person who has chosen the same holiday as him/her.
● They should compare the reasons they have for choosing that holiday.
● If there are students who do not find partners, they can go on directly to the second part of the exercise.
● Ask students (still in pairs if possible) to find other students who have chosen different holidays.
● They should tell one another what they *should* do and what they *will have to* do for the holidays they have chosen.

Optional activity

● In groups of three or four, students decide on another holiday destination (it does not have to be in America).
● They make detailed plans – when they're going, how they're travelling, what they will do there – and each group then presents its plans to the class.

Summary

● Remind students to look over the Summary and learn the new material.

Practice Book

● Tell students which exercises you want them to do.

Tapescript for Exercise 2

OPERATOR: Operator. May I help you?
JOAN: Yes, I'd like to make a collect call to England.
OPERATOR: To England. What number, please?
JOAN: The STD code is 0223.
OPERATOR: 0223.
JOAN: and the number is 103.
OPERATOR: 103.
JOAN: 493.
OPERATOR: 493. That's 0223 103493.
JOAN: That's right.
OPERATOR: And what number are you calling from?
JOAN: Er, area code 512.
OPERATOR: 512.
JOAN: 442–9006.
OPERATOR: 442–9006. And your name, please?
JOAN: Joan Perry.
OPERATOR: Is that Perry, with a P?
JOAN: Yes, that's right.
OPERATOR: Thank you, Ms Perry, I'll try to connect you.
JOAN: Thank you.
(Operator dials number and it rings)
HELEN: 103493.
OPERATOR: Hello, I have a reverse-charge call from Joan Perry in the United States. Will you pay for the call?
HELEN: Yes.
OPERATOR: Thank you. Go ahead please.
JOAN: Hello, Mum.
HELEN: Hello, darling, how are you?
JOAN: Fine, been having a wonderful time, and you?
HELEN: Fine.
JOAN: I'm just phoning to see if you can pick us up at the airport tomorrow. Do you think you can?
HELEN: Well, it depends on the time.
JOAN: Our plane lands at 19.46 – that's 7.46 in the evening.
HELEN: Oh, yes, that should be fine. 7.46?
JOAN: That's right. Pan Am flight 52.
HELEN: OK, darling, I'll be there.
JOAN: Thanks, Mum. See you then. Bye-bye.
HELEN: Bye, darling.

5 Going to Miami. Make some sentences with *You'll have to . . .* and *You should . . .* for somebody who's going to Florida on holiday.

Examples: *'You should take sunglasses.'*
'You'll have to have a passport.'

You should
You'll have to

have
take
watch out for
go through
buy

a passport.
light clothes.
pickpockets.
customs.
a visa.

traveller's cheques.
medical insurance.
immigration control.
sunglasses.

NEW YORK, NEW YORK!
Spend two weeks in exciting New York City. Theatre, dance, opera, museums,...

WINNER TAKE ALL!
Come to Las Vegas and try your luck. When you're tired of winning at the casino, relax by the pool or go to watch a fabulous show...

WHITE WATER MAGIC
If you are a confirmed sportsman or sportswoman, spend an exciting two weeks with us canoeing in the beautiful Rocky Mountains...

DO IT YOURSELF
We provide the car or camping van, maps and advice, and you go your own way, discovering the America you want to discover.

ALOHA
You will never forget the warm welcome of Hawaii. Beautiful sunny beaches, friendly people, luscious tropical food...

FLOAT ALONG
Enjoy beautiful Texas scenery and wildlife while relaxing on a raft on the Rio Grande. Comfortable tent accommodation at night...

6 Which one of these holidays would you most like to win in a competition? Don't tell anyone else, but write down the reasons for your choice.

7 Try to find someone else in the class who has chosen the same holiday as you. Tell each other the reasons for your choices.

Then find people who have chosen another holiday. Tell them what you think they will have to do and should do.

Problems

A Emergency

1 Match the pictures and the sentences.

1. My baby has just eaten some aspirins.
2. There's a fire in my kitchen.
3. There's been an accident. A man is hurt. He's bleeding badly
4. There's been a burglary.
5. Smoke is coming out of my neighbour's kitchen window.
6. Somebody has stolen my motorbike.

2 The same or different? You will hear nine pairs of words. If the two words are the same, write 'S'. If they are different, write 'D'.

3 Can you hear a *th*? Copy the list; then listen and circle the words you hear.

1. then / den
2. there / dare
3. think / sink
4. thing / sing
5. those / doze

4 Practise saying these after your teacher or the recording.

There's a   There's a fire
There's a fire in my kitchen.

There's been
There's been an accident.
There's been a burglary.

through   put you through
I'll put you through.

there   right there
We'll be right there.

think   I think
I think his leg is broken.

Unit 9: Lesson A

Students learn to talk about emergencies.
Principal structures: present perfect for announcing that things have just happened; contrast between this use of the present perfect and the simple past; *there has been*.
Words and expressions to learn: *fire; neighbour; kitchen; burglary; smoke; window; instructions; ambulance; emergency; bleed; steal; cover* (verb).
Phonology: /θ/ and /ð/.

Language notes and possible problems

1. The present perfect tense   Remind students that the present perfect is often used to report recent events which are 'news' (emergencies, for example). It is not used in narratives about the less recent past (as when students talk about things that happened to them when they were younger, in Exercise 8). Nor is it used with finished-time adverbials, even when reporting 'news'.

It may be necessary to remind students that this use of the present perfect is not only confined to emergencies.

2. There has been   Students are likely to have difficulty with some of the tenses of *there is*; make sure they use this form in their practice.

3. Steal, rob, burgle   You may want to point out the differences between these three verbs (and the corresponding nouns *theft, robbery* and *burglary*).

4. Students' reticence about real emergencies
Some classes enjoy Exercise 8 very much; some students choose to talk about serious accidents and some about trivial ones. But you may feel that your students do not wish to talk about distressing experiences they have had. If this is the case you can replace Exercise 8 with Exercise 3 from the Practice Book, to ensure that students work on the contrast between present perfect and simple past tenses.

If you are short of time
You can leave out Exercises 2 and 3 or Exercise 7.

1 Matching sentences and pictures
● Students will not know all the words in the exercise, but they should be able to match the sentences and pictures and make a good guess at the meanings.
● Give them a few minutes to do the exercise individually, and then let them compare notes in pairs or groups before checking the answers with the whole class.
● Explain new vocabulary, being careful to point out the difference between *stealing* and *burglary*.
● Make sure students understand what each of the contractions (*there's*) stands for.

2 /θ/ and /ð/: ear-training
● Here students listen for the difference between /θ/ and /s/ and between /ð/ and /d/.
● They must simply write *S* if the two words they hear are the same, and *D* if they are different.
● You may want to play the recording more than once.

Tapescript and answers to Exercise 2
1. than, Dan (*D*)
2. that, that (*S*)
3. then, then (*S*)
4. there, dare (*D*)
5. think, think (*S*)
6. thing, sing (*D*)
7. those, doze (*D*)
8. through, through (*S*)
9. throw, throw (*S*)

3 Can you hear a *th*?
● Students continue practising discrimination of *th* sounds.
● Ask them to copy the list from their books.
● Then play the recording, more than once if necessary, while they circle the words they hear.

Tapescript for Exercise 3
1. then   2. dare   3. think   4. sing   5. those

4 Pronunciation practice
● Students practise /θ/ and /ð/ in sentences from the lesson.
● Get the students to repeat after you or the recording, chorally and individually.
● You may want to remind students that when they make these sounds their tongues should be touching the bottom of their top front teeth.

5 Practice: reporting emergencies

- Ask the class to suggest possible sentences to go with the second picture (for example, *Someone has stolen my car*).
- Then put the students in groups and ask them to work out sentences for the rest of the pictures (imagining that they have to report the emergencies by phone).
- Walk round and help where necessary.
- Do not discourage students who want to use passive constructions; this will give you a chance to see how well they master them. But do try to get a *There's been* sentence in each group.
- You may want to introduce the word *rob* and contrast it with *steal* and *burgle*.
- When students have finished, discuss the answers with the class.

Possible answers to Exercise 5
3. Smoke is coming out of the travel agency.
4. There's been a car accident. A woman is hurt.
5. I think there's been a burglary at a chemist's. The window is broken.

6 Listening practice

- Explain that the illustration is from a British phone box, and give the students a few minutes to read it.
- You may want to precede the listening exercise proper with a prediction exercise. If so, put the students into small groups. They should be able to predict some, but not all, of the words and expressions that go in the blanks. Point out that one blank can represent one or more words.
- After five minutes or so, let students compare notes with their neighbours before playing the recording.
- Play the recording while students listen and read the incomplete conversation.
- Students may want you to play it more than once before you check the answers.
- If you have done the prediction exercise, discuss the students' predictions. Students may have put perfectly suitable words into the blanks, even though they are not those used in the actual recording.

Tapescript for Exercise 6
OPERATOR: Emergency. Which service, please?
FATHER: Ambulance.
OPERATOR: What number are you ringing from?
FATHER: 744 6972.
OPERATOR: Hold on. I'll put you through.
OFFICER: Ambulance service. Can I help you?
FATHER: My son has fallen off a wall, and I think his leg is broken.
OFFICER: Your name and address, please?
FATHER: Colin Jackson, 7 Latton Close.
OFFICER: All right, Mr Jackson, we'll be right there. You can cover your son to keep him warm, but don't move him.
FATHER: Thank you.

7 Improvising conversations

- Demonstrate the exercise with three volunteers.
- Ask them to stand with their backs to one another (so that it is more like a phone conversation).
- Tell one of them to be the emergency operator, one to phone, and one to be the officer.
- Tell the caller to choose one of the situations in Exercise 1 or Exercise 5.
- When the caller is ready, the operator should answer the phone and the three students should improvise their conversation.
- Then divide the whole class into groups of three or four, and get them to do the same, switching roles for each new conversation.
- Walk round the room as they are working, and help with any problems.
- Let them continue until they find it easy to speak fluently.
- After you have stopped them, ask if there are any problems that need clearing up.

8 Personalisation

- This exercise is designed both to give fluency practice with the vocabulary used in the lesson and to contrast the simple past tense with the use of the present perfect that students have been working on.
- If you feel students do not wish to talk about emergencies in their own lives, do Exercise 3 in the Practice Book instead.
- Look at the example with the students and explain what they have to do.
- Tell them that they can talk about serious emergencies or unimportant ones.
- Point out that they will have to use the simple past tense, not the present perfect, because the emergencies they are talking about are not related to the present.
- Let students work individually for a few minutes to prepare their stories.
- Tell them they can make notes of words they want to use, but they are not to write out whole sentences.
- They can consult you about new words and/or use dictionaries.
- Then divide the class into groups of six or so and let them tell each other their stories.
- Make yourself available to help with problems, but make it clear that you are not correcting mistakes, aside from verb tense mistakes, at this point. (In this kind of exercise, effective communication is more important than accuracy.)
- You may want each group to choose the most interesting story to be retold to the entire class.

Summary
- Remind students to look over the Summary and learn the new material.

Practice Book
- Tell students which exercises you want them to do.

5 Look at the pictures and report the emergencies. Your teacher will help you.
Example: 1. *'There's a fire in the bedroom.'*

6 Phoning about an emergency. Here are some instructions from a British phone box.

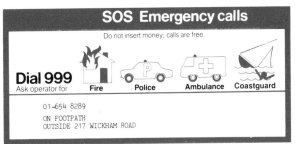

SOS Emergency calls

Do not insert money; calls are free.

Dial 999
Ask operator for   Fire   Police   Ambulance   Coastguard

01-654 8289
ON FOOTPATH
OUTSIDE 217 WICKHAM ROAD

' (Reproduced by permission of British Telecommunications.)

Now listen to the conversation and fill in the blanks.

OPERATOR: Emergency. .... service, ...?

FATHER: Ambulance.

OPERATOR: What .... are you ringing ....?

FATHER: ....

OPERATOR: Hold on. I'll .... you through.

OFFICER: .... Can I .... you?

FATHER: My ....: has fallen off a ...., and I think his .... is broken.

OFFICER: Your .... and ...., please?

FATHER: Colin Jackson, ... Latton Close.

OFFICER: All right, ..., we'll be right there. .... cover your .... to keep him ...., but don't .... him.

FATHER: ....

7 Form groups of three. Choose emergencies from Exercises 1 and 5, or think of other emergencies. Invent and practise new conversations like the one in Exercise 6.

8 Think of an emergency in your life. Ask the teacher for any words you need to talk about it. Then tell the students around you what happened. Example:

'I wasn't very old, about 12. I was at home with my little brother. He pulled a very hot saucepan of soup on himself. I phoned.. '

B You made me do it

1 Study and practise the dialogue. Your teacher will help you. Then work with a partner and make up a new dialogue, using some of the words and expressions you have learnt.

A: I'm sorry. I didn't mean to do it.
B: That's all right.
A: You see, I was thinking about something else. And I forgot what I was doing.
B: I see.
A: Actually, you made me do it.
B: I made you do it?
A: Yes. You coughed. You made me jump.
B: Yes. Well, it doesn't matter. We can get a new one.
A: I mean, it wasn't really my fault, was it?
B: No, it wasn't your fault.
A: I didn't do it on purpose.
B: No. Be careful!
A: It was an accident, you see.
B: Look out! Look out!!!
A: I mean, – **(CRASH!!!!!!!)**

2 Which picture? Listen to the sentences and write the answers.
Example:

2. *music*

Then try to remember the sentence that goes with each picture.

| a light switch | a brake | music | hard work |
| an accelerator | rain | chocolate | a kiss |

3 Write four sentences of your own using *make*, like the ones in Exercise 2. Other students will try to guess what you have written about.

40

Unit 9: Lesson B

Students learn to talk about causation, blame and responsibility, and to excuse themselves.
Principal structures: *make* + object + adjective; *make* + object + infinitive; past progressive; *I didn't mean to.*
Words and expressions to learn: *cough; switch; brake; kiss* (nouns); *mean* (= intend); *see* (= understand); *burn; It doesn't matter; That's all right; my/your fault; on purpose; than usual;* other words to be chosen by the students.
Phonology: decoding conversational expressions spoken at speed.

Possible problem

Make   The structure *make* + object + infinitive without *to* may cause some difficulty, and you may want to make sure that students do Exercise 3 in the Practice Book.

If you are short of time

You can give Exercise 5 for homework and/or drop Exercise 7.

1 Dialogue

● The situation in the dialogue is deliberately vague: students can imagine what they like.
● This has the advantage that the words and expressions can be adapted to a wide variety of purposes when the students come to use them themselves.
1. Books closed, play the recording once or twice. Ask students to recall words or expressions from the dialogue – any items at all, in any order.
– See if the class can build up some of the dialogue together from memory (with you writing it on the board).
2. Books open, go through the dialogue with the students, explaining where necessary.
– Encourage them to ask you questions (e.g. *What does ... mean?, How do you pronounce ...?*)
3. Give students practice in saying some of the sentences which contain weak forms, e.g.
I was thinking about something else.
And I forgot what I was doing.
We can get a new one.
It was an accident, you see.
(Stress and weak forms are practised again in Practice Book Exercise 1.)
– Point out the contrast between *was* (/wəz/) and *wasn't* (/wɒznt/).
– Run through the recording, so that students can imitate the sentences.
4. Tell students to choose a sentence from the dialogue and say it to you. You will repeat it with a correct pronunciation (but not indicate how correct their version was).
– If they wish, they repeat the same sentence again for you to say after them, until they are satisfied with their pronunciation.

– Then get the students to practise the dialogue in pairs.
5. Divide the class into groups of two to four, and tell them to make up new conversations, using as much as possible of the language from the dialogue they have just studied.
– The subject can be left to their imaginations – obviously it must involve some kind of accident.
– You may want to make suggestions for students who can't think of a situation for themselves. Possible ideas: breaking a cup or ornament; a car crash; dropping a baby; breaking a window; breaking a bottle of wine.
– Don't encourage students to be too ambitious: it's probably best to aim at short six- or eight-line sketches that can be prepared in a few minutes.
– If it is motivating for your class, you may want to tape-record or video-record the final products.

2 Listening: *make*

● Go through the pictures with the students, making sure they understand what is represented in each one.
● Ask them to take out a piece of paper and write down the numbers 1 to 8.
● Play the recording, pausing after each sentence, while students decide which picture is being described.
● You may want to play the recording more than once.
● Let students compare answers before checking with you.
● Then ask them to try to remember the exact words of the sentences on the recording.
● The pictures will help them; you may want to let them work in small groups to try to remember all the sentences.
● When you are checking the answers, point out the two constructions, *make* + object + adjective and *make* + object + 'bare' infinitive (without *to*).

Tapescript and answers to Exercise 2
1. It makes a car go faster. (*an accelerator*)
2. It makes me want to dance. (*music*)
3. It makes the light go on and off. (*a light switch*)
4. It makes flowers grow. (*rain*)
5. It makes a car stop. (*a brake*)
6. It makes you tired. (*hard work*)
7. It makes you feel happy. (*a kiss*)
8. It makes you fat. (*chocolate*)

3 Further practice with *make*

● Ask each student to write four sentences like those in Exercise 2.
● Each sentence must use one of the two constructions with *make* and should describe something well enough so that other students can make an intelligent guess at what is described.
● Walk round while students are writing to give any help that is needed, but encourage students to use words from their own vocabulary.
● Get students to stand up and walk round, exchanging questions and guesses with as many other students as possible; or if this is difficult, to exchange with as many students as they can without moving from their seats.
● (Practice Book Exercises 2 and 3 give more work on these points.)

4 Reading

• Tell the students that their first task is to work individually at putting the pictures in the right order.
• It is not important at this point that they understand every word in the story.
• If there are important words that they do not know, let them use their dictionaries or ask you (you might consider declining to define words that are not essential for the task of ordering the pictures).
• Let students compare answers in small groups before conferring with you.

(The correct order is: D E B A F C)

• Then divide the class into groups of three or four and ask them to try and put the linking words from the box into the correct places.
• This will involve their reading the story with a bit more care.
• Walk round as they work to give help where needed. Watch out especially for confusion between *so* and *because.*
• When all the groups have finished (the quicker groups can compare answers with one another while the slower groups finish), check the answers: *because, so, As, but, because, and, which.*

5 Writing

• Students can do this exercise individually or in small groups.
• Give them a few minutes to look at the pictures and then ask them to begin writing the story.
• They can ask you for words that they really need, but they should try as far as possible to rely on words that they already know.
• Remind them that they should try to use words from the box in Exercise 4.
• If the students have worked individually, they can get into small groups and compare versions; or you can get individuals or groups to pass their stories around for the others to read.
• In either of these processes you should make yourself available to answer questions about the correctness of items in the stories.
• Alternatively, you may want to collect the stories right away and correct them before handing them back to the students. (In a mature and motivated class that is not too large you can hand over the tape recorder to the students for Exercise 7 while you correct the stories, so as to give them back immediately.)
• More writing practice is given in Practice Book Exercise 5.

6 How many words?

• Stop the recording after each sentence so that students can work out the number of words and write it down.
• Students may want you to play the recording more than once so that they can be sure of their answers.
• Check the answers right away; ask the students if they can tell you what the words are, and play the recording again until they have understood as much as they are going to.

Tapescript and answers to Exercise 6
1. 'I'm sorry.' 'That's all right.' (3,4)
2. It doesn't matter. (4)
3. We can get a new one. (6)
4. My daughter's just hurt her arm. (7)
5. There's a fire in the post office. (8)
6. There's been a terrible accident. (6)
7. Somebody has taken my bag. (5)

7 *You Made Me Love You*

• Depending on the time you have available, you can choose how to treat this song.
• If you don't have much time, you may just want to play the recording once and ask students to tell you anything they understand.
• Then get them to turn to page 156 and read the lyrics as you play the recording again.
• Alternatively, if you have more time, you can follow this procedure:
• Play the first verse (down to *You made me feel so sad*) once and ask students to tell you any words they understand.
• You may want to explain that *wanna = want to.*
• Put the words or phrases on the board in the approximate position they hold in the song.
• You may want to play the song one more time so that students can complete the verse.
• Then turn to page 156, explain the difficult words in the second verse (*sigh, grand, 'deed = indeed,* and *gimme = give me*), and play the entire song as students listen.

Summary

• Remind students to look over the Summary and learn the new material.

Practice Book

• Tell students which exercises you want them to do.

4 Read the story and put the pictures in order. Do not worry about the blanks.

A man had a row with his wife .... his breakfast was burnt. This made him leave home later than usual, ... he drove to work very fast. .... he was going round a corner, a dog ran across the road. The man stamped on the brakes, ... the car skidded (the road was in a very bad condition .... the City Council had not repaired it for a long time). The man lost control of his car .... crashed into a lorry .... was parked on a double yellow line.

Now put one of these words in each blank.

and	as	because	because	but
		so	which	

5 Write the story that goes with these pictures. Try to use some of the words from the box in Exercise 4.

6 How many words do you hear? (Contractions like *there's* count as two words.)

7 Listen to the song. How much can you understand? (Words on page 156.)

If and when

A If you see a black cat, …

1 Match the beginnings and the ends of these sentences.

If you are travelling at 80kph in a car,
If your ancestors' language was Choctaw,
If the score is 40–15,
If today is your golden wedding anniversary,
If your great-grandparents all had blue eyes,
If you travel from England to Scotland,
In the 18th century, if someone saw a dodo,
If last year was a leap year (with 366 days),
If you can speak French,

next year won't be a leap year.
they were on the island of Mauritius.
you have been married for 50 years.
you can understand at least a bit of Italian.
you have blue eyes.
you can stop safely in 52m.
you do not go through immigration control.
you are probably playing tennis.
they lived in America.

2 Superstitions. Do you believe in luck? Complete the sentences with words and expressions from the box.

1. If .... a black cat, you'll have good luck.
2. If .... some wine, ... some salt over your left shoulder to keep bad luck away.
3. If the sky .... this evening, the weather is going to be fine tomorrow.
4. If your first visitor in the New Year .... dark hair, ... good luck all year.
5. You'll have bad luck if you: .... under a ladder, ... an umbrella in the house, or .... a hat on a bed. If you .... a mirror, you'll have seven years' ....
6. If the palm of your .... hand itches, you're going to .... some money.

bad luck	break	get	has	is red
left	open	see	throw	walk
you'll have	you see	you spill		

3 Do you know any other superstitions?

Unit 10: Lesson A

Students learn to talk about conditions and probability.
Principal structures: *if*-clauses in open conditions; distinction between *if* and *when* in subordinate clauses; affirmative and negative imperatives.
Words and expressions to learn: *score; wedding; great-grandparents; century; island; superstition; luck; shoulder; hat; New Year; spill; itch* (verb); *close* (verb); *drunk; safely.*
Phonology: pronunciation of /ɪ/.

Language notes and possible problems

1. Conditionals Textbooks often talk about the 'first', 'second' and 'third' kinds of conditional sentence. This is rather misleading. A more realistic analysis is as follows:

A Open conditions In one kind of sentence with *if* (which we can call 'open conditions'), we use the tenses which are normal for the situation, whatever they are. Examples:
*If Mary **came** yesterday, she **won't come** again today.*
*If you **love** me, why **did** you **call** me a fool?*
The only restriction is that it is unusual to have *will* in the *if*-clause; after *if*, a present tense is usually used to express a future idea (as in many other kinds of subordinate clause).
*If you **come** tomorrow, I'**ll see** what I can do.*

B Hypothetical conditions In the other kind of sentence with *if*, we use special verb forms to stress that we are talking about something that might not happen, or might not be true. In the *if*-clause we use a past tense to talk about the present or future; in the main clause we use a modal auxiliary (usually *would*). This is the so-called 'second conditional'.
*If I **knew** I **would tell** you.*
*If you **came** tomorrow, I **might be able** to help.*
To talk about the past (so-called 'third conditional') we use the past perfect tense and a 'modal perfect'.
*If you **had been** on time, we **would have caught** the train.*

In this lesson, students practise understanding and expressing open conditions. The only thing they need to learn about is the use of a present tense to refer to the future in an *if*-clause.

2. Punctuation When an *if*-clause or a *when*-clause begins a sentence, we usually follow the clause with a comma. The comma can be dropped in shorter sentences, but for the moment it might be best to advise students to put a comma in all cases.

3. *If* and *when* Speakers of some languages have difficulty in seeing clearly the difference between *if* and *when* in certain contexts. Exercise 5 is designed to help them; you may want to leave it out if your students have no problems here.

4. Pronunciation: /ɪ/ This lesson, in which the word *if* comes up repeatedly, is a good opportunity to revise the pronunciation of /ɪ/. There is no specific exercise on this point; you can help students with their pronunciation as problems arise.

Optional extra materials
Cards with sentence beginnings and endings for optional exercise after Exercise 3.

If you are short of time
You can leave out Exercise 7; or if your students do not need it, you can leave out Exercise 5.

1 Open conditions: sensitisation
● This exercise helps students to become familiar with the way *if* is used.
● The exercise can be done in groups. Get the students to write out the complete sentences.
● If your students are competitive, ask them to see which group can work out all the right answers first.
● They will need to use dictionaries or consult you for some of the vocabulary.

Answers to Exercise 1
If you are travelling at 80kph in a car, you can stop safely in 52m.
If your ancestors' language was Choctaw, they lived in America.
If the score is 40–15, you are probably playing tennis.
If today is your golden wedding anniversary, you have been married for 50 years.
If your great-grandparents all had blue eyes, you have blue eyes.
If you travel from England to Scotland, you do not go through immigration control.
In the 18th century, if someone saw a dodo, they were on the island of Mauritius.
If last year was a leap year (with 366 days), next year won't be a leap year.
If you can speak French, you can understand at least a bit of Italian.

2 Superstitions
● Here students work on sentences using future and imperative forms in the main clause.
● Let them do the exercise individually, using dictionaries or asking you about difficult vocabulary.
● Get them to compare notes; discuss the answers.
● You may want to point out that the present tense is used to express a future idea in these sentences.

3 Discussion
● Ask students what they think about the superstitions in Exercise 2. Most students will probably tell you that they don't believe in them.
● Ask them if they know of any other superstitions; get them to tell the class about them if possible.
● Watch the pronunciation of *if*.
● Watch out, too, for a future tense in the *if*-clause, and correct it if it comes up.

Optional activity Beginnings and endings
● Before the lesson, prepare cards or slips of paper. On each one, write one half of one of the sentences listed below.
● Hand out half-sentences to students and tell them to learn them by heart.
● When they are ready, tell them to walk round saying their half-sentences and trying to find their 'other halves'.

• When students think they have made a complete sentence they should check with you. Note that one or two alternative combinations are possible.

Half-sentences
If you heat ice,   it changes into water.
If it rains this afternoon,   I'm going to stay at home.
If you're going to the shop,   could you get some carrots?
If you go to the US,   you need a visa.
If you buy me a drink,   I'll buy you one tomorrow.
If anybody telephones,   tell them I'm not at home.
If you love me,   why did you call me a fool?
If you ever go to Australia,   you must go and see my
                                                brother in Perth.
If you drop this glass,   it won't break.
If you're making coffee,   I'd like some.
If you stayed up late last night,   you must be tired.

4 Listening: *What will happen if...* 🔲

• This is a simple, not very serious dramatised serial story with seven episodes.
• Students listen to each part and then try to guess what will happen next.
• Play each part one or more times, explaining difficulties if necessary, and then ask students to answer the questions in their books.
• Encourage discussion and disagreement.
• You may like to revise expressions which students have learnt for expressing degrees of certainty (*I think, I'm sure, I believe; certainly, probably, possibly*).

Tapescript for Exercise 4: see page 180

5 *If* or *when?*

• Go through the examples with the students, and help them see that *when* is used to talk about things that *will* happen, whereas *if* is used to talk about things that *may* or *may not* happen.
• Students can do the exercise individually in writing and then discuss their answers in pairs or groups. Point out the use of the present tense to refer to the future in the subordinate clauses. Students will get more active practice of this point in the next lesson.

6 Listening: imperatives with *if* 🔲

• Students listen to a series of conditional instructions and try to do what they are told.
• The instructions become more difficult as the exercise goes on.

Tapescript for Exercise 6
1. If you can understand this sentence, write your name.
2. If today is Tuesday, write the number 12. If not, don't write anything.
3. If your arms are longer than your hair, draw a circle. If not, draw a square.
4. If you can see the sun, stand up.
5. If it's raining, look at your feet. If not, look at another person – but don't look at the teacher.
6. If Edinburgh is in the north of England, close your eyes for ten seconds.
   (NOTE: Edinburgh is in Scotland, not in England.)
7. If stamps are not sold in pubs, don't say hello to another student.
8. If there are more than fifteen students in your class, put your pen on the floor. If not, put it in your mouth.

9. If your eyes are blue, raise your right hand. If they are brown, raise your left hand. If they are neither blue nor brown, don't raise either hand.

7 Imperatives with *if*: further practice

• Put students into groups of four or five and ask them to write instructions with *if* like the ones in Exercise 6.
• Each group should write four or five instructions.
• Walk round while they are working to give any help that is needed; make sure that each group has at least one instruction with *don't* in its list.
• When they have finished writing, they should read out their instructions for other groups to follow.
• If you have an even number of groups, pairs of groups can work at the same time; otherwise it is probably best to get each group to give its instructions to the whole class in turn.
• If your class is competitive you may want to get them to vote for the best instructions.

8 *Song for a Rainy Sunday* 🔲

• The song is recorded twice: once complete and then once with gaps where some of the words go. (The words are on page 156.
• Play the first version while students listen to it.
• Then ask them to tell you any words they remember; you may want to put these on the board.
• Tell them that they will hear the song again, with some words left out, and they are to try to remember the words.
• You can pause at each blank for students to say the word; or you can play the song through once while students try to write the missing words, and then again for them to say the words in the right places.
• You may want them to look at the words in their books as you play the complete version a last time, and answer any questions they may have.

Summary
• Remind students to look over the Summary and learn the new material.

Practice Book
• Tell students which exercises you want them to do.

4 What will happen if ...?
Listen to the recording and
answer the questions.

5 *If* or *when*? Look at the difference.

When I go to bed tonight, I'll ...
  (I *will* go to bed.)
If I go to Scotland, I'll ...
  (I *may* go to Scotland.)

When you are on holiday, think of me.
  (You *will* be on holiday.)
If you are ever in London, come and see us.
  (You *may* be in London.)

1. .... I get rich, I'll travel round the world.
2. .... that's all you can say, I'm leaving.
3. .... I go to bed, I usually read for a few minutes.
4. .... you say that again, I'll hit you.
5. .... it rains this afternoon, we'll stay at home.
6. I'll close the curtains .... it gets dark.
7. .... I get older, I'll stop playing rugby.
8. Be patient; we can go home .... the game's finished.
9. Get on quickly .... the train stops.
10. .... you drive when you're drunk, you'll probably crash.

6 Listen to the recording
and do what the speaker tells
you.

7 Work in groups. Write
instructions like those in
Exercise 6 and give them to
another group.

8 Listen to the song once.
Then listen again and try to
remember the words that
have been left out.

B How to fill a kettle

1 Put a word or expression from the box into each blank. Then use the picture to help you put the sentences in order.

as soon as	then	then
until	when	when

.... it does this, it will turn the tap off.
When you do this, the cat will run, turning the tap on.
.... you want to fill the kettle, hook its handle to the string and turn the small wheel .... the kettle is under the tap.
.... lower the fish to the right side of the cat's wheel.
.... turn the small wheel again to get the kettle back.
.... the kettle is full, move the fish to the left side of the wheel, and the cat will run the other way.

2 Look at the pictures and say what will happen. Example:

1. 'When / As soon as she opens the door, the light will go on.'

Unit 10: Lesson B

Students learn more about describing processes and giving instructions.

Principal structures: present tense with future meaning in subordinate clauses; *when* and *until* in subordinate clauses.

Words and expressions to learn: *tap; tin; fridge; knife; butter; onion; turn on/off; fill; cry; full; sharp; hard; last* (= final); other words to be chosen by the students.

Phonology: pronunciations of the letter *a* (revision).

Language notes and possible problems

Present tense with future meaning in subordinate clauses When the main clause of a sentence has a future tense (*will* or *going to*), or an imperative, the subordinate clause often has a present tense with a future meaning:

*I'll let you know as soon as she **gets** here.*
*What are you going to do when you **leave** school?*
*Stir it until it **thickens**.*
*I'll give you as much time as you **need**.*

In this lesson only clauses with *when, as soon as,* and *until* are dealt with; other uses will be studied later in the course.

Some students may have problems with this, especially if the equivalent conjunctions in their own language are followed by other tenses.

If you are short of time

You can leave out Exercise 4; or you can do Exercise 7 as a whole-class activity, with you drawing the suggestions together.

1 Presentation: filling a kettle

● Give the students a few minutes to look at the picture in their books and understand it.
● Then ask them to work individually, putting a word or expression from the box into each blank.
● Let them compare answers before checking with you.
● Then put them into groups of three or four and get them to try and put the text in order by looking at the picture. Each group should copy the sentences in the right order so they end up with a complete correct text.
● Walk round while they are working to give any help that is needed.
● Check their answers by getting each group to read out a sentence in order.
● After going over the answers you may want to point out how the verbs are used in the sentences.

Answers to Exercise 1

When you want to fill the kettle, hook its handle to the string and turn the small wheel *until* the kettle is under the tap. *Then* lower the fish to the right side of the cat's wheel. When you do this, the cat will run, turning the tap on. *As soon as* the kettle is full, move the fish to the left side of the wheel, and the cat will run the other way. *When* it does this, it will turn the tap off. *Then* turn the small wheel again to get the kettle back.

2 Practice: *what will happen?*

● Let students work in pairs to make up a sentence for each picture. They can consult you or their dictionary for new words.
● Walk round while they are working to make sure they have all understood how to use the tenses.
● You may not want to bother checking the answers with the whole class.
● Practice Book Exercise 1 gives additional work on this point.

Some possible answers to Exercise 2

2. As soon as / When he closes the door, all the toys will fall down.
3. When / As soon as he opens the door, the bell will ring.
4. When they drive away, the tins will make a terrible noise.
5. When anyone sits on the chair, they'll fall on the floor.
6. When he falls down, he won't get hurt.

3 When or until

- Get students to work individually, using their dictionaries or consulting you and each other about new words.
- If they do ask about new words, make sure that they use correct question forms (*What does* sharp *mean?*, *Does* asparagus *mean* asperge? etc.).
- Practice Book Exercise 2 gives additional work on this point.

Answers: 1. until 2. when 3. When 4. until 5. until 6. When

4 Writing cooking tips

- Put the students in groups of four or five.
- Each group must come up with a list of three or more cooking tips – perhaps in the form of a poster to put on the classroom wall if this is easy.
- Walk round while they are working to give any help that is needed, but encourage them to try and use the English at their disposal.
- When they finish they can read their tips out to the others and answer questions about them; or stick them on the wall or notice board so everyone can read them and ask questions.
- Practice Book Exercise 3 revises some of the vocabulary areas covered here.

5 Listening

- Ask the students to read the sentences in their books, and not to worry about words they don't understand.
- Then play the recording as they try to write down the words that will complete each sentence.
- Play the recording again, more than once if necessary, and let them compare answers before checking with you.

The sentences are:
1. Stick a needle in and see if *it comes out clean.*
2. Press it on the top and if it springs up again, *it's done.*
3. Tap *the bottom.*
4. Cut *a piece and try it.*
5. Listen to it to see *if it's bubbling.*
6. See if it's shrunk *from the sides.*

- Then let the students work in small groups to try and match pictures and sentences.

Answers: 1B 2D 3A 4C 5E 6F

- From the listening and the pictures, they should now be able to guess what the listed words mean. Let them discuss it in small groups and then explain, translate or demonstrate the words.

Tapescript for Exercise 5
KATY: How do you tell if a cake's done? You're baking a cake, how do you tell if it's done?
ALEX: Stick a needle in and see if *it comes out clean.*
JANE: Press it on, press it on the top and if it springs up again, *it's done.*
KEITH: Or I suppose on the bottom (*mumble mumble*) if it's scones or bread you press the bottom and if it springs out, –
SUE: Tap *the bottom.* Tap it. (*mumble*)

MIKE: Cut *a piece and try it.* (*laughter*)
SUE: By that time it's too late!
MIKE: If it runs off your plate, then it's done. (*laughter; general mumbling*)
SUE: Listen to it to see *if it's bubbling.* (*laughter*) See if it's shrunk from the sides. That's what I do.
KATY: See if it's shrunk *from the sides?*
SUE: See if it's shrunk from the sides.
KATY: Mm.

6 Pronunciations of the letter *a*

- Ask students to look at the numbered lists of words (all of which come from the previous exercises).
- See if they can remember how to pronounce the words; you may want to ask them if they remember the rules from Lesson 3B.
- Note that for most Americans and for people from some parts of Britain *class* and *last* will be pronounced like the words in the first group.
- Go through the unnumbered list, with volunteers pronouncing the words.
- You can use the recording as a check if you wish; the exercise is recorded in a southern British, a northern British and an American version, for purposes of comparison.
- If you think it will be useful for students, they can say which of the five groups each word belongs to. Here is the way they would be grouped by a speaker from the south of Britain.

1 /æ/	2 /eɪ/	3 /ɑ:/	4 /ɔ:/	5 /ɒ/
crack	failing	bark	paw	swab
angle	delayed	craft	stall	wand
flash	tray	harm	balk	
nap	sprain	vast		
	rate	shaft		

7 Students' inventions

- Put students into groups of three or four. Give each group three minutes to choose one of the tasks or decide on another similar apparatus to invent.
- It is probably best to give a time limit for the exercise, which can be extended if things are going well.
- Walk round while the groups are working to give any help that is needed.
- When they are ready, each group should present its invention to the class, with appropriate illustration if they have produced it.
- In a competitive class, you may want the students to vote on the best invention.

Summary
- Remind students to look over the Summary and learn the new material.

Practice Book
- Tell students which exercises you want them to do.

3 Cooking tips. Put *when* or *until* in each blank.

1. Cook asparagus .... you can easily put a sharp knife through the middle of the stems.
2. If you need unsalted butter, pour boiling water over salted butter which has been cut into pieces, and then put it all into the fridge. .... the butter is hard, the salt will be left in the water.
3. .... you only need the yellow skin of a lemon, cut it with a potato peeler; this will cut it thinner than a knife.
4. If you are cooking whole onions, remember that they won't make you cry .... they lose their roots. So peel them from the top and cut the roots off last.
5. Serve vodka very cold. Keep it on ice .... the moment you pour it.
6. .... a melon is ready to eat, the end opposite the stem will be fairly soft.

(from *Supertips* by Moyra Bremner – adapted)

4 Work in groups. Make a list of three or more cooking tips to tell the class.

5 How do you tell when a cake or a loaf of bread is done? Listen, and complete the sentences.

1. Stick a needle in and see if...
2. Press it on the top and if it springs up again, ...
3. Tap...
4. Cut...
5. Listen to it to see...
6. See if it's shrunk...

Now match the numbered sentences to the pictures.

6 Pronunciation. Pronounce these words.

1. handle   cat   back   tap
2. way   make   cake
3. sharp   hard   class   last
4. small   all
5. want   water   what

You probably don't know these words. How do you think they are pronounced?

bark   failing   crack   delayed
craft   angle   harm   flash   swab
tray   wand   sprain   paw   rate
stall   nap   vast   balk   shaft

7 In groups, invent a way of doing one of these things. Describe your invention to the other groups; you can draw pictures if you want.

1. Putting your shoes on without bending down
2. Opening and closing a window
3. Picking apples
4. Cleaning high windows
5. Washing socks

Now can you guess what these words mean?

needle   spring   tap   bubble   shrink

45

Revision and fluency practice

A A choice of activities

> Look at the exercises in this lesson. Try to decide which of them are most useful for you, and do three or more.

GRAMMAR REVISION

1 Choose the correct tense (present or present perfect).

1. How long *do you know / have you known* Mary?
2. *I live / I've lived* here for eight years.
3. *I'm going / I've been* home on Sunday.
4. *I have / I've had* this car since 1982.
5. Sorry I'm late. *Are you waiting / Have you been waiting* long?

2 Choose the correct tense (present perfect or simple past).

1. *Have you ever seen / Did you ever see* a boxing match?
2. *Have you ever been / Did you ever go* camping when you were a child?
3. Where *have you had / did you have* lunch yesterday?
4. Where's the telephone? *There's been / There was* an accident!
5. *I've never travelled / I never travelled* by air.
6. Can you help me? *I've lost / I lost* my watch.
7. *I've lost / I lost* my glasses the other day.
8. '*Have you had / 'Did you have* breakfast?' 'Not yet.'

3 Choose the correct tense (simple or progressive).

1. 'Could I speak to Linda?' 'I'm afraid *she puts / she's putting* the baby to bed. Could you ring back in about half an hour?'
2. I first met my wife when I *worked / was working* in Detroit.
3. How often *do you see / are you seeing* your parents?
4. My father *worked / was working* in Nigeria for a long time when he was younger.
5. *Do you know / Are you knowing* my friend Alex Carter?
6. 'Would you like a cigarette?' 'No, thanks, *I don't smoke / I'm not smoking.*'
7. 'What *do you do / are you doing?*' '*I try / I'm trying* to mend my bicycle. Would you like to help?'
8. 'What *do you do / are you doing?*' 'I'm a chemical engineer.'
9. 'I called at your house yesterday evening, but you weren't there. What *did you do / were you doing?*' 'I was at a party.'
10. 'What *did you do / were you doing* after the party?' 'I went straight home.'

LISTENING

4 Listen to the news broadcast and answer the questions.

1. The Distillers' Company are planning to 'axe' some jobs. How many – more than a hundred or less than a hundred? And how many plants are they going to close?
2. Three youths attacked a nineteen-year-old airman. Did he have to go to hospital? Was any money stolen, and if so, how much?
3. Two women tried to use a stolen credit card. What did they try to buy? a) wine b) spirits c) cigarettes d) a car.
   What colour car did they drive away in? Can you describe them at all?
4. People in Amport go to church for an unusual reason. What is it?
5. What has been stolen in Cassington, near Witney? a) camping equipment b) cooking equipment c) a camera from a kitchen d) camera attachments.
6. Which of these words do you hear in the weather forecast?
   cool cold clouds cloudy snow showers sunny intervals wet dry nineteen ninety north-westerly north-easterly winds strong Tuesday

Unit 11: Lesson A

Students revise the use of tenses and practise various skills. No new material is taught.

Note: choice

You may like to get students' views about which exercises are most useful for them, before choosing a suitable selection. If they do not all have the same priorities, groups can work on different exercises.

● Exercises 1–3 can be done individually in writing or by general class discussion, as you prefer.
● Exercise 1 reminds students of the use of the present perfect for states continuing up to the present (sentences 1, 2, 4 and 5).
● Note that in 3 *I've been* is impossible (if Sunday was past, the correct form would be *I went*).

2 Present perfect or simple past

● Students are reminded that the present perfect:
a. is used to talk about finished actions when we are thinking of an unfinished time (1, 5, 8)
b. is used to give 'news' (4, 6)
c. is not used with adverbials of finished time (2, 3, 7).

3 Simple or progressive

● The following rules are revised here.
a. Present progressive for temporary actions going on at the moment of speaking (1, 7).
b. Simple present for permanent states, habits and repeated actions (3, 5, 6, 8).
c. Past progressive for 'background' actions that were going on when something else happened (2, 9).
d. Simple past for other past actions and events (4, 10).

4 Listening for specific information

● Make sure students understand the questions. (Note the journalistic use of *axe* to mean *cut* or *abolish*.)
● Tell students that they will not understand everything, but that if they listen carefully they will be able to answer most of the questions.
● Play the recording through once without stopping and see if students can answer any of the questions.
● Then play it again, stopping after each news item while students write their answers. (Get them to copy the words from the weather forecast beforehand; then they can just circle the appropriate items.)
● Play the broadcast a third time if necessary.
● The text is on page 181. It is probably not very useful to go right through it explaining every word.

Answers to Exercise 4

1. more than a hundred (715); 2
2. yes; no
3. spirits; either white or blue; both in late twenties, one six feet tall with dyed blonde hair, one five feet five, both have London accents
4. to buy stamps
5. camping equipment
6. cool, cloudy, showers, sunny intervals, dry, nineteen, north-westerly, winds

5 Listening for particular items

● Make sure students understand the task.
● Play the dialogue once without stopping (telling the students not to write anything this time).
● Ask if they noticed any items of food or drink.
● Then play the dialogue again, stopping once or twice to give students time to write if necessary.

Answers: Food: *tomatoes, bread, eggs, butter, steak, chops*
Drink: *milk, coffee, orange juice, wine*

● Go over the instructions for the second part of the exercise and continue as before.

Tapescript for Exercise 5

A: Hello. Did you get everything?
B: Nearly. I forgot the milk, though.
A: It doesn't matter. I'll borrow some from Jenny next door.
B: Here you are, then. A tin of tomatoes, bread, coffee, orange juice and a dozen eggs.
A: What about the butter?
B: Butter, butter. Oh, yes. Here it is in my pocket.
A: And the steak?
B: You didn't ask me to get steak.
A: Yes I did.
B: No you didn't.
A: Well, it doesn't matter. There are some chops in the fridge.
B: I got a bottle of wine.
A: Oh, great!
B: And some matches – we've run out.
A: Clever. Did you get the washing-up liquid?
B: You didn't ask me to get washing-up liquid.
A: Yes I did.
B: No you didn't.
A: Well, it doesn't matter...

46

6 Perceiving *there's* and *there are* 🔲

- Tell students to write THERE'S and THERE ARE at the heads of two columns.
- Ask them how they think they are usually pronounced.
- Practise the correct unstressed pronunciations (/ðəz/ and /ðərə/) a few times.
- Tell students to listen to the recording.
- Each time they hear *there's* or *there are* they should put a tick under the appropriate heading.
- You may need to play the recording more than once.

Tapescript for Exercise 6
Downstairs at the front *there's* a living room and a dining room. At the back *there's* a big kitchen. *There are* three bedrooms on the first floor, and *there are* two small bedrooms on the top floor. *There's* a toilet on each floor, and *there are* bathrooms on the first and second floors. *There's* a big garden, but the garage isn't very big. Come and see the house if you like – we're usually there at weekends.

7 Questionnaire
- Students should realise that there is no scientific basis to the test, and that it is not to be taken seriously.
- Before starting, ask them to say whether or not they think they are peaceful.
- Then tell students to read through the text and note down their scores.
- Let them use their dictionaries or ask you if they have problems with vocabulary.
- If they disagree with the results, or are critical of any of the questions, ask them if they can suggest improvements.

8 Students' questionnaires
- Put students in groups of three or four.
- Each group should choose one of the subjects and make up a questionnaire with ten or so questions.
- Possible beginnings for questions: *Have you ever...?, Do you ever...?* or *How often do you...?*
- You will probably need to help with vocabulary.
- When questionnaires are ready, groups can exchange them and answer the questions.

9 Mime: *What am I?*
- Give students a minute or two to choose their jobs and work out how to mime them.
- Then let them take turns to do their mimes for the rest of the class.
- Make sure students remember to put the indefinite article *a/an* before the name of the job when they make their guesses.

10 Mime: *What am I playing?*
- Tell students to look at the illustration and note how the definite article *the* is used: with the names of musical instruments, but not with sports and games.
- The exercise can be done in the same way as Exercise 9, but it is very effective if students work in pairs or groups of three and prepare collective mimes.

11 Mime: *What are we talking about?*
- Students work in groups of three. (Pairs are also possible.)

- Give them 15 minutes to work out a short and simple conversation in which somebody asks for something or asks somebody else to do something.
- They must write down the text of their conversation.
- When they are ready, one group mimes its conversation (without speaking) for the rest of the class, or for one of the other groups. Groups must try to make it clear by their actions what they are talking about.
- One or more of the other groups then repeats the first group's mime, adding the words that they think have been left out.
- Finally, the first group repeat their sketch; this time they say the words as well.
- Continue until every group has performed.
- If you have video, this can be used very effectively (record the mime and play it back several times while the class try to decide what the words might be).

12 Descriptions
- Go over the dialogue practising pronunciation and explaining difficulties.
- Note the use of *leave*, not *forget*, when the place is specified (*I left it on the bus*).
- Give students about a quarter of an hour to make up and practise similar conversations, using as many of the underlined words and expressions as possible.
- Then get students to perform their conversations for the rest of the class.
- If you are planning to tape- or video-record the performances, tell students in advance – this will give them an incentive to produce good quality work.

13 Question-box
- This is a very successful discussion activity at all levels.
- Encourage students to ask questions which can lead to discussion.
- Before students put their questions in the box, check them for serious mistakes.
- Don't correct the English while students are playing, but note points for attention later if you wish.
- Make sure students don't put their questions back in the box when they have answered them.
- If a student doesn't want to answer a particular question, he or she can say *I'd rather not answer* (put this on the board), put the question back, and take another – but students are only allowed to do this once.
- In a large class, play the game in two or more subgroups.

Summary
- There is no Summary for this lesson.

Practice Book
- There are no Practice Book exercises for this lesson. Students should spend their homework time studying for the Revision Test which follows Unit 11.

5 Listen to the conversation. Every time you hear the name of a food, write 'F'; every time you hear the name of a drink, write 'D'.
Listen a second time. Write down an example of each of these: a hard thing, a soft thing, a liquid, a solid, a countable noun, an uncountable noun.

6 Pronunciation. Listen to the conversation. How many times do you hear *there's* and *there are*? Make a note each time.

READING AND WRITING

7 Are you a peaceful person? Answer the questions as honestly as you can and then find out your total score. (But don't take the test too seriously!)

1. If you have ever been in a political demonstration, score 2.
2. If you have lost your temper during the last three days, score 3.
3. If you have ever driven at over 160kph, score 2.
4. If you have ever broken a cup, glass or plate on purpose, score 1.
5. If you have been in a fight in the last three years, score 3.
6. If you have seen a war film, gangster film, western or other violent film in the last month, score 1.
7. If you have ever been in love with two people at the same time, score 2.
8. If you ever have violent dreams, score 1.
9. If you have ever walked out of a job, score 2.
10. If you have ever watched a boxing-match, score 2.
11. If you like the town better than the country, score 1.

Your score:

0–7:   You are a very peaceful person.
8–13:   Average.
14–20:   You are not at all peaceful!

8 Now make up your own questionnaire.
Suggestions: find out whether people are energetic, polite, cultured, generous, honest, shy, careful with money, fashion-conscious, interested in sport, interested in politics, sociable.

SPEAKING

9 'What's my job?' Choose a job and mime it (act it without speaking) to the other students. They will say what they think you are.

10 'What am I playing?' Choose a game or a musical instrument. Mime it to the other students. They will say what you are playing.

11 'What are we talking about?' Work in groups of three. Prepare a conversation in which somebody asks for something, or asks somebody else to do something. When you are ready, mime your conversation (without using the words) for the other students. They will try to find the words.

Are you a painter?

You're a conductor.

I think he's a policeman.

You're playing the harp.

Are you playing cricket?

Perhaps she's playing tennis.

12 Descriptions: revision. Read the conversation. Then work with a partner and make up a similar conversation about something that has been lost. Try to use the words and expressions in italics.

A: *I've lost* a briefcase.
B: Oh, yes? *What's it like?* Can you describe it?
A: It's brown, *with* a handle on top, and *it's got* a brass lock. It's about this big.
B: Anything inside it?
A: Yes. *There are* some books *with* my name *in*, and there's a pen *that* I bought yesterday. And a pint of milk.
B: *Where did you lose it?*
A: I think *I left it* on the number 14 bus.
B: Well, *I'll see what I can do* . . .

13 Question-box. Each student writes three questions on separate pieces of paper. One of the questions must begin *Have you ever. . .?*, and one must begin *Do you. . .?* The questions are folded up and put in a box. Students take turns to draw out questions and answer them.

47

B Knife-thrower's assistant wanted

WELL-KNOWN NORTHERN MANUFACTURER
requires
SALES MANAGER
for district between Liverpool and Carlisle.
Very good .....1..... and conditions.
Use of new company car.
.....2..... between 25 and 40.
Previous selling .....3..... essential.
.....4..... to: Managing Director, Domestic
Engineering Services Ltd, 417 North Way,
Whitehaven, Cumbria WN6 4DJ.

1 Read the advertisement and the two letters. Fill in the numbered gaps with words and expressions from the box. (You can use a dictionary, or ask your teacher about difficult words.)

advertised	age	apply	companies
engineering	experience	faithfully	
look forward	salary	Sales Manager	
several	should like	worked	write

17 Grove Crescent
Greendale
Cumbria CU6 7LY

May 24, 1985

The Managing Director
Domestic Engineering Services Ltd
417 North Way
Whitehaven
Cumbria WN6 4DJ

Dear Sir

I ..5... to apply for the post of ...6... advertised in the Guardian of 22 May. I am 36 years old and have experience of selling in ...7... firms. I also have qualifications in ..8...

I look forward to hearing from you.

Yours faithfully

Roger Parsons

35 Allendale Road
Carlisle
CA2 4SJ.

23 May, 1985

Dear Sir,
I wish to ...9... for the job of Sales Manager ...10... in yesterday's Guardian. I have a Higher National Diploma in Business Studies, and have ...11... as a Sales Manager for two large ...12... I am 29. I ...13... to hearing from you.
Yours ...14...,

Andrew Jardine

2 Here are some sentences from four letters from **Domestic Engineering Services Ltd to Mr Parsons and Mr Jardine.** (The sentences are not in order; some of them come in more than one letter.) Can you write one of the letters?

Dear Mr ......
Yours sincerely
Please come for an interview on .... at .... a.m.
Thank you for your letter of .... May.
Please confirm your acceptance as soon as
  possible.
Thank you for coming for an interview yesterday.
We regret that we are unable to offer you the
  post.
We are pleased to offer you the position of
  Sales Manager, starting on 1 August, at a
  salary of £12,500 a year.

Unit 11: Lesson B

Students revise and practise letter-writing conventions in a communicative writing exercise; they conduct simulated job interviews.
Principal structures: revision of tenses.
Words and expressions to learn: *experience; salary; interview; canteen; conditions; Managing Director; qualifications; advertise; apply; essential; previous; full-time; Yours faithfully; Yours sincerely; I look forward to hearing from you; as soon as possible.*

Language notes and possible problems
1. Tenses This lesson will require the use of simple past and present perfect tenses in appropriate situations. You may like to revise the relevant rules at a suitable moment – for instance, before Exercise 4.
2. Letters This is a good opportunity to revise basic letter-writing conventions. Students should note:
– position of the address and salutation
– layout of the letter
– use of *Yours faithfully* in conjunction with *Dear Sir*, and *Yours sincerely* when the addressee's name is used.
3. Curriculum vitae In real job applications, of course, applicants normally enclose detailed c.v.'s. This is avoided here in order to ensure that information about applicants' supposed experience is exchanged orally during Exercise 4.

If you are short of time
This lesson involves a small-scale simulation activity (Exercises 3 and 4) which will probably take over an hour; the lesson as a whole will take two hours or more. If you do not have this much time, just do Exercises 1 and 2.

1 Text completion
● The purpose of this exercise is to introduce some of the vocabulary students will need, and to help them revise letter-writing conventions.
● Give students a minute or two to look through the advertisement, and then get them to try to write down the four words that are needed to complete the text.
● Let them use dictionaries or ask you about the words in the box.
● Get them to compare notes in groups before giving them the answers.
● Then work on the two letters in the same way.
● Finally, you may wish to discuss some of the language points and rules for letter-writing (see *Language notes*). Ask students which of the two letters they feel is more 'businesslike', and why. Which applicant do they feel is more likely to get the job?

Answers to Exercise 1
1. salary 2. age 3. experience 4. write (*or* apply)
5. should like 6. Sales Manager 7. several
8. engineering 9. apply 10. advertised 11. worked
12. companies 13. look forward 14. faithfully

2 Writing a letter
● This exercise can be done individually (with students choosing which letter they want to write), or in groups

of four (with each student in a group writing a different letter).
● In a slow class, students may need help to work out the situation (there are two letters offering interviews, one letter of rejection, and one offering a job).
● When students are ready, you can get them to give you the text for each letter while you write it on the board.

Answers to Exercise 2
After the firm's printed address and the date, and the applicant's address (at the top on the left), the four letters should continue more or less as follows:

Dear Mr Parsons

Thank you for your letter of 24 May.
Please come for an interview on (date) at (time) a.m.

Yours sincerely

(signature)

Dear Mr Jardine

(similar text to previous letter)

Dear Mr Parsons (or Jardine)

Thank you for coming for an interview yesterday. We regret that we are unable to offer you the post.

Yours sincerely

(signature)

Dear Mr Jardine (or Parsons)

Thank you for coming for an interview yesterday. We are pleased to offer you the position of Sales Manager, starting on 1 August, at a salary of £12,500 a year. Please confirm your acceptance as soon as possible.

Yours sincerely

(signature)

---

3 Reading advertisements

- Give students a few minutes to look through the advertisements, either using their dictionaries or asking you for help with difficult words.

4 Interviews

1. *Organising the exercise*

- Divide the students into groups of about six.
- In each group, there should be three or so applicants for jobs and three or so interviewers. (Exact numbers are not important.)
- Tell each group to agree on one of the jobs in the group of small ads.
- When students are ready, the three applicants should go and sit separately from the interviewers.

2. *Writing letters*

- The applicants (working individually), write their letters of application for the job. (Tell them that they can invent as many 'facts' as they like, but that the language they use should be taken largely from the letters in Exercise 1.)

3. *Preparing interviews*

- Meanwhile, the interviewers in each group work together to prepare suitable questions. The illustration will give them some ideas, but they will need to ask some questions appropriate to the particular job.
- Make sure they don't ask questions which the applicants will be unable to understand.

4. *Replies*

- When the letters of application are ready, the applicants should deliver them. The interviewers will then write offering interviews.
- Meanwhile, the applicants should start preparing their roles.
- Tell them to decide what jobs they have at present, what experience and qualifications they have, and so on.

5. *Interviews*

- Applicants go to be interviewed in turn. (The order is determined by the times given in the letters they have received.)
- You may want to put a time-limit on interviews (e.g. five minutes).

6. *Offer of job*

- When the interviews are finished, the interviewers in each group must decide who they are going to offer the job to.
- They then have to write appropriate letters to all the applicants.
- You will need to give the applicants something to do while they are waiting for their letters.

Summary

- Remind students to look at the Summary and learn the new material.

Practice Book

- There are no Practice Book exercises for this lesson. Students should revise for the Test.

NOW DO REVISION TEST ONE.
(See page 162 and the Test Book.)

3 Read the advertisements with a dictionary.

ROSTON TIMES

MANAGER FOR SMALL NEWSAGENTS

Applicants must have experience of running a small shop.
Good knowledge of accounting desirable.
Aged 25–40.
Apply in writing to:
Personnel Manager
Chambers and Wren
Chambers House
High Street
Barbury BA6 10S.

Efficient
SHORTHAND TYPIST/SECRETARY
needed for small friendly company.
Apply to Office Manageress, Ann Harper Ltd,
6 Newport Road, Roston RS1 4JX.

FULL-TIME GARDENER
wanted for Roston General Hospital.
Experience essential.
Good wages and conditions.
Apply: The Administrator.

TEACHER REQUIRED
for private language school.
Teaching experience unnecessary.
Apply: The Director of Studies
Instant Languages Ltd
279 Canal Street, Roston.

CLEANER
required for our Roston office,
hours by arrangement. Apply The
Manager Coleman and Stokes 33
South Parade Roston RS1 5BQ.

Full-time
DRIVERS
required
Clean driving licence
Must be of smart appearance
Aged over 25.
Apply
CAPES TAXIS
17 Palace Road
Roston.

SECRETARY
(good Audio/Shorthand)

CABIN STAFF
Southern Airlines require cabin staff for
intercontinental flights. Applicants must be
between 20 and 33 years old, height 1m60 to
1m75, education to GCE standard, two
languages, must be able to swim. Apply to
Recruitment Officer, Southern Airlines,
Heathrow Airport West, HR3 7KK.

PART-TIME JOB
Circus has an unexpected vacancy for a
knife-thrower's assistant. Excellent pay. Apply in
writing to City Show Office, 13 Rose Lane, Roston.

SECRETARIES

Methodist Ch
Overseas Div

SECRETA ASSISTA

PA/SECRE

4 Job interviews. Work in groups of about
six (three interviewers and three applicants)
1. Applicants write letters of application for
   one of the jobs advertised; interviewers
   prepare interviews.
2. Applicants are interviewed in turn.
3. Interviewers choose the best applicant and
   write letters to all three.

Where do you work? How long have you been there?
Why do you want to change your job? Where did
you go to school? Have you any experience of
selling? Can you speak any foreign languages?
Have you ever lived abroad? Have you ever been
dismissed from a job? What are your interests?
Are you married?

What's the salary? What are the hours?
Is there a canteen?

Causes and origins

Paper-making centuries ago

A From tree to paper

1 Read the text with a dictionary, and put one of these words into each blank: *paper, wood, trees.* Ask the teacher for help if necessary.

> *Excuse me. What does 'invented' mean?*

> *Excuse me. I don't understand this.*

> *Excuse me. Can you explain this word?*

> *Excuse me. How do you pronounce this?*

Wood fibres magnified

......1...... was invented by the Chinese in the first century AD. The art of ......2......-making took 700 years to reach the Muslim world and another 700 years to get to Britain (via Spain, southern France and Germany).

Most ......3...... is made from ......4....... When ......5...... are cut down, they are transported by land or water to paper mills. Here they are cut up and the ......6...... is broken up into fibres, which are mixed with water and chemicals. This ......7...... pulp is then dried on a machine and made into ......8.......

Paper-making today

Future paper

......9......-making is an important British industry, and ......10...... from Britain is exported to South Africa, Australia and many other countries. Some of the ......11...... used in the British paper-making industry comes from ......12...... grown in Britain, but ......13...... is also imported from other countries such as Norway. One tree is needed for every 400 copies of a typical forty-page newspaper. If half the adults in Britain each buy one daily ......14......, this uses up over 40,000 ......15...... a day. ......16...... are being cut down faster than they are being replaced, so there may be a serious paper shortage before the year 2000.

2 Close your book and listen to the sentences. Are they true or false?

3 The word *America* (/ə'merɪkə/) has the sound /ə/ twice. Which ten of the following words also contain the sound /ə/?

iron century paper
correct Germany adults
fibre replaced pulp
machine industry exported
Africa countries Norway
needed serious shortage

4 Make some true sentences.

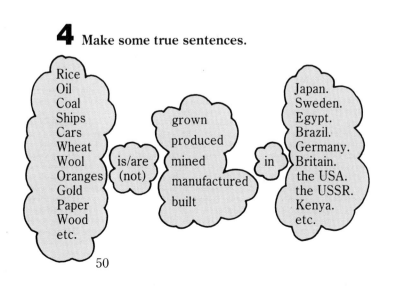

Rice
Oil
Coal
Ships
Cars
Wheat
Wool
Oranges
Gold
Paper
Wood
etc.

is/are
(not)

grown
produced
mined
manufactured
built

in

Japan.
Sweden.
Egypt.
Brazil.
Germany.
Britain.
the USA.
the USSR.
Kenya.
etc.

Unit 12: Lesson A

Students learn to talk about manufacturing and other processes.
Principal structures: simple present passive; preview of simple past and present progressive passives; no article with 'general' reference.
Words and expressions to learn: *industry; page; adult; dry* (verb); *use; grow; reach; get to; AD; by land; daily; serious; Muslim;* other words as chosen by students.
Phonology: perceiving /ə/.

Language notes and possible problems

1. The passive   Not all languages contain passive verb forms, and some students may have difficulty in grasping the meaning of the passive at first. But the exercises will give students a feeling for the use of the forms, and by the end of the lesson they should have a reasonable understanding of the point.

You may wish to explain how the 'same' idea can be expressed by active or passive structures, by comparing, for instance, *The Chinese invented paper* and *Paper was invented by the Chinese*. Note, however, that these two sentences don't really have the same meaning. (In the first one we are talking about the Chinese; in the second we are talking about paper.) So active and passive structures should not be presented as exact equivalents.

2. Zero article   Students may have difficulty in remembering to omit the article with nouns used in a very general sense (e.g. *paper, wood, paper mills*).

3. Other points   The main purpose of this lesson is to give students plenty of experience of passive structures, but it may be worth saying a word about one or two of the following points from the text:
- The difference between *made from* (talking about process) and *made of* (talking about material).
- The use of sequencing and connecting words in the second paragraph (*when, here, and, which, then*).
- The use of *up* to mean 'completely' in *cut up, broken up* and *used up*.
- Difficult structures which are previewed here include: present progressive passive (*trees are being cut down*); *there may be*; past participle introducing a descriptive phrase (*the wood used in the British paper-making industry*).

4. Phonology   Encourage students to improve their pronunciation of /eɪ/ in *paper* and *made*.

5. Vocabulary   This lesson contains a large number of new words. Make it clear to students that they do not need to learn them all (see Summary).

1 The text
● Tell students to read through the text once without dictionaries, so as to get a general idea.
● Then get them to read it slowly again, looking up words or asking you questions and deciding which of the three words goes in each blank.
● Go round helping where necessary.
● Once the text has been read, you may want to talk about the use of the passive, and other language points arising (see *Language notes*).

Answers to Exercise 1
1. Paper   2. paper   3. paper   4. trees (*or* wood)
5. trees   6. wood   7. wood   8. paper   9. Paper
10. paper   11. wood   12. trees   13. wood   14. paper
15. trees   16. Trees

2 Listening and recall
● This can be done in two ways: *either* ask students to tell you their answer after each sentence; *or* get them to write the number of each sentence followed by *T* or *F*, and wait till the end to discuss answers.

Answers: 1F   2T   3F   4F   5F   6F   7F   8T   9F   10T

Tapescript for Exercise 2: see page 181

3 Pronunciation (/ə/)
● It is important for students to realise that /ə/ is the commonest vowel sound in English, and that it is very often pronounced in unstressed syllables where we write *a, e, o* or *u*.
● If students can become sensitive to this point they will find it much easier to understand spoken English (since they will not be confused by hearing /ə/ when they expect a different vowel).
● It is not so important for them to *pronounce* /ə/ in every case where it is required; they can be understood perfectly well without doing this.
● Give students a few minutes to try the exercise individually and compare answers in groups.
● Then play the recording or read the words and help them to correct their answers.

The words containing /ə/ are: iron, century, paper, correct, Germany, fibre, machine, industry, Africa, serious

4 Making sentences
● Start by explaining the vocabulary, or by letting students find out the meanings of the words by using dictionaries or consulting each other.
● Practise the pronunciation of the new vocabulary.
● This activity depends on students having a certain amount of general knowledge. If yours do not, you will need to give prompts (e.g. *'Gold – Russia'*).
● You might ask students to write their first sentence before continuing the exercise orally.
● Alternatively, you can turn this into a question-making exercise, with students asking each other, for instance, *Is rice grown in Britain?* This provides an opportunity to practise expressions like *I don't know, I think so, I don't think so, I'm not sure*.
● Pay attention to linking (e.g. *rice is*) and to the pronunciation of /ɪ/ in *ships, is, built* and *Britain*.
● Practice Book Exercise 4 gives additional work on these structures.

50

5 Listening: natural resources

- Before starting the exercise, spend some time going over the map and key with the students, explaining any new words which are not clear.
- Then play the recording and ask students to say or write their answers.
- Encourage them to use full 'short answer' forms like *Yes, it is* and *No, it isn't* rather than just *Yes* and *No*.
- If students are speaking, pay attention to the vowel /ɪ/ in *it is* and *it isn't*.
- You will need to pause for some time after each sentence to give students time to search for the answer and write it down.

Tapescript and answers to Exercise 5
1. True or false? Oil is produced in Texas. (*T*)
2. True or false? Cars are manufactured in Montana. (*F*)
3. True or false? Gold is mined in North Dakota. (*F*)
4. True or false? Maize is grown in Nebraska. (*T*)
5. True or false? Wheat is grown in Kansas. (*T*)
6. True or false? Aircraft are manufactured in Oklahoma. (*F*)
7. Are oranges grown in California? (*Yes, they are.*)
8. Is wheat grown in Arizona? (*No, it isn't.*)
9. Is rice grown in Oregon? (*No, it isn't.*)
10. Are aircraft manufactured in Kansas? (*Yes, they are.*)
11. Is silver mined in Idaho? (*Yes, it is.*)
12. Is paper made in Utah? (*Yes, it is.*)

6 Guessing countries

- Demonstrate the exercise by thinking of a country yourself. Think of a country and say four sentences about it, using verbs from Exercise 4 in three of the sentences.
- As students try to guess, give them clues to help guide them (e.g. *No, it's a bigger country than that; No, it's not in Europe*).
- Then divide the class into groups of four or so and let each student take a turn at thinking of a country. (Point out the verbs in Exercise 4.)
- Walk round while they are working to give any help that is needed.
- Do not correct all the errors students make, but try to ensure that they omit the article before words used in a general sense.
- Practice Book Exercise 2 gives additional practice on the use of the article.

7 *Made of*

- You may wish to put the students into different groups for this exercise.
- Tell them that they can use their dictionaries, and that they must try to answer the questions as quickly as they can.
- Most of the questions have more than one possible answer. Number 4 is meant to be a credit card, but your students may come up with another perfectly plausible answer.
- Practice Book Exercises 1 and 6 give more work on this point.

Summary

- Remind students to look at the Summary and learn the new vocabulary.

Practice Book

- Tell students which exercises you want them to do.

5 Look at the map. Then listen to the recording and answer the questions. Examples:

True or false? Oil is produced in Texas.

True.

Is wheat grown in Arizona?

No, it isn't.

6 Think of a country. Write four sentences about it; use verbs from Exercise 4 in three of the sentences.
Read your sentences to some other students. They will try to guess the country; you can help them if you want. Example:

Wool is produced there. Coal is mined there. Paper is manufactured there. Some good Olympic runners have come from there.

Is it the USA? *No, it's in Europe.*

Is it East Germany? *No.*

Britain? *Yes.*

7 Work in groups. See which group can finish the questions fastest. Use your dictionaries if you need to.
Write the name of:

1. something made of wood that you can play a game with
2. something made of iron that is found in a house
3. something made of china
4. something made of plastic that helps you buy things
5. something made of glass that helps you see
6. something made of leather that you can carry things in
7. something made of wool that people wear on their feet
8. something in the classroom that's made of steel
9. something made of cotton that someone in the group is wearing
10. something made of synthetic fibre that someone in the group is wearing

B Who killed Harrison?

1 Grammar. Look at the examples. Then write the infinitives and past participles of the verbs below.

INFINITIVE:	Can you **make** an omelette? I want **to see** the manager. We need **to import** less.
PAST TENSE:	She **made** that dress herself. I **saw** Alan yesterday. We **imported** 4m tons last year.
PAST PARTICIPLE	I've **made** you a cake. I haven't **seen** her today. Paper is **made** from wood. He was last **seen** in Cairo. This was **imported** from Taiwan.

1. know   steal   go   drink
2. find   build   think
3. mix   question   kill   arrest   need   export
4. manufacture   use   dry

2 Put the *-ing* form or the past participle.

1. 'What are you doing?' 'I'm .... bread.' (*make*)
2. Paper is .... from wood. (*make*)
3. When was that church ....? (*build*)
4. Mary and John are .... their own house. (*build*)
5. Why are you .... up that chair? (*break*)
6. I think the window was .... by a stone. (*break*)
7. Too many trees are .... down every year. (*cut*)
8. When we arrived, she was .... his hair. (*cut*)
9. The police are .... him now. (*question*)
10. When she was ...., she said nothing. (*question*)

7 Read the following text, but do *not* look at the text on the opposite page. Then work with a partner, and ask him or her questions to get more complete information about Harrison's death.

HARRISON was last seen alive at 9.30 p.m. (*Where?*) He was found dead in his flat by his wife Mary when she came home from a dance. (*What time?*) He was killed with a revolver. A small French-English dictionary was found by his body. (*Anything else? Was anything stolen?*)

The police suspect Haynes, MacHale and Cannon. All three were arrested the next morning.

HAYNES once worked for Harrison, but was sacked. (*Why?*) He has often said he hates Harrison, and would like to kill him. He was seen by three witnesses at 10.30. (*Where?*) When he was arrested, a revolver was found in his car. (*Where were his fingerprints found?*)

MacHALE is known to the police as a thief, but not as a killer. (*Where is he from?*) He is an old friend of Harrison's. (*Does he know Mrs Harrison?*) When he was arrested, £2,000 in cash was found in his wallet. (*Anything else?*)

CANNON works in an import-export business. (*Where?*) Harrison owed him a lot of money. When he was questioned, he said that he was at his hotel from 9.30 to 11.30. (*What did his wife say?*) He was seen earlier coming out of Harrison's flat. (*What time?*) Cannon's wife is an old friend of Mary Harrison's.

WHO DO YOU THINK KILLED HARRISON?

Unit 12: Lesson B

Students practise talking about the causes of past events.

Principal structures: simple past passive; irregular verb forms; present and past participles contrasted.

Words and expressions to learn: *stone*; *dance* (noun); *body* (= corpse); *thief*; *business*; *invent*; *direct* (verb); *arrest*; *sack* (verb); *owe*; *search*; *import*; *export*; *alive*; *central*; *earlier*.

Phonology: /h/; decoding rapid speech.

Language notes and possible problems

1. Information gap exercise Note that the success of Exercise 7 depends on students' not having read the texts before they do the exercise. Try to make sure your students do not have the time to look at these two texts in advance.

2. Passive verb forms Students are already reasonably familiar with passives. Exercises 1 and 3 should help to consolidate their understanding of the structure of passive verb forms.

3. 'Past participle' You may like to point out that this is a confusing name (the form can be used to refer to the past, present or future).

4. Present progressive and present passive Students tend to confuse forms such as *is breaking* and *is broken*, especially in the early stages of learning English. Exercise 2 will help them discriminate between the two forms.

5. *With* and *by* You will probably want to point out that in passive sentences we use *by* to indicate the *agent* of an action and *with* to indicate the *instrument* which the agent uses to do the action. Compare:

*She was killed **by** her lover.*
*She was killed **with** a knife.*

Practice Book Exercise 2 gives work on this point.

If you are short of time

You can leave out Exercise 4 if you think your students have no problems with question-words; you can leave out Exercise 5 or Exercise 6.

1 Regular and irregular past participles

● Go over the examples with the students to make sure they understand what the terms *infinitive*, *past tense* and *past participle* mean.

● Then ask them to write the infinitives and past participles of the verbs in the four lists. You may want them to compare answers in groups before checking with you.

● Point out that lists 1 and 2 contain irregular verbs with three and two different forms respectively.

● Lists 3 and 4 are of regular verbs. Note the pronunciation /ɪd/ of the endings in *arrested*, *needed* and *exported*, and the spellings of the endings in list 4.

● Finally, point out that it is the past participle that is used with *am/are/is/was/were* to form the passive, which students met in the last lesson.

2 Progressive and passive

● Ask students to do at least two or three sentences in writing to make sure that everybody has grasped the point.

● Then continue orally if you like.

● Practice Book Exercise 1 gives more work on this point.

Notes for Exercise 7 are on the next page

3 Making past passive sentences

- This exercise requires a certain level of general knowledge, and will be easiest for well-educated students with a European-type cultural background.
- You may want to let the students work in groups first to see how many facts they know or can deduce.
- If you think your students will find the exercise too difficult altogether, you can either give them help ('*America – Columbus*') or replace the exercise with one of your own, containing references that are more familiar to the students.
- Be sure to point out that sentences can end with a name or a date, or both.
- You will probably want to let students work individually at first, writing one or two sentences, and then continue orally.
- If time allows, you might get the students to make up 'true or false' sentences in groups and then try them out on the rest of the class.
- When they have finished the exercise, let them listen to the recording of native speakers trying it. (There is no task.)
- Practice Book Exercise 4 gives more work on forming passive sentences.

Facts from Exercise 3
America was discovered by Columbus in 1492; the Taj Mahal was built by Shah Jehan; J.F. Kennedy was assassinated in 1963 by Oswald; *Psycho* was directed by Hitchcock; the *Pastoral Symphony* was written by Beethoven in 1808; paper was invented in the first century by the Chinese; TV was invented by Baird in 1923; radium was discovered in 1898 by the Curies; Everest was first climbed by Hillary and Tensing in 1953; *Hamlet* was written by Shakespeare around 1600; the *Communist Manifesto* was written in 1848 by Marx and Engels; the 1974 World Cup was won by West Germany.

Tapescript for Exercise 3: see page 181

4 Question-words

- This is a revision exercise designed to help students who confuse *who* and *how*, *when* and *where* etc. under pressure.
- Go over the examples with them and then play the recording, telling them to say the question-words as fast as they can. (The recording gets faster and faster.)

Tapescript for Exercise 4
in 1982   in Africa   with a knife   to learn English   a book
Ann and Peter   by train   Shakespeare   on Monday
in Paris   now   because I was tired   a new car   very fast
tomorrow   here   my mother   a pen   to get more money
in the bank   by car   slowly   because it's late
the President   a pair of shoes

5 Making questions

- Ask students to suggest the answers to the first two sentences.
- Then put the two questions on the board:
  What time does she get up?
  When was it built?
- Point out that they both have the same structure:
  auxiliary verb + subject + main verb.
- It is probably best to do this exercise in writing, so that students get enough time to work out the right answers if they are confused.

6 Pronunciation

- The first part of the exercise can be dropped if students are able to pronounce /h/ without difficulty.
- The phrases in the second part of the exercise will appear in the story in Exercise 7, but none of them contain new words. They give students practice in hearing linking between words.

Tapescript for Exercise 6
from a dance   anything else   he was arrested
he often said   to kill him   in his car   not as a killer
an old friend   a lot of money   he was at home

7 Information-gap exercise

- This exercise is done in pairs, but you may wish students to do the initial work in small groups.
- Get half the students (for example, the right-hand side of the class) to cover the right-hand page of their books; and the other half of the class to cover the left-hand page.
- Students should read the portion of Exercise 7 that is uncovered, using their dictionaries or consulting you about new words.
- Tell students to prepare the questions they are going to ask; give help with word order if needed.
- When everyone is ready, get students from one half of the class to pair off with students from the other half, and let them start asking questions. It does not matter if there is one group of three.
- Students should keep one side of the book covered, and *not* show one another their books.
- They should make notes of the answers they get.
- When the question-and-answer session is finished, ask students to try to decide who murdered Harrison. This may lead to discussion: help with vocabulary and structures if necessary, but don't correct mistakes at this point unless it is essential.

Answer to Exercise 7
The police arrested Mary Harrison and charged her with Harrison's murder.

They think she came back from the dance some time between 9.30 and 11.30 and shot her husband, leaving a French-English dictionary and a Paris underground ticket by the body to throw suspicion on Cannon. She got her friend Mrs Cannon (who hates Cannon) to give the police false information about Cannon's movements. She took her husband's wallet and threw it away, but gave the money to MacHale, who is her lover.

But your students may think the police are wrong: do let them argue their case if they think it is a better one.

Summary
- Remind the students to look over the Summary and learn the new words.

Practice Book
- Tell students which exercises you want them to do.

3 Make some true sentences.

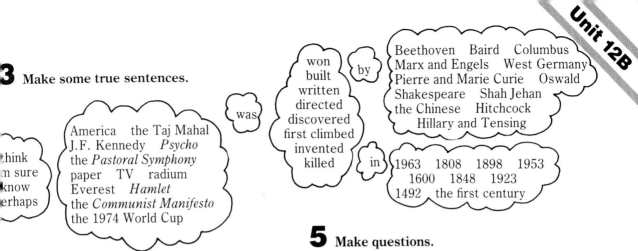

think
m sure
know
erhaps

America   the Taj Mahal
J.F. Kennedy   *Psycho*
the *Pastoral Symphony*
paper   TV   radium
Everest   *Hamlet*
the *Communist Manifesto*
the 1974 World Cup

was

won
built
written
directed
discovered
first climbed
invented
killed

by

Beethoven   Baird   Columbus
Marx and Engels   West Germany
Pierre and Marie Curie   Oswald
Shakespeare   Shah Jehan
the Chinese   Hitchcock
Hillary and Tensing

in

1963   1808   1898   1953
1600   1848   1923
1492   the first century

Now listen to the recording.

4 Who, what, when, where, why, how?
Listen to the answers and write the
question-words. Examples:

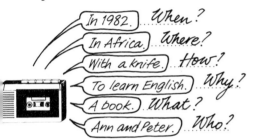

In 1982.   *When?*
In Africa.   *Where?*
With a knife.   *How?*
To learn English.   *Why?*
A book.   *What?*
Ann and Peter.   *Who?*

5 Make questions.

1. Gloria gets up very early. (*'What time...?'*)
2. The church was built by Wren. (*'When...?'*)
3. I'm waiting. (*'What...?'*)
4. He was sacked last week. (*'Why...?'*)
5. We're going on holiday in July. (*'Where...?'*)
6. I don't usually sit here. (*'Where...?'*)
7. He never travels by car. (*'How...?'*)
8. My father was killed when I was six.
   (*'How...?'*)

6 Pronunciation. Pronounce these words.

here   half   home   Harrison   hated   who
hand   hungry   happy

Listen and write what you hear.

7 Read the following text, but do *not* look at the text on the opposite page. Then work with a
partner, and ask him or her questions to get more complete information about Harrison's death.

HARRISON was last seen alive talking to a woman in the street outside his flat in
central London. (*What time?*) He was found dead by his wife (*Name?*) when she
came home from a dance at 11.30. (*How was he killed?*) A Paris underground
ticket was found by his body. (*Anything else?*) His wallet had been stolen.

The police suspect Haynes, MacHale and Cannon. All three were
arrested the next morning.

HAYNES once worked for Harrison, but was sacked for stealing.
He has often said he hates Harrison, and would like
to kill him. He was seen by three witnesses 50km
from Harrison's home. (*What time?*) His fingerprints
were found in Harrison's flat. When he was arrested,
his car was searched by the police. (*Was anything found?*)

MacHALE is from Scotland. He is a very old friend of Mrs Harrison's. (*Did he
know Mr Harrison?*) When he was arrested, a love letter (signed '*Mary*') was found in his
pocket. (*Anything else? Find out if MacHale is known to the police.*)

CANNON works in Paris. (*What does he do? Find out if he owed Harrison money.*)
He was seen coming out of Harrison's flat at 9.15. When his wife
was questioned, she said that he was out of his hotel all evening.
(*What did he say? Find out if Cannon's wife knows Mary Harrison.*)

WHO DO YOU THINK KILLED HARRISON?

Descriptions

A Places

1 Look at the picture. Which word goes with which number?

hill   mountain   valley   wood   stream
waterfall   island   river   lake   bridge
path   road

2 How do you get from A to B? Use the words in Exercise 1 with these prepositions.

across   through   along   up   down

Example: '*You go down the hill, . . .*'

3 Look at the map and listen to the recording. Decide whether the sentences are true or false. Example:

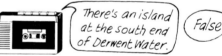

There's an island at the south end of Derwent Water.

False.

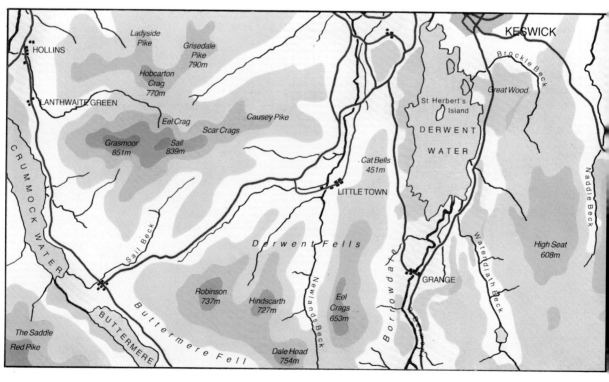

Unit 13: Lesson A

Students practise talking about places: they learn the words for some features of landscape, revise the expressions used for asking and giving directions, and revise the names of rooms.
No new structures
Words and expressions to learn: *hill; valley; stream; waterfall; wood; path; lake; town hall; college; park; central heating; through; straight ahead.*
Phonology: decoding rapid speech.

Language notes and possible problems

1. Conditional structures The use of conditionals and past tenses to talk about imaginary situations is previewed in Exercise 5 (*Imagine that somebody asked you... What would you say?*). The point will be studied in detail later, but you may want to say a word about it now.

2. Irony The dialogue in Exercise 8 contains several ironic remarks which mean the exact opposite of what the words say (e.g. *Oh, good. Let's buy it at once!*). This rhetorical device is not common to all cultures, and it may be necessary to explain it carefully.

If you are short of time
Drop the song.

1 Vocabulary extension: landscapes
● Practise the pronunciation first of all (make sure students don't say an *s* in *island*).
● Then let students pool their knowledge in groups. When they have done what they can, go over the answers with them.
● Answer any questions they may have about other vocabulary in this area, within reason. (But if a student wants to learn a large number of words, he or she probably ought to work at home with a dictionary.)

2 Prepositions
● Get students to write the answer (so that everybody has to try).
● Then let them compare notes before you check the answer with them.
● If necessary, explain the exact meanings of the prepositions.

Answer: You go down the hill, along the road, across the bridge, through the wood and up the other hill.

3 Listening
Note The map shows a part of the Lake District, a wild and beautiful area of moorland and mountain in north-west England.
● Look at the map with the class. Not all students may be used to reading maps; check that they know the meaning of the main symbols, can identify roads and rivers, and understand the use of colour and contour lines to show height (darker shades of brown mean higher ground).
● Check that students remember the words *north*, *south*, *east* and *west*, and can identify the directions on the map.

● When students are familiar with the map, play the recording and ask them to note their answers. (You will need to stop the recording after each sentence to give them time to think and write.)
● Play the recording once more if necessary. Then let students compare notes before telling them the answers.

Tapescript and answers to Exercise 3
1. There's an island at the south end of Derwent Water. (*F*)
2. There are three big lakes on the map. (*T*)
3. Dark colours on the map mean high ground. (*T*)
4. Cat Bells is a hill just east of Derwent Water. (*F*)
5. Cat Bells is higher than High Seat. (*F*)
6. St Herbert's Island is in the middle of Derwent Water. (*T*)
7. There's a wood to the east of Derwent Water. (*T*)
8. Buttermere is in a deep valley. (*T*)
9. The map shows three high waterfalls between Crummock Water and Buttermere. (*F*)
10. There's a road on the south-west side of Buttermere. (*F*)

54

4 Perceiving unstressed syllables

- Play the sentences one by one, letting students discuss the answer before going on to the next.
- Don't play a sentence more times than necessary: students must learn to cope with real-life speech.

Tapescript and answers to Exercise 4
1. There are three big lakes on the map. (8)
2. There's an island at the south end of the lake. (11).
3. Go across the bridge and through the wood. (8)
4. Can you tell me the way to the post office? (10)
5. You have to turn right after the police station. (9)
6. It's about half a mile from here. (8)
7. I went to look at a flat this afternoon. (9)
8. What was it like? (4)
9. Is the kitchen big enough? (5)
10. How much does it cost? (5)

5 Giving directions (introduction)

- Give students a minute or two to think about this, and then let them compare notes in groups.
- Discuss the answer and explain any difficulties.

Answer: Go straight ahead for about 200 metres, then turn right at the first crossroads. Then take the first left. Keep straight on past the station; you'll see it on your left.

6 Giving directions (continued)

- This is a straightforward exercise. You may like to start it off yourself by asking a bright student for directions to one of the places on the map.

Optional activities Giving directions
1. Students work in groups, using the map from Exercise 5. Each student in turn gives directions to the others, and then asks where they think they are. For example: *You are at the car park. Go straight ahead for 200 metres, turn left at the crossroads,* (various other directions) *and take the first right. Where are you?*
2. Students work in pairs making conversations in which a tourist asks somebody the way.
3. Get students to tell you how to get to various local places, starting from the classroom.
4. One student stands in the middle of the room pretending to be in a well-known place which everybody knows well (don't forget to agree on which way he/she is supposed to be facing). The others come up and ask for directions to various places.

7 Names of rooms

- Get students to work individually at first, then to compare notes in groups.
- Check that they know the names of the most important rooms (*kitchen, living room, bedroom, bathroom, toilet/lavatory*).

8 House-agent's advertisement

- Let students read through the advertisement. Give whatever help is necessary.
- You may want to point out the typical use of impressive synonyms: *residence* instead of *house*; *cloakroom* instead of *toilet*; *lounge* instead of *sitting/living room*; *mature garden* instead of *garden with plants growing*.

- When students are ready, tell them that they will hear a conversation between John, who has just been to look at the house advertised, and his wife Sally.
- The students' task is to see how many differences they can find between what John says about the house and the advertiser's description.
- You may like to play the recording twice, letting students compare notes after the first hearing.
- Note that they are *not* expected to understand every word, and neither you nor they should worry if there are passages they cannot understand. This is quite normal at this stage.
- It would be a mistake to go through the recording explaining low-priority words and structures.

Tapescript for Exercise 8
JOHN: Hi, darling.
SALLY: Hello, John. Well, did you see the 'magnificent town residence'?
JOHN: Yes.
SALLY: So what's it like?
JOHN: Well, first of all it's four miles out of the town centre.
SALLY: Oh, no!
JOHN: And it's not all that big. Three bedrooms: one quite big, one smallish, and one that would be OK for the cat. The luxury bathroom doesn't have a shower, and the downstairs cloakroom is at the end of the garden – at the end of the jungle, I should say. The sitting and dining room are both pretty small.
SALLY: What about the kitchen? Is it big enough to have breakfast in?
JOHN: Oh, yes. Easily. If you sit on the fridge and put your feet out of the window there's plenty of room.
SALLY: The garage?
JOHN: Fine for a bicycle. A bicycle, mind. Not two bicycles. And there's oil-fired central heating, which doesn't work. And the walls and roof are in a very bad state. Apart from that it's fine.
SALLY: Oh, good. Let's buy it at once!

9 Personalisation

- Encourage students to make this a genuine piece of communication. They should try to make the others 'see' the place they are describing.

10 Song

- The song contains a lot of the vocabulary from the first part of the lesson.
- Play it once right through, and ask students what they have understood.
- Then play one section, stopping and repeating if necessary, while students try to work out the words.
- Finally, let students look at the words on page 157 while you play the song once more. Encourage them to sing along with the recording.

4 Pronunciation. Listen to the recording. How many words do you hear in each sentence? What are they? (Contractions like *there's* count as two words.)

5 Look at the town plan. Imagine that somebody asked you how to get from the car park to the post office. What would you say? If you don't know the answer, put these sentences in order.

Then take the first left.
You'll see it on your left.
Then turn right at the first crossroads.
Go straight ahead for about 200 metres.
Keep straight on past the station.

6 Work in groups. Ask and give directions from the car park to other places on the map. Example:

'Excuse me. Can you tell me the way to the Rainbow Theatre?'
'Yes. Go straight ahead . . .'

7 Can you write down the names of all the rooms in a typical house?

8 Read the advertisement and listen to the recording. How many differences can you find between the two descriptions of the house?

Map labels:
Rainbow Theatre
Post Office
Swimming Pool
Goldberg Close
Railway Station
Town Hall
STATION ROAD
HIGH STREET
MAHON STREET
ANTONIO AVENUE
Lennox Way
Police Station
OSBORNE ROAD
LORD CHANCELLOR'S DRIVE
Edward VIII Way
Superb Cinema
Caplan Road
Agricultural College
Sir Percy Shorter Park
Jonah's Way
Franklyn Road
JOYCE AVENUE
SHORTER DRIVE
JAMES
Romainville Hospital
Car Park

Metres
0   50   100   150   200

Central York
MAGNIFICENT TOWN RESIDENCE

Four double bedrooms, luxury bathroom, upstairs and downstairs cloakrooms, lounge, dining-room, kitchen/breakfast room, double garage, beautiful mature garden, gas-fired central heating. In first-class condition.

£90,000

9 Work in groups of three or four. Tell the other students in the group about a place that you like. It can be somewhere in the country, a town, a street, a building, or any other kind of place.

10 Listen to the song, and see how much you can understand. Then look at the words on page 156, listen again, and sing along.

B | Things

1 Listen to the conversation and learn the new words and expressions.

A: Funny, isn't it?
B: Yes. I didn't think it would be so big.
A: No.
B: Do you like it?
A: I don't know. I'm not sure. Give me time.
B: It looks heavy.
A: Yes, it's quite heavy. Try and pick it up.
B: Ooooh! My back!
A: See?
B: It feels really cold. Like ice.
A: I know.
B: And it smells funny.
A: Sort of sweet.
B: Yes. What's that thing on the top? What's it for?
A: I don't know. Perhaps it's to open the lid with.
B: Fred.
A: Yes, Pete?
B: What *is* it?

2 Put these words and expressions into the sentences.

a bit	feel	funny	isn't it	like	looks
smells	so	sort of	sure	think	with

1. 'Is that Mary?' 'I'm not ....'
2. 'Do you like my hair like this?' 'Not really. I think it looks a bit ....'
3. It was a good film. But I didn't .... it would be .... long.
4. Your sister looks .... you.
5. My brother looks .... like my father.
6. 'The house .... funny.' 'Yes, I've been cooking fish.'
7. I .... funny. .... hot and cold all over.
8. It's cold today, ... ?
9. That baby .... like a football .... arms and legs.

3 Listen to the recording and say what you think the things might be. Begin *It sounds like...* Example:

'It sounds like a train.'

4 What are these?

1. A thing that takes you from place to place.
2. A thing that tells you the time.
3. A thing (that) you read to find out what has happened in the world.
4. A thing (that) you sit on.
5. A thing (that) you open the door with.
6. A thing (that) you drink out of.
7. A small animal with long ears.
8. An animal that has a very long neck.
9. An animal that has black and white stripes.
10. A very big animal with a very long nose.

In sentences 3–6, the word *that* can be left out. In sentences 1 and 2, it can't. Why?

5 How quickly can you match the words and the descriptions?

boat	calendar	envelope	gun	hairbrush
ice-cream	microphone	pillow		suitcase
tap	tongue	wrist		

1. A thing water comes out of.
2. A thing you tidy your hair with.
3. Something that makes you cool in hot weather.
4. Something you put a letter in.
5. A part of your body that joins your hand to your arm.
6. A thing you can travel in across water.
7. Something you put your head on at night.
8. A thing you speak into.
9. A thing that can kill people.
10. Something that tells you the date.
11. A thing that is useful when you travel.
12. Something you use for talking and tasting.

Unit 13: Lesson B

Students learn to describe and define things.
Principal structures: *feel, smell* + adjective; *it sounds like...*; relative *that* in definitions (*a thing that...*); omission of object pronoun (*a thing you sit on*); preposition at end of relative clause; 'universal' *you*.
Words and expressions to learn: *back; ice; tongue; envelope; feel; smell; funny* (= strange); *sweet; some of these: lid; calendar; suitcase; hairbrush; pillow; sheet; wrist; queue; sandwich; microphone; lipstick; magazine; nail; overcoat; rose; umbrella; beer; litre; oil; pig.*
Phonology /iː/, /ɪ/ and /aɪ/; pronunciations of the letter *i*.

Language notes and possible problems

1. Linking verbs Note the use of adjectives after the 'linking' or 'copula' verbs *look, feel* and *smell*.
2. Relative pronouns In Exercises 4–6, students practise structures in which the object pronoun *that* is left out. Many students will find this difficult.
3. End-position of prepositions. In these exercises, students also practise relative clauses ending in prepositions. This structure, too, is likely to cause difficulty.
4. With Note how *have* and *with* can be used to express identical meanings. Compare (Exercise 4):
An animal that has a very long neck.
An animal with a very long nose.
5. You Students may need help to understand the 'universal' use of *you* to mean *people in general* (as in *A thing you tidy your hair with*).
6. Pronunciation The word *thing* comes up very often in this lesson. Encourage the correct pronunciation of /θ/ and /ɪ/.

If you are short of time

Drop Exercise 7 if these pronunciation points are not important for your students; drop one or more of Exercises 8–10.

Optional extra materials

● Objects for further practice in defining (Exercise 6). Suggestions: clothes-brush, corkscrew, tin-opener, knife, fork, spoon, alarm clock, torch, map, credit card, key, soap.
● Small objects for the *Optional activity* after Exercise 8. Suggestions: key, paper-clip, diary, comb, ring, piece of soap, sweet, egg, light bulb, battery, paper tissue, grape, tie, credit card, pocket knife, stamp, toy car.

1 Dialogue

● Play this while students listen (books closed).
● Stop the recording after A's fifth utterance (*See?*) and ask students what they think the thing is.
● After they have heard the whole dialogue, see how much they can remember about the mysterious object.
● Play the dialogue again, and see if this time they can remember some complete sentences.
● Then get the class to build up the whole dialogue on the board.

● Let them open their books, and play it once more while they follow the text.
● Give whatever explanations are necessary.

2 Vocabulary

● Students can either do the exercise individually (comparing notes when they have finished), or orally round the class.

Optional activity

● A good way of activating the language from the dialogue is as follows:
1. Ask a group of four or five students to prepare a mimed sketch (lasting a minute or so), in which they are having difficulty with a heavy object. It is up to them to decide what the object is; they must not tell the others.
2. The rest of the class watch the mime and try to guess what the object is.
3. Now the rest of the class divide into groups. Each group 'takes over' the mime of the first group, repeating it as well as they can *but adding words*. They should use some of the vocabulary from the original dialogue. Very fluent students may be able to do this as an improvisation; others should be given a few minutes to prepare.

3 Identifying sounds

● Play each sound and ask students what they think they hear. They should start *It sounds like...*
● Encourage them to discuss and disagree with each other. (The sounds are deliberately chosen so as to be difficult to identify unambiguously.)

The sounds are: a train; a typewriter; a cup breaking; a car crash; a bath running; rain; people watching football; a fire; an egg frying; a lawnmower

4 Definitions and descriptions

● This introduces the structures that are used for defining and describing.
● After students have discussed the answers to the questions (more than one answer is possible in some cases), you may want to go over the grammar with them (see *Language notes*).
● See if they can work out for themselves why *that* can be left out in some sentences but not in others.

5 Matching exercise

● This can be done in small groups, with students sharing their knowledge of vocabulary.
● When they have finished, go over the pronunciation of the new words with them.
● Students should notice that in these sentences *that* has been left out when it is the object pronoun.

56

6 Students' definitions

● Ask students to choose two or three of the pictures and write definitions of them (similar to those in Exercises 4 and 5).
● Let them give their definitions and see if other students can decide which pictures they are talking about.
● The exercise can be continued orally in groups.
● If you wish, you can bring in some more things for students to define (see suggestions in *Optional extra materials*); or you can ask students to make up definitions for things they have thought of themselves, and see if the class can guess what they are talking about.

7 /iː/, /ɪ/ and /aɪ/; pronunciation of *i*

● If students have difficulty with the difference between /iː/ and /ɪ/, practise the words and expressions in groups 1 and 2.
● Then get students to look at groups 3 and 4. Practise the pronunciation of /aɪ/ if necessary, and ask students if they can see when the letter *i* is pronounced /aɪ/. Get them to find a few more words to go in groups 3 and 4.
● Make sure they are clear about the pronunciation of the exceptions in group 5. Can they think of any more words like *give*? (*Live.*)

8 Characteristics of things

● Students have to interpret data presented in a table in order to make a choice between seven different things or substances.
● You may like to do this as a competition, asking students to see how fast they can finish.

The answers are: 1. a boiled egg 2. a pint of beer 3. a cat 4. a sweater 5. a bicycle 6. a litre of oil 7. a pearl

● If you have a lot of time available, you could ask students to work in groups and make up their own version of this exercise to try on the rest of the class.

Optional activity

● Get a volunteer to come out in front of the class (preferably somebody with a good vocabulary).
● The student's hands should be behind his or her back, and he or she should face the class.
● Put a small object into the student's hands without letting anybody see it.
● The class have to ask questions to find out what it is.
● The person holding the object can give any information asked for except the name of the object (if he or she knows what it is).
● When the class have identified the object, put its name on the board if necessary.
● Ask for another volunteer and do the same thing again.
● See *Optional extra materials* for suggestions of objects that can be used.

9 Twenty questions

● Students may already know this game, which is excellent for revising interrogative structures.

● Start off yourself; when the students have guessed (or failed to guess) your object, let them continue in groups.

10 Listening to native speakers

● Students may find it amusing to listen to the recording of some native speakers playing 'Twenty questions'.

Tapescript for Exercise 10
'I'll start if you like.'
'OK.'
'You've got to tell us whether it's animal, vegetable or mineral.'
'I have to tell you?'
'Yes.'
'You don't have to ask me?'
'No, you have to tell us that and then we have to ask the rest.'
'OK. It's mineral.'
'Is it manufactured?'
'Yes.'
'Is it smaller than a loaf of bread?'
'Yes.'
'Can you burn it?'
'It wouldn't burn well, no.'
'Is it something to do with the hospital?'
'No, not necessarily.'
'Does it have moving parts?'
'Not usually. No, it doesn't.'
'Is it useful?'
'Yes.'
'In the home?'
'Yes.'
'Is it edible?'
'No.'
'Is it a kitchen implement?'
'I wouldn't call it an implement.'
'Have you got one in your house?'
'Yes.'
'More than one?'
'More than one.'
'More than ten?'
'More than ten.'
'Does it always come in a group –'
'No.'
' – quantity?'
'No, it can come as a single –'
'Anything to do with electrics?'
'No.'
'Are there any on this table?'
'Yes.'
'Is it a glass?'
'Yes.'
(Laughter)
'I knew it was a glass from the very beginning.'

Summary

● Remind students to study the Summary on page 144. Encourage them to learn some of the optional extra vocabulary if possible.

Practice Book

● Tell students which exercises you want them to do.

6 Now describe these.

a church

a lipstick

a nail

an overcoat

a pig

a rose

a magazine

a suit

a sheet

a sandwich

an umbrella

Make up descriptions of some more things. See if the other students can work out what they are.

7 Pronunciation. Say these words and expressions.

1. is   it   didn't   think   big   thing   with   lid   pick   liquid
2. It feels cold.   Eat it.   What is it?   Is it liquid?
3. like   time   quite   alive   white   mine
4. light   high   tight   might   right   flight
5. give   pint   bicycle   litre

9 Twenty questions. One student thinks of something. The student doesn't tell the others what it is; he/she only tells them that it is 'animal', 'vegetable', 'mineral' or 'abstract'. (For example: a leather handbag is animal, a newspaper is vegetable, a glass is mineral and an idea is abstract.) The other students must find out what the thing is by asking questions (maximum 20); the only answers allowed are *Yes* and *No*. Useful questions:

Can you eat it?
Is it made of wood/metal/glass?
Is it useful?
Can you find it in a house/shop/car?
Is it liquid?
Is it hard/soft/heavy/light?
Have you got one of these?
Is there one in this room? In this building?
Is it manufactured?

8 Match the numbers and the pictures.

	LIQUID OR SOLID?	ALIVE?	USEFUL?	CAN YOU EAT/ DRINK IT?	MANUFAC- TURED?	CAN YOU WEAR IT?
1	S	NO	YES	YES	NO	NO
2	L	NO	YES	YES	YES	NO
3	S	YES	YES	NO	NO	NO
4	S	NO	YES	NO	YES	YES
5	S	NO	YES	NO	YES	NO
6	L	NO	YES	NO	YES	NO
7	S	NO	NO	NO	NO	YES

10 Listen to the recording of some people playing 'Twenty questions'.

a sweater

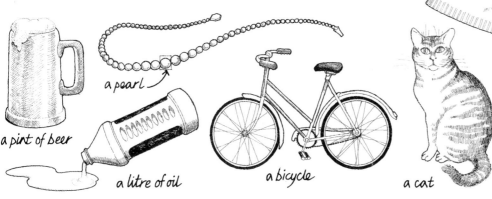

a pint of beer

a pearl

a litre of oil

a bicycle

a cat

a boiled egg

Families

A Different kinds of families

1 Match the texts and the pictures. You can use a dictionary.

1. Don and Lola are Kenny's grandparents. Kenny has lived with them since he was a baby. Last year they adopted him as their own child.
2. Kim and May are married, but they do not want to have children. Although they enjoy playing with their nieces and nephews, they do not want to be full-time parents.
3. John and Christine have got three children – Simon, Lucy and Emma. There are a lot of couples with young children in their neighbourhood, so they often help one another out.
4. Anamita has got four children. Besides her husband, Surendra, and the children, she also shares her home with her mother-in-law, her brother-in-law and his wife. The children get on well with their aunt and uncle, and like listening to their grandmother's stories.
5. Claire and Bridget live together. They both work outside the home and share the care of Beth, Bridget's six-year-old daughter.
6. Ann has been divorced for ten years. Her two children, Jason and Ruth, live with Ann, and see their father almost every week.
7. Because Jack is too ill to live alone, he lives with his son Barry, who is 25. Barry is getting married soon, and Jack will continue to live with the young couple. He hopes to have grandchildren to look after soon.

2 Pronouncing words together. Some words change their pronunciation before vowels. Listen to the differences in pronunciation.

1. they   they adopted him
2. who   who is 25
3. Claire   Claire and Bridget

Now pronounce these.

4. she also shares
5. too ill to live alone
6. their aunt and uncle
7. Barry is getting married
8. see their father almost every week
9. the care of Beth

3 How many words do you know for talking about relatives? Make a list beginning *mother, father,...* and see how many words you can add.

4 Tell other students about your family or other families you know. Examples:

'My uncle is divorced. His son...'
'My neighbours have got six children. ...'

Unit 14: Lesson A

Students learn to talk about family relationships, practise asking about and expressing preferences, and learn some ways of connecting sentences in a written text.
Principal structures: *Would you rather*; paragraph linking.
Words and expressions to learn: *relative; aunt; uncle; niece; nephew; cousin; grandmother; grandfather; granddaughter; grandson; mother-in-law; father-in-law; brother-in-law; sister-in-law; parents-in-law; in-laws; society; rule* (noun); *adopt; continue; universal; healthy; proud; although; besides.*
Phonology: linking with /r/, /j/ and /w/.

Language notes and possible problems

1. Talking about families You will probably want to make very sure, in Exercise 4, that students understand that they do not have to speak about their own families if they don't want to, as this may be difficult for some students.

2. Pronunciation: linking Exercise 2 helps students to realise and practise the differences in pronunciation that occur when two vowels are pronounced one after another. Three cases are studied:

a. words ending in written *-r* or *-re*: when these are followed by a vowel. /r/ is pronounced.

b. words ending in /iː/, /i/, and /eɪ/ (this rule also applies for words ending in /ɔɪ/ and /aɪ/): when these are followed by a vowel, a very slight /j/ is pronounced between the two words.

c. words ending in /uː/ (and /əʊ/ and /aʊ/): when these are followed by a vowel, a very slight /w/ is pronounced between the two words.

You may wish to make these rules explicit for the students; guidance for this is given in the notes for the exercise.

If you are short of time

You can leave out Exercise 4 and/or Exercise 7.

1 Vocabulary presentation

● Put students into groups of three or so.
● Encourage them to pool their knowledge and to use their dictionaries in order to read the texts and match them with the pictures.

The answers are: 1D 2A 3F 4G 5C 6E 7B

2 Pronouncing words together 📼

● Play or read the first example to the students.
● Ask them to tell you what the difference is when the words are pronounced together, and then get them to practise saying the example.
● Do the same with the other two examples.
● You may wish to elicit or point out the fact that in the first example, /j/ is the closest consonant to /ɪ/, which is why it is lightly pronounced to separate the two words; and that in the second example /w/ is lightly pronounced because it is the closest consonant to /uː/.

● Get volunteers to pronounce the next six lines. Get the class to listen; the volunteers should continue trying until the class decides that their pronunciation is acceptable.
● Afterwards, put the students in pairs to practise all nine lines for a minute or two.

3 Vocabulary revision and extension

● Divide the class into groups of three or four.
● Ask each group to try and add as many words as they can to the list that begins *mother, father, . . .*
● Walk round while they are working to give any help that is needed.
● Let groups compare answers when they have finished.
● You may want to point out the plural forms *sisters-in-law* and *brothers-in-law.*
● Practice Book Exercise 3 revises kinship terms once again.

4 Personalisation

● Ask the students to work individually, making up five or six sentences about a family they know.
● Make sure they understand that they do not necessarily have to talk about their own families – this may make some of them uncomfortable for one reason or another.
● When most of the students have finished, divide the class into groups of three or four.
● They should take turns telling each other about the family they have chosen; after each person has had his or her turn, the others try to report back what has been said.
● In quicker groups, you may want to make this more difficult by getting all three or four students to give their information before they all try to report back.
● Groups who finish early can form new groups and begin again.

5 Sentence and paragraph connectors

- Get the students to look back at the texts in Exercise 1 and find the words from the box.
- Make sure they understand how the words are used.
- Then ask them to read the text in Exercise 5, trying to put one of the words from the box into each blank.
- They can use their dictionaries or consult you about difficulties. Point out that one of the words from the box is used twice.
- Walk round while they are working to give any help that is needed.
- After working individually, they should compare answers and try to reach a consensus before checking with you.

Answers:
Although but besides so also because and

- Practice Book Exercise 2 gives more work on these words.

6 Class survey

- Go over the questions with the students, making sure they understand each one.
- You may have to remind or teach students the meaning of *Would you rather*.
- Then tell them they can ask *you* any of the questions they want.
- Try to answer truthfully: it will help them enjoy the exercise more.
- You can take this opportunity to help them with pronunciation, and to point out the reply forms *I'd rather . . .* and *I'd rather not*.
- Then tell each student to choose one question to ask as many other class members as possible. They should note the answers. (It does not matter if two students choose the same question.)
- Ideally, this will be done as a walk-round activity so everyone can ask everyone else.

7 Reporting the survey

- Go over the example with the students, and then get each student to report the results of his or her survey to the class.

8 Listening: native speakers doing the survey

- Ask students to write the numbers 1 to 5 on a piece of paper, and to keep their books open so they can see the questions in Exercise 6.
- Then play the recording, pausing after each item so that students can look at Exercise 6, decide which question the people are answering, and write its letter down.
- Remind the students that it is not necessary to understand every word, but just to decide which question is being answered.
- You may want to play the recording through a second time so that students can check their answers.

Answers: 1c 2f 3b 4h 5e

Tapescript for Exercise 8: see page 181

9 Song *My Old Dad*

- Ask the students to close their books.
- Play the recording through once, and then ask the students to tell you any words they remember.
- Let them open their books and read the lyrics, and answer any questions they have about meaning.
- You may wish to point out the use of *I guess* for *I reckon* and *mad* for *angry*. These are Americanisms that are beginning to be heard in British English; British pop songs, especially, contain many Americanisms.
- Play the song again so the students can try to hear the missing verbs (mostly irregular past tense forms).
- Let them compare answers with one another before checking with you.
- After going over the answers, the students may want to hear the song one more time.

Tapescript for Exercise 9: *My Old Dad*
We never *saw* him in the mornings
And he always *came* home late
Then he *sat* and *read* the paper
And *did* the crossword while he *ate*

He never *helped* us with our homework
But he *taught* me how to swim
And he *taught* me to be patient
I guess I *learnt* a lot from him

   My old dad
   He was one of the good guys
   He was nobody's hero
   But he was special to me

Every summer we *went* to Blackpool
Except when he *was* unemployed
He *loved* to *sit* and *watch* the sunset
That *was* one thing we both *enjoyed*

He *was* always very gentle
Nothing ever *made* him mad
He *was* never rich or famous
But I *was* proud of my old dad

   My old dad
   He was one of the good guys
   He was nobody's hero
   But he was special to me

Jonathan Dykes (lyrics)
Robert Campbell (music)

10 Personalisation: *proud of*

- Tell the students briefly about someone in your family that you are proud of, for whatever reason.
- Then divide the class into groups of two or three so that each student can do the same.
- Exercise 4 in the Practice Book gives students an opportunity to write about this topic.

Summary
- Remind students to look at the Summary and learn the new words.

Practice Book
- Tell students which exercises you want them to do.

5 Find these words in the texts in Exercise 1.

| also | although | and | because |
| besides | but | so |

Now put one of the words into each blank in this text.

.... there are many different kinds of families in the world, there are some things that are the same everywhere. Not all societies have western-type marriage with one wife and one husband, ... some kind of marriage is universal. And when a person marries, ... the new wife or husband, he or she also gets a complete new family of in-laws. Marriages with close relatives do not always produce healthy children, ... all societies have rules about who can marry who. Each society .... has a division of work based on age and sex. In modern western societies, there is a move to change this last rule .... it can be unfair to women, ... it will be interesting to see if this succeeds.

6 Class survey. Make sure you understand the questions. Then choose one question to ask the other people in the class.

a. Would you like to live alone part of the time – say, one week a month?
b. Would you rather have more or fewer brothers and sisters than you have?
c. Would you like to have children? How many? OR: Would you like to have more or fewer children than you have?
d. Would you rather live in the same town as your parents or not?
e. Would you rather spend less time working and more time with your family?
f. Would you rather give your parents the money to have a nice holiday on their own, or take them on holiday with you?
g. Would you rather invite your in-laws to spend a week with you, or stay at home while your husband/wife visits them?
h. What's the best age for having children? Is it better to be young or a bit older?

7 Report the results of your survey. Example:

'Nine people would rather spend less time working and more time with their families, and six people think they see enough of their families.'

8 Listen to the recording. Some British people are answering questions from the survey. As you hear their answers, write the letters of the questions they are answering.

9 Listen to the song and try to write down the verbs.

MY OLD DAD

We never .... him in the mornings
And he always .... home late
Then he .... and .... the paper
And .... the crossword while he ....

He never .... us with our homework
But he .... me how to swim
And he .... me to be patient
I guess I .... a lot from him

My old dad
He was one of the good guys
He was nobody's hero
But he was special to me

Every summer we .... to Blackpool
Except when he .... unemployed
He .... to .... and .... the sunset
That .... one thing we both ....

He .... always very gentle
Nothing ever .... him mad
He .... never rich or famous
But I .... proud of my old dad

My old dad
He was one of the good guys
He was nobody's hero
But he was special to me

10 Tell other students about someone in your family that you are proud of.

59

B Family life

Dear God,
Are boys better than girls. I know you are one but try to be fair.

Sylvia.

My mother said she won't get maried again it's too much truble.

my mum only likes little babies. when they get old Like me she smacks them.

1 Listen to the conversation. Can you fill in the missing words?

MIKE: Do you think housewives .... be .... in the same .... as other people ....? I mean, everybody .... who does a regular job .... a salary.

SUE: Yeah, but who .... them? That's the trouble. I mean, who .... they be paid by? The only way you could do it is by .... the man enough of a wage to pay you as well. And that, that, er, I mean, in our .... age, in my parents' age anyway, my .... was paid ...., um, to pay, to support his wife and .... Nowadays that's not always ....

JOHN: There's no, there's no way you could pay a .... now. She's doing about ten jobs.

2 Listen to the conversation. You will hear four of the expressions listed below. Which ones?

the wife stays at home   comes home to work
the end of his day's work
the end of the wife's working day
to work until midnight   If you both share
Well, that's it   I'll pick my feet up
I'll read the newspaper

If they don't want you to make your own breakfast they should say so before

Timmy

Unit 14: Lesson B

Students learn more ways of expressing agreement and disagreement, while talking about family life.
Principal structure: *should.*
Words and expressions to learn: *housewife; wage; housework; support; own* (determiner); *regular; upset; special; free; nowadays; pocket money; (fifteen)-year-old; you're right.*
Phonology: sentence stress in expressions of agreement and disagreement.

Language notes and possible problems
1. Should You may like to remind students that *should* is followed by the infinitive without *to.*
2. Half and half dialogue If you are not used to the technique of dialogue construction used in Exercise 6, you should follow the directions for setting it up very carefully. Students usually enjoy this exercise very much, but it must be organised well in order to work properly.

If you are short of time
You can leave out Exercise 2 and/or Exercise 4.

1 Listening and completing a text 📼 Ⓐ
• This is an extract from a discussion between several native speakers about housewives' work.
• Ask students to copy out the text, leaving the blanks.
• Play the recording once and tell students to try to fill in some of the blanks.
• Play it a second time and see if they can fill in some more.
• Play it again, as many times as you feel are appropriate. Then let students compare notes before checking with you.
• (Note that John has a strong northern accent.)

Tapescript for Exercise 1
MIKE: Do you think housewives *should* be *paid* in the same *way* as other people *are*? I mean, everybody *else* who does a regular job *gets* a salary.
SUE: Yeah, but who *pays* them? That's the trouble. I mean, who *would* they be paid by? The only way you could do it is by *paying* the man enough of a wage to pay you as well. (*She means: to pay his wife as well.*) And that, that, er, I mean, in our *parents'* age, in my parents' age anyway, my *father* was paid *enough*, um, to pay, to support his wife and *children*. Nowadays that's not always *true*.
JOHN: There's no, there's no way you could pay a *housewife* now. She's doing about ten jobs.

2 Listening for specific expressions 📼 Ⓐ
• Go over the expressions with the students. Practise the pronunciation and explain any difficulties.
• Play the recording and ask students to note the four expressions they think are exactly the same in the box and in the conversation.
• Get them to compare notes; play the recording again if necessary.

• Then (playing the recording as many more times as necessary) get students to correct the other six expressions

The four 'correct' expressions are: *the wife stays at home; the end of the wife's working day; Well; that's it;* and *If you both share.* The other six expressions are as in the tapescript below.

Tapescript for Exercise 2
KATY: If the husband works and *the wife stays at home,* when the husband *comes home from work,* do you think that should be *the end of his working day?*
EVERYBODY: No, no, no, no.
SUE: It's not *the end of the wife's working day.* Otherwise the wife goes on *working until midnight,* and the husband sits on his backside, you know. *If you both share,* then perhaps you could both sit down by nine o'clock. I'm talking about the husband who comes home and says, '*Well, that's it, I'll put my feet up*'; sits by the fire and puts his feet up, *reads the newspaper* and that's it.
JOHN: No, no, I don't agree with that.

3 Agreeing and disagreeing

- Ask each student to draw three columns on a piece of paper, and to try and classify the expressions in the box according to whether they have one, two or three stresses.
- Let them compare answers with one another, and then play the recording for them to listen to before checking their answers with you.
- When you have checked the answers, get the students to say the expressions after you or the recording.
- Then divide the class into groups of three or four and ask them to write the expressions down again, this time in order from the ones that express strong agreement to the ones that express strong disagreement.
- There is not, of course, one right answer. See below for one way the expressions can be grouped.
- You might want to ask students if they can think of other ways of expressing agreement or disagreement. They may come up with good answers like *Mm, Yeah,* or *Well, . . .*

Answers to Exercise 3: pronunciation

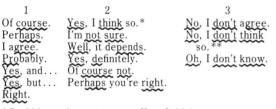

1	2	3
Of course.	Yes, I think so.*	No, I don't agree.
Perhaps.	I'm not sure.	No, I don't think
I agree.	Well, it depends.	so.**
Probably.	Yes, definitely.	Oh, I don't know.
Yes, and. . .	Of course not.	
Yes, but. . .	Perhaps you're right.	
Right.		

*Could have three stresses: Yes, I think so.
**Could have four stresses: No, I don't think so.

Possible answers to Exercise 3: degree of agreement
1. Of course.   Yes, and. . .   Yes, definitely.   Right.
2. Yes, I think so.   I agree.
3. Probably.
4. Perhaps.   Perhaps you're right.
5. I'm not sure.   Oh, I don't know.
6. Well, it depends.   Yes, but. . .
7. No, I don't think so.
8. No, I don't agree.
9. Of course not. (*This can alternatively be strong agreement with a negative statement.*)

4 Reactions to opinions
- In this exercise responsibility for a fair discussion is shared among the members of a group.
- Go over the statements with the class, dealing with any difficulties in understanding.
- Then divide the class into groups of four to six.
- Each person in a group should choose a different point.
- Students read out their points in turn; the student who has chosen a point should make sure that all the others express their opinions on it.
- Walk round while students are working to give any help that is needed.
- It is not a good idea to correct mistakes while the discussions are going on, but you may want to note down mistakes in the use of *should* or of one of the expressions focused on in Exercise 3, and point out the correct usage to the class after the groups have finished working.

- Exercise 1 in the Practice Book gives some written work on *should*.

5 Students' opinions
- This can be done as a whole-class exercise in a small class, in groups of four to six, or as a walk-round activity. If you decide to work in groups it is best to have different groups from Exercise 4.
- Get each student to write an opinion about family life on a piece of paper. Walk round to help with vocabulary where needed.
- When students are ready, let them read out what they have written and see whether the others agree.

6 Half and half dialogues
- Divide the class in half. If possible get the halves of the class to move their chairs away from one another.
- Tell *only* the right-hand side of the class to turn to the dialogue marked Unit 14B, Dialogue A on page 158 of their books. They must not let students on the other side of the class see the dialogue.
- Tell *only* the left-hand side of the class to turn to the dialogue marked Unit 14B, Dialogue B on page 157 of their books. They must not let students on the other side of the class see the dialogue.
- Tell the students on both sides of the class to invent the other half of the dialogue they have, writing *only* the new half on a sheet of paper. They must not copy the other half from the book.
- They can work in pairs or threes providing they work with students from the same side of the classroom.
- Walk round to help while they are working, but speak quietly so that students from the other side of the class will not hear.
- You may want to indicate when something they have written does not 'fit' with the lines of dialogue that go before and after it, and explain why.
- Students who finish quickly can help others on their side of the class or work on a Practice Book exercise.
- When all the students have finished, tell them to close their books and take the half-dialogues they have written.
- Put them in pairs. Each pair should contain one student from each side of the class.
- They should read the two halves of the dialogue to one another, beginning with the student who had Dialogue A. You may want to demonstrate with one pair in front of the class first.
- Most dialogues will make good sense. In cases where they don't, encourage students to see why and to make small changes.
- Students can try out their half-dialogues with several partners.

Summary
- Remind students to look at the Summary and learn the new words.

Practice Book
- Tell students which exercises you want them to do.

3 One, two or three stresses? Put the expressions from the box into three lists. Example:

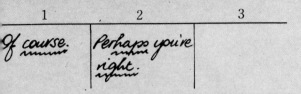

1	2	3
Of course.	Perhaps you're right.	

Of course. Perhaps. Yes, I think so.
No, I don't agree. I'm not sure. I agree.
Well, it depends. Probably. Yes, and...
No, I don't think so. Yes, definitely.
Of course not. Oh, I don't know.
Yes, but... Right. Perhaps you're right.

Now put the expressions in order, going from strong agreement to strong disagreement.

4 Work in groups. Each student should choose one of the sentences below, and make sure that all the other group members say what they think about it.

1. Housewives should be paid a salary.
2. Husbands should do some of the housework.
3. Children should do some of the housework.
4. Even young children should get regular pocket money.
5. Children should be free to choose their own friends.
6. When children are 16, they should be free to do what they like.

5 Write a sentence yourself about family life. See if other students agree with it.

6 Turn to the page your teacher tells you. Invent the other half of the dialogue. Write *only* the invented half on a sheet of paper. Then close your book and find a partner to make a complete dialogue with.

mothers and other nasty people frighten children to make them be good

You should never hit a baby because it can't hit back

Women do the washing up and cleaning and tidying and men go on the train and get tired.

Hopes and wishes

A Would you like to have a white Rolls Royce?

1 Listen to the recording and write down a phrase from the box for each blank.

> I'd like to   I'd like to   I'd like to
> I'd really like to   I'd really like
> I would like to   I *would* like
> I'd love to   I'd just like to

KEITH: .... work in a museum.
JOHN: I think .... own me own gardening centre. I'd love that. (*Yeah*) Yeah. .... that.
SUE: .... be a really good potter. (*Hm-hm. Yeah.*) Be on my own. (*Yeah*)
JANE: .... be really good at something.
ALEX: Actually with the job I've chosen, the police force, ... go into dog handling in that. That's what ....
KATY: I think .... teach again.
MIKE: What .... spend my time doing isn't really classed as jobs.

2 Work in groups. Make some true sentences.

> I'd / I would
> My sister would
> My husband would
> etc.

> (really)

> like to
> love to

> work...
> own...
> be a really good...
> be really good at...
> go into...
> ... again.
> spend my time...

Now close your books and tell some people from other groups what was said in your group. Examples:

'*Michiko would like to go into accounting.*'
'*Kurt's sister would love to own a horse.*'

3 Pronunciation. Listen to the words, and try to pronounce them correctly.

no   so   go   hope   know   broke   spoke   over   don't   won't
open   closed   Rome   phone

Now listen to the definitions, and say which words the speaker is talking about.

Example:

The past of 'speak'. (*spoke*

4 Look at the questions and prepare your answers. You can answer as follows:

> '*Yes.*'   '*I think so.*'   '*I don't think so.*'
> '*I hope so.*'   '*I hope not.*'   '*I don't know.*'
> '*No.*'   '*No, I don't.*'   '*No, I won't.*'

When you are ready, close your book, listen to the questions, and answer them.

1. Will you live to be 100 years old?
2. Will you get married next year?
3. Is it going to rain tomorrow?
4. Will everyone come to the next English class?
5. Will you be ill next week?
6. Are there going to be any Olympic Games in the year 2000?
7. Do you hope to travel to America some day?
8. Do you dream in English?
9. What did your teacher want to do when he/she was younger?
10. Will you be very rich one day?
11. Did anyone in your class want to be a doctor when they were younger?
12. Would you like to go to the moon?

Unit 15: Lesson A

Students learn and revise ways of expressing wants, hopes and intentions.
Principal structures: *want, would like* and *would love; want* + object + infinitive; *hope to, going to* and *try to*.
Words and expressions to learn: *museum; the moon; Japan; magazine; patience; artist; midday; own* (verb); *good at; open* (adjective); *different* (= other); *political; really; again* (= as before); *everyone; by* (with time expressions).
Phonology: pronunciation of /əʊ/.

Language notes and possible problems

1. *Would like* and *want* Students are shown a slightly simplified version of the difference between the two verbs. They should see that *would like* is more tentative than *want*. *I want* can sound like an order in English, and *I'd like* is used in requests.

2. Object + infinitive The structure with an object and infinitive after *want* and *would like* (e.g. *They wanted me to be a doctor*) is highly idiomatic. In general, other languages do not have a similar structure, and students are likely to find it difficult. They may try to say, for instance, **My parents wanted that I...*

3. *Before* Students have already met the use of a present tense with a future meaning after *when* and *if. Before* is followed by a present tense in Exercise 6.

If you are short of time

If pronunciation is not an important priority for your students, you can leave out Exercises 3 and 4; you can leave out Exercise 8.

1 Listening: *I'd like/love to* Ⓐ

● Ask the students to read over the gapped sentences and use their dictionaries or ask you for help with difficult words.
● You will probably want to point out that John's use of *me* for *my* is a common substandard usage.
● Get the students to write the seven names on a piece of paper. As you play the recording, they should write down the expression(s) they hear.

Answers to Exercise 1

KEITH: I would like to
JOHN: I'd love to; I'd really like
SUE: I'd like to
JANE: I'd like to
ALEX: I'd like to; I *would* like
KATY: I'd just like to
MIKE: I'd really like to

2 Personalisation

● Put the students into groups of three or four and ask them to make some true sentences about themselves, friends or family with the elements in the table.
● You may want to demonstrate by making a few sentences of your own.
● Walk round while the students are working, to give any help that is needed.

● After each student has had a chance to make at least one sentence, get the students to close their books and walk round the classroom, reporting what they have found out in their groups.

3 Pronunciation revision: /əʊ/

● If you are working with students for whom pronunciation is not an important priority, or if time is short, you may prefer to drop Exercises 3 and 4.
● If you do work on /əʊ/, remember that an easy way to help students get the sound right is to break it up into its two parts: /ə/ (as in ***mother***) and /uː/ (as in ***too***).
● If these two sounds are put together quickly, the result is a good British /əʊ/.
● Let students prepare the answers to the questions (without consulting one another) and help them to practise the words.
● Then play the recording or read the following definitions.
● Students should decide which word each definition refers to and say it, taking care over the pronunciation.

Tapescript for Exercise 3

1. the past of *speak*
2. the opposite of *open*
3. *do not*
4. the opposite of *come*
5. the capital of Italy
6. the past of *break*
7. the opposite of *yes*
8. the opposite of *closed*
9. the opposite of *under*
10. *will not*

4 Expressions with /əʊ/

● Practise the pronunciation of the various expressions.
● Then ask students to look at the questions and decide what answer they would like to give to each one (without saying anything for the moment).
● The questions are framed so that one of the listed answers should usually be appropriate, though there may be exceptions in individual cases.
● When students are ready, get them to close their books and ask the questions or play the recording, picking students to answer.
● They should take reasonable care over the pronunciation of /əʊ/.

5 _When I was younger_

● Ask each student to write three sentences using the elements provided. Students should not write their names on their papers.
● Walk round as they are working to give any help that is needed.
● Collect the papers, shuffle and number them.
● Then either read them out yourself or pass them out for students to read aloud. It does not matter if a student gets his or her own paper.
● The number should be read, followed by the three sentences.
● The other students write down the number followed by the name of the person they think wrote the sentences.
● When they have finished, call out the names and the numbers so they can see how often they were right.
● More practice on this point of grammar is given in the next lesson.

6 Letters: guessing other students' ambitions

● Ask students to pair off, each choosing a partner who is not sitting nearby.
● Then go over the two letters with the class, and make sure they understand what they are to do.
● Each student should write down at least two guesses about his or her partner's ambitions.
● Walk round while they are working to give any help that is needed.
● Deliver the letters as they are completed so that students can answer them. Students who finish very quickly can choose new partners to write to.

7 Class survey

● This is best done as a walk-round exercise.
● You may want to practise the pronunciation of the question form _Would you like . . . ?_ and the short answers _Yes, I would_ and _No, I wouldn't_ before starting.
● Get each student to choose a different item from the list.
● Tell students to get up and walk round, trying to ask everyone else if they would like the thing in question. They should note the answers.

8 Reporting the survey

● This is straightforward, provided students have succeeded in noting the answers they were given.
● The example sentences will help students to get the grammar right: make sure they notice the use of a singular verb form with _everyone_.

Summary

● Remind students to look at the Summary and learn the new vocabulary.

Practice Book

● Tell students which exercises you want them to do.

5 What did you want to be or do when you were younger? Write three sentences and give them to the teacher. Then try to guess whose sentences the teacher is reading.

> I wanted to be...
> I wanted to study...
> I wanted to...

> but
> and

> my parents wanted me to...
> my teachers wanted me to...
> I changed my mind.
> I still want...
> now I...

6 Choose another member of the class. Write a letter.

> Dear ....,
> I think you *want to / are going to / hope to / are going to try to* .... *by 1995 / by the end of the year / before you are 80* etc.; and I think
> .... Am I right?
> Yours,
>
> ....

Now answer the letter(s) you have received.
Example:

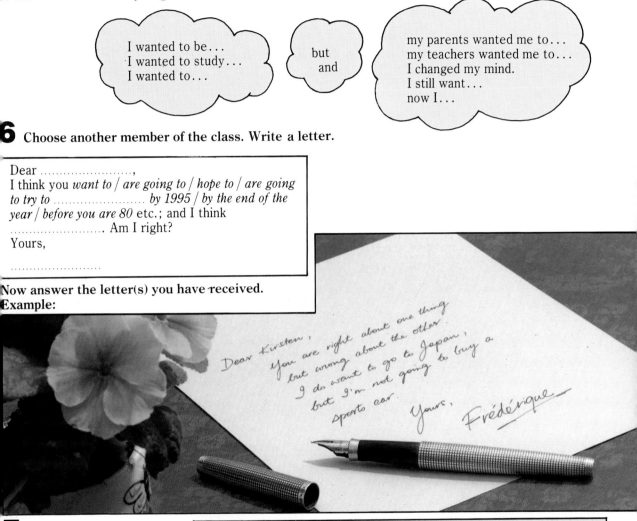

> Dear Kirsten,
> You are right about one thing
> but wrong about the other.
> I do want to go to Japan,
> but I'm not going to buy a
> sports car.
> Yours,
> Frédérique

7 Class survey. Choose one of the things in the list and ask the other students if they would like it. Examples:

'Would you like to have a white Rolls Royce?'
'Yes, I would.'

'Would you like to be famous?'
'No, I certainly wouldn't.'

to have:	more money a different job more free time a better love-life (more) children more patience your picture in a magazine political power in your country a different house/flat more friends a private plane a white Rolls Royce a big motorbike two wives/husbands
to be:	famous an artist three years old
to:	sleep until midday every day live to be 100 speak a lot of languages travel a lot own a museum

8 Report the results of your survey. Examples:

'Three people out of twelve would like to travel a lot.'
'One person would like to be famous.'
'Everyone would like to speak a lot of languages.'

'Nobody would like to have a yacht.'
'Most people would like to have a private plane.'
'Not many people would like to live to be 100.'

B Could you do me a favour?

1 Complete the two conversations with the words and expressions in the boxes.

PAUL: Hey, John.
JOHN: Yeah?
PAUL: ....?
JOHN: Sure. What is it?
PAUL: Well, ..., I'm
.... until Friday.
........................, do you think?
JOHN: Yes, OK.
PAUL: ...., John. ....
JOHN: ....

> the thing is   Thanks a lot
> Could you do me a favour
> That's all right   short of money
> Could you lend me a fiver
> That's very nice of you

ANNIE: ....
We've got a problem.
MR OLIVER: Oh yes? ....?
ANNIE: Well, ...,
.... We're cycling, and
we haven't got ....
tonight.
MR OLIVER: ....
the Crown Hotel?
ANNIE: Yes. It's .... too
expensive. So .... sleep
in your barn.
MR OLIVER: Yes, ...
.... You don't smoke,
do you?
ANNIE: Oh, no. Neither of us do. Well,
....
MR OLIVER: ....
come into the house for a wash?
ANNIE: ....
MR OLIVER: ....

2 Can you find some examples of informal and formal language in the two conversations?

INFORMAL	FORMAL
Hey	Excuse me.
Yeah?	Oh, yes?
. . .	. . .

3 Practise the conversations with a partner.

> Have you tried   much   all right   you see
> Excuse me   Not at all   Would you like to
> thank you very much   I don't mind
> This way   I'm sorry to trouble you
> What's the matter
> I see   we wondered if we could
> it's like this   anywhere to sleep
> That's very kind of you

Unit 15: Lesson B

Students learn ways of asking for favours, agreeing to requests, thanking and replying to thanks; they study differences between formal and informal language.

Principal structures: more practice of *want* + object and infinitive; *I/We wondered if* + past.

Words and expressions to learn: *favour; Could you do me a favour?; letter; post* (verb); *Sure* (= of course); *well,...; the thing is,...; Thanks a lot; short of money; That's all right* (reply to thanks); *you see,* (asking someone to be understanding); *it's like this; We wondered if we could...; Not at all* (reply to thanks); *this way.*

Phonology: decoding rapid speech.

Language notes and possible problems

1. Neither In the second dialogue, *neither of us* is used with a plural verb. A singular verb is also possible, and would be more common in a formal style of written English.

2. 'Softeners' Note the use of *well, the thing is, you see,* and *it's like this* in the dialogues to introduce and 'ease the way' for a difficult explanation which the speaker may find embarrassing.

3. All right Compare *all right* (used in the second dialogue for agreement) and *That's all right* (used in the first dialogue as an informal reply to thanks).

4. I/We wondered if + past In lesson 6B students came across *I wondered if you were free.* Here they practise *We wondered if you could...* You will probably want to point out to them a) the 'tentative' use of the past tense in *wondered* and b) the use of the past tense after the expression *I/We wondered if.*

If you are short of time

You can leave out Exercise 3; or the students can write the conversations in Exercise 6 out for homework, and practise them after correction.

1 Dialogues

● This is a prediction exercise, intended to get students thinking about the various words and expressions before being told how they are used.

● You may like to start by running over the pronunciation of the words and expressions in the boxes, so that students don't make up their own wrong pronunciations.

● Take each conversation separately, giving students time to fill in the gaps and compare notes before you play the dialogue and let them check their answers.

● The first dialogue is easy. The second is a good deal more difficult, and you should allow more time for it. It may be best done in groups.

● Note that slight variations in the order of the expressions are possible at one or two points.

Tapescript for Exercise 1
(Answers are in *italics.*)

PAUL: Hey, John.
JOHN: Yeah?

PAUL: *Could you do me a favour?*
JOHN: Sure. What is it?
PAUL: Well, *the thing is,* I'm *short of money* until Friday. *Could you lend me a fiver,* do you think?
JOHN: Yes, OK.
PAUL: *That's very nice of you,* John. *Thanks a lot.*
JOHN: *That's all right.*

ANNIE: *Excuse me. I'm sorry to trouble you.* We've got a problem.
MR OLIVER: Oh yes? *What's the matter?*
ANNIE: Well, *you see, it's like this.* We're cycling, and we haven't got *anywhere to sleep* tonight.
MR OLIVER: *I see. Have you tried* the Crown Hotel?
ANNIE: Yes. It's *much too expensive.* So *we wondered if we could* sleep in your barn.
MR OLIVER: Yes, *all right. I don't mind.* You don't smoke, do you?
ANNIE: Oh, no. Neither of us do. Well, *thank you very much.*
MR OLIVER: *Not at all. Would you like to* come into the house for a wash?
ANNIE: *That's very kind of you.*
MR OLIVER: *This way.*

2 Informal and formal language

● Students probably already realise that there are differences in the language people use to talk to strangers and to friends when greeting and making requests.

● Explain what is meant by *formal* and *informal,* if necessary.

● Then see if students can suggest other words and expressions for the two lists.

● Note the following contrasts:

INFORMAL	FORMAL
Hey	Excuse me
Yeah?	Yes?
OK	All right.
Thanks a lot	Thank you very much.
That's all right	Not at all
Could you...	We wondered if you could...
That's very nice of you	That's very kind of you

● Note also the informal expressions *Sure, a fiver,* and the formal expression *I'm sorry to trouble you.*

● Point out to the students that the past tense follows *I/We wondered if.*

3 Practice

● When students understand the dialogues clearly, get them to practise one or both of them in pairs.

● You may like to play the dialogues again first so as to provide a model for pronunciation and intonation.

4 Pictures

- In the first part of the exercise, students simply have to decide which pictures go with the four sentences in their books (L, F, H, and A).
- Next, they have to listen to four further sentences and decide which pictures these refer to.

The sentences (which you can play or read, as you prefer) are:
5. He wants his mother to mend his bicycle. (K)
6. She wants her sister to lend her a dress. (B)
7. He wants somebody to take him to Manchester. (E)
8. He wants her to lend him some sugar. (C)

- Finally, students have to work out sentences appropriate to pictures D, G, I and J.

Possible answers are:
D. They want the man to sell them some petrol.
G. She wants him to post some letters for her.
I. He wants her to cut his hair.
J. She wants them to clean the car.

- Look out for confusions between the names of the letters of the alphabet (especially with A and E, E and I, G and J).

5 Decoding rapid speech

- The recording contains a number of expressions from the dialogues in Exercise 1.
- They are spoken at 'fast colloquial' speed, with all the contractions and alterations in pronunciation that this implies.
- Although students should by now be very familiar with the expressions, they may have to work hard to catch them all.
- Play each one and then pause so that students can write it down.

The expressions are:
Excuse me.
Thanks a lot.
What's the matter?
Could you do me a favour?
That's very nice of you.
All right.
I see.
It's like this.
Not at all.
Would you like to come into the house?
I'm sorry to trouble you.
I don't mind.

6 Making up conversations

- Ask students to choose one of the situations shown in the pictures in Exercise 4, and to make up conversations in pairs to illustrate their chosen situations.
- They should use as many of the expressions from Exercise 1 as possible.
- If time allows, let students practise the conversations and perhaps act them out for other students.
- You may want to tape-record or video-record the conversations; the knowledge that they are to be recorded can act as an incentive for some classes.

Summary

- Remind students to look at the Summary and learn the new vocabulary.

Practice Book

- Tell students which exercises you want them to do.

4

Look at the pictures. In each picture, somebody wants somebody else to do something.
(i) Which pictures go with sentences 1–4?   (ii) Listen to the four spoken sentences.
Which pictures go with them?   (iii) Make sentences yourself for the last four pictures.

1. He wants them to sign a petition.
2. They want him to give them some water.
3. He wants her to take the dog for a walk.
4. He wants his father to lend him his car.

5

Pronunciation. Listen to the recording and write the words and expressions that you hear.

6

Work in pairs or groups of three. Make up a conversation for one of the pictures. Use some of the words and expressions from the conversations in Exercise 1.

Money

A Where does all the money go?

1 How much (approximately) is £1 in your currency? How much is £10? £50? $1? $20? $100? Make a note and try to remember. Then complete the table by guessing an amount for each blank. Listen to the recording and check your answers.

AVERAGE BRITISH HOUSEHOLD EXPENDITURE 1983	
(Pounds per week after taxes and insurance)	
Housing	£24.62
Fuel, electricity	7.24
Food	
Alcoholic drink	10.14
Tobacco	
Recreation, entertainment, education	13.03
Clothing, footwear	
Household goods and services	10.14
Other goods and services	17.38
Transport and communication	

2 Look at the table in Exercise 1 and answer the questions as quickly as you can.

1. What did the average family spend most on in 1983?
2. Which of the things in the table did they spend least on?
3. True or false? They spent more on alcohol than on heating and electricity.
4. Did they spend more on food than on housing?
5. Did they spend less on clothing than on transport and communication?
6. True or false? They spent nearly twice as much on alcohol as on tobacco.
7. True or false? Alcohol and tobacco together cost more than half as much as housing.

Unit 16: Lesson A

Students learn to talk about personal expenditure and budgets.
Principal structures: *must* and *can*; quantifiers; revision of present perfect and past; omission of article for general reference; saying numbers; use of *this*, *next* and *last* in time expressions.
Words and expressions to learn: *electricity*; *goods*; *transport*; *opinion*; *currency*; *budget*; *rent* (noun); *savings*; *income*; *earn*; *spend*; *miscellaneous*; *personal*; *exchange rate*; other words of students' choice.

Language notes and possible problems

1. *Must* and *can* Students are asked to use *must* and *can* in Exercises 4 and 6. This should be revision for most students, but you might want to check and make sure they all understand the exact meanings of these two verbs.

2. Quantifiers Once again, this should be revision; but if you think your students are weak on this point you may wish to do a preliminary presentation of the meanings of the different quantifiers (*more, less, too much, not enough, how much, a lot of, much, a lot*) used in the lesson.

3. Zero article You may have to be careful that your students do not insert *the* when speaking about things in general (e.g. *She spends too much on books*, not **...on the books*).

4. Singular verb with amounts of money Some students may find it strange to use a singular verb in a sentence like *How much is £20 in your currency?*

If you are short of time

You can leave out Exercise 3; you can get students to do Exercise 5 as individual homework and then do Exercise 6 in class individually.

Optional extra materials

Newspapers with the exchange rates in them, for Exercise 1, if you think your students will not have any idea of what the exchange rates are. You will need one newspaper for every three or four students (or copies of the exchange rate section).

1 Listening: British household expenditure

- Help students decide how much the various amounts of money are worth in their own currency or currencies.
- If they are all from the same country, they can work in groups of three or four to answer the questions before comparing answers with the rest of the class.
- If you do not think your students will have any notion of exchange rates, bring in a few copies of newspapers with the rates in and let the students look them up.
- In a class where the students are from different countries, let them work individually or in national groups and then report to the class.
- Make sure they notice that you use a singular verb even when the money is 'plural' (e.g. *£10 **is** 85 francs*).
- Then go through the table explaining any unknown words. (*Communication* covers telephone and postal services.)

- Let students work for a few minutes guessing what the missing figures might be, roughly.
- You may want to suggest they allow for 7% to 8% inflation per year since 1983, to get a better idea of what the figures might be.
- When students have made their guesses and compared notes, ask them to copy the table; then play the recording and let them complete the table.
- You may want to play the recording a second time if all the students have not got all the answers.

Tapescript and answers to Exercise 1

A: And how much did they spend on food, Dave?
B: Well, this was not as high as we'd expected, actually only the third highest figure in the table at £21.72; not very high compared with housing at £24.62. We aren't sure why, but there has been a trend towards spending less on food over the past few years.
A: Were there any other surprises?
B: No big ones, really. Expenditure on transport and communication came to £23.17, which reflects the steady climb in petrol prices. Clothing and footwear cost £8.69; that is only slightly less than last year, in real terms. And the tobacco figure of £5.79, again slightly up on last year, didn't surprise us greatly.
A: Why? Is this a long-term trend?
B: Well, yes. Since 1979 we've seen...

Answers: food £21.72, tobacco £5.79, clothing and footwear £8.69, transport and communication £23.17.

2 Scanning

- Tell the students to write the answers to the questions as quickly as possible. This gives practice in rapid comprehension.
- Let them compare notes and discuss the answers if necessary.
- During the discussion, make sure they are saying the figures correctly (e.g. *five pounds and seventy-nine pence*).

Answers: 1. housing   2. tobacco   3. true   4. no   5. yes   6. true   7. true

3 Reactions

• Ask the students for their reactions to the expenditure figures in Exercise 1, and encourage discussion.
• As a follow-up exercise students might be asked to imagine what the figures might be for a typical household in their own country, or for a typical student.

4 Personalisation

• Go over the examples with the students, pointing out:
– that the present perfect is used with *this year* and the past with *last year*
– that *must* and *can* can be used with future meanings with *next year*
– that *a lot of* (and not *much*) is used after affirmative verbs (so we don't say **I spent much on transport last year*).
• Then ask the students to write at least three sentences each; walk round while they are working to make sure everyone has understood and is using the quantifiers correctly.
• Get them to volunteer sentences orally; they need not be the same sentences as they have written down.
• In a large class, the oral part of the exercise can be done in groups of six or more.
• In the Practice Book, Exercise 1 gives additional work on quantifiers and Exercise 2 revises *must* and *can*.

5 Making a personal budget

• Go through the instructions, making sure the students understand any new words and know what they are to do.
• Put them in pairs to work, while you walk round the class to give any help that is needed.
• Try not to advise them on how to make up their budgets, but only to help with language problems.

6 Cutting down expenditure

• Explain that Alice has had to change her job for personal reasons, and her salary is now 25% lower than it was before.
• Get each pair to give their budget to another pair.
• Each pair must take the budget they have been given and cut it by 25%.
• When they have finished, go through the examples that show them how to explain the changes to the authors of the original budget. You may have to do a little extra work on *must* if some of the students are not very familiar with it.
• Then let the students explain their changes to one another.

Summary

• Remind students to look at the Summary and learn the new words.

Practice Book

• Tell students which exercises you want them to do.

3 Say what you think about the figures in Exercise 1. Does the average British family spend too much on some things and not enough on others, in your opinion?

4 Make some sentences about your own expenditure this year, last year and next year. Examples:

'This year I've spent a lot of money on...'
I've spent too much on...'
I haven't spent much on...'

'Last year I spent a lot on...'
I spent too much on...'
I didn't spend much on...'

'This year I've spent less/more on... than last year.'

'Last year I spent less/more on... than this year.'

'I must spend less on... next year.'
'I can spend more on... next year.'

5 Budgets. Alice Calloway is a 25-year-old sales manager. She earns quite a good salary (you decide how much), and lives alone in a small flat. Work with another student and make a budget for Alice. You must decide how much she spends every week (in pounds or dollars) on the following items (you can add more if you want to).

rent	clothing and shoes
electricity and gas	alcohol
food and household	cigarettes
travel	entertainment
books	miscellaneous
telephone	savings

6 Cutting down expenditure. Alice has had to change her job for personal reasons. Her income is now 25% lower than it was. Exchange budgets with another pair of students. Your job now is to cut down Alice's expenditure by 25%. When you have done this, explain your changes to the two students who made the budget. Examples:

'We think Alice spends too much on...'
'She must spend less on...'
'She must travel less.'

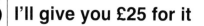

B I'll give you £25 for it

1 Listen to the conversation. Learn the new words and expressions. Then close your book, listen again, and try to write down the missing words.

A: How much do you want for it?
B: Forty.
A: Forty pounds?
B: Yes. It's worth fifty, but I'm in a hurry.
A: I don't know. It's not in very good condition. Look. This is broken. And look at this. I don't think it's worth forty. I'll give you twenty-five pounds.
B: Twenty-five? Come on. I'll tell you what – I'll take thirty-five. Since you're a friend of mine. You can have it for thirty-five.
A: No, that's still too much. To tell you the truth, I can't afford thirty-five.
B: I'm sorry. Thirty-five. That's my last word.
A: Come on, let's split the difference. Thirty pounds.
B: Thirty. Oh, very well. All right, thirty.
A: Can I give you a cheque?
B: Well, I'd prefer cash, if you don't mind.

2 Say these sentences from the dialogue. Remember to link the marked words.

How much do you want for it?
I'm in a hurry.
I don't know.
I don't think it's worth forty.
Since you're a friend of mine.
You can have it for thirty-five.
Come on, let's split the difference.
Can I give you a cheque?
Well, I'd prefer cash, if you don't mind.

3 Work with a partner. Each of you tries to sell something to the other, and you try to agree on a price. But you can't buy or sell until each of you has used at least two of the words or expressions you wrote down in Exercise 1.

4 Grammar revision. Put *too*, *too much* or *too many* in each blank.

1. 'How much are the carrots?' 'Forty pence a pound.' 'That's ....'
2. She doesn't go skiing any more. She's .... old.
3. You're driving .... fast. Please slow down.
4. If you eat .... chocolate, you'll get fat.
5. I've got .... books – I don't know where to put them all.
6. You've given me .... meat. I can't eat it all.

Unit 16: Lesson B

Students learn to bargain, and revise ways of talking about quantity.

Principal structures: *will* for making proposals (e.g. *I'll give you £25*); quantifiers; *too...to*; *(not) ...enough to...*

Words and expressions to learn: *pound* (weight); *cover*; *drawer*; *chest of drawers*; *portable*; *worth*; *since* (= because); *a friend of mine*; *can('t) afford*; *in...condition*; *Come on*; *I'll tell you what*; *To tell you the truth,...*; *Oh, very well*; *I'd prefer...*; *if you don't mind*.

Phonology: linking between words: vowel liaison and consonant assimilation.

Language notes and possible problems

1. Quantifiers Quite a few of the quantifiers (*much, many, enough, too much, too many*) are revised in this lesson. You may have to check that all the students are familiar with them, and teach them more thoroughly if some are not.

2. Too...to; ...enough to... Adjectives with infinitive complements are common structures in English; here students learn to use two of these structures. Most of them will have learnt *too...* and *...enough* without infinitives; so the concept should not be difficult. Some students may have trouble with the form, however.

3. Linking between words Students have already practised vowel liaison earlier in the book. What may be new to at least some of them is the consonant assimilation that occurs in combinations like *don't know*, where the *t* is not exploded. This is a useful point to master for students who are aiming at a very good standard of pronunciation.

If you are short of time

You can leave out Exercise 2 if pronunciation is not a high priority for your students; you can get students to do Exercise 4 for homework; you can leave out Exercise 7.

Optional extra materials

The alternative procedure suggested for Exercise 3 is much more interesting for students than the simple exercise proposed in the Student's Book. For this alternative you will need some play money. This can be 'Monopoly' money or just pieces of paper you have cut up and labelled. There should be eight £5 notes and ten £1 notes for each student, plus twenty £1 notes for you to use as change. If you are short of time you can get the students to make their own play money in class by tearing up and labelling pieces of paper.

1 Conversation: listening

- Get the students to close their books and play them the recording without stopping as far as the words, *You can have it for thirty-five.*
- Then stop the tape and ask the students what they think is happening.
- When they have told you, ask them to guess what the final price will be.

- Rewind to the beginning and play the entire conversation.
- Ask the students to tell you any words or phrases they remember.
- Then let them open their books and look at the conversation as you play it again.
- Help them with the new words and expressions.
- Ask them to close their books again and listen to the gapped conversation, writing down the missing words and expressions during the pauses. You may want to play the gapped conversation twice.
- Let them compare answers before you rewind and play the complete conversation again.
- Practice Book Exercise 4 revises some of the expressions from this activity.

Tapescript and answers to Exercise 1
A: How much do you want for it?
B: Forty.
A: Forty pounds?
B: Yes. *It's worth* fifty, but I'm *in a hurry.*
A: I don't know. It's not *in very good condition.* Look. This is broken. And look at this. I don't think it's worth forty. *I'll give you* twenty-five pounds.
B: Twenty-five? Come on. *I'll tell you what* – I'll take thirty-five. *Since* you're *a friend of mine.* You can have it for thirty-five.
A: No, that's still too much. To tell you the truth, *I can't afford* thirty-five.
B: I'm sorry. Thirty-five. That's *my last word.*
A: Come on, *let's split the difference.* Thirty pounds.
B: Thirty. Oh, very well. All right, thirty.
A: Can I give you a cheque?
B: Well, *I'd prefer* cash, if *you don't mind.*

2 Pronunciation: linking between words

- Ask the students to say the sentences after you or the recording, paying special attention to the marked links.
- You may want to explain or demonstrate that the *t* is not exploded in the combinations *don't know, don't think, split the* and *don't mind.*

3 Improvisations

- Tell each student to think of something they want to sell, and to fix two prices – the price they want to sell it for and the lowest price they'll take.
- Then put them in pairs and get them to take turns trying to sell each other their objects.
- Tell them that they can't buy or sell until both buyer and seller have used at least two of the words or expressions they wrote down in Exercise 1.
- They can leave their books open during this exercise to help with words and expressions.
- Walk round while they are working to give any help that is needed, but do not correct mistakes at this time – the aim is fluency, not accuracy.

Alternative to Exercise 3 and notes for Exercise 4: see the next page (page 69)

Alternative to Exercise 3

- You will need play money (see *Optional extra materials*) for this alternative.
- Tell students they are going to play a game, and that the winner will be the person who buys the most objects.
- First of all, each student must invent or choose five possessions to sell – real things like their pens or combs, or imaginary objects.
- Tell them that they will each have £50 to spend.
- Distribute the play money or ask students to make their own (eight £5 and ten £1 notes apiece, plus twenty £1 notes for you for change).
- Then let students begin buying and selling, preferably by walking round the classroom. The aim is to buy more objects than anyone else.
- You may want to put the list of expressions from the dialogue onto the board so they can see them as they are working.
- Walk round yourself, to help with language problems and to serve as a 'bank': teach *Can you change £5 for me?* and *Here's your change* when the occasion arises.
- When the game runs down, find out who has the most possessions. In the event of a tie, the winner is the one with the most money left over.

4 *Too, too much and too many*

- This is just a quick revision of these three forms, which sometimes get confused.
- If you have noticed that students have been making mistakes with these expressions, you may want to precede the exercise with more direct teaching of the differences between the three.
- Ask students to work individually so that you can walk round and help anyone who is having trouble.
- Let them compare answers with one another before checking with you.
- Practice Book Exercises 1 and 2 give more work on *too much* and *too many*.

5 *Enough, not... enough and too*

- Another revision exercise: let students work in twos or threes to write one sentence for each of the numbered pictures.
- There may be more than one correct answer for some of the pictures.

Possible answers to Exercise 5

2. tall enough	6. slim enough
3. too big	7. too thin *or* too heavy
4. too small	8. thick enough
5. too fat	9. too low

6 Listening: an auction

- Students hear excerpts from a village auction.
- Make sure they understand what an auction is. You may want to explain the expression 'lot number' (the items are listed by lot number; a lot may be one item or several).
- Get the students to copy the list of names and tell them that they must try to write down how much each person paid for the item bought.
- Play the recording without stopping while they try to do this.

- You may want to play it a second time before checking the answers.
- Then ask the students to look at the second part of the exercise in their books.
- Ask them to read the list of items; explain any new words. Tell them that there are some items on the list that they will not hear mentioned on the recording.
- Play the recording again while students try to note who bought what.
- Let them compare answers, and play the recording again if necessary before checking the answers with them.

Answers to Exercise 6

Hunt	£5	Blue and white bowl and cover (d)
Holtby	£3	Small bedroom chair (g)
Crowther	£5	Portable lights (f)
Day	£6	Two boxes of miscellaneous (b)
Drew	£3	White chest of four drawers (e)

Tapescript for Exercise 6: see page 182

7 Adjective + complement

- Go over the situation with the students, and explain any new words.
- Get them to work in threes or fours to match the pictures with the sentences.

The answers are: 1J 2E 3I 4H 5A (though some variation is possible).

- Then let students work individually to try and write sentences about other things in the picture.
- Each student should write two sentences with *too...* and two sentences with *not... enough*.
- Walk round to help with vocabulary problems.
- Let students compare answers, and then ask for a few volunteers to read their sentences to the class.
- You may want to collect the papers to check that everyone has understood.
- Practice Book Exercise 3 gives more work on this.

5 *Enough, not . . . enough* or *too?* Example:

1. *too short OR not tall enough.*

1

2

3

4

5

6

7

8

9

6 Copy the list of names; then listen to the recording of an auction. How much did each person pay?

Hunt Holtby Crowther Day Drew

Here is a list of some of the items sold at the auction. Listen again and match the items to the names of the people who bought them. There are some extra items.

a. Cigarette box, lighter and ashtray
b. Two boxes of miscellaneous
c. Espresso coffee maker
d. Blue and white bowl and cover
e. White chest of four drawers
f. Portable lights in excellent condition
g. Small bedroom chair

7 Ian and David have just rented a flat. They are going to an auction to buy some furniture. But they can't find anything they want. Match the sentences below with some of the lettered objects in the picture.

1. It's too heavy to carry.
2. It's too long to fit in the living room.
3. It's not big enough to hold all my books.
4. It's not strong enough to put anything on.
5. It's too difficult to clean.

Now imagine why Ian and David aren't buying some of the other things in the picture. Write two sentences with *too...* and two sentences with *not...enough.*

B

C

D

E

F

G

H

J

K

L

I

M

PURE SILK

69

Before and after

A Do you get up as soon as you wake up?

1 Choose one of these questions (or make up a similar question) and ask as many people as possible. Make a note of the answers.

1. Do you get up as soon as you wake up?
2. Do you have breakfast before or after you get dressed?
3. Do you put your left shoe on before your right?
4. Do you make the bed before or after you have breakfast?
5. Do you undress before you brush your teeth at night?
6. Do you put the light out before or after you get into bed?
7. Do you go to bed at a fixed time, or do you wait until you're tired?
8. Before you go to sleep, do you usually read in bed?
9. Do you pay bills as soon as you get them?
10. Before you buy something, do you always ask the price?
11. Do you put salt on food before or after you taste it?
12. Do you read the newspaper before or after you arrive at work?
13. Do you address an envelope before or after you close it up?
14. Do you answer letters as soon as you get them?
15. Do you wait until your hair is too long before you go to the hairdresser?
16. Do you have to translate English sentences before you can understand them?
17. What are you going to do after the lesson has finished?
18. Are you going to study English before you go to bed tonight?
19. Will you study any more languages after you have learnt English?
20. Will you keep on working until you're 60?

2 Report the answers to the class.
Examples:

'*Four students out of twelve have breakfast before they get dressed.*'
'*Sixty per cent of the students read the newspaper after they arrive at work.*'
'*Most people put their left shoe on before their right.*'

3 How do you usually spend the evening? Write a paragraph using this skeleton.

When I ...., I .... Then
I .... and .... After that
I .... Then I .... until
.... Before I ...., I
....

4 Pronunciation. Say these words.

1. possible   on   long   not   stop   want
2. before   more   report   always   salt
   saw   course   caught   bought
3. note   go   envelope   close   coat

Now put these words into groups 1, 2 or 3. (One word does not belong in any of the groups.)

no   off   short   got   home   other   fall
thought   draw   lost   horse   open   boat
gone   don't

Can you find any more words to put in the three groups?

Unit 17: Lesson A

Students learn more about expressing time relations.
Principal structures: time clauses with *as soon as, before, after, until*; sequencing markers; the use of *still, yet* and *already*; *such* and *so*.
Words and expressions to learn: *postman; mat; commercial traveller; make a bed; undress; brush one's teeth; put out* (a light); *go to bed; address* (verb); *answer* (a letter); *translate; keep on...ing; report; as many as possible.*
Phonology: /ɒ/, /ɔ:/ and /əʊ/ and their spellings.

Language notes and possible problems

1. Time clauses Students who speak European languages will have little difficulty in understanding or constructing complex sentences containing time clauses. Speakers of other languages may have problems, particularly in cases where the time clause begins the sentence. Practice Book Exercises 1 and 2 provide extra work for those who need it.

2. Tenses You may need to remind students that present tenses are normally used to refer to the future in time clauses (see the last four questions in Exercise 1). Note also the occasional use of a present perfect tense to stress the idea of completion (see Exercise 1, questions 17 and 19). For the use of the past perfect, see Lesson 17B.

3. *Yet, still* and *already* These words can cause difficulty: other languages do not always have three separate words with exactly the same range of meaning. Simple rules:
– *Still* expresses continuation. Position: with the verb.
– *Yet:* used in questions and negative sentences to talk about something which is expected to happen, but is not known to have happened (or has not happened) so far. Position: at end of clause.
– *Already:* used especially in affirmative sentences to say that something expected has happened (perhaps earlier than expected). Position: with verb or at end of clause.

Another way of looking at it is to consider that these three words show whether something belongs to the past, present or future:
– *Still* says that something belongs to the present, not the past.
– *Not yet* says that something belongs to the future, not to the present; in questions, *yet* asks whether something belongs to the present or the future.
– *Already* says that something belongs to the present or past, not the future.

If you are short of time
Drop Exercise 4 if pronunciation is not a high priority; drop Exercises 7–9 or give Exercise 7 for homework.

1 Time clauses: survey
• Tell students to look through the questions, asking you (or using their dictionaries) if they have any difficulty.

• Then tell them each to choose a question (or to make up a question of a similar kind). Try to ensure that students choose different questions as far as possible.
• Get students to walk round (or to talk to as many other students as possible) asking their questions. They should note the number of 'yes' and 'no' answers.

2 Reporting the survey
• Go over the examples and make sure students can use all the structures involved.
• Then get them to report on their findings.
• Make sure they use singular verbs with *nobody* and *everybody* if the occasion arises.

3 Linking sentences into paragraphs
• Here, students practise using conjunctions and simple adverbial markers (*then, after that*) to show the sequence of a series of events.
• Some students will find this exercise easy: encourage them to make more complex paragraphs using other sequencing markers (e.g. *as soon as, next, finally*) if they want to. Other students may need a good deal of help.

4 Pronunciation
• Many students find it difficult to distinguish the three vowels /ɒ/, /ɔ:/ and /əʊ/. This exercise should help students to tell them apart and to know which spellings correspond to each vowel. (But note that the analysis applies to British English only – the pronunciation and distribution of these sounds is very different in American English.)
• Get students to try the words in the first group. Then demonstrate them and get the class to practise them. (A common mistake is to make the vowel without rounding the lips – this makes it sound rather similar to /ʌ/, so that for example *not* and *nut* are confused.)
• Point out that this vowel is usually spelt *o*, but can be spelt with *a* after *w*.
• Try the words in the second group. This vowel is longer; the jaws are further apart, but the lips are more tightly rounded.
• Make sure students notice all the different ways in which /ɔ:/ can be spelt: the most common are *or, au, aw* and *al*.
• The third vowel (/əʊ/) should be familiar. Students should note the common spellings: final *o*, *o* followed by silent *e*, and *oa*.
• When students can pronounce the sounds well, get them to try the second and third parts of the exercise (preferably before they hear the words pronounced). Let them compare notes in groups before you discuss the answers with them.

Answers to Exercise 4
Group 1 (/ɒ/): off, got, lost, gone.
Group 2 (/ɔ:/): short, fall, thought, draw, horse.
Group 3 (/əʊ/): no, home, open, boat, don't.
The word that does not belong is *other* (/'ʌðə(r)/).

5 *Still, yet* and *already*

- Let students look at the first illustration and think about the meanings of the three adverbs.
- Then ask them to look at the second illustration and try to fill in the right words.
- If necessary, explain the meanings of the adverbs (see *Language notes*).
- Continue the exercise as an individual or group activity, as you wish.

6 Listening practice: itinerary

- Make sure students understand what they have to do.
- Go over the pronunciation of the place names, to make sure students will recognise them:

Birmingham /'bɜːmɪŋəm/
Coventry /'kɒvəntri/
Dudley /'dʌdli/
Leamington /'lemɪŋtən/
Wolverhampton /wʊlvə'hæmtən/

- Play the recording and ask students to try to note down the order in which the traveller visits the places.
- Play the recording again once or twice if necessary, but don't stop in the middle or give explanations.
- Let students compare notes in groups before giving them the answer.

Answer to Exercise 6

Dudley, Wolverhampton, Birmingham, Leamington, Coventry.

Tapescript for Exercise 6

SWITCHBOARD: Cooper and Johnson. Can I help you?
COMMERCIAL TRAVELLER: Hello. This is Henry Douglas. Could I speak to Mr Cooper, please?
SWITCHBOARD: One moment. I'll put you through.
BOSS: Arthur Cooper here.
CT: Hello, sir. This is Douglas.
BOSS: Oh, hello Henry. How's it going? Finished yet?
CT: No, not yet, sir. It's going rather slowly, I'm afraid. The meeting with Fisher and Dennis took half the morning. Those people are so slow!
BOSS: Yes, they are a bit sleepy, aren't they? How were things in Coventry?
CT: I haven't been there yet, sir. I went to Dudley first.
BOSS: I see. So you're going to Coventry next?
CT: No. I want to go to Leamington before I go to Coventry, because Mr Singleton won't be there after three o'clock.
BOSS: Oh, right. And then you'll go on to Wolverhampton, I suppose.
CT: I've already been to Wolverhampton, sir. I went there before I came to Birmingham.
BOSS: Oh, I see. Right. Well, good luck. I hope things go a bit faster now. Give my regards to John Walsh in Coventry, will you?
CT: Yes, of course, sir. See you tomorrow.
BOSS: Right you are. Goodbye.
CT: Goodbye, sir.

7 Story

- Give students a few minutes to read through the story. Explain any difficulties.
- Point out the difference between *such* (used with a noun phrase, as in *such a good dancer*) and *so* (used with an adjective alone, as in *so handsome*). (Practice Book Exercise 5 deals with this point.) You may also like to

comment on the use of the past perfect, which is previewed here before being studied in detail in Lesson 17B.

- Tell students to close their books and see if they can remember some of what happened.

8 Story: students as co-authors

- This story is a collaborative effort: the beginning and end are provided, and students have to make up the middle.
- This is probably best done in groups. Give students ten minutes or so to work out how Alison's life could have changed so dramatically. One person in each group should make notes.
- If you wish, you can then ask students to write out the new chapter (though this will probably take a long time, and might be better done for homework).
- One person from each group should tell the rest of the class about their plan for Chapter 2.
- Alternatively, get one person from each group to go to another group and pass on their version.

Summary

- Remind students to look over the Summary and learn the new material.

Practice Book

- Tell students which exercises you want them to do.

5 Look at picture 1 and study the examples. Then put *still, yet* or *already* into the sentences.

1

John's still in bed.
He hasn't got up yet.
Susan is already dressed.

The postman has .... been.
Jane hasn't picked up her letters ....
They are .... on the mat.

Alice's taxi is .... waiting in front of her house.
Alice isn't ready ....
She is .... in the bath.

'Have you had lunch ....?'
'No, I'm .... working. What about you?'
'I've .... eaten.'

Peter and Ann are both 19.
Ann is .... at school.
Peter is .... married.
He hasn't got any children ....

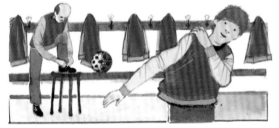

Jake is nearly 40, but he .... plays football every Saturday.
His son Andy is not 15 ...., but he is .... a good footballer, too.

6 Listen to the conversation between a commercial traveller and his boss. The traveller has to visit five places: Birmingham, Coventry, Dudley, Leamington and Wolverhampton (not in that order). Can you list the towns in the order in which he has visited them or will visit them?

7 Read the story.

ALISON BOGLE

Chapter 1
Alison Bogle lived in Exeter and worked in a bookshop. She was 23 – slim and pretty, rather shy and very quiet. She spent most of her spare time reading; at the weekend she went walking on the moors, or drove over to see her parents in Taunton.

Alison was quite happy, but sometimes she wished she didn't have such a quiet life. Exeter was not really a very exciting place. At half past ten at night, all the lights went out. Nobody ever danced in the streets – at least, Alison had never seen it happen. And it rained all the time. *All* the time.
There were so many things Alison would like to do. So many things she hadn't done. For example, she had never been in an aeroplane.

Chapter 2
....
....
....

Chapter 3
Alison poured herself another glass of champagne and smiled at Carlos. What a man! He was so handsome. And such a good dancer. And so kind to her. Alison had never met anybody like him. She wondered what he was thinking.
The sun, shining down through the palm trees, made a moving pattern of light and shade on the sand. Carlos smiled back at her and stood up. He took her hand. 'Come on, let's have another swim,' he said.

8 Work with two or three other students. Make up Chapter 2 of the story. Then tell your Chapter 2 to another group.

B I hadn't seen her for a very long time

1 Choose the correct words and expressions to put in the gaps.

I .... down the street one day   *walked / was walking*
Looking at the shops
When someone asked me if I .... the way.   *know / knew*
I gave the girl directions
And then saw who it was.
I couldn't .... of anything to say.   *think / to think*

I hadn't seen her .... a very long time   *since / for*
Since the day we said goodbye.
She .... changed,   *hasn't / hadn't*
She .... looked young and shy.   *still / yet*
I thought perhaps .... changed so much   *I / I'd*
She didn't .... it was me,   *realise / realised*
Then I saw the recognition in her eye.

We stood in silence for a while,
Then I led her to a bar.
I felt as if I .... with a ghost.   *was walking / had walked*
We drank and began to talk
And then her eyes met mine.
Her eyes .... always shown her feelings most.   *have / had*

We .... about the good old days   *talked / have talked*
About family and friends
About the hopes we'd shared .... it all went   *before / after*
    wrong.
She seemed quite pleased to see me
So I .... two more drinks,   *ordered / had ordered*
But when I got back to the table she .... gone.   *has / had*

I hadn't seen her for a very long time *etc.*

2 Listen to the song and check your answers.

3 Past perfect tense. Look at the examples and then do the exercise.

PAST (THEN):	I **saw** who it was.
EARLIER PAST (BEFORE THEN):	I **hadn't seen** her for a very long time.
PAST:	We **talked** about…
EARLIER PAST:	…the hopes we**'d shared**.

Put in the correct tense (simple past or past perfect).

1. When we .... talking, I realised that we .... before. (*start; meet*)
2. When I .... at my suitcase, I could see that somebody .... to open it. (*look; try*)
3. When we got to the restaurant, we found that nobody .... to reserve a table. (*remember*)
4. The doctor ....him, and found that he .... his arm. (*examine; break*)
5. Before my 18th birthday I .... out of England. (*not be*)
6. We were a few minutes late, so the film .... when we .... to the cinema. (*already start; get*)
7. When she got to England, she found that the language was quite different from the English that she .... at school. (*learn*)
8. 'Good afternoon. Can I help you?' 'Yes. I .... my watch to you for repair three weeks ago. Is it ready yet?' (*bring*)

Unit 17: Lesson B

Students learn more about narrative and the expression of past time relations.
Principal structures: past perfect tense.
Words and expressions to learn: *the way* (to somewhere); *directions; recognition; silence; ghost; feelings; the good old days; hope* (noun); *meeting; look* (= appear); *realise; lead; go wrong; reserve; examine; repair; pleased.*
Phonology: decoding rapid speech.

Language notes and possible problems
Past perfect tense   This may cause problems for students who do not have an equivalent tense in their own language. A simple rule of thumb: the past perfect is used when one is already talking about things that happened at some time in the past, and one wants to go back for a moment to an earlier past time. Note the following points:
1. The past perfect is only used to talk about an earlier past which is not the main focus of attention; if our main interest moves to the earlier period, we start using the simple past to talk about it.
2. We don't always use the past perfect in sentences with conjunctions like *before* or *after*, where the time sequence is already explicit.

---

1 Song: completing the text
● Give students a few minutes to look at the text and decide which are the correct forms.
● Let them compare notes in groups.

2 Listening to the song
● Play the song, and tell students to check their answers.
● Explain any difficulties.
● See if students can understand the reason for the use of the past perfect in the song.
● If students like the idea, play the song again and let them sing along.

3 Past perfect tense
● Look at the examples with the students and make sure they understand the use of the past perfect.
● It is probably best to get students to do at least part of the exercise individually in writing, so that you can check that everybody has grasped the point.
● Practice Book Exercise 1 gives further work on the past perfect if needed.

Answers to Exercise 3
1. started; had met   2. looked; had tried
3. had remembered   4. examined; had broken
5. had not been   6. had already started; got
7. had learnt   8. brought

4 How many words?

- Play the recording, stopping after each sentence while students try to decide how many words there are, and what they are.
- Play the recording two or three times if necessary.

Tapescript and answers to Exercise 4

1. This all happened about three years ago. (7)
2. I had to go to London. (6)
3. The station's about five miles away. (7)
4. My train was at nine o'clock. (6)
5. By eight thirty I'd already packed everything. (8)
6. We went out to the car. (6)
7. I got into the car. (5)
8. I realised that I'd forgotten my coat. (8)
9. I drove back home as fast as I could. (9)
10. I arrived at the station just in time. (8)

5 Listening practice: anecdote

(This is a true story, which happened to the authors.)

- Look over the pictures first of all. Explain that they are in the wrong order, and that students have to listen to a story and then try to put the pictures in the right order.
- Teach the word *anorak*.
- Play the recording once without stopping.
- Ask students to make a start on the exercise, working individually.
- After a few minutes, play the recording again one or more times.
- When students have done what they can, tell them to continue in groups, trying to agree on a final version.
- Then discuss the answer with them.

Answer to Exercise 5

F I D G B H J C A E
or
F I D G H B J C A E

Exercise 5: summary of story

(The story is too long and rambling to give the complete tapescript. A summary is provided for reference.)

1. Speaker had to go to Zürich for conference. Train from Didcot to Reading, coach Reading to airport. Train at 9.00. By 8.30 had packed and was ready to drive to station (five miles away). Feeling calm and relaxed.
2. Getting into car, hit head on roofrack. Blood started running down forehead. Started driving to station (accompanied by girlfriend, who would take car back home afterwards). Feeling less calm.
3. Halfway to station, realised had forgotten anorak (essential in Zürich in winter). Turned round and raced back to house. Picked up anorak. Drove back to station at enormous speed. Forehead still bleeding. Feeling much less well organised.
4. Kissed girlfriend goodbye and rushed into station. Just managed to jump onto train as it was moving out.
5. Sitting in train (forehead still bleeding) realised had forgotten to give girlfriend car keys. Girlfriend would not be able to take car back home.
6. Saw Oxford through train window instead of Reading. Realised was on wrong train.

6 Conversation

- In a fluent and confident class (especially if numbers are small), you can do this as a whole-class activity.
- Otherwise, put students in groups of four or five.

- Ask if the song, or the story in Exercise 5, reminded them of incidents that have happened to them.
- If so, get them to tell the class or their group about the incident.
- If students are working in groups, finish by asking for one of the stories from each group to be told to the whole class.
- You may have to help with vocabulary, but try not to interrupt students with corrections unless it is absolutely necessary.

Summary

- Remind students to look at the Summary and learn the new material.

Practice Book

- Tell students which exercises you want them to do.

4 Pronunciation. Listen to the recording. How many words do you hear in each sentence? What are they? (Contractions like *I'd* count as two words.)

5 Listen to the story and then put the pictures in the right order.

6 Can you talk about one of these?

1. A day in your life when everything went wrong.
2. A meeting with somebody that you hadn't seen for a very long time.

Facts and opinions

A They thought the sun went round the earth

1 What did people believe hundreds of years ago?
Make sentences.

'They used to think that…'

the sun	was flat
the sky	could be made into gold
the earth	were born from mud
heavy things	was the centre of intelligence
lead	was made of crystal
the heart	went round the earth
insects	fell faster than light things

Do you know any other strange things that people used to believe?
Did you believe any strange things when you were a child?

2 Who found out what?

Pasteur proved that
Fleming found out that
Harvey showed that
Darwin said that
Newton proved that
Lucretius believed that

light
everything
people
penicillin
the blood
illnesses

were caused by very small living creatures.
was made up of colours.
circulated round the body.
was made up of atoms.
would kill bacteria.
were related to monkeys.

Can you think of other things that famous scientists have found out?

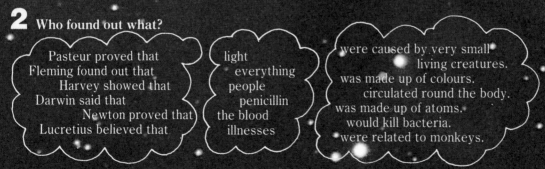

Unit 18: Lesson A

Students learn to talk about other people's knowledge, beliefs and opinions.
Principal structures: 'reported speech' with past reporting verb and sequence of tenses; word order in reported questions; *used to.*
Words and expressions to learn: *the blood; illness; star; scientist; religion; politics; animal; war; experiment; cause; tell a lie; discover; flat; living; equal; impossible.*
Phonology: rhythm.

Language notes and possible problems

1. Reported speech and direct speech Not all languages have the equivalent of the English 'reported speech' construction (in which the grammar of the original direct speech is changed so as to make it part of the 'reporter's' sentence). Some students may therefore find it easier to report using direct speech (*She said 'I am tired'*); or they may be tempted to use a mixed construction (**She said that I am tired*).

2. Tenses In some languages, past statements, questions, beliefs etc. may be reported without changing the tenses which would have been used by the original speaker. This may lead students to make mistakes like **She said that she is tired*; **They thought that the earth is the centre of the universe.*

Students must learn that we normally use past tenses to report past utterances and ideas: *She said that she **was** tired*; *They thought that the earth **was** the centre of the universe.*

Note, however, that present tenses are often possible when we are reporting statements or ideas which were, and still are, true. Compare: *They thought that the sun **went** round the earth*; *He proved that the earth **went**/**goes** round the sun.*

3. Reported questions You will need to explain the use of *if* and *whether* in Exercise 6. Students are also likely to have problems with the word order of reported questions: look out for mistakes like **Do you know what is his name?*.

4. Omission of *that* Note that the conjunction *that* is often left out (especially in speech) after the most common reporting verbs such as *say, think*. It is less usual to omit *that* after other verbs such as *prove, complain, comment*.

5. Vocabulary and level This is a more difficult lesson, and students whose vocabulary is poor may go rather slowly, especially if the ideas are unfamiliar to them. Dropping Exercise 4 (or giving it for homework) will make things easier. Make sure students realise that they do not need to learn all the new words.

If you are short of time
Drop one or more of Exercises 3–6.

1 Presentation: old beliefs
• Get students to do the exercise in groups, pooling their knowledge and using dictionaries where necessary.

• If they do not have any background knowledge of 'popular science' you may need to help out a bit.
• Go over the answers and explain any remaining vocabulary problems.
• Then explain the grammar of 'reported speech', showing how the tense of the idea or statement that is reported is made to 'match' the tense of the reporting verb:
> *They **thought**: 'The earth **is** flat'.*
> *They **thought** that the earth **was** flat.*

• Continue with the exercise, getting students to try to talk about other old beliefs and their own childhood beliefs.

Answers to Exercise 1
They used to think that:
– the sun went round the earth.
– the sky was made of crystal.
– the earth was flat.
– heavy things fell faster than light things.
– lead could be made into gold.
– the heart was the centre of intelligence.
– insects were born from mud.

2 Scientists
• This exercise can also be done in groups, with students pooling their knowledge and using dictionaries.
• If students don't have enough background knowledge to do the exercise as it stands, give them the first part of each answer (*Pasteur proved that illnesses...*; *Fleming found out that penicillin...* etc.). The rest then becomes relatively easy.
• Ask students if they can suggest the direct speech sentences that the scientists might actually have said (e.g. *'People **are** related to monkeys'*).
• Then see if students can think of any other things that scientists have found out.

Answers to Exercise 2
Pasteur proved that illnesses were caused by very small living creatures.
Fleming found out that penicillin would kill bacteria.
Harvey showed that the blood circulated round the body.
Darwin said that people were related to monkeys.
Newton proved that light was made up of colours.
Lucretius believed that everything was made up of atoms.

3 Rhythm

- Ask students to try saying the first three sentences.
- Then demonstrate or play the recording, pointing out how the unstressed syllables are pronounced more quickly and less distinctly than the others.
- Get students to practise until they can say the sentences easily with a good rhythm.
- They may need a lot of practice to achieve a good natural pronunciation of *that the* (/ðət ðə/).
- Next, get students to try to find the stresses in sentences 4–6 themselves, before they practise saying them. Make sure they realise that stresses are usually found on content words (nouns, verbs, adjectives and adverbs), but rarely on grammatical words (articles, pronouns, prepositions, conjunctions, auxiliary verbs and *be*).

4 Quotations

- This exercise will help students to become more aware of the way tenses are used in reported speech.
- Look over the examples, explaining any difficulties, and pointing out the change from *is* to *was* and from *cannot* to *could not*.
- Then get students to try to change some of the other quotations. (There is no need to do them all, if the vocabulary or ideas need too much explanation.)

5 Listening to continuous speech

- In this exercise, students are asked to listen to a very short and simple lecture.
- Before you start, pre-teach the words in the box (or let students look them up) and deal with any difficulties in the sentences.
- Students may already be able to suggest some of the answers, but tell them not to write anything down yet.
- Play the recording once.
- Tell students to write out any of the sentences that they can complete.
- Play the recording once or twice more, and give students another minute or two to finish as much as they can.
- Let them compare notes in groups and then discuss the answers with them.

Answers to Exercise 5

(Variations in the wording are possible.)

1. ... Aristotle said that heavy things fell *faster than light things*.
2. ... everybody believed that Aristotle *was right*.
3. ... scientists started to wonder if Aristotle's beliefs *were true*.
4. ... Galileo did some experiments which proved that Aristotle *was wrong*.
5. He showed that heavy things *and light things fell at the same speed*.
6. Galileo was the first person to *study the sky with a telescope*.
7. He found out that Jupiter *had satellites*
8. and that Saturn *had rings*
9. and that there were mountains *on the moon*
10. and spots *on the sun*.

Tapescript for Exercise 5

The Greek philosopher Aristotle, who lived in the fourth century BC, was interested in a large number of different subjects. In one of his books he dealt with the movements of physical objects, and here he said that heavy things fell faster than light things. It is unlikely that Aristotle tried to prove this by experiment; he was probably just repeating a common belief.

For 2,000 years, everybody thought that Aristotle was right. However, in the 16th century scientists began to question a large number of old beliefs, and the Italian scientist Galileo Galilei carried out various experiments on the dynamics of falling bodies. He is said to have dropped a cannon-ball and a pebble from the top of the leaning tower of Pisa to see which would reach the ground first. This may not be true, but we do know that Galileo proved that Aristotle was wrong; he showed that light and heavy things fell at the same speed.

Galileo was also interested in astronomy and optics. He improved the telescope, which had recently been invented, and was the first person to use one of these instruments to study the sky. He found out that Jupiter had satellites, that Saturn had rings, that there were mountains on the moon and spots on the sun.

Galileo got into serious trouble with the Italian universities and the Catholic Church, which preferred Aristotle's picture of the universe, and he was made to stop telling people about his new discoveries.

6 General knowledge quiz

- Look over the examples and make sure students understand how reported questions are constructed.
- Then get students to prepare questions in groups (preferably on subjects that most of the class will know something about and be interested in).
- When each group has a reasonable number of questions, get them to take turns asking the rest of the class. Join in yourself if you like.
- In a competitive class, you may like to organise the exercise as a team game (with points for correct answers, and perhaps points deducted for word order mistakes).

Summary

- Remind students to look over the Summary and learn the new material.

Practice Book

- Tell students which exercises you want them to do.

3 Pronunciation. Say these sentences with the correct stress.

1. **People thought** that the **earth** was **flat.**
2. They be**lieved** that the **sky** was **solid.**
3. They **thought** that the **sun went round** the **earth.**

Where are the stresses in these sentences? Can you say them?

4. They thought that the stars were holes in the sky.
5. They didn't know that the sun was a star.
6. They believed that mountains were the homes of gods.

4 Change the quotations from direct speech to reported speech. Examples:

Marx: 'Religion is the opium of the people'.
Marx said that religion was the opium of the people.'
The young George Washington: 'I cannot tell a lie'.
Washington said that he could not tell a lie.'

1. Stevenson: 'To travel hopefully is better than to arrive'.
2. Dorothy Parker (of another woman): 'She speaks 18 languages, and she can't say "no" in any of them'.
3. Somebody (of President Gerald Ford): 'He can't walk and chew gum at the same time'.
4. Anita Loos: 'Gentlemen prefer blondes'.
5. Oscar Wilde: 'It is better to be beautiful than to be good'.
6. The British Prime Minister Harold Wilson: 'A week is a long time in politics'.
7. Calderon: 'Life is a dream'.
8. *The Daily Express* in 1938: 'There will be no war in Europe'.
9. Dr Dionysus Lardner (1793–1859): 'Rail travel at high speed is impossible because people will not be able to breathe'.
10. Professor J.H. Pepper: 'The electric light has no future'.
11. Simon Newcomb, American astronomer: 'Artificial flight is impossible'.
12. Professor Tait: 'The telephone is physically impossible'.
13. Admiral Leahy, US Navy, June 1945: 'The atom bomb will never go off, and I speak as an expert in explosives'.

5 Listen to the recording and try to complete the sentences. The words in the box will help you.

| light | right | ring | satellite | speed |
| telescope | true | wrong | | |

1. The ancient Greek philosopher Aristotle said that heavy things fell...
2. For 2,000 years everybody believed that Aristotle...
3. In the 16th century, scientists started to wonder if Aristotle's beliefs...
4. The Italian scientist Galileo did some experiments which proved that Aristotle...
5. He showed that heavy things...
6. Galileo was the first person to...
7. He found out that Jupiter...
8. and that Saturn...
9. and that there were mountains...
10. and spots...

6 Work in groups of about four. Prepare some 'general knowledge' questions to ask other students. Begin *Do you know...?* or *Can you tell me...?* Examples:

'Do you know if gold is heavier than lead?'
'Can you tell me whether Britain has a king or a queen?'
'Do you know what his or her name is?'
'Do you know who Marco Polo was?'
'Can you tell me who Robert Redford is?'
'Do you know where the President was born?'
'Can you tell me who discovered radium?'
'Do you know who invented the telephone?'
'Do you know where Toronto is?'

B Probability

1 Look at the information about Fred Smith. Then listen to the recording of a conversation between Fred and a girl at a party. What did he say that was not true? Example:

'Fred said that he lived in Paris and California.'
'He told the girl that he had been to Venice.'

FRED SMITH
Full name: Frederick George Smith.
Age: 25
Address: 17 Victoria Terrace, Highbury,
    London N5.
Profession: van driver.
Interests: photography, model aeroplanes.
Education: Finsbury Park Comprehensive
    School.
Qualifications: none
Father: Albert Eric Smith, 52, shop
    assistant.
Mother: Florence Anne Smith, née
    Henderson, 48, housewife.

2 Here are some of the things that Fred said in the conversation. Do you think they are true? Use one of the expressions in the box.

| It must be true. It's probably true. |
| It could be true. It might be true. |
| It's probably not true. It can't be true. |

1. My friends call me Fred.
2. I photograph famous people.
3. I travel all over the world.
4. I've been photographing the President for *Time* magazine.
5. Famous people are all the same.
6. I find you interesting.
7. I want to photograph you.
8. I love poetry.

LLANDYFRDWY

3 Look at the picture. What can you say about the time and place? Examples:

'It might be morning, because...'
'It can't be in Germany, because...'
'It must be during the day, because...'

Unit 18: Lesson B

Students learn more ways of expressing the concept of probability. They practise the intelligent use of dictionaries.

Principal structures: modal verbs used to express probability and certainty; *likely to*; *there is likely to be*; *say* and *tell*; more practice of reported speech.

Words and expressions to learn: *full name*; *profession*; *poetry*; *parking place*; *photograph* (verb); *likely*; *none*; other words chosen by students.

Phonology: initial consonant clusters beginning with *s*.

Language notes and possible problems

1. Modal verbs This lesson practises the use of certain modal verbs (*must*, *could*, *might*, *can't*) to express degrees of probability and certainty. Students should already know the grammar of modal verbs, but you may need to revise the basic facts:
– the verbs have no *-s* in the third person singular.
– they are followed by the infinitive without *to*.
– questions and negatives are formed without *do*.

2. Must and can't Note that the opposite of *must* (when it expresses logical certainty) is *can't*, not *mustn't*. Compare *It must be true* and *It can't be true*. Students may have difficulty with this.

3. Likely Students may not have an adjective in their language which corresponds to *likely*; they may also find the structures difficult, especially *there is likely to be...*

4. Say and tell The distinction between these two verbs often causes problems. In Exercise 1, students practise using them with a following *that*-clause. They will need to note that *tell* must have a personal object (*He told her that...*) while this is unnecessary with *say* (*He said that...*).

5. Initial consonant clusters with s Speakers of certain languages find clusters like *st*, *sp* very difficult to pronounce at the beginning of a word. Look out for mistakes like **estudent*, **espeak*.

6. Lying Some of the optional activities here rely on getting students to 'tell lies' for fun. In some cultures, it is not usual to say things which are not true in order to tease or amuse people, and certain students may find the situation slightly shocking.

If you are short of time

This lesson is longer than average. You can drop Exercise 4 if the pronunciation point is not important for your students; Exercises 5 and 6 can be done for homework or dropped; Exercise 7 can be done for homework.

Optional extra materials

If you are going to do the 'two envelopes' *Optional activity*, you will need two envelopes, one empty and the other containing a picture which students can easily describe.

1 Listening; reporting discrepancies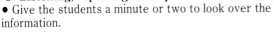
● Give the students a minute or two to look over the information.

● Point out the difference in the way *say* and *tell* are used in the examples.
● Tell students to close their books while you play the recording.
● Then ask if they can remember any of Fred's lies. Encourage them to make sentences beginning *He said that...*, *He told her that...* or *He asked her if/whether...*; make sure the tenses are all right.
● Play the recording again once or twice until students have understood the main points of the conversation and picked out most of the lies.

Tapescript for Exercise 1: see next page (page 77)

2 Degrees of certainty
● Look through the expressions in the box, giving whatever explanations are needed.
● The expressions are arranged in order: see if students can see the basis for this.
● The exercise can be done individually round the class or by group discussion, as you like.

3 Picture: making deductions
● Let students look at the picture for a minute or two.
● Go over the examples with them, and see if they can find ways of completing the sentences.
● Ask them to write one sentence each about the picture, using the same modal verbs as in the last exercise.
● After hearing their sentences, see if they can make some more deductions orally.
● You may like to finish by telling the class that the scene is in Wales (not England). Mention that Wales has its own language, Welsh, which is quite different from English – the word *Llandyfrdwy* in the picture (pronounced roughly /hlænd∧vrdu:i/) is a typical Welsh place name. You might also want to point out that pubs in England and Wales are only open at certain times (and pubs in some parts of Wales are closed all day on Sundays).

Optional activity: two envelopes
● Ask for two volunteers, or choose two students who speak quite well.
● Give them each an envelope: one will contain a picture, and the other will be empty, but do not let the class know which is which.
● Tell them to go out of the room for two minutes; the one who has a picture will prepare to describe it to the class; the other will prepare a description of an imaginary picture.
● When the students return, they each give their description, without letting the class know which description is real and which is invented.
● The class ask questions about the pictures.
● Finally, the class decide who was telling the truth.

Optional activity: find the lies
● Tell the students something about yourself; warn them in advance that you are going to include three lies in what you say, and see if they can pick them out.
● Alternatively, ask students to write three sentences about themselves, including at least one lie. Then let them listen to each other's sentences and try to find the lies. (Encourage the use of *must*, *could*, *can't* etc.)

Optional activity: 'alibi'

• Ask for two volunteers.

• Tell them that they are going to be questioned (separately) by the police, who are investigating a crime which was committed yesterday between 4.30 and 5.30.

• The two volunteers must go out of the room for five minutes and prepare a joint alibi for the time of the crime – they must say that they were together, and they must agree on the details of where they were and what they were doing.

• While they are preparing their story, the rest of the class (the police) prepare an interrogation.

• They must try to think of questions which the volunteers will not have foreseen (weather; clothes; who arrived first at the meeting place; . . .).

• Bring in one of the volunteers while the other stays outside out of earshot.

• Let the class ask their questions for a maximum of five minutes. They should note the answers.

• Then bring in the second volunteer and let the class question him/her, trying to break the alibi by finding contradictions between the two stories.

• While this is going on, the first volunteer can listen, but should not be able to signal to the one being questioned.

• When students are used to the game it can be played in groups of six to eight. It gives excellent practice in asking past tense questions.

4 Pronunciation: initial clusters with *s*

• Students who speak Spanish may have difficulty in making *st(r)*, *sp(r)* and *sc(r)* without putting a vowel in front; the same is true of speakers of Arabic, Farsi, and many oriental languages.

• If your students have this problem, get them to practise the words in the exercise until they find it easier, and encourage them to be careful when they come across words of this kind later on. (There are several in the next exercise.)

5 *Likely*

• Go over the examples and practise the pronunciation of *likely*.

• You may like to get students to do some of the questions in writing and the others orally.

• If they did Exercise 4, look out for the pronunciation of *Spain*, *spend*, *stop*, *strange*, *start*, *speak*, *spring*, *snow*, *Scotland* and *street*.

6 Personalisation

• If students are stuck for ideas, ask them what is likely to happen to other people in the class in the future; whether there is likely to be another war soon; what is likely to happen to prices; whether students are likely to travel in the near future.

7 Reading and dictionary use

• The purpose of this exercise is to show students how much of a text they can understand without using dictionaries.

• First of all, give them five to ten minutes to read the text. Do not allow questions or dictionaries. Tell students to write down the words they don't know.

• Get them to read the text again and tell you how well (or badly) they understand it.

• Ask them what words they have listed.

• Pick out some words which can be guessed from the context, and ask students if they can get an idea of what these words mean from looking at the text.

• Ask which words they think they really need to look up.

• Let them look up only the really essential words.

• Then let them read the text once more.

• Finally, tell them to choose some words and expressions from the text to learn.

Summary

• Remind students to look at the Summary and learn the new material.

Practice Book

• Tell students which exercises you want them to do.

Tapescript for Exercise 1

'Hello, then. What's your name?'
'Oh, er, Janet. Janet Parker.'
'Oh, yes? I'm Frederick. Frederick Getty Onassis. But my friends call me Fred.'
'Oh. What do you do, er, Fred?'
'Oh, I'm a photographer. I photograph famous people: film stars, pop singers, people like that.'
'Oh yes? Where do you work, then? Are you based in London?'
'Oh, no. I live in Paris. Paris and California. But I travel all over the world.'
'Oh, yes?'
'I've just got back from Washington. I've been photographing the President for *Time* magazine.'
'Oh, have you?'
'Before that, I was in Venice for the film festival. In a few days, I'll be in Tokyo for a fashion show. It's a busy life, you know. A busy life.'
'It must be terribly interesting. All that travelling. All those famous people.'
'Oh, no. Famous people – they're all the same, really. I was saying to Paul McCartney only last week – I get so tired of famous people. Sometimes I just want to be with ordinary simple people. Ordinary people have more character. More real beauty. Now you, Janet. I find you interesting. You have a very unusual face.'
'Oh, yes? Have I really?'
'Yes, Janet. You have wonderful eyes. Wonderful. Very expressive. Tell me, what do you do? Are you an actress? A model?'
'Oh. no. I work in a shop.'
'Really. In a shop. You surprise me. Janet, I want to photograph you. I'll put your face on the covers of the world's fashion magazines. We'll do some pictures in my London studio first of all. And then probably I'll take you to Paris – or perhaps to California: the light is better in California. Yes. We'll go to California in my Boeing 747.'
'Oh! You've got a Boeing 747?'
'Well, it's really my father's. He's quite a rich man.'
'What does he do?'
'Oh, oil, diamonds, gold, ship-building – boring things like that. I'm not interested in business myself. I'm more the artistic type. Like my mother. She's a Shakespearean actress, you know. I'm like her. I love nature, poetry, ideas, beauty.'
'Oh, yes. So do I. So do I.'
'Janet. This isn't a very interesting party. We'll go to my studio now . . .'

4 Pronunciation. Say these words.

1. star   stop   stand   studio   start   student
2. speak   spoke   Spain   spend
3. score   Scotland   Scottish
4. spring   spread   strange   street   straight
   screw   scratch   scream

5 Look at the examples to see how *likely* is used.

She **is likely to** come soon. = She **will probably** come soon.

I **am likely to** need help. = I **will probably** need help.

Now express these ideas using *likely*.

1. I will probably go to Spain soon.
2. She will probably spend next week in London.
3. It will probably stop raining soon.
4. You will probably meet some strange people at John's house.
5. If you start learning English now, you will probably speak it quite well by next summer.
6. They say the spring will probably be wet this year.

Now look at these examples.

There is likely to be a phone call for me.
   = **There will probably be** a phone call for me.
There are likely to be about 20 people at the party. = **There will probably be** about 20 people at the party.

Now express these ideas using *there is/are likely to be...*

1. There will probably be an election in June.
2. There will probably be some problems.
3. There will probably be snow in Scotland.
4. There will probably be a parking place in this street.

6 What is likely to happen in your life? In your country? In the world? Make sentences with *likely*.

7 Reading and dictionary use.

1. Read the text and write down the words you don't know. Do *not* use a dictionary.
2. Read the text again. How well can you understand it? (*Very well/quite well/not very well/not at all.*)
3. Look at the words you wrote down. Have you got any idea what some of them mean? Look at the text and see if you can guess.
4. Which of the words do you really need to look up in a dictionary, to understand the text well? Look them up and read the text once more.
5. Choose some of the new words to learn.

THE AMAZON FOREST AND THE FUTURE OF THE WORLD

The Amazon forest, in Brazil, covers five million square kilometres – an area as big as the whole of Europe excluding Russia. It contains one third of the world's trees.

However, the trees are disappearing. By 1974, a quarter of the forest had already been cut down. In the following year, 1975, 4% of the remaining trees went. If the destruction of the forest continues at the same rate, there will be nothing left by the year 2005.

Scientists say that the disappearance of the trees is already causing changes in the climate. In Peru, there is less snow than before on the high peaks of the Andes mountains. In Bolivia, there is less rain than before and more wind. In some parts of north-east Brazil there is now very little rain.

What will happen if more of the Amazon forest is cut down? According to climatologists, two things are likely to happen: there will be serious effects on the world's climate, and the air that we breathe will lose some of its oxygen. Why is this?

Trees absorb the gas carbon dioxide from the air, and give out oxygen into the air. The trees of the Amazon rain forest are chemically very active, and some scientists believe that they provide 50% of the world's annual production of oxygen. If we lose the tropical forests, the air will contain much less oxygen and much more carbon dioxide. It will become difficult – perhaps even impossible – to breathe.

With more carbon dioxide in the air, the temperature will rise; the ice-caps at the North and South Poles will melt; the sea level will rise, and hundreds of coastal cities will be flooded.

Scientists do not all agree about the exact figures – the calculations can be done in different ways with different results. But all scientists agree that if we destroy the Amazon forest it will be environmental suicide – like losing an ocean. Life on earth will become difficult, and it may become impossible.

Small talk

A Hello, nice to see you

1 Listen to Dialogue 1, and write the numbers and letters of the expressions you hear.

1. A I go.
   B I'm going.
   C I'll go.

2. A Nice to see you.
   B It's nice to see you.
   C Nice seeing you.

3. A Are we late?
   B We're late.
   C Aren't we late?

4. A You're first
   B You're the first
   C You're not first

5. A Who is coming?
   B Who ever's coming?
   C Who else is coming?

6. A Can I take your coat?
   B Let me take your coat.
   C Shall I take your coat?

7. A You know Lucy, do you?
   B You know Lucy, don't you?
   C You don't know Lucy, do you?

8. A I think we've met her once.
   B I think we met her once.
   C I think we'll meet her one day.

9. A What can I get you to drink?
   B What can I give you to drink?
   C What would you like to drink?

10. A The room doesn't look nice, John.
    B The room does look nice, John.
    C Doesn't the room look nice, John?

11. A You've changed it about
    B You've changed it round
    C You've changed it over

2 Listen again. Which of these do you hear?

A don't you?   D wasn't it?
B do you?   E aren't we?
C isn't it?   F haven't you?

3 Real questions or not? Listen to the sentences. Does the voice go up or down at the end? Examples:

The piano was over by the window, wasn't it?
You know Lucy, don't you?

1. It's a lovely day, isn't it?
2. You're French, aren't you?
3. She's got fatter, hasn't she?
4. The train leaves at 4.13, doesn't it?
5. Children always like cartoon films, don't they?
6. It's your birthday next week, isn't it?
7. Hotels are expensive here, aren't they?
8. Ann said she'd phone, didn't she?

4 Work with two or three other students. Act out a 'greeting' scene like the one in Dialogue 1.

Unit 19: Lesson A

NOTE
● The whole of this Unit (19A and 19B) is based on a series of five dialogues which portray different stages in a dinner party. Each dialogue generates a good deal of work, and students are led up to the point where they can improvise their own 'social' conversations in groups. Although the Unit is divided into the usual two lessons for the sake of convenience, it really consists of five mini-lessons, and should be handled as such. The Teacher's Book instructions are organised accordingly.
● The Unit will probably take longer than usual to work through, particularly if you have time to make a detailed study of the language of the dialogues. This is not, however, essential; much of the new language is 'preview' material which will come up again.
● The texts of all the dialogues in the Unit are at the end of the Student's Book, on pages 157–158. Ideally, students should not look at these until they have finished work on Dialogue 5. But some students are very uncomfortable if they cannot see the written word fairly soon. If it is necessary, let them look at the text of each dialogue after work on it is finished – but try and get them to mask the following dialogues while they read. It is important to do each set of exercises before reading the dialogue.

▬▬ DIALOGUE 1 ▬▬

Students learn some conventional 'social' language used in greeting and welcoming people and asking for confirmation.
Principal structures: question-tags with affirmative sentences.
Words and expressions to learn: *sofa*; *coat*; *move* (= change address); *ask for*.
Phonology: intonation of question-tags.

Language notes and possible problems
Question-tags The *meaning* of the question-tag structure will probably be easy for students to grasp. Many languages have an expression which is added to a sentence in order to invite the hearer's agreement. But students will probably find the *structure* difficult to learn, and the intonation will certainly cause problems. Students will need to learn these 'rules of thumb':
a. that the tag is negative if the sentence is affirmative.
b. that the tag repeats the auxiliary verb of the sentence; or if there is no auxiliary, the tag contains *do/does/did*.
c. that the intonation of the tag depends on the speaker's intention: a rising intonation means that the speaker wants information (it is a real question); a falling intonation means that the speaker is sure of the hearer's agreement.

If you are short of time
You can leave out Exercise 2.

1 Listening comprehension 🔲
● Ask students to look at the pictures and tell you as much as they can about them.

● Play the dialogue once while students just listen.
● Tell them to write down the numbers 1 to 11 on a piece of paper and play the dialogue again.
● Students should listen for the numbered expressions and try to write the correct letter each time.
● You may need to play the dialogue once more.
● Let them compare notes; then give them the answers.

Answers: 1C 2A 3A 4B 5C 6B 7B 8A 9A 10C 11B

2 Identifying question-tags 🔲
● See if students can tell you the answers before they listen again.
● Then play the dialogue so they can check. (The tags they hear are *don't you?*, *haven't you?* and *wasn't it?*.)

3 Intonation of question-tags 🔲
● You may need to play the sentences several times before students can agree on the intonation.
● Check the answers with them (1, 3, 5 and 7 go down; 2, 4, 6, and 8 go up).
● Elicit or explain the meaning of the two intonation patterns (see *Language notes*), and get students to imitate them.
● Point out how question-tags are constructed.

4 Improvisation
● Ask for three or four volunteers.
● Get them to improvise a scene similar to the one in the dialogue. (Start by getting two of the students to go out of the room and knock on the door.)
● Then get the class to do it in groups. Walk round listening, and help if necessary.

DIALOGUE 2

Students learn ways of giving and eliciting personal information and asking for repetition.
Words and expressions to learn: *ground; weekday; a change; I beg your pardon; I should think; hard work; How do you mean?; somewhere else.*
Phonology: more practice on the intonation of question-tags.

Possible problems
Handling the dialogue The main purpose of the dialogue is to provide listening practice. Do not go through the text in detail unless students particularly want to. If you do decide to study the text, the time to do it is before Exercise 9. Try to get students to mask dialogues 3–5 while they read.

If you are short of time
You can spend a minimum of time on Exercise 6, and leave out or shorten Exercise 9.

5 Listening comprehension
- Play the dialogue; then ask students to read the sentences and note their answers.
- Play the dialogue again while they check answers.
- Let them compare notes; then give them the answers.

Answers: 1T   2T   3F   4F   5F   6T   7F   8F   9DK
10T   11T

6 Recall
- Play the dialogue once again.
- Ask students what they can remember.
- You may like to try to rebuild the dialogue on the board, or let students do it in groups.

7 Real questions: rising intonation
- Get students to repeat the sentences.
- Make sure everyone can manage the intonation reasonably well.
- Remind students that a rising intonation on a question-tag indicates a real question.

8 Asking for agreement: falling intonation
- Get students to repeat the sentences.
- Make sure they understand the meaning of a falling intonation here – the speaker expects agreement.

9 Improvisation
- Make a 'compartment' at the front of the class, with two rows of four chairs opposite each other.
- Ask for six volunteers to 'get onto the train'.
- Tell them that they're on a long train journey; they're bored, so they should start a conversation.
- Every few minutes, stop the train at a station and let a few people get off and few new ones get on.
- If things are going well, establish a second compartment; appoint ticket collectors, etc.

DIALOGUE 3

Students learn polite formulae for mealtimes.
Principal structures: questions with prepositions at the end of the clause; more work on the structure of question-tags.
Words and expressions to learn: *delicious; Could you pass me...?; I've had enough; How stupid of me;* other words as chosen by the students.

Language notes and possible problems
Clause-final prepositions Students have seen variou examples of this structure. In this lesson they take a mor formal look at questions ending in prepositions. It is a d ficult structure for most students; the best way of explair ing it is to tell students that an expression like *look at c listen to* is almost like one word. So we like to keep the tw parts together, even if this means separating a prepositic from its object.

10 Listening for specific information
- Students may not be familiar with all the words for food and drink in this dialogue.
- Play it once through while they listen, and then once again (perhaps pausing once or twice) while they try to note the words they recognise.
- Give them a few moments to finish writing, let them compare notes, and give them the answers.

Answers: salt   mustard   beef   potato   meat   beans
carrot   bread   wine

- Explain the meanings of the new words and practise their pronunciation.

11 Prepositions at the end of questions
- Get students to complete the two examples, and check that everybody has the same answer.
- Let them do the exercise individually before comparing notes in groups; then go over the answers with them and explain any problems.
- Note that *who*, and not *whom*, is used as an object form in this structure (sentences 2–4).

12 Construction of question-tags
- Explain that students are to say the question-tag for each sentence, as if asking for agreement.
- Remind them that their voices should fall at the end of the question-tags.
- (With unconfident students, play the recording twice and let them write the answers the first time.)

Tapescript for Exercise 12: see page 182

Summary
- Remind students to study the Summary.

Practice Book
- Tell students which exercises you want them to do.

5 Listen to Dialogue 2. Then look at the following sentences. Are they true or false? Write 'T' (true), 'F' (false), or 'DK' (don't know).

1. Lucy works in a pub.
2. She likes her work.
3. She doesn't meet many interesting people.
4. Lucy's job is always hard work.
5. There is only one barman in her pub.
6. John works in a bank.
7. He likes his job very much.
8. He has just been made manager.
9. He's going to move to another town soon.
10. Lucy wouldn't like to move to another town.
11. John has lived in the same place for six years.

6 Listen again. Can you remember some sentences from the dialogue?

7 Real questions. Listen and repeat.

1. That's hard work, isn't it?
2. You're an accountant, aren't you?
3. You have to move round, don't you?
4. It'll be in another town, won't it?

8 Asking for agreement. Listen and repeat.

1. It's a nice day, isn't it?
2. She's very pretty, isn't she?
3. Good clothes are expensive, aren't they?
4. You're tired, aren't you?

9 Work with four or five other students. You are all in the same compartment on a long train journey. Act out a conversation in which you get to know one another.

10 Listen to Dialogue 3. Write down all the words you hear for things that you can eat or drink.

11 Can you complete these questions from the dialogue?

What are you looking ....?
What are John and Lucy talking ....?

Now read the following answers and write the questions.

1. They're talking about politics.
   What are they talking about?
2. I went with Henry.
3. I'm looking for Alice.
4. I bought it for you.
5. I'm thinking about holidays.
6. I'm listening to some piano music.
7. I'm looking at your ear-rings.
8. The letter was from Andy.

12 Asking for agreement. Listen, and say the 'question-tags'. Example:

It's a nice day, . . .

. . . isn't it?

79

B I didn't think much of it

1 Listen to Dialogue 4.
What do you think they were
talking about?
Can you remember any of the
things they said?

2 Which of these words and expressions come in the dialogue?
Write down your answers; then listen again and see if you were
right.

I liked it all   lovely   nonsense   I didn't think much of it
I cried   I couldn't help it   It made him laugh
It didn't say anything to me   I may be very old-fashioned
So am I   I like violence   Why did you like it?
It was really really boring   three old men   Who wrote it?
I've never heard of him

3 Write down the names of a food, a sport,
an animal and a person (singer, actor,
writer, ...) that you like. Tell another student,
and listen to his or her answers.

Write down the names of a food, a sport, an
animal and a person (singer, actor, writer, ...)
that you don't like.
Tell another student and listen to his or her
answers.

I like ...
I quite like...
I really like...
I like ... very much.
I love...

So do I.
I don't.
I quite like him/her/
it/them.
I've never heard of
him/her/it/them.

I don't like...
I don't much like...
I really don't like...
I don't like ... at all.

Neither do I.
I do.
I don't mind him/her/
it/them.
I've never heard of
him/her/it/them.

Unit 19: Lesson B

━━━━━━━━ DIALOGUE 4 ━━━━━━━

Students learn more ways of expressing opinions, and of agreeing and disagreeing with other people's opinions.
Principal structures: *so/neither do I.*
Words and expressions to learn: *sex; violence; complete; awful; old-fashioned; I didn't think much of it; I couldn't help it.*

Language notes and possible problems
So do I, etc. Students have already met *So do I* (and *So am I, So have I,* etc.). They have not yet met the negative equivalent *Neither do I.* Note that *neither* is usually pro-nounced /'niːðər/ in American English. The alternative form *Nor do I* is common in British English.

If you are short of time
Leave out Exercise 4.

1 Listening comprehension
Play the dialogue once while students listen, and see they have an idea of what the conversation is about.
Ask if they can remember any words or expressions.

2 Recall
Get students to write the words and expressions which they think come in the dialogue.
Then get them to compare notes in groups.
Play the dialogue again, more than once if they want, and let them check.
Then discuss the answers with them, explaining any difficulties.

Answers to Exercise 2
The expressions which occur in the dialogue are:
lovely   nonsense   I didn't think much of it   I cried
I couldn't help it   It didn't say anything to me
It was really really boring   Who wrote it?

3 Expressing and reacting to opinions
  Go over the instructions for the first part of the exercise and make sure students understand *So do I* and the other expressions illustrated.
• Then get them to write down their four words.
  Call on one or two students to tell their neighbours what they like. The neighbours should answer truthfully, using the expressions illustrated.
• When you are satisfied that everybody understands what to do, divide the class into pairs and let them go ahead.
• To get additional practice, you can tell students to change partners once or twice.
  Go on to do the second part of the exercise in the same way.

4 Books, films, plays, etc.

● This can be done in groups, or as a whole-class exercise.
● Go over the expressions first, and make sure there are no problems.
● Opinions can be expressed in the same ways as in the previous exercise. There is a wider choice of expressions for conveying reactions.
● It is best if students talk about things which the others are likely to have read or seen – for example, recent films or TV programmes.

5 Discussion

● If the class is sufficiently confident and fluent, they may be able to say more things about some of the books, films etc. that they mention.
● Encourage them to talk as freely as possible.
● Don't correct mistakes unless they are a serious obstacle to communication (though you may wish to note points for attention at another time).

▄▄▄ DIALOGUE 5 ▄▄▄

Students learn expressions used in leave-taking. They practise listening comprehension, and finish with a large-scale improvisation.
Principal structures: *ought to* and *had better* are previewed.
Words and expressions to learn: *whose; It's getting late; We've got a long way to go; We ought to be on our way* (= leaving); *I suppose; We'd better be going; enjoy oneself; Thank you for coming; I'll give you a ring; Thank you so much.*
Phonology: fluency practice.

Language notes and possible problems
1. Ought to is previewed here. You may like to explain that *ought* means practically the same as *should*, but that it is used with a *to*-infinitive.
2. Had better You will need to explain that the *'d* in *We'd better* is a contraction of *had*, not *would* or *should*, and that *better* does not really mean 'better' (the expression simply means the same as *should* or *ought to*).
3. Enjoy oneself You will probably want to point out the use of the reflexive pronoun here.

If you are short of time
Leave out Exercise 9.

---

6 Detecting differences   🔲▶

● Look at the sentences in the list first of all. Explain any difficulties.
● Then play the recording, and ask students to write the versions of the expressions that actually occur in the dialogue. (Note that none of the expressions in the list are incorrect.)
● Play the dialogue once more, and give students time to finish writing.
● Then let them compare notes in groups, before discussing the answers (see *Language notes*).

Answers to Exercise 6
It's getting late.   We've got a long way to go.
Yes, we'd better be going, too.   Thank you so much, Ann.
We really enjoyed ourselves.
Thank you for coming.   You must come over to us soon.
I'll give you a ring.
That's not mine. (*or* This is mine.)
Well, whose is this, then?   Is it old and dirty?

7 Fluency practice

● Give students time to read through the texts.
● Each student should choose at least one sentence whose pronunciation he or she wants to check.
● Students should say their sentences to you, trying to get a good intonation and rhythm.
● You should simply say the sentences after the students without making any comments or corrections.
● Tell students to try the sentences again, making any changes they want to and comparing their pronunciation with yours until they are satisfied.

8 Student choice   🔲▶

● Play the whole set of dialogues while students listen, following in their books if they want to.
● Then tell them each to write down five to ten useful expressions which they have not yet learnt, but which they think it would be good for them to know.

9 Improvisation

● This can be done either with one group at a time 'performing' for the others, or with several groups working simultaneously.
● The first approach is more demanding, but will probably achieve greater concentration, especially if you tape-record or video-record the performances.
● Students should act out their scenes properly, with appropriate movements.
● Give each group a minute or two to divide up the roles, but don't allow them time to prepare what they are going to say.
● If you have students who tend to go on and on, you may want to impose a time-limit on each sketch, say five minutes.

Summary
● Remind students to go over the Summary and learn the new vocabulary.

Practice Book
● Tell students which exercises you want them to do, and make sure they know what is required.

4 Write down the names of three books/films/plays etc. that you liked and three that you didn't.
Tell other students and listen to their answers.

> I liked...
> I really liked...
> etc.

> So did I.
> I didn't.
> I didn't think much of it.
> I haven't seen it.
> I've never heard of it.
> etc.

> I didn't like...
> I didn't much like...
> etc.

> Neither did I.
> I did.
> I quite liked it.
> I haven't read it.
> etc.

5 Talk some more about books/plays/films etc. that you have read or seen.

6 Listen to Dialogue 5. The following sentences are like sentences in the dialogue, but they are not exactly the same.
What are the exact sentences in the dialogue?

It's late.
We've got to go a long way.
We'd better go, too.
Thank you very much, Ann.
I really enjoyed myself.
Thanks for coming.
You must come and see us soon.
I'll phone you.
This isn't mine.
Well, who is this, then?
It's old and dirty.

7 Look at the dialogue texts on pages 156–158.
Choose a sentence and try to say it with a good pronunciation.
The teacher will say it for you correctly.

8 Listen to Dialogues 1–5 again.
Read the texts, and write down some useful expressions to learn.

9 Improvisation. Work in groups of six to eight. Act out a dinner party. How long can you go on for?

Do it

A How to do it

1 Match the words and the pictures.

cover	peel	rub
scratch	shake	stick

2 Here are some useful practical tips for everyday life. Unfortunately, the beginnings and ends have got mixed up. Can you sort them out?

To make tomatoes easier to peel,   rub them with lemon first and then wash them.
If you want to pick up a rabbit,   rub it with liquid brass cleaner.
To get cigarette stains off your fingers,   cover them with very hot water for a minute or two.

If you catch German measles,   put cold water in one and stand the other in hot water.

You can clean dirty saucepans   by packing them with wet newspaper and leaving them overnight.

To get dust out of a guitar,   don't hold its ears.
If two glasses are stuck together,   don't visit anyone who is pregnant unless you're sure she's already had them.

To get small scratches off your watch glass,   put rice inside it, shake it and empty it.
You can make tight shoes more comfortable   by filling them with cold water and vinegar and letting them boil for five minutes.

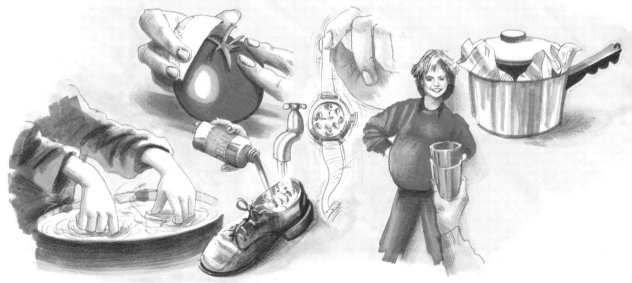

Unit 20: Lesson A

Students learn more about giving instructions and giving their opinions on courses of action to take.
Principal structures: infinitive of purpose; *by ...ing*; negative imperatives; *had better*.
Words and expressions to learn: *finger; rabbit; saucepan; dust; rice; scratch; luggage; examination; peel* (verb); *rub; cure* (verb); *shake; stick* (verb); *scratch* (verb); *catch* (a disease); *empty* (verb); *tight; pregnant*.
Phonology: consonant clusters in words beginning *ex-*.

Language notes and possible problems

1. Infinitive of purpose In the first exercise there are four examples of the *to*-infinitive used to express purpose. Students may need to be reminded about the structure; point out that no preposition is used before the infinitive, and look out for the common mistake *For to...*

2. By ...ing This structure may be difficult for students to get used to. There is some more work on it in Practice Book Exercise 1.

3. *Had better* Some students may not know this structure. You will probably want to point out that it does not compare two courses of action, but simply says what should be done.

Students may also be tempted to use a *to*-infinitive with *had better*, so you will have to watch out for mistakes like *I had better to go now.*

If you are short of time

You can leave out Exercises 3 and 4; if good pronunciation is not a high priority for your students you can leave out Exercise 6.

Optional extra materials

Slips with the beginnings and ends of the tips in Exercise 2 (if you want to try the 'split-halves' option). Scissors (for students to use in Exercise 5).

1 Vocabulary

- Let students try the exercise individually.
- Then get them to compare notes.
- Discuss the answers with them; practise the pronunciation of the words and make sure students understand how they are used (give the past tense and past participle of *stick* and *shake*).

2 Tips

- This can be done in groups. If your students are competitive, ask them to see which group can work out all the right answers first. They should write out the sentences.
- They will need to use dictionaries for some words.
- When you are checking the answers with them, put one example of a sentence with *by ... ing*, one example of a sentence beginning with a *to*-infinitive, and one example of a sentence with a negative imperative on the board. Point out how the structure is formed and how the sentence is punctuated.

Alternative to Exercise 2: split halves

- If you prepare slips of paper with the half-sentences from Exercise 2 on them, it can be done as a walk-round activity.
- Hand out the slips, and tell the students to learn by heart what is written on them.
- They should then walk round saying their half-sentences and trying to find the person who has the other half.
- Finish off by pointing out how the structures in the tips are formed, and how the sentences are punctuated.

Answers to Exercise 2

To make tomatoes easier to peel, cover them with very hot water for a minute or two.

If you want to pick up a rabbit, don't hold its ears.

To get cigarette stains off your fingers, rub them with lemon first and then wash them.

If you catch German measles, don't visit anyone who is pregnant unless you're sure she's already had them.

You can clean dirty saucepans by filling them with cold water and vinegar and letting them boil for five minutes.

To get dust out of a guitar, put rice inside it, shake it and empty it.

If two glasses are stuck together, put cold water in one and stand the other in hot water.

To get small scratches off your watch glass, rub it with liquid brass cleaner.

You can make tight shoes more comfortable by packing them with wet newspaper and leaving them overnight.

3 Beginnings of tips

- Divide the class into groups of three or four.
- Tell them they must imagine or invent beginnings for the four ends of tips in the exercise. They should write the whole tip down.
- Tell them their beginnings can be serious or funny.
- Walk round while they are writing to make sure they are forming and punctuating their sentences correctly, but don't make suggestions about what they should write down; the humour or invention in the exercise should come from the students.
- When they have finished, get the groups to read out their tips and let the class vote on a) the most sensible and b) the funniest tip.
- (Some of the tips the students invent may be just as sensible as the original ones.)

The original tips were:

If you're travelling abroad, don't put your address on the outside of your luggage. (Thieves hang around airports to see who's going abroad so they can go to the houses and burgle them while the owners are away.)

You can keep a mirror from misting up by rubbing it with a cut potato or apple.

To keep wasps away from a picnic, put a glass of beer a few yards away.

To get chewing-gum off a piece of clothing, hold the back over the steam from a kettle.

4 Endings for tips

- This can be done as a whole-class exercise: ask students to volunteer suggestions.

Possible answers

The night before an examination, you should do something relaxing and then get a good night's sleep.

To find out how far away a thunderstorm is, count the time between the flash and the bang: five seconds = one mile; three seconds = one kilometre.

You can get a tight ring off by putting soapy water on your finger.

5 Students write tips

- Put the students into small groups. Each group should write four tips.
- Walk round while they are working to help with any problems.
- Then the students should *either* copy their tips down in mixed-up fashion (as in the Student's Book, Exercise 2) *or* cut them apart so that each half is on a separate slip of paper.
- Groups exchange sets of tips and see how fast they can unscramble them.

6 Pronunciation: clusters with ex-

- This is a sensitisation exercise to help students to deal with clusters of several consonants (some students' languages may contain no consonant clusters at all).
- Get students to pronounce the lists of words after you or the recording. If there are particular difficulties you may want to repeat this sort of exercise from time to time.

7 Desert island: *had better*

- This is best done as a whole-class activity.
- Explain the situation to the students.
- Go over the examples with them and make sure they understand what *had better* means and how to form sentences with it.
- Then let students volunteer suggestions about the things that should be done. Write the suggestions up on the board in note form as they do.
- Try to make sure that most students volunteer a suggestion.

8 Planning life on the island

- Make groups of six or seven students.
- Each group is to submit a plan of how they think the work they talked about in Exercise 7 should be organised.
- They should say who in the class (not just in their group) should do what work and why.
- Walk round while they are working to help if needed.
- When the groups have finished let them submit their plans to one another and discuss the relative merits of each plan.

Summary

- Remind students to look at the Summary and learn the new words.

Practice Book

- Tell students which exercises you want them to do.

3 **How do you think these tips begin?**

.. don't put your address on the outside of your
luggage.
.. by rubbing it with a cut potato or apple.
.. put a glass of beer a few yards away.
.. hold the back over the steam from a kettle.

Can you complete these tips?

The night before an examination, ...
To find out how far away a thunderstorm is, ...
You can get a tight ring off by ...

5 **Work in groups. Each group writes four
tips (serious or funny ones). Then copy the tips,
with the beginnings and ends out of order, and
give them to another group to put in order.**

6 **Say these words. Notice the stress.**

1. side   ex**ci**ting   said   ex**cept**
2. pen   spend   ex**pen**sive   speak
   ex**per**ience   sport   **ex**port
3. rest   press   ex**pre**ssion
4. late   play   ex**plain**
5. shave   change   ex**change**

7 Imagine your plane has just crashed on an
island where no one lives. You may not be
rescued for months. Talk about what there is to
do. Examples:

'We'd better build a place to sleep in.'
'We should make a fire that planes can see.'

8 Work with six or seven other students.
Make a plan for the class's life on the island.
Decide who should do what part of the work
and why, and report to the class. Examples:

'We think Giovanna should plan the houses, because
she's an architect.'
'Ahmed had better not do any hard work, because
he's been ill.'

83

B If I were you,...

1 Match the expressions and the pictures.

| back to front face downwards inside out |
| sideways underneath upside down |

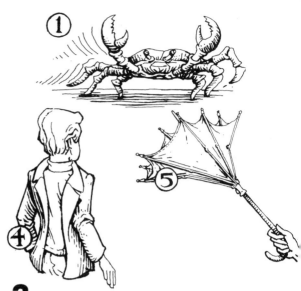

2 Listen to the dialogue. Are there any differences between the version on the recording and the version in the book?

A: If I were you, I'd turn it the other way round.
B: Well, I think I'll try it this way first.
A: I mean, –
C: Hello. I wouldn't do it like that if I were you.
B: Wouldn't you?
C: No, I think you ought to turn it upside down.
B: Oh, really? I'll think about it.
C: Yes, and put a blanket underneath first, or it'll get dirty.
D: Hi. Why don't you turn it sideways?
B: You think so?
D: Oh, yes, and remember to cover it, or it'll get wet.
B: Get wet?
A: You really ought to take the wheels off first, you know.
B: Well, I –
E: I think it would be much better if he turned it back to front, don't you?
A: That's just what I said.
D: Don't forget to tighten all the screws up.
C: You're not getting anywhere like that.
D: If I were you, I'd go back to the beginning and start again.
C: And I still think you should turn it upside down.
E: Let's help him.
B: It's quite all right. I can do it by myself, thank you very much.
E: No, it's no trouble.
A: Come on, everybody.

3 Look through the dialogue and write down some useful expressions and structures to learn.
Exchange lists with one or more other students and see if you have thought of the same expressions.

4 Fluency practice. Choose a sentence from the dialogue and practise saying it. Try for accurate intonation and rhythm.

5 Put a verb from the box into each blank (or set of blanks). Use some verbs more than once; use the correct tenses.

| be change do explain have know |
| look make read ring stop take |

A: I don't know what to do. If John *were* here, he ....

B: Yeah, if John .... here, he .... what to do, but .... he .... how to do it? If I .... you, I' .... the instructions again.

A: I've read them twice already. Do you think it .... a good idea if I .... the top off and .... inside?

B: I don't know. I don't think I' .... that if it .... mine.

A: Wouldn't you? What .... you .... if you .... this mess in your kitchen?

B: I' .... worrying about it for the moment; I' .... Pat and .... the problem; I' .... my plans for this evening.

A: Yeah, I suppose you're right. If I .... the top off, I' .... probably just .... it worse. Pour me a drink while I ring Pat, will you?

Unit 20: Lesson B

Students learn more ways of suggesting, persuading and warning; they learn to express the notion of orientation.

Principal structures: hypothetical conditions in the present (so-called 'second conditional'), including *If I were you,...; ought to;* warnings with *or; Let's; Why don't you; remember* and *forget* + *to*-infinitive.

Words and expressions to learn: *screw; law; drug; give up; seem; immediately; back to front; face downwards; inside out; sideways; underneath; upside down; the other way round; this way; I'll think about it; It's no trouble.*

Phonology: final consonant clusters.

Language notes and possible problems

1. Conditionals Students have worked with 'open conditions' in Unit 10. (See Teacher's Book Unit 10, Lesson A for a general discussion of conditionals.) Now they are introduced to 'unreal' or 'hypothetical' conditions, where a past tense is used in the *if*-clause to talk about the present or future, and a modal auxiliary (usually *would*) is used in the main clause. You will probably want to stress that this form is used to talk about something that might not happen, or might not be true.

2. If I were you,... You will need to explain that *were* is sometimes used instead of *was* after *if*, especially in this particular expression.

3. Or Warnings can be given in English by using *or* + a future tense to predict the unwelcome consequences of an action (e.g. *Cover it, or it'll get wet*). Not all languages have an equivalent structure, so it may need explanation.

4. Remember to; forget to You will probably want to point out that the infinitive is used after these verbs when the meaning is *remember/forget that one has to do something.*

If you are short of time

(Note: this is a longer than average lesson.) If pronunciation is not a high priority, leave out Exercise 4 and/or Exercise 7; get students to do Exercise 5 for individual homework; get students to do the preparation phase of Exercise 8 for homework.

1 Matching

- Let students do the exercise individually and then compare notes before checking with you.
- Explain the exact meanings of the expressions where necessary, and practise the pronunciation.

2 Dialogue: detecting differences

- Tell students to close their books, if possible before they have a chance to look closely at the printed version of the dialogue.
- Play the recording once without stopping and then ask them what they can remember.
- Tell them to open their books and read the dialogue.
- Ask if they think this is exactly the same as the recorded version, or if there are a few differences, or a lot of differences.

- Ask if they can see any specific differences.
- Tell them to close their books and listen again; see if they can identify some more differences.
- Finally, let them listen while they follow the text in their books. This time they should be able to pick out virtually all the differences.

Tapescript for Exercise 2: see the next page (page 85)

3 Students choose items to learn

- Give students plenty of time to look through the dialogue and ask you questions.
- Leave them free to make their own decisions as to what items they want to learn.
- When students are ready, let them compare notes.
- They may want to add things to their lists after they have seen what other students have chosen.
- If they have left out any of the more important structural points (see *Language notes*), you may want to draw their attention to them.

4 Fluency practice

- Ask each student to choose a sentence from the dialogue and say it to you.
- Explain that you will repeat the sentences after the students without comment; they should try to hear whether there is any important difference between your version and theirs.
- Let students say sentences as many times as they want to (with you repeating them) until they are satisfied.

5 Conditional: practice of forms

- You may want to go over the formation and use of the hypothetical conditional if you did not do so during Exercise 3.
- Then let students work through the exercise individually, walking round to make sure everyone has understood.
- Let them compare answers before checking with you.

Answers: (were), would know, were, would know, would, know, were, d read, would be, took, looked, d do, were, would, do, had, d stop, d ring, explain, d change, took, d, make

6 Freer practice: writing advice letters

- Make sure students understand that there are four bits of letters from different people to the same person (Christine), and four bits of her answers.
- The students' task is to match the problem letters with the replies. Tell them they can use dictionaries or ask you for help with vocabulary. (You may need to explain that in Britain people who cannot afford lawyers can apply for Legal Aid and, if their application is accepted, obtain financial assistance towards the cost of a lawyer.)
- Let them work individually for a few minutes before comparing answers in groups of three or four and checking with you.
- Then ask each group to choose one of the pairs of fragments, imagine the situation, and invent the rest of Christine's letter.
- Ask them to try to use some of the language they have learnt in this lesson.
- Walk round while they are working to give any help that is needed.
- You may want to put the letters up in the classroom so the students can read one another's; or if there is time they can pass their letters around or read them out to the class.

7 Pronunciation: final consonant clusters

- Some languages contain no final consonant clusters at all, and speakers of these languages will have problems with this aspect of English pronunciation.
- Ask students to repeat the words after you or the recording.
- Then go round the room letting each student say one word in turn until you think they have had sufficient practice.
- This exercise will not be enough to help students with real problems in this area, but will serve as sensitisation so that you can work on clusters as they come up in future lessons.

8 Speeches

- Give students ten minutes or so to collect ideas for their speeches.
- They will probably need help with vocabulary, but they should not use a lot of expressions that the rest of the class will not understand.
- Let them take notes, but discourage them from writing out complete scripts.
- When they are ready, put them in groups of four or so. Each student in turn should make his or her speech to the group.
- When they have finished, each group should choose the most persuasive speech to be repeated to the whole class.
- Don't make corrections while students are making their speeches, but note mistakes for future treatment if necessary.
- Alternatively, your students may prefer to do this as a one-to-one exercise, with each student walking round and trying to convince as many other individuals as possible.

Summary

- Remind students to look at the Summary and learn the new words.

Practice Book

- Tell students which exercises you want them to do.

Tapescript for Exercise 2

(The differences are in *italics*.)

A: If I were you, I'd turn it *upside down*.
B: Well, I think I'll try it this way first.
A: I mean, –
C: Hello. I wouldn't do it like that if I were you.
B: Wouldn't you?
C: No, I think you ought to turn it *inside out*.
B: Oh, really? I'll think about it.
C: Yes. And put a *sheet of paper on top* first, or it'll get dirty.
D: Hi. Why don't you *take it to pieces*?
B: You think so?
D: Oh, yes. And remember to cover it, or it'll get *dusty*.
B: Get *dusty*?
A: You really ought to *put* the wheels *on* first, you know.
B: Well, I –
E: I think it would be much better if he turned it back to front, don't you?
A: That's just what I *was thinking*.
D: Don't forget to *undo* all the screws.
C: You're not getting anywhere like that.
D: If I were you, I'd *give up and go home*.
C: And I still think you should turn it *inside out*.
E: Let's help him.
B: It's quite all right. I can do it by myself, thank you very much.
E: No, it's no trouble.
A: Come on, everybody.

6 Four friends wrote to Christine asking for advice. Here are bits of their letters and bits of her answers. Match the problem to the answer.
Then work in groups: imagine one of the situations and invent the rest of Christine's letter. Try to use some of the expressions you have learnt in this lesson.

has ever been in trouble with the law before

the only time I've been interested in another man, and it's finished now. Should I tell Steve or

parents just don't understand. Just because he's younger than me, they think

must be drugs. She won't talk to us about it, and we don't know who to

you, I would go to the family doctor immediately

were you, I wouldn't say anything to him. I've known him since long before you were married,

as bad as it seems. If you can't afford a good lawyer, she ought to be able to get one free by

Why don't I talk to your mother? Perhaps her feelings wouldn't get in the way so much if I spoke to her

7 Pronunciation. Say these words.

1. ask   asks
2. ghost   ghosts   post   posts
3. find   finds   mend   mends   sound   sounds
4. tap   taps   envelope   envelopes
5. bank   banks   drink   drinks
6. aunt   aunts   invent   invents
7. tap   tapped   hope   hoped   help   helped
8. like   liked   work   worked   sack   sacked
9. isn't   doesn't   wasn't   hasn't
10. hadn't   wouldn't   couldn't   shouldn't

8 Prepare a short speech (maximum two minutes). In your speech, you must try to make other students do something. For example: stop studying English; leave the room; give up smoking; become vegetarians; change their religion; give you a lot of money; buy you a car; change their jobs.

Technology

A Electricity

1 Look at the pictures. Do you know the names of some of these things? Work in groups of three or four and try to list as many as possible.

2 In all of these words, the last syllable is pronounced /ə/. Look at the spellings. Then say the words after the recording or your teacher.

heater   cooker   computer   calculator
transistor   mirror   similar   sugar
centre   theatre   departure   figure
there   here   where   hear   wear   hair
their   Africa   cinema   idea   visa

3 If you could have just five of the things in the picture (plus leads, plugs and sockets), which would you choose? Which five are the least important?

4 Which of the things in the picture can you see now? Which of them are somewhere else in the building?

5 Look at the pictures below and listen to the recording. Which thing is described in each sentence? Example:

It's plugged in and switched on. It's black and white.

The radio.

Unit 21: Lesson A

Students learn to talk about everyday electrical appliances.
Principal structures: *must, mustn't, should, shouldn't*; phrasal verbs; *which* (*of*) (interrogative).
Words and expressions to learn: *plug in; unplug; turn up; turn down*; the names of some everyday electrical appliances.
Phonology: various spellings of the vowel /ə/ in final unstressed syllables.

Language notes and possible problems

1. Must and must not   Here students practise the use of *must* to talk about actions which are considered very important or necessary. Note that *must not* expresses negative obligation, not the absence of obligation. German speakers, among others, will find this confusing (the German expression *ich muss nicht* means *I don't need to*, not *I mustn't*).

2. Must and should   Note that there is not always a very clear difference between these two verbs. *Must* expresses a stronger degree of obligation than *should*, but the choice of verb may depend on the speaker's attitude rather than the objective facts.

3. Phrasal verbs   Note that *switch on/off, turn up/down* and *plug in* are phrasal verbs – the particle (*on/off* etc.) follows a pronoun object. Compare:
    I switched the TV off.
OR *I switched off the TV.*
BUT *I switched it off.*
NOT **I switched off it.*

4. Which   *Which* occurs several times in the exercise instructions; you may like to point this out, and to explain that *which of* is used before articles, demonstratives, possessives and pronouns.
    Which is more common than *what* when we are choosing between a limited number of things.

5. Vocabulary   A good deal of new vocabulary is presented in this unit. Students should choose a reasonable number of items to learn (see Summary), but you should make it clear that they don't need to learn everything if they find it difficult.

If you are short of time
Drop Exercise 2 and/or Exercise 8.

---

1 Vocabulary: pooling information
● Students should work in groups, sharing their knowledge.
● If they do not know a word they should use a dictionary, ask other students, or ask you.
● Put on the board:
Excuse me, what's this called?
What do you call a thing for drying hair?
How do you say... in English?
How do you pronounce...?
How do you spell...?
● When students have done as much as they can, give them the answers and practise the pronunciation of the words. (Note especially *iron* (/'aɪən/.)

Answers to Exercise 1
1. tape recorder   2. record player / gramophone
3. personal stereo   4. cassette player / recorder
5. calculator   6. vacuum cleaner / hoover   7. hair dryer
8. electric kettle   9. washing machine   10. dishwasher
11. (food) mixer   12. fridge / refrigerator
13. tumble dryer   14. cooker   15. (convector) heater
16. iron   17. toaster   18. computer   19. (light) bulb
20. switch   21. knob   22. plug   23. lead (/liːd/)
24. socket   25 torch / flashlight   26. battery   27. lamp

2 Pronunciation
● Students may find it difficult to believe that all the words are pronounced /ə/ at the end.
● Play or demonstrate the first few words; try to persuade the students not to pronounce the *-r* at the end if they are aiming at a standard British accent.
● Let them try the other words themselves; give them the correct pronunciation as a check.

3 Priorities
● Give students a few minutes to make their choices and compare notes among themselves.
● Then ask them to explain their decisions.

4 Which ones can you see?
● Tell students to count the electrical appliances, leads, sockets, plugs, bulbs etc. that they can see.
● Get them to compare notes with their neighbours.
● See who can find most.

5 Listening: identifying items
● Get students to look at the picture for a moment.
● Explain *plugged in* and *switched on/off*.
● Then play the recording, pausing after each sentence while students write their answers.
● Let them compare notes, then play the recording again and discuss the answers.

Tapescript and answers to Exercise 5
1. It's plugged in and switched on. It's black and white. (*radio*)
2. It's not plugged in. It's got a three-pin plug. (*electric kettle*)
3. It's plugged in but it's switched off. It's white. (*TV*)
4. It's plugged in and switched on. It's white. (*food mixer*)
5. It's plugged in but it's switched off. It's black. (*iron*)
6. It's not plugged in. It's got a two-pin plug. (*hair dryer*)
7. It's plugged in and switched on. It's black. (*vacuum cleaner*)

6 What should you do?

- Go over the six boxed expressions.
- Explain the meanings of any expressions which are not clear.
- Make sure students understand the rule for word order in expressions like *switch it off, turn it up*.
- Go through the exercise orally, and then consolidate by asking students to write the answers to one or two of the questions.
- Note that more than one answer is often possible.

7 Grammar: *should* and *must*

- Explain (or see if students can explain) the difference between *should* and *must* (see *Language notes*).
- Make sure students understand the meaning of *mustn't* (see *Language notes*).
- Note that in many of the sentences two answers are possible, depending on how strongly people feel.
- Go through the exercise, asking students which word they think is the best in each case.

Optional activity: memory test

- Do a series of ten or a dozen actions which illustrate the expressions which have just been learnt.
- For example: switch on the light; switch on the cassette player; switch off the light; turn up the cassette player; unplug a heater; turn down the cassette player; switch on the light; plug in the heater; unplug the cassette player.
- Ask students what you did; see if anybody can remember the exact sequence.
- Get a student to do the same thing.

8 What does it cost?

- Look through the information with the students and explain any difficulties.
- Ask which electrical appliances they use regularly.
- Then get them to try to answer the first question. They will need to make a rough guess at the number of hours a week they use each appliance; they can calculate the cost by looking at the tables of information.
- (It will be more interesting if you can find out and tell them the cost of a unit of electricity in their own currency.)
- When they have done this, tell students to go round the class trying to find out the answers to the other two questions.

Summary

- Remind students to look over the Summary and learn some of the new material.

Practice Book

- Tell students which exercises you want them to do.

6 Look at the sentences and say what you should do. Use these verbs.

switch on	switch off	turn up
turn down	plug in	unplug

Example:
What should you do if you've finished using your calculator? *'Switch it off.'*

What should you do if:
1. the radio isn't loud enough?
2. the record player's too loud?
3. you see in the newspaper that there's an interesting TV programme just starting?
4. you don't want to watch TV any more?
5. the TV's on fire?
6. the cooker's too hot?
7. you want to use your calculator?
8. the iron isn't getting the creases out of your clothes?
9. the iron's burning your clothes?
10. you've finished with the iron?

7 Put in *should, shouldn't, must* or *mustn't*.

1. You .... always switch electrical appliances off when you are not using them.
2. Small children .... watch violent programmes on TV.
3. In Britain, before you start using a new electrical appliance, you .... put the right kind of plug on.
4. When you put a plug on, you .... be careful to put the wires in the right places.
5. You .... touch electrical appliances when you are in the bath.
6. When you move into a new house or flat, you .... check the electrical wiring.
7. You .... plug too many things into the same socket.
8. You .... wash white and coloured clothes separately.
9. You .... clean out the fridge from time to time.
10. You .... let the iron get too hot if you are ironing silk.
11. You .... turn your radio up loud at night.
12. In Britain, you .... buy a licence every year if you have a TV.

8 Look at the information and then answer these questions.
1. **How much would your use of electricity cost you every week if you paid British prices?**
2. **Which electrical appliance do people in the class spend the most money on?**
3. **Who spends the most on electricity?**

THE COST OF ELECTRICITY
1. Electricity is sold by the 'unit'. (You use one unit if you use 1 kilowatt [1,000 watts] of electricity for one hour, or 500 watts for 2 hours, or 100 watts for 10 hours.)
2. In Britain in 1984, one unit cost about 5p.
3. To see what you get for one unit, look at the information below.

WHAT YOU GET FOR ONE UNIT

electric blanket: 2 nights
convector heater: ½ hour
food mixer: over 60 cakes
hair dryer: 3 hours
iron: over 2 hours
kettle: 12 pints of water (7 litres)
light (100w bulb or 1,500mm tube): 10 hours
radio: 20 hours
record player: over 24 hours
fridge: 1 day

clothes dryer (tumble dryer): ½ hour
stereo: 8–10 hours
tape recorder: over 24 hours
black and white TV: 9 hours
colour TV: 6 hours
toaster: 70 slices of toast
vacuum cleaner: 2–4 hours cleaning
electric razor: 2,000 shaves.
hot water: 1 bath, 4 showers or 10 bowls of washing-up water

LARGER APPLIANCES
cooker: it takes 20–25 units to cook one week's meals for a family of four.
dishwasher: one full load uses 2½ units.
freezer: ½ unit per 10 litres per week.
washing machine: it takes 9 units to do the weekly wash for a family of four.

B It doesn't work

1 Match the objects with the problems. You can use a dictionary. The first two answers are done for you.

a. It makes a funny noise. _2,4,7,9_

b. It won't start. _4,7_

c. It won't wind on.

d. It doesn't work.

e. The dial's broken.

f. It won't record.

g. It's started going very fast.

h. It won't stop dripping.

i. One of the buttons is stuck.

j. It won't turn off.

k. I can't hear anything.

l. It smells funny.

m. There's no colour.

n. It keeps flooding.

o. There's something wrong with the engine.

p. It won't ring.

q. It's stopped.

r. It's leaking.

s. The rewind's stuck.

t. It's slow.

u. The flash won't work properly.

v. It keeps sticking.

2 Put in an infinitive or an *-ing* form.

1. My watch has stopped .... (*work*)
2. I would like .... a better stereo. (*buy*)
3. I very much enjoy .... photos of animals. (*take*)
4. Do you like .... sport on TV? (*watch*)
5. I must ask Harry .... my cassette player. (*mend*)
6. We hope .... a new car soon. (*get*)
7. I don't want .... Judy – will you do it? (*telephone*)
8. Our dishwasher keeps .... (*flood*)
9. Thanks very much for .... my bicycle. (*mend*)
10. Don't forget .... some oil in the car. (*put*)
11. I can't stand .... advertisements on TV. (*watch*)
12. We must .... the mixer back to the shop – it doesn't work. (*take*)

3 Listen to the recording. How many words do you hear in each sentence? What are they? (Contractions like *What's* count as two words.)

Unit 21: Lesson B

Students learn to talk about breakdowns and faults.

Principal structures: *start, keep* and *stop* + *...ing*; *won't* (= refuses to).

Words and expressions to learn: *flash* (on a camera); *engine*; *dial* (noun); *drip*; *record*; *wind* (verb); *flood*; *keep ...ing*; *ring*; *leak*; *rewind*; *take a photo*; *properly*; *there's something wrong with...*

Phonology: perception of unstressed syllables.

Language notes and possible problems

1. Won't   Note that *won't* is used for both people and things which 'refuse' to do what we want (see Exercise 1).

2. -ing forms   Most students will only have one form in their language corresponding to the English infinitive with *to* (as in *Do you want **to mend** it?*), the infinitive without *to* (as in *Can you **mend** it?*), and the *-ing* form (as in *Thank you for **mending** it*). Some of the most common cases are revised in Exercise 2; you may want to take the opportunity to test and consolidate students' knowledge of this point.

3. Tenses   Both simple and continuous tenses occur in Exercise 1 (compare *It makes a funny noise* and *It's leaking*). The choice will depend on whether one is complaining about a repeated problem or one that is going on at the moment; in some cases both are true and both tenses are possible. Note, however, that *smell* is a 'non-progressive' verb; we could not usually say **It's smelling funny*.

If you are short of time

Start Exercise 1 in class and leave students to finish it for homework. Drop Exercise 3.

1 Problems

● Go over the examples with the students and make sure they understand what to do.

● Check that they know what *'s* is short for in sentences *e*, *g*, *m*, *o*, *q*, *r*, *s* and *t*.

● They should realise that each object can have several things wrong with it, and that some problems can apply to more than one object.

● Let students work individually. Help them when necessary, but encourage them to rely on their dictionaries so as to practise reference skills.

● When about half the students have finished, divide the class into groups of three or four and let them compare answers.

● Then go over the answers with the whole class, practising the pronunciation of the sentences.

2 Infinitives and -ing forms

● It may be best to let students do this exercise individually, so that you can see how many people need to revise the point. If necessary, go over the main rules:

– Modal verbs like *must* are followed by an infinitive without *to*.

– Many other verbs can be followed by an infinitive with *to* (e.g. *hope, want, forget, would like*).

– Some verbs are followed by an *-ing* form, not an infinitive (e.g. *enjoy, keep, can't stand, stop*). *Like* is most often followed by an *-ing* form in British English.

– Prepositions are followed by *-ing* forms (e.g. *thank you for ...ing*).

3 How many words?

● Play the recording, stopping after each sentence while students try to decide how many words there are and what they are.

Tapescript and answers to Exercise 3
1. Can I help you? (4)
2. I've got a problem with a cooker. (8)
3. How long have you had it? (6)
4. Where did you buy it? (5)
5. What colour is it? (4)
6. I don't remember how much it cost. (8)
7. Can I bring it into the shop? (7)
8. What's your address? (4)

4 Listening for specific information

- Students hear a man telephoning a department store to complain about a pressure cooker that is not working properly.
- Begin by pre-teaching the words in the box, or let students use their dictionaries to find out the meanings.
- Then tell them that they are going to hear a phone conversation, and that they must try to write the answers to the questions as they hear them.
- Warn students that the woman's voice is rather faint, and that they will not understand everything that is said; this does not matter.
- Point out that the information in the recording will be in the same order as the questions in their books.
- Play the recording through once. There is a great deal of repetition and redundancy in the conversation, and one playing should be enough for most students to answer most questions.
- Ask them to compare their answers in groups; then check to see if there are many differences of opinion within the groups.
- If there are, play the recording again so that they can try to resolve their differences before checking their answers with you.
- You may want to play the tape a final time after checking the answers so that they can hear what they have missed.

Answers to Exercise 4
1. Yes   2. Yes   3. It won't release all the pressure when they finish cooking with it, and they can't get the top off
4. Yes   5. No   6. Yes   7. Patterson
8. East Hagbourne   9. Yes   10. About a year
11. Tower   12. About £34

Tapescript for Exercise 4: see page 183

5 Making new conversations

- Ask students to work in pairs preparing and practising their conversations.
- Go round and help as necessary.
- When students are ready, get them to perform their dialogues to other pairs (or to the whole class if time allows).
- Don't worry about mistakes: it is fluency and not accuracy which is the aim here. Only deal with mistakes which seriously interfere with communication; note others for treatment on another occasion if you wish.

Summary
- Remind students to look at the Summary and learn the new material.

Practice Book
- Tell students which exercises you want them to do.

4 Look these words up in a dictionary or ask
your teacher what they mean.

| guarantee   pressure   pressure cooker |
| receipt   release   stainless steel |

**Now listen to the telephone conversation and
answer these questions.**

1. Is the pressure cooker stainless steel?
2. Is it automatic?
3. What's the problem?
4. Is it under guarantee?
5. Can the man find the guarantee papers?
6. Does the man have the receipt?
7. What is the man's name?
8. Where does the man live: East Hagby, East
   Hadley or East Hagbourne?
9. Does the woman think she can help him?
10. How long has he had the pressure cooker?
11. What make is it?
12. About how much did the pressure cooker
    cost?

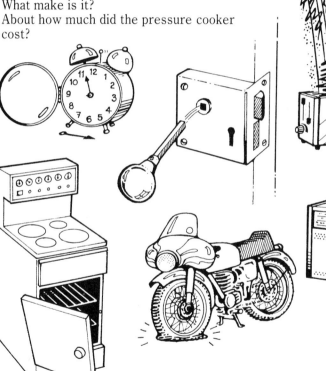

5 Work with a partner, and make up a conversation about something that has gone wrong. You
can talk about one of the things in Exercise 1, about one of the things in the pictures on this page,
or about something else if you prefer.
Use some of the expressions from Exercise 1, and some of these expressions from the telephone
conversation.

Can I help you?
I hope so.
I've got a problem with...
How long have you had it?

What make is it?
Is it under guarantee?
I'll take your name.
Thank you very much for your help.

Revision and fluency practice

A A choice of activities

> Look at the exercises in this lesson. Try to decide which of them are most useful for you, and do one or more.

LISTENING

1 Listen to the recording. You will hear some sentences with mistakes in. Answer by saying the correct sentences (below) with the right stress. Examples:

'You lost a briefcase, didn't you?'
'*No, I* **found** *a briefcase.*'

'Sally found a briefcase, didn't she?'
'*No,* **I** *found a briefcase.*'

'You found a handbag, didn't you?'
'*No, I found a* **briefcase**.'

1. No, I found a briefcase.
2. No, my mother lives in London.
3. No, it's John's birthday on Tuesday.
4. No, I'm a teacher of German and Arabic.
5. No, I live at 37 Edinburgh Road.

2 Listen to the football results and answer the questions.

1. Did Manchester City win?
2. Who lost against Swansea?
3. How many goals did Manchester United score?
4. What was the score between Liverpool and Arsenal?
5. Did Nottingham Forest play at home or away?
6. How many draws were there?

3 Try to fill in the missing words. Then listen to the song and see if you were right.

A BIGGER HEART

His arms are stronger than mine
His legs are .... than mine
His car's always cleaner
And his grass is always ....

But my heart is .... than his
And my love for you is stronger than his.

His shirts are .... than mine
His soufflés are lighter than mine
His video is ....
And his faults are fewer

But my heart is .... than his
And my love for you is stronger than his.

He's more ...., much more elegant
More charming and polite than me
He's more responsible, much more dependable
He's everything I long to be.

His office is .... than mine
His martinis are drier than mine
His roses are ....
And his overdraft is smaller

But my heart is .... than his
And my love for you is stronger than his.

SPELLING AND PRONUNCIATION

4 Do you know how to pronounce these words?

Two syllables, not three: asp(i)rin, bus(i)ness, cam(e)ra, diff(e)rent, ev(e)ning, ev(e)ry, marri(a)ge, med(i)cine.

Three syllables, not four: comf(or)table, secret(a)ry, temp(e)rature, veg(e)table, usu(a)lly.

Silent letters: shou(l)d, cou(l)d, wou(l)d, ca(l)m, wa(l)k, ta(l)k, ha(l)f, i(r)on, i(s)land, lis(t)en, (w)rite (w)rong, (k)now, (k)nife, (k)nee, (k)nock, (k)nob, dau(gh)ter, hei(gh)t, li(gh)t, mi(gh)t, ri(gh)t, ti(gh)t, strai(gh)t, throu(gh), wei(gh), nei(gh)bour, ou(gh)t, thou(gh)t, g(u)ess, g(u)ide, g(u)itar, (h)our, (h)onest, We(d)n(e)sday, san(d)wich, si(g)n.

(For a more complete list of spelling and pronunciation problems, see the Summary.)

Unit 22: Lesson A

Students practise various skills.

Language notes and possible problems

Contrastive stress (Exercise 1) Languages have different ways of emphasising a word or phrase. In English this is often done by 'contrastive stress' – by saying words louder, on a higher pitch, and perhaps more slowly. Not all students will find this easy, and practice may be necessary.

Optional extra materials

Questions for Exercise 5; cards for *Optional activity*.

1 Contrastive stress

- Look over the examples; help students to see how stress can determine meaning.
- Play the examples, and practise the three pronunciations of *No, I found a briefcase*.
- Then tell students that they will hear three or four sentences for each answer.
- Play the recording, stopping while students try to say the answers with the right stress.

Tapescript for Exercise 1

1. You lost a briefcase, didn't you?
   Sally found a briefcase, didn't she?
   You found a handbag, didn't you?
2. Your sister lives in London, doesn't she?
   Your mother works in London, doesn't she?
   Your mother lives in Manchester, doesn't she?
3. John's getting married on Tuesday.
   It's John's birthday on Wednesday.
   It's Helen's birthday on Tuesday.
4. So you're a student of German and Arabic?
   So you're a teacher of German and French?
   So you're a teacher of Russian and Arabic?
5. You live at 37 Edinburgh Street, don't you?
   Now your address is 35 Edinburgh Road, right?
   So you live at 37 Liverpool Road?
   What's your address? 27 Edinburgh Road?

2 Listening for specific information

- Look over the instructions and the questions.
- Explain that the first team mentioned in a football result is playing 'at home' (on its own ground); the second team is said to be playing 'away'.
- Mention the use of *nil* for a zero score.
- Play the recording once without stopping and tell students to answer as many questions as they can.
- Play it again once or twice if necessary.
- Let students compare notes; give them the answers.

Tapescript for Exercise 2

Football League, Division 1:
Norwich 2, Sunderland 0.
Aston Villa 3, Watford 1.
Manchester City 2, West Ham 0.
Ipswich 3, Luton 3.
Tottenham Hotspur 4, Stoke 0.
Southampton 1, Swansea 4.
Manchester United 1, Everton 1.
Brighton 2, Coventry 0.
Notts County 1, Birmingham 3.
Liverpool 0, Arsenal 2.
Nottingham Forest 3, West Bromwich 4.

3 Song

- Let students look over the text.
- Get them to guess at the missing words, individually at first and then in groups. If necessary, point out that rhyme is a clue.
- When they are ready, play the song.

Answers to Exercise 3
longer, greener, bigger, whiter, newer, bigger, intelligent, higher, taller, bigger

4 Misleading spellings

- This exercise gives a few common words with misleading spellings, which students may mispronounce.
- Go through the list section by section, asking students how they think the words are pronounced. Play the recording or demonstrate the pronunciation, and practise words which cause difficulty.
- See the Summary for a more complete list.

5 Question-box

- Write some simple questions on slips of paper – preferably questions which *can* be answered in a sentence, but about which more can be said.
- Fold the slips and put them in a bag or box. Students sit in a circle and take it in turns to draw questions, read them aloud and answer them.
- Answers may lead to discussion – several students may talk about their earliest memories, for instance.
- Help with words and structures where necessary, but don't correct if you can avoid it.
- Make sure students don't put their questions back in the box when they have answered them.
- In a large class, make two or three groups.
- For an alternative approach, see 11A Exercise 13.

Suggested questions
What is your earliest memory?   Would you like to be a bird? Why?   What did you do on your last birthday?   Do you believe in God? Why?   What is your father or mother like? Are you ever bored? How often? Why?   Where would you like to be at this moment?   Do you like living in...? Why? What do you do when you're alone at home?   What did you dream about last night?   What would you do if you only had one more week to live?   Who do you like most in the world?   Would you like to be very rich? Why?   Is it better to be beautiful or intelligent? Why?   If you were an animal, what animal would you like to be? Why?   How do you feel if you are alone for a long time?   Where would you like to live?   Do you like children? Why (not)?   Are you more awake in the early morning or the late evening?   Do you like dancing? Why (not)?

6 The *yes/no* game

- This game practises short answer forms.
- Students have one minute to answer as many questions as possible.
- They may not say *yes* or *no*, or nod or shake their heads. But they can say, for example, *I am, I do, it is, I have, she will.*
- Make sure students understand the rules; then demonstrate the game with a volunteer. (Suggested questions for demonstration purposes are given below.)
- You will need one student who has a stop-watch or a watch with a second hand, to make sure that each session lasts for exactly one minute, and a second assistant to count the number of questions answered.
- The winner is the student who answers most questions; anybody who says *yes* or *no* is out.
- Useful tricks:
1. Ask several questions about the same subject and then suddenly throw in a question that looks as if it's 'outside the game' (e.g. *Am I speaking too fast?*).
2. Ask a question-word question (e.g. *How old are you?*) and reply to the student's answer by repeating it as if asking for confirmation (*Twenty-three?*).
3. Make a remark followed by a question-tag (e.g. *Warm, isn't it?*).
- After one or two volunteers have tried it out, get groups to prepare lists of questions.
- A good way to play is to get students from group A to go to group B to be questioned, and vice versa.
- You can finish by having the whole class question you.

Demonstration questions

Are you ready?   Do you like speaking English?   How old are you?   Did you say twenty?   Really?   Have you got a watch?   You have?   Am I speaking too fast?   Are you nervous?   Do you like driving?   You haven't got a car, have you?   How did you come to school?   I beg your pardon – by bus?   How much did the ticket cost?   Really?   Would you like to have a lot of money?   It's difficult to answer without saying *yes* and *no*, isn't it?   Are you married?   Have you got any children?   *How* many?   Four?   It's cold today, isn't it?   Aren't you cold?   Can you sing?   Sing us a song.   Go on.   Would you like to?   Are you sure?   No?   Do you smoke?   Never?   How many?   Twenty?   This is difficult, isn't it?   Do you think you can go on for one minute?   Look – you see this paper?   Can you see this word here?

Optional activity: improvisation

- Prepare cards with sentences – one for each participant. (For suggested sentences, see below.)
- Ask for six to eight volunteers.
- Get them to sit in two rows facing each other.
- Tell them that they are strangers, in the same carriage on a railway journey. They must start talking and keep on for at least five minutes.
- Give each student a card (tell them not to show the cards to each other).
- They must try to direct the conversation so that they can introduce their sentences naturally.

Suggested sentences:

My father speaks ten languages.   I think her name's Barbara.   Umbrellas are very expensive.   Nobody knows what happened.   It's very good with cheese.   I was only

seven at the time.   I don't believe it.   I prefer dogs to cats.   Why would you like to go to the moon?   There are six hotels in my village.   It's not easy.   Singing makes you tired.   Scotland is full of strange people.   I would like a new one.   I'll kill him if I see him.   It was under the piano.

7 Reading strategies: dictionary use

- Some students look up every unknown word in their dictionaries. Many words that students don't know can be guessed from the context; others do not contribute very much to the meaning of a text, and can be ignored. It is important to develop the skill of 'selective reference' when learning to read in a foreign language, so that one can find out the meanings of key items without slowing oneself down (and losing the thread of the argument) by worrying about every single unknown word. This exercise helps students to think about this skill.
- The text contains seven to ten difficult words. If students can learn the meanings of four of them, they can find the money and get it away safely.
- The four words are *furlong* (= 220 yards), *beehive*, *fence* and *jiggle* (= shake).
- Students should work in groups (without dictionaries) deciding which four words to look up.
- When they are ready, ask which words they chose.
- Let them look their words up.
- Then see if they can decide where the treasure is.
- Help students to see why the four words mentioned above are essential, while others are less important.
- Explain that by choosing the right words to look up in a dictionary, one can understand the main point of a text without looking up everything one doesn't know.

8 Selective use of dictionaries: more practice

- Tell students to read the text without using their dictionaries or asking questions.
- When they have done this, ask how much they have understood – most of the text, more than half, about half, less than half, not much?
- Tell them to write down the words they don't know.
- Then tell them to underline the words which they think they can guess (more or less).
- Ask which words they think they *must* look up in order to get a reasonable understanding of the text.
- Encourage students to discuss the question, and to disagree with each other's selections if they want to.
- Then let them look up the words they have chosen.
- Finally, tell them to read the text once more.

Practice Book

- There is no Practice Book work for this unit. Students should prepare for the Revision Test.

SPEAKING

5 Question-box. Take a question out of the box, read it aloud and answer it. Say at least one sentence; if you like, you can say more. If you don't like a question, you can say *I'd rather not answer*, but you must take another question and answer it.

6 The *yes/no* game. Work in groups. One person has to answer questions for one minute; the others ask him or her as many questions as possible. The person who answers must not say *yes* or *no*.

READING

7 Use your dictionary and get rich. Look at the paper and the map, and try to decide where the money is buried. You can look up *four* words (maximum) in your dictionary. Which four words will you look up?

THE MONEY IS CONCEALED IN A BOX IN A HOLLOW TREE. THE TREE IS HALF A FURLONG NORTH-EAST OF THE LARGE BEEHIVE BY THE SOUTH FENCE. BEWARE! JIGGLE THE BOX FOR TEN SECONDS BEFORE YOU OPEN IT OR IT WILL BLOW UP.

SCALE
YARDS 0 50 100 150 200

8 Read this text and write down the words you don't know.
How well can you understand the text without looking up the words?
Can you guess what any of the words mean?
How many of the words do you *have* to look up?
Look them up and read the text again.

BLACKBEARD'S TREASURE
In the 17th century Spanish ships sailed regularly to Central and South America to fetch gold for the Spanish government. The ships were often attacked by pirates, who infested the 'Spanish Main' (the sea area north-east of Central and South America).

As the pirates could obviously not bank their stolen gold, they buried it. A famous pirate called Blackbeard, who operated on the Spanish Main from 1690 to 1710, hid his treasure somewhere on the coast of North Carolina. He then killed everyone who knew where the treasure was, and boasted 'Only the Devil and myself know the hiding place'.

Perhaps the Devil told somebody, because it seems likely that Blackbeard's treasure was dug up on Christmas Day 1928, at a place called Plum Point in North Carolina. But the gold disappeared again at once: nobody knows who found it, or where it has gone.

B What do you say when you...?

1 Here are some pairs of sentences. In each pair, the two sentences mean the same, but one is more formal than the other. Can you divide them into formal and informal?

Hello. ...... *F*
Hi. ...... *I*

How's it going?
How are you?

Can't complain.
Very well, thank you.

Goodbye.
See you.

Hey!
Excuse me.

Have you got a fiver?
Could you lend me five pounds?

Thank you very much.
Thanks a lot.

Do you mind if I smoke?
Is it OK if I smoke?

How much is that?
What do you want for that?

2 Can you match the expressions and the situations?
Example:

'Can I look round?' Shop

EXPRESSIONS	SITUATIONS
Can I look round?	Shop
I'll put you through.	Doctor's surgery
Fill up with four-star, please.	Lost property office
A single for two nights.	Thanking somebody
Single to Manchester.	Making an appointment
Check in at 9.30.	On the telephone
Second on the left.	Pub
It was green, with a red handle.	Hotel reception
That's very kind of you.	Complaining about faulty goods
I'll give you twenty-five for it.	Garage / petrol station
Pint of bitter, please.	Bank
It won't switch off.	Replying to thanks
Could we make it a bit later?	Hairdresser
How would you like it?	Airport
It hurts when I bend down.	Giving directions
Not at all.	Bargaining
Not too short, please.	Station

Unit 22: Lesson B

Students revise differences between formal and informal usage, and the language characteristic of various situations.

1 Formal and informal usage

● Students should find this exercise easy. Give them a minute or two to think about the expressions, and then let them compare notes before giving them the answers.

● In some cultures the rules governing formal and informal language are very elaborate and rigid compared with the more flexible European conventions. Students from such cultures may have problems in this area (they may worry unnecessarily, for instance, about exactly how they should speak to a teacher in English). Help them to understand the factors that determine whether we speak formally or informally.

Answers to Exercise 1

The more formal sentences are:

Hello.   How are you?   Very well, thank you.   Goodbye. Excuse me.   Could you lend me five pounds?   Thank you very much.   Do you mind if I smoke?   How much is that?

2 Situational language

● This, too, is an easy exercise. It can be done in the same way as Exercise 1. You may need to help a little with vocabulary.

Answers to Exercise 2

Can I look round? – Shop.
I'll put you through. – On the telephone.
Fill up... – Garage/petrol station. ('Four-star' petrol is the top grade generally used for cars.)
A single for two nights. – Hotel reception.
Single to Manchester. – Station.
Check in at 9.30. – Airport.
Second on the left. – Giving directions.
It was green... – Lost property office.
That's very kind of you. – Thanking somebody.
I'll give you twenty-five... – Bargaining.
Pint of bitter, please. – Pub.
It won't switch off. – Complaining about faulty goods.
Could we make it...? – Making an appointment.
How would you like it? – Bank.
It hurts when... – Doctor's surgery.
Not at all. – Replying to thanks.
Not too short, please. – Hairdresser.

3 Situational language (continued)

- This gives students a chance to see how well they know the language characteristic of various everyday situations.
- If they find the exercise interesting, let them try to find expressions for as many of the situations as possible.
- You may like to take some of the more useful situations and list the students' expressions for each one on the board.

4 Focusing on one situation

- Now students have to study one situation in detail.
- Tell them to choose the situation they wish to study, and to join up with other students who have chosen the same situation.
- Get them to think of all the things they would typically say in their own language in the situation they have chosen, and to see whether they know how to say these things in English.
- Give them whatever help is necessary.

5 Sketches

- When students have drawn up their lists, get them to prepare typical conversations for their situations.
- Let them practise the conversations (with appropriate gestures and movements).
- Then get them to perform their conversations for other groups or for the class.
- You may wish to tape- or video-record the conversations. If so, warn the students beforehand; this will encourage them to aim at a high standard.

Summary

There is no Summary for this lesson.

NOW DO REVISION TEST TWO.
(See page 167 and the Test Book.)

3 Choose five of the
situations and see if you can
think of another typical
expression for each one.

4 Work with two or three other students.
Make a list of typical expressions for one of the
situations. Your teacher will help you.
Useful questions:

How do you say...?
What do you say when...?
What's the English for...?
How do you pronounce...?
How do you spell...?
What does...mean?

5 Prepare and practise
a conversation for the
situation which you studied
in Exercise 4.

93

Feelings

A Not exactly calm

1 Match the words with the faces. You can use your dictionary.

| afraid amused angry cross |
| pleased relaxed sad |
| surprised upset worried |

2 How many different words from Exercise 1 can you use to complete these sentences?

People frown when they're...

People smile when they're...

People cry when they're...

People laugh when they're...

Unit 23: Lesson A

Students learn to talk about and practise expressing positive and negative emotions.

Principal structure: *let* + object + infinitive without *to*.

Words and expressions to learn: *mood; secret; smile; frown; build up; get over; shout; let; hide; afraid* (= frightened); *relaxed; amused; sad; easygoing; good/bad times*; other words chosen by students.

Phonology: /ə/.

Language notes and possible problems

1. Past participles are often used in English to talk about emotional reactions (*upset, amused, worried, ...*). This is not the case in all languages, and some students may have trouble on this point.

2. *Let* + object + infinitive Students should not have trouble with the concept behind this structure, though some students may confuse the meanings of *let* and *make*. You will also probably have to watch out that your students do not use a *to*-infinitive with *let*. Practice will be needed to avoid mistakes of this sort, and it is a good idea to get students to do Practice Book Exercise 1 for homework.

If you are short of time

Leave out Exercise 3 if pronunciation is not a high priority; leave out Exercise 4 or give it for homework.

Optional extra materials

Sentences on strips of paper as described in the *Optional activity* after Exercise 2; sentences and phrases on strips of paper for the improvisation alternative in Exercise 4; pictures from magazines as described in the *Optional activity* after Exercise 6.

1 Vocabulary presentation: matching

• Put students into groups of three or four, and let them pool their knowledge and use their dictionaries to match the words with the faces.

• When they have finished, check the answers. (Some variation in the answers is possible.)

Possible Answers: 1. amused   2. pleased
3. relaxed   4. afraid (*or* worried)   5. worried (*or* upset)
6. upset (*or* worried)   8. surprised   9. angry   10. cross

2 Facial expressions

• Make sure the students understand the meanings of the four verbs.

• Get them to copy the four sentence beginnings, and then let them work individually to finish the sentences in as many different ways as they can.

• Get them to compare answers with one another before checking with you.

• They may want to discuss the answers when you are checking; some variation is possible.

Possible answers to Exercise 2
People frown when they're angry, or cross, or upset, or worried, or sad, or surprised.

People smile when they're pleased, or relaxed, or amused, or surprised.
People cry when they're sad, or afraid, or upset, or angry.
People laugh when they're amused or surprised.

Optional activity

• Prepare strips of paper, each with a sentence on it in the pattern, *You've just got a* (some present) *for your birthday and you're* (some emotion). For example, *You've just got a book for your birthday and you're cross*; or *You've just got a new car for your birthday and you're very pleased.*

• Each student in turn draws a strip of paper and mimes the situation to the other students, who must try to guess both the present and the emotion.

3 Pronunciation: stress and /ə/

- Go over the example with the students and make sure they understand about word stress and resultant /ə/.
- Get them to copy the words and then try and mark them as in the example.
- Read the words or play the recording, so they can try and hear if they were right before checking their answers with you.

Answers to Exercise 3
1. amused surprised correct about
2. never even problem children

4 Expressing emotions

- Let students work in small groups to try and classify each one of the sentences and phrases in the list.
- Then check the answers with them (see below for possible answers).
- The second part of the exercise can be done as prepared sketches or as improvisations.
- For prepared sketches, put the students into groups of two to four.
- Tell them to prepare a conversation using at least two of the sentences and phrases in the list.
- If you tape- or video-record the sketches when they are ready, it will give them more of an incentive to prepare seriously.
- Walk round while they are working to give any help they need; some of their dictionaries may not help them with *build up* and *get over*.
- For improvisations, copy the sentences and phrases out on strips of paper so that there are at least as many strips as students.
- Let students each draw a sentence.
- Tell them they are all sitting in an airport waiting for their planes.
- Choose two of the more confident students and tell them they are to begin a conversation.
- Anyone can join in the conversation at any time, as long as only one person is talking at once.
- Each student must try to manage the conversation so as to be able to fit in the sentence he or she has drawn.

Possible answers to Exercise 4 (first part)
1. surprised, cross, angry
2. relaxed, pleased, surprised
3. angry, cross
4. worried, cross, afraid
5. surprised and upset, worried
6. pleased, surprised
7. surprised, amused, cross
8. cross, angry
9. afraid, worried, upset

5 Personalities: reading and listening

- Let the students work with their dictionaries, individually or in groups, to read the text and try to fill the blanks.
- Walk round while they are working to give any help they need; some of their dictionaries may not help them with *build up* and *get over*.
- Then play the recording so that they can check their answers.
- You may want to play it more than once if students are not sure of themselves the first time.

- Answer any questions students may have about the new words and expressions in the exercise.
- Practice Book Exercise 5 gives more work on the vocabulary in this exercise.

Tapescript and answers to Exercise 5
(The answers are in *italics*.)
I'm not exactly *calm*. In fact, I'm a fairly emotional person. I express my *emotions* easily, and never let them build up *inside* me. I enjoy the good times more, and get over the *bad times* more *quickly*, when I can talk or shout or *cry* about them. So the people *around* me usually know what kind of mood I'm in. Strangely enough, this *helped* me keep a secret once. I had a *problem* that *upset* me terribly, and for once I didn't want to share it with anyone. No one ever *imagined* that I was hiding *anything*!

6 Class survey (*let*)

- Point out the construction of the sentence *I never let them build up inside me* from Exercise 5; you may want to say that it is constructed in the same way as sentences with *make*, which the students are familiar with.
- Then go over the questions in Exercise 6 with the students, making sure that they understand them.
- Assign a question to each student, who should ask it of as many others as possible (getting up and walking round the room if this is feasible).
- When students have finished, ask them to report on the results of their survey. See if students can account for any differences in the reports of two people asking the same question.
- Practice Book Exercise 1 gives additional work on *let*.

Optional activity
- Find magazine pictures of people's faces – preferably unknown people, from advertisements.
- You should have a picture for every three students or so.
- Number the pictures.
- Divide the students into groups of two to four, give each group a picture, and ask them to write a few lines about what they think the person is like (using vocabulary from Exercises 5 and 6).
- Then they should pass their picture, but not their text, to another group, for them to do the same.
- Groups that finish quickly can work on a third picture.
- When the students have finished, show each picture to the class and get the two (or three) groups that have worked on it to read their texts. (The differences can sometimes be startling.)

Summary
- Tell students to study the Summary and learn the new words.

Practice Book
- Tell students which exercises you want them to do.

3 Underline the stressed syllables, and then circle the vowels that are pronounced /ə/. Say the words after the recording or your teacher. Example:

afraid

1. amused   surprised   correct   about
2. never   ever   problem   children

4 How might you feel if you said these things? Example:

What was that noise? *Surprised or afraid*

1. Where have you been?
2. Isn't this nice!
3. Damn you!
4. He should be more careful.
5. Oh dear!
6. What a lovely idea!
7. You're kidding!
8. You'd better not do that again.
9. I can't see a thing.

Now invent a short conversation using at least two of the sentences above.

5 Fill the blanks with the words from the box; you can use your dictionary. Then listen and see if you were right.

anything	around	bad times	calm
cry	emotions	helped	imagined
inside	problem	quickly	upset

I'm not exactly .... In fact, I'm a fairly emotional person. I express my .... easily, and never let them build up .... me. I enjoy the good times more, and get over the .... more ...., when I can talk or shout or .... about them. So the people .... me usually know what kind of mood I'm in. Strangely enough, this .... me keep a secret once. I had a .... that .... me terribly, and for once I didn't want to share it with anyone. No one ever .... that I was hiding ....!

6 Choose one of these questions to ask other students. Note the answers and report to the class.

Do you sometimes let small things upset you very much, or are you usually easy-going?
Do you ever let emotions build up inside you and then express them too strongly?
Do you usually let the people around you know how you feel about things?
Can you think of a time when you were very upset but didn't let anyone know?
Would you let your children know if you were very worried about something?
OR: Would you let your parents know if you were very worried about something?

B In love

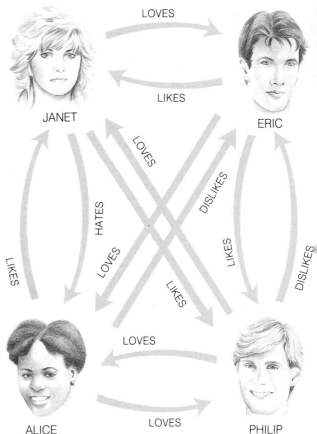

1 Who loves who? Look at the picture and answer the questions as fast as you can.

1. Who does Janet love?
2. Who loves Janet?
3. Who does Eric love?
4. Who likes Eric?
5. Who dislikes Eric?
6. Who does Eric dislike?
7. Who loves Alice?
8. Who does Alice love?
9. Who does Janet hate?
10. Who hates Janet?
11. How does Eric feel about Philip?
12. Does Philip feel the same about him?
13. Do Philip and Janet love each other?

2 Listen to the recording. You will hear Philip, Eric, Alice and Janet (not in that order). Can you decide who you are listening to each time?

3 Pronounce these words and phrases after your teacher or the recording.

1. slowly   strongly   special   stand   smell
2. slowly   as slowly   not slowly
3. special   as special   had special
4. strongly   as strongly   not strongly
5. stand   she's standing   don't stand
6. smile   this smile   that smile

"This could be difficult. They say they're all together."

Unit 23: Lesson B

Students learn to say more about interpersonal relationships and emotions.

Principal structure: *who* as subject and object in questions.

Words and expressions to learn: (radio) *programme*; *relationship*; *dislike*; *admire*; *grow* (= become); *last* (verb); *get to know*; *fond of*; *close*; *lucky*; *silly*; *guilty*; *whole*; *strongly*; *in love*.

Phonology: initial consonant clusters *sl*, *st*, *str*, *sp*, and *sm*.

Language notes and possible problems

1. Who In modern English (especially in speech and informal writing) *whom* is rarely used; *who* functions as both subject and object. Note that when *who* is the subject of a question the verb has an affirmative form; when *who* is the object the verb is interrogative. Exercise 1 helps students get used to this.

2. Reading skills Exercises 4 and 5 help students practise reading skills: getting the general meaning of a text without understanding every word, and guessing words from context. Both these skills are important for students who want to read in English, but will not know all the words they come across.

If you are short of time

Leave out Exercise 8; if pronunciation is not a high priority, leave out Exercise 3.

1 Who loves who?

● If you tell students to keep their books closed until the exercise begins, this can be done as a contest.

● Tell students to open their books, look at the illustration and answer the questions as fast as they can.

● They should write the numbers of the questions followed by the briefest possible answers.

● The winner is the first student to write all the answers correctly.

● Check the first few students to finish, to make sure they are right.

● Stop everybody after five minutes if they have not all finished yet, and let them compare notes.

● Then go over the answers with the class and answer any questions.

● Exercise 1 in the Practice Book gives more work on this point.

Answers to Exercise 1

1. Eric   2. Philip   3. Alice   4. Nobody
5. Philip and Alice   6. Nobody   7. Eric and Philip
8. Philip   9. Alice   10. Nobody   11. He likes him
12. No   13. No

2 Listening

● Tell students to look at the illustration while you play the recording.

● Explain that they have to decide who is speaking each time.

● Play the recording a second time if necessary.

● Then let students compare notes before giving them the answers.

Tapescript and answers for Exercise 2

1. I know he loves me. But he says he loves Janet too. Can you really love two people at the same time? (*Alice is speaking.*)

2. 'Mother.'
   'Yes, darling?'
   'I'm in love.'
   'Not again, dear. Who with this time?'
   'Eric, of course. He's the most wonderful man in the world. But I don't know if he loves me.' (*Janet is speaking.*)

3. I really like her; I mean, she's a very nice person. But it's not love. (*Eric is speaking.*)

4. 'What do you think of Eric?'
   'Don't like him much.'
   'No. I don't like him either.'
   'I think he fancies you, you know.'
   (*Philip and Alice are speaking.*)

3 Pronunciation: initial consonant clusters

● You may want to leave this exercise out if your students have no difficulty with initial consonant clusters.

● Otherwise, get students to repeat the words and expressions after you or the recording. They should try to make an effort not to insert a vowel before the initial *s*.

96

4 Comprehension skills

- Tell students to read the letter *without* using a dictionary, and without asking questions.
- Their task is to see how much they can understand despite the fact that some words have been left out.
- When they have finished reading, ask for a show of hands to see who has understood most, half, less than half, or not much of the text.
- Ask if they think they would understand the letter very much better if the missing words were there.

5 Words and definitions

- Tell students to read the words and their definitions. Don't give any additional explanations.
- Then tell them to look back at the text and decide which word goes in each gap.
- The exercise can be done either in groups, or individually with students comparing notes afterwards.
- When they have finished, go over the answers and give additional explanations if necessary.

Answers: 1. real   2. admire   3. relationship
4. fond   5. closer   6. lucky   7. in love   8. silly
9. silly   10. last   11. get to know   12. guilty

- Ask students if the definitions helped them to understand the meanings of all the words clearly, or if translations would have been more useful in some cases. (In a class where all the students speak the same language they may suggest the translations.)

6 Writing letters

- Explain the exercise to the students. Organise things so that roughly a third of the students are writing letters from each of the three people.
- Give them a time limit – ten minutes should be enough for them to write short letters.
- Go round helping with words and expressions where necessary, but encourage students to keep to language they have already learnt as far as possible.
- Exercise 3 in the Practice Book gives another opportunity to write a letter, for students who are weak in this area or could do with more vocabulary revision.

7 Giving advice

- Collect the letters. Tell students that they are now going to imagine they are the radio programme advisers.
- Put all the students who imagined they were Janet in Exercise 6 into one group, and give them the letters from Eric. (Or, in a large class, make two groups and divide the 'Eric' letters between them.)
- Give the 'Janet' letters to the group of students who imagined they were Alice, and the 'Alice' letters to the students who wrote letters from Eric.
- Each group has to read the letters, choose one of them and decide on what advice to give.
- Give them ten or fifteen minutes to do this. Then get each group to elect a spokesperson to tell the class what advice they have decided on.
- Get the three spokespeople to come to the front of the class and play out the radio programme (each one in turn reads a letter and then gives advice).
- Alternatively, record the spokespeople in their groups and play the final recording to the whole class.

8 Song *Trying to Love Two Women*

- (Note that this song is sung in a strong western American accent.)
- Before listening to the song, you will probably want to explain these expressions to students:
  - *ball and chain:* attached to a prisoner's leg to keep him from running away
  - *long old grind:* tiring, tedious business
  - *stock two shelves:* fill two shelves; here, satisfy two women
- Play the first verse once and ask students to tell you any words they understand.
- Put the words or phrases they guess correctly on the board in the approximate position they hold in the song.
- Play the verse again and let them see how much more they can complete; help them to guess words from context.
- If students are still interested you can deal with the second and third verses in the same way, before they turn to page 158 and listen to the entire song again.
- Answer any questions they have.
- Alternatively, if you are short of time, you may just want to play the song twice: once without looking at the words, after which the students tell you any words they have understood; and then again while they look at the words.
- Again, you will probably want to answer their questions about some of the words.

Tapescript for Exercise 8: see page 158

Summary
- Tell students to look over the Summary and learn the new words and expressions.

Practice Book
- Tell students which exercises you want them to do.

97

4 Here is a letter that Philip wrote to an advice programme on the radio. Read it without worrying about the blanks. How much can you understand – most, more than half, half, not much?

Dear Radio Helpline,

Please help me. I have got a ...1... problem. I am in love with two women at the same time!

I met Janet through my work about a year ago, and we began going out together. I love and ...2... her a lot, and would like to think we might decide to spend our lives together. We share so many things; it is a very special ...3... . She does not feel as strongly about me as I do about her, but she is certainly very ...4... of me. We have been growing ...5... over the year, and I have been hoping that she will slowly realise how ...6... we are to be together.

Then, three weeks ago, at a party, I met Alice. It was love at first sight – I feel as if I have known her all my life. She is very much ...7... with me, too. I have told her about Janet.

What should I do? My problem must sound ...8... to some people, but it is not ...9... for me. I think of both of them all the time. The feeling I have for Alice is more exciting, but will it ...10...? I haven't had the time to ...11... her very well yet. Should I just wait and see what happens? I feel a bit ...12... about the whole thing. Please help.

Yours,

Philip

5 Here are the words that go in the blanks in Exercise 4. Try to put each word in the right place. One word is used twice.

admire	You *admire* someone when you think he or she is a good person.
closer	nearer to each other
fond	If you like someone, you're *fond* of them.
get to know	learn to know well
guilty	A *guilty* person has done something wrong.
in love	When you are *in love* with someone, you want to be with them as much as possible and find them sexually exciting.
last (verb)	not stop
lucky	Someone with good luck is *lucky*.
relationship	the way in which people get on with one another
real	true
silly	the opposite of *serious*

6 Imagine you are one of the other people in the picture (Janet, Alice or Eric). You are also upset about the situation. Write a letter to the radio programme asking for help.

7 Work in groups of three or four. Prepare the radio advice programme answer to one of the letters. Don't write it down! Tell the other students, or record it for them.

8 Listen to the song. See how much you can understand, with your teacher's help.

Authority

A Government in Britain and the USA

1 Read the text without a dictionary.

HOW BRITAIN IS GOVERNED

Britain consists of four countries: England, Scotland, Wales and Northern Ireland. London, the capital, is the centre of government for the whole of Britain, but local authorities are partly responsible for education,
5 health care, roads, the police and some other things.

Laws are made by Parliament. There are two 'houses': the House of Commons and the House of Lords (which has little power). Members of the House of Commons are called MPs (Members of
10 Parliament); an MP is elected by the people from a particular area.

Parliamentary elections are held every five years or less. The leader of the majority party in Parliament becomes Prime Minister, and he or she chooses the MPs who will run the different departments of government – the ministers. The Prime Minister and the most important ministers make up the Cabinet, which is the real government of the country.

There are three main political parties: the Labour Party (left-wing), the Conservative Party (right-wing), and the Social Democrat-Liberal Alliance (centre).

Britain has a ceremonial Head of State, the King or Queen, who has no political power.

2 Read this entry from a dictionary. It gives several meanings for the word *authority*. Which of the meanings is the one used in the first paragraph of the text in Exercise 1? Which one do you think is used in the title of Unit 24?

respected store of knowledge or information: *We want a dictionary that will be an authoritative record of modern English* —compare DEFINITIVE — **~ly** *adv*
au·thor·i·ty /ɔːˈθɒrɪ̩ti, ə-‖əˈθɑ-, əˈθɔ-/ *n* **1** [U] the ability, power, or right, to control and command: *Who is in authority here?|A teacher must show his authority* **2** [C *often pl.*] a person or group with this power or right, esp. in public affairs: *The government is the highest authority in the country.|The authorities at the town hall are slow to deal with complaints* **3** [U] power to influence: *I have some authority with the young boy* **4** [U9] right or official power, esp. for some stated purpose: *What authority have you for entering this house?* **5** [C *usu. sing.*] a paper giving this right: *Here is my authority* **6** [C] a person, book, etc., whose knowledge or information is dependable, good, and respected: *He is an authority on plant diseases* **7** [C] a person, book, etc., mentioned as the place where one found certain information
au·thor·i·za·tion, -isation /ˌɔːθəraɪˈzeɪʃən‖ˌɔːθərə-/ *n* **1** [U] right or official power to do something: *I have the owner's authorization to use his house* **2** [C] a paper giving this right

(from the *Longman Dictionary of Contemporary English*)

Unit 24: Lesson A

Students learn some facts about British and American government, together with the associated lexis. They practise dictionary use and note-taking.

Principal structures: revision of simple present active and passive for processes; countable and uncountable nouns; *who* and *which*.

Words and expressions to learn: *authority; government; capital; Parliament; power; MP; area; leader; majority; party; Prime Minister; department; news; elect; local; responsible for; main.*

Language notes and possible problems

1. Countable and uncountable nouns Some students may not be very clear about the distinction, which is revised and extended in Exercise 4. Strictly speaking, it is more accurate to talk about countable and uncountable *uses* of nouns – there are several examples in the lesson of words which can be both, depending on the exact meaning (for instance *government, authority*). Look out for mistakes like **a good English, *a terrible weather, *informations, *furnitures.*

2. *Who* and *which* Students have not so far paid much attention to relative *which*. The difference between *which* and *who* may cause difficulty to students whose mother tongues do not make the distinction. Note also that in most of the sentences in Exercise 6, *who* and *which* come after commas (in 'non-identifying' clauses), and cannot be replaced by *that*.

3. Vocabulary in context Students vary very widely in their command of basic reading skills in a foreign language. Some will find it difficult to appreciate, for instance, that the meaning of a word is determined by its context, while for others the point will be self-evident. Exercises 1–3 will show whether there are problems in this area.

4. Dictionary use Students should now be losing their dependence on their mother tongues as they become more able to learn English through English. A good bilingual dictionary will continue to be an essential tool, but students should also have a good English-English dictionary. The *Oxford Advanced Learner's Dictionary of Current English* and the *Longman Dictionary of Contemporary English* are both excellent, though rather advanced. An extremely good lower-level dictionary is Longman's *Active Study Dictionary*. Not all learners are used to finding their way through dictionary entries. If your students have difficulty here, Exercise 2 provides an opportunity to give some useful information and advice.

5. Study skills: note-taking Exercises 7–9 provide an introduction to this skill for students who need it.

If you are short of time

Exercises 4–6 can be dropped if your students do not need to work on these points of grammar. Students with good reading comprehension skills may not need Exercise 3. If your students are not interested in government and/or study skills, you may wish to drop other exercises or miss out the whole lesson.

1 Reading for information

● Before starting work on the text, ask students to tell you anything they know – facts or words – about British and United States government.

● Write the words on the board as they mention them, and see how far students' contributions can be built up into a description of the two systems of government.

● Then ask students to spend five to ten minutes reading the text, without dictionaries and without asking questions.

● The text is quite difficult – there is a fair amount of new vocabulary – but students should get a reasonable idea of the meaning of most of it.

2 A dictionary entry

● If students are not used to English-English dictionaries they may find this entry initially baffling.

● Look through the entry with the class, explaining the main conventions used if necessary.

● At this stage, students need only realise that numbers are used to distinguish different meanings/uses, and that each meaning is demonstrated by an explanation followed by examples.

● When the structure of the entry is reasonably clear, ask students to decide on their answers to the question (meanings 2 and 1 respectively), and to compare notes with other students to see if they all agree.

● If students are interested, you may like to ask them what they think is meant by the various abbreviations: *n(oun), sing(ular), pl(ural), C(ountable), U(ncountable)* and *usu(ally)*. (The figure *9* after *U* in the fourth definition is a code used in this dictionary to show that a word needs to be modified by a descriptive phrase.)

● Students may also like to try to decipher the phonetic transcriptions, if they are not yet used to these. (The first transcription gives the British pronunciations, the second the American pronunciations.)

3 Alternative definitions

• In order to do this exercise students need to search the text for the words in question and see how they are used.

• It is a very simple exercise, and students with reasonable comprehension skills will probably find it too easy. It is, however, useful for students who have little experience of reading continuous text, or who find it difficult to transfer their mother-tongue comprehension skills to English.

• After students have decided on their answers to each question, see whether they all agree and give any explanations that may be necessary.

• When students have finished the exercise, tell them to read the text once more.

Answers to Exercise 3

country: 1   capital: 2   house: 3   power: 5
member: 1   hold: 2   majority: 1   run: 1
cabinet: 1   wing: 4   head: 2

4 Countable and uncountable nouns (introduction)

• Find out whether students understand the difference between countable and uncountable nouns (or uses of nouns). Make sure they realise that countable nouns have plurals and can be used with the article *a/an*, while uncountable (or mass) nouns only have singular forms and cannot be used with *a/an*.

5 Examples of countable and uncountable nouns

• Get students to list the words in the first group under the headings *C*, *U* or *B*.

• Let them compare notes before you discuss the answers with them.

Answers

C	U	B
road	education	glass
house	power	
member	water	
difference	money	
cabinet	music	
idea		
piano		

• Ask students what they think about the words in the second group. They may be surprised to learn that *travel*, *English* and *weather* are uncountable and cannot be used with *a/an*; that *information*, *luggage*, *hair* and *furniture* are not plural countable (as they are in some other languages); and that *news*, despite the final *-s*, is also singular and uncountable. They may also be confused by the fact that *money* is grammatically uncountable, since money can of course be counted.

6 *Who* and *which* (relative)

• This easy exercise can be done individually or by class discussion, as you wish.

• Give whatever explanations are necessary (see *Language notes*).

7 Introduction to note-taking

• In this and the next two exercises, students will hear a simple lecture (in three parts) on the United States system of government.

• Look over the notes and ask students what they think they mean. Explain *federation* if necessary.

• Teach the word *abbreviation*.

• Ask if students can think of ways of abbreviating the notes.

• Play the recording of the first part of the talk.

8 Completing notes

• Look over the incomplete notes and explain any difficulties.

• Get students to abbreviate the notes.

• Play the recording of the second part of the talk (more than once if necessary) and ask students to complete the notes, using abbreviations as much as possible.

• Let them compare notes with each other and then discuss the answers.

9 Taking notes

• Look at the five words listed in the exercise instructions; demonstrate the pronunciation (so that students will recognise them when they hear them) and ask students to decide on abbreviations for them (so that they can make quick notes). It is not necessary to discuss their meanings; if students do not know them already, the text will give them clear explanations.

• Play the first sentence of the third part of the talk and tell students to make a note. Write some of their notes on the board and discuss the different approaches, suggesting improvements if necessary.

• Then continue, either playing the whole of this part while students take notes (if they are fluent), or breaking it into sections and stopping after each (if they are less good at note-taking).

• They will not of course understand everything they hear; their job is simply to note what they do understand. Don't help them out by explaining things or saying the sentences more slowly for them – this would destroy the purpose of the exercise.

Tapescript for Exercises 7–9: see page 183

Summary

• Remind students to look over the Summary and learn the new material.

Practice Book

• Tell students which exercises you want them to do.

3 All of these words come in the text in exercise 1. There are two or more explanations with each word. Which explanation gives the meaning that the word has in the text?

country
(line 1)
1. land occupied by a nation
2. open land without buildings – the opposite of *town*

capital
(line 2)
1. (of letters) not small
2. town or city from which a country is governed
3. money used to start a business

house
(line 7)
1. building for people to live in
2. building made or used for some particular purpose
3. political assembly

power
(line 8)
1. ability to do or act
2. faculty of the body or mind
3. physical strength
4. energy
5. authority over people

member
(line 8)
1. one of a group
2. part of the body
3. part of a construction

hold
(line 12)
1. have in one's arm or hand
2. organise
3. believe

majority
(line 13)
1. greater number or part
2. legal age of adult responsibility

run
(line 15)
1. govern, organise, control
2. move quickly on foot
3. (of machines) work

cabinet
(line 17)
1. governing group
2. piece of furniture for storing things

wing
(line 20)
1. part of bird or aeroplane
2. part of building
3. part of car
4. category of political belief

head
(line 24)
1. part of body above shoulders and neck
2. leader; person at the top

4 Countable or uncountable? Look again at the dictionary entry. The first meaning of *authority* is marked *U* (uncountable); the second meaning is marked *C* (countable). Do you know what this means?

5 Are these words countable or uncountable (or both)?

1. road education house power member difference cabinet water glass idea money music piano

2. English information luggage news travel hair weather

6 Look at how *who* and *which* are used in the text in Exercise 1, and then complete the sentences.

1. San Fantastico, ... is the capital of Fantasia, is the centre of government.
2. The Fantasian Parliament, ... has little real power, has 300 members.
3. Our MP, ... is a woman, has a majority of 15,000.
4. Fantasia has 17 parties, ... are all very different.
5. The party .... our MP belongs to is called the New Radical Alliance.
6. The last election, ... took place five years ago, was won by the Progressive Democratic Party.
7. Cabinet ministers are the people .... really govern the country.
8. The President of Fantasia, ... is paid a very high salary, is elected for life.

7 You will hear part of a talk on the government of the United States. Before you listen, look at these notes.

US federation 50 states
48 between Canada/Mexico, + Alaska, Hawaii.
fed cap Washington, S of N Y, near E coast.

8 Now listen to the next part of the talk and try to complete these notes.

Washington centre federal govt, but each state has own...
State govts make own laws, responsible for..

9 Now listen to the rest of the talk and try to make notes yourself. (You will need abbreviations for these words: *Congress, Representatives, Senate, Democrats, Republicans.*)

B All right, I suppose so

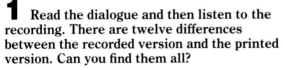

1 Read the dialogue and then listen to the recording. There are twelve differences between the recorded version and the printed version. Can you find them all?

TONY: Mum, can I have a party next weekend?

MOTHER: Well, I don't know. How many people?

TONY: About 20, I think.

MOTHER: You're not going to invite that Edwards boy, are you?

TONY: Well, –

MOTHER: Because I'm not having him in the house.

TONY: All right, Mum, Well, can I?

MOTHER: You remember what happened last time?

TONY: Oh, go on, Mum. We'll be very careful. I promise.

MOTHER: Well, all right, I suppose so. But you *must* tell me exactly how many are coming, and you *must* tidy up afterwards.

TONY: OK, Mum.

MOTHER: And do be careful of the carpet.

TONY: All right, Mum.

MOTHER: And you won't play your father's jazz records, will you? You know he doesn't like you to.

TONY: No, Mum, OK.

MOTHER: And you *must* get everybody out by midnight.

TONY: Yes, Mum.

MOTHER: And don't make too much noise, will you?

TONY: No, Mum.

MOTHER: And don't...

Unit 24: Lesson B

Students learn more about the language of requests and commands, and replies to these.
Principal structures: affirmative, negative and emphatic imperatives; reported requests and commands; question-tags after negative clauses.
Words and expressions to learn: *carpet; jazz; noise; order; delivery; part; invite; promise; tidy up; urgent; last time; I suppose so; see that...; exactly; out of the question.*
Phonology: strong and weak forms of *must.*

Language notes and possible problems

1. Imperatives Students should by now have little difficulty with ordinary affirmative and negative imperatives, but the emphatic imperative with *do* (e.g. *Do be careful*) may need a little practice. Encourage students to use it in Exercise 6.

2. Reported requests and commands Students have already worked on the structure *verb + object + infinitive* (e.g. *They want him to sign a petition*). Here they use it to report commands and requests that somebody should do something (e.g. *She told him to tidy up afterwards*). Make sure students get the right word order in reported negatives (e.g. *She told him not to invite the Edwards boy*). Students should also note that requests for permission are not reported in the same way as requests for somebody to do something (compare *He asked her if he could give a party* and *He asked her to give a party*).

3. Question-tags Students have already done extensive practice on negative question-tags (e.g. *You will do it, won't you?*). The reverse structure (*You won't do it, will you?*) should not be too difficult. Note that we use a falling intonation in requests and commands, but not necessarily in questions – compare *You won't play your father's jazz records, will you?* and *You're not going to invite that Edwards boy, are you?*

After affirmative imperatives, we often use a nonnegative tag (e.g. *will you?, could you?*) with a rising intonation.

4. *Must* and *have to* Both these verbs occur in the dialogues. It is probably enough at this level if students regard them as equivalent, though this is not quite true. (*Must* is used more often to impose or question obligation; *have to* is used more objectively to talk about obligation which already exists.) The Practice Book has an exercise on *had to* and *will have to*.

If you are short of time

Drop Exercise 2 (and miss out the last three sentences of Exercise 3). Drop Exercise 4 if your students are not aiming at a high standard of pronunciation.

---

1 Dialogue: detecting differences

● Give students a few minutes to read the dialogue and ask questions.
● Then play the recording without stopping. Ask students if they noticed any differences.

● Play it two or three more times and see if they can find all the differences (perhaps combining in groups to share information).
● Note that the differences do not substantially affect the meaning; they are simply stylistic variants or minor changes on points of detail.

Tapescript and answers to Exercise 1

TONY: Mum, can I have a party next Saturday?
MOTHER: Well, I don't know. How many people?
TONY: About 20 or so, I think.
MOTHER: You're not going to invite that Johnson boy, I hope.
TONY: Well, –
MOTHER: Because I'm not having him in my house.
TONY: All right, Mum. Well, can I?
MOTHER: You remember what happened last time, don't you?
TONY: Oh, go on, Mum, We'll be really careful, I promise.
MOTHER: Well, all right, I suppose so. But you *must* tell me exactly how many people are coming, and you *must* tidy up afterwards.
TONY: OK, Mum.
MOTHER: And do be careful of the carpet, please.
TONY: All right, Mum.
MOTHER: And you won't play your father's jazz records, will you? You know he doesn't like you doing that.
TONY: No, Mum, OK.
MOTHER: And you *must* have everybody out by midnight.
TONY: Yes, Mum.
MOTHER: And don't make too much noise
TONY: No, Mum.
MOTHER: And don't...

2 Completing a dialogue

● This can be done individually or as a whole-class exercise, as you prefer.
● A good approach is to ask students to note each answer individually and then discuss it round the class.

Tapescript and answers to Exercise 2

MR L: Er, Miss Collins.
MISS C: Yes, Mr Lewis?
MR L: I'd like *you to* do a couple of letters for me, *if* you don't mind.
MISS C: Well, er, Mr Martin has just asked *me to* do a letter for him. He says it's *urgent*.
MR L: Well, I'm *afraid* he'll *have to* wait. I've *been trying* to get these letters written all week, and they *must* go today. I *won't* keep you long.
MISS C: Right, Mr Lewis.
MR L: This letter is *to* John Barlow, at Barlow and Fletcher, in Manchester.

'Dear Mr Barlow

Thank you for your letter of April 14, in which you ask *us to* wait a further six weeks for delivery of our order. I am afraid that this is out of the question. We have already *been waiting* eight weeks *for* these urgently needed parts, and we *must* have them by the end of the *month*. If they do not arrive *by* April 30, I regret to say that we shall *have to* cancel the order and look elsewhere.

Yours sincerely

Paul Lewis'

See that that *goes* today, Miss Collins, would you?
MISS C: Yes, of course, Mr Lewis.
MR L: And now a letter to...

3 Reported commands and requests
- The first two or three sentences can be done by class discussion.
- Then get students to work individually, comparing notes when they have finished.

Answers to Exercise 3
1. Tony's mother told him *not to* invite the Edwards boy.
2. She told him *to tell* her how many were coming.
3. She *told him to* tidy up afterwards.
4. She *told him to be careful* of the carpet.
5. She *told him not to* play his father's jazz records.
6. *She told him to get* everybody out by midnight.
7. *She told him not to make too much* noise.
8. Mr Lewis asked Miss Collins *to do* a couple of letters for him.
9. Mr Barlow had *asked* Mr Lewis *to wait* six more weeks.
10. Mr Lewis *asked/told Miss Collins to* see that the letter went the same day.

4 Weak and strong forms of *must*
- Play the recording or say the sentences in both ways and let students imitate them.
- Make sure students realise the effect of using the strong form – it expresses insistence on the importance of the action referred to.

5 Choice of vocabulary
- Give students a few minutes to look through the dialogues and pick out items they think it will be useful to learn.
- Answer questions if necessary.

6 Sketches
- Students will probably need 20 minutes or so to prepare and practise their conversations. Encourage them to use the expressions they wrote down in Exercise 5.
- When they are ready, let them perform them for other groups or the rest of the class.
- You may like to tape- or video-record the performances. If so, let students know in advance: this will motivate them to aim at a high standard.

Summary
- Remind students to look over the Summary and learn the new material.

Practice Book
- Tell students which exercises you want them to do.

Next lesson
- If you are planning to do the *Optional activity* in Unit 25 Lesson A, warn students in advance that they should bring postcard or other reproductions of paintings to class.

2 Try to complete this dialogue with the words and expressions from the box. Then listen to the recording and see if you were right.

> afraid been trying been waiting by for goes have to have to if me to month must must to urgent us to won't you to

MR L: Er, Miss Collins.

MISS C: Yes, Mr Lewis?

MR L: I'd like .... do a couple of letters for me, ... you don't mind.

MISS C: Well, er, Mr Martin has just asked .... do a letter for him. He says it's ....

MR L: Well, I'm .... he'll .... wait. I've .... to get these letters written all week, and they .... go today. I .... keep you long.

MISS C: Right, Mr Lewis.

MR L: This letter is .... John Barlow, at Barlow and Fletcher, in Manchester.

'Dear Mr Barlow

Thank you for your letter of April 14, in which you ask .... wait a further six weeks for delivery of our order. I am afraid that this is out of the question. We have already .... eight weeks .... these urgently needed parts, and we .... have them by the end of the .... If they do not arrive .... April 30, I regret to say that we shall .... cancel the order and look elsewhere.

Yours sincerely

Paul Lewis'

See that .... today, Miss Collins, would you?

MISS C: Yes, of course, Mr Lewis.

MR L: And now a letter to...

3 Can you complete the sentences?

1. Tony's mother told him .... invite the Edwards boy.
2. She told him .... her how many were coming.
3. She .... tidy up afterwards.
4. She .... of the carpet.
5. She .... play his father's jazz records.
6. .... everybody out by midnight.
7. .... noise.
8. Mr Lewis asked Miss Collins .... a couple of letters for him.
9. Mr Barlow had .... Mr Lewis .... six more weeks.
10. Mr Lewis .... see that the letter went the same day.

4 Say these sentences in two ways: first with an ordinary pronunciation of *must* (/ms/) and then with an emphatic pronunciation (/mʌst/).

1. You must tell me.
2. You must tidy up afterwards.
3. You must get everybody out.
4. They must go today.
5. We must have them by the end of the month.

5 Look at the dialogues and write down ten or so expressions that you want to learn and remember.

6 Work with another student and prepare a conversation for one of the following situations. Use some of the expressions that you have learnt from the dialogue.

1. A fifteen-year-old asks his or her father or mother for permission to go on a cycling holiday abroad.
2. A boss asks his or her secretary to do something; the secretary has too much work.
3. A fourteen-year-old wants to go to an all-night party; father or mother doesn't like the idea.
4. A shop assistant asks the manager for a day off.

Note: For the next lesson (Unit 25 Lesson A) you may need to bring pictures. Ask your teacher.

Look and listen

A I don't know much about art, but I know what I like

1 Listen to the first part of the recording. Which picture do you think the people are talking about?
Now listen to the second part. Which picture are they talking about?

2 Do you like any of the pictures? Which do you like best (or least)? What kind of pictures do you like?

Unit 25: Lesson A

Students practise talking about their responses to visual stimuli.

Principal structures: adverb position in sentences; contrast between *very* and *too*; formation of words ending in *-er*; passive questions with final preposition.

Words and expressions to learn: *snow*; *leaf*; *painting*; *writer*; *director*; *actor*; *art*; *statue*; *play* (noun); *return* (verb); *modern*; *real*; *public*; *great*; *so-called*; *work of art*.

Phonology: pronunciations of the letter *r*.

Language notes and possible problems

1. Position of adverbs   Some students may have problems with the position of adverbs and adverbial phrases like *much*, *very much*, and *best*. In this lesson they learn that in English an adverb cannot come between the verb and its object; they learn to put these adverbs after the object. (*Much* and *very much* can go before the main part of the verb in some circumstances, but it is probably best to avoid sentences like *I very much like that painting* for the moment.)

2. Too   Not all languages have two different words corresponding to *too* and *very*. You may need to help students to see the difference. Point out that *too* has a kind of comparative meaning: it suggests *more than we want*, or *more than is good*, or a similar idea.

3. Pronunciation of the letter r   In standard southern British English pronunciation (often called 'RP' or 'received pronunciation'), the sound /r/ is only made before a vowel. In words where the letter *r* is written before a consonant or at the end of a word, either no sound is pronounced for this letter or it is realised as /ə/. (Compare *red* /red/, *hurry* /'hʌri/, *arm* /ɑ:m/, *fire* /faɪə/.) Students often tend to pronounce every *r* that is written. Note, however, that this is not an important problem; students will still be understood perfectly well if they pronounce *r* when they shouldn't. (Indeed, in most varieties of English other than 'RP', including standard American, *r* is pronounced whenever it is written.) You may also want to point out that *rr* is pronounced in exactly the same way as *r*.

Optional extra materials

Art postcards for the *Optional activity* after Exercise 2.

If you are short of time

If the difference between *very* and *too* does not present a problem for your students, leave out Exercise 4. If pronunciation is not a high priority, you can leave out Exercise 6. You can leave out Exercise 7 and/or Exercise 8.

1 Which picture?   📼 Ⓐ

- Give students a moment to look at the three pictures.
- Play Part 1 of the recording (the first four speakers). Pause after each person speaks and ask the students for their guesses as to which picture is being discussed.
- Don't tell them the answer at this stage if they haven't guessed it, and don't tell them if their answers

are wrong or right; but let them listen to the four speakers again if they wish.
- Deal with Part 2 of the recording in the same way.

Tapescript for Exercise 1

PART 1

1. I've gotta like it, there's that much on it to see that you, you've gotta, you've gotta like it, you could study it for ages...
2. Oh, I like this very, very much, because it's so active. It's got an older atmosphere too, which is nice.
3. It's very well presented, plenty of depth, nice contrasts in colour, in fact, I like it, yeah... And it, and it gives the impression of being very cold, even, even up here.
4. Well, I don't like the winter very much for a start, and this, I like the winter if, if it's cold and crisp and sort of skiing and what-have-you. This is sort of dirty and dingy to me. Um, you know, they don't seem to be having much fun, do they?

PART 2

1. It's not a style of painting I like a lot. Um, I kind of agree with Pat, I think it was, that you said it was, um, too stylised? (*Yes, or, angular, er, ...*) Too angular and distorted.
2. I like this one because it's er, I think it portrays the character well. There's depth and feeling in the painting, and I like that.
3. I don't like this one so much, because they're very, very sharp features, I mean, everything seems to be, um, exaggerated. The nose is terribly long. All the features are angular (*Yeah*), and it doesn't appeal because of that.
4. This lady, I don't much care for the painting generally. Er, the painting itself is very dull, and the lady herself is very dull. Not too impressed.

2 Discussion

- Ask students for their reactions to the pictures. They may want to know something about them. They are:
  - *Winter Scene with Skaters*, by the Dutch painter Hendrick Avercamp (1583–1634). The painting is in the National Gallery, London.
  - *Youth Leaning against a Tree among Roses*, by the English painter Nicholas Hilliard (1547–1619). The painting is in the Victoria and Albert Museum, London.
  - *Portrait of the Journalist Sylvia von Harden*, by the German artist Otto Dix (1891–1969). The picture is in the Musée d'Art Moderne, Paris.
- If students are interested, get them to talk about pictures, painters and galleries that they like.
- To generate more discussion, you may like to bring reproductions of other pictures into class and get students to talk about them. (See *Optional activity*.)

Optional activity: discussing pictures

- Bring postcard reproductions (or slides) of some other pictures into the classroom – as wide a variety as possible.
- Get students to work in groups. Each group should have several pictures to talk about. Get them to exchange reactions, saying what they like, what they don't like, and if possible why.
- When they have said all they want to about their pictures, tell them to exchange pictures with another group.
- You may like to put on the board some useful words and structures for expressing likes, dislikes and preferences. For instance:

I like...very much.
1 quite like...
I don't much like...
I really like...
I can't stand...
I don't understand...
1 like...better than...
I prefer...to...
I like...best.
...is my favourite painter.
I think...is wonderful/terrible/interesting/etc.

3 Position of adverbs
● Go over the examples with the students. If they are used to grammatical terminology, you may want to tell them that the adverb or adverb phrase cannot separate the verb from its object.
● Then ask the students to work individually to try and put the sentences in order.
● Let them compare answers before checking with you.
● Practice Book Exercise 1 gives more work on the position of adverbs.

4 Very and too
● Give students a few minutes to work on the exercise individually, writing down their answers. Walk round while they are working to make sure no one is having too much difficulty.
● Then go through the exercise asking for volunteers to answer.
● After the first few sentences, you may like to stop and see if students can explain the difference between *very* and *too*.
● Practice Book Exercise 2 gives additional work on *very* and *too*.

5 Word formation with *-er* and *-or*
● Get students to try the matching exercise by themselves to start with; they can use their dictionaries.
● When they have finished, let them compare notes in groups.
● Explain any language problems and practise the pronunciation of the words. (Discourage students from pronouncing the *r* at the end of *composer, potter,* etc.)
● Point out that three of the words are spelt with *–or,* but tell students that most words of this kind are spelt with *-er.*
● Go on with the rest of the exercise.
● Finish by asking students if they can think of any other words of the same kind. (They ought to be able to suggest *teacher,* if nothing else.)
● It may be worth pointing out that it is not always possible to form a noun referring to a person who does something by adding *-er* to the verb. (For instance, a person who types is a *typist,* not a **typer,* and a *cooker* is not a person.)

6 Pronunciations of letter *r*
● Students may not realise that *r* is only pronounced before a vowel (see *Language notes*).
● Give them a minute or two to try to decide which are the words in which *r* is pronounced.

● Then play the recording or say the words.
● Let students compare notes and then tell them the answers.
The words are: pottery, runs, hurry, real, try, foreign
● See if students can work out the rule.
● Go on with the rest of the exercise. Students should note that *r* is not pronounced in the ending *-ered* (because there is no *pronounced* vowel after *r*); and that a final *r* may be pronounced before a following word that begins with a vowel (as in the second group of expressions with *painter*).

7 Quiz
● This exercise practises a form which many students find difficult: most languages do not have clauses ending with prepositions.
● It can be done as a competition, with the class divided into two teams.
● Give students a few minutes to prepare questions.
● Help them with vocabulary if necessary, but discourage them from preparing questions which other students will not understand.
● Get the students to decide on a scoring system before they start.
● Practice Book Exercise 3 gives more work on passive questions ending in *by.*

8 Discussion
● Divide the class into groups of four to six.
● Explain that in each group, each student must choose one statement to be responsible for. This means that he or she must make sure that everyone else in the group expresses an opinion on the statement.
● Walk round while students are working to give any help that is needed, but do not correct their English at this time. You can note down common or important mistakes to work on in a later class.

Summary
● Remind students to study the Summary and learn the new words.

Practice Book
● Tell students which exercises you want them to do.

3 Look at these sentences.

I like modern painting very much.
  (NOT ~~I like very much modern painting.~~)
I like the Hilliard picture best.
  (NOT ~~I like best...~~)
I don't like bright colours much.
  (NOT ~~I don't like much...~~)

Now put the words in order to make sentences.

1. painting much Otto Dix like the very I .
2. best snow I picture the like .
3. don't picture I this much like .
4. much the picture man don't of I like the very young .
5. I colours the Hilliard the much picture like in very .

4 Put in *very* or *too*.

1. I think Sylvia von Harden's face is .... interesting.
2. I don't like the colours in the picture of the woman; they're .... strong.
3. There are some .... amusing people in the snow picture.
4. The leaves and the clothes in the Hilliard picture are .... well painted.
5. The Avercamp picture has .... many things happening in it; it's not easy to look at.
6. A lot of modern painting is .... abstract for me; I like pictures of real things and people.

5 Match words from the two columns.

statues   composer
plays   potter
films   writer
music   actor
books   sculptor
pottery   director
pictures   painter

Can you find words ending in -er for the following?

a person who drives
somebody who dances
a person who climbs
a person who builds houses
somebody who looks after a garden
somebody who plays football
a person who sings
somebody who runs
somebody who cleans

6 Pronunciation. The letter *r* comes in all of these sixteen words. In standard British English, *r* is only pronounced in six of the words. Which six?

picture   potter   pottery   painter   runs
hurry   first   part   far   real   try   word
fourteen   foreign   tired   modern

Pronounce these words and expressions.

ordered   wondered   answered   preferred
remembered   covered   mattered

painter has   painter takes   painter makes
painter leaves   painter covers
painter asks   painter empties
painter isn't   painter orders
painter understands

7 Work in groups. Write ten questions ending in *by* about books, films, music, etc. Then test other students. Examples:

'Who was **The Third Man** directed by?'
'Who was **Tom Sawyer** written by?'
'Who was **Carmen** composed by?'

8 Work with three or four other students. Choose one of the statements below. You must make sure that all the other students in your group express their opinions on the statement you have chosen.

1. If a painting is really good, you don't have to be educated to like it.
2. A lot of so-called 'great art' is rubbish.
3. Too much public money is spent on art museums.
4. No individual should be able to own a great work of art.
5. The statues and other works of art that have been taken from places like Greece and Nigeria should be returned to them.
6. A great photograph can be as fine a work of art as a great painting.

B Quite a choice

Dolly Parton

1 Try to fill the blanks with words from the box. Then listen to the recording and see if you were right.

about	at	but	don't	for
	let's	one	then	

A: Where shall we go, ...?
B: How .... a concert?
A: OK. .... see what's on near here. Here we are. We've got quite a choice. Bach, Haydn and Mozart; or Stravinsky; or Ewan MacColl – he's a folk singer, isn't he?
B: Yeah.
A: Or Dolly Parton.
B: Which .... do you prefer?
A: Don't mind, really. I'm not mad about country and western, ... otherwise I'm easy.
B: What about Stravinsky, then – I haven't heard any Stravinsky .... a long time.
A: OK. It's .... eight, so we've got plenty of time.
B: Great. Why .... we have a drink somewhere first?

Now choose four or more useful words or expressions from the dialogue. Write them down.

2 Listen to the recording. You will hear three songs: *The Riddle Song, Logger Lover* and *What Did You Learn in School Today?* Copy the table and mark your reactions to each song ($\sqrt{}$ = like; χ = dislike; $-$ = no opinion).

	Tune	Words	Singer
Riddle Song			
Logger Lover			
What Did You...			

Compare your reactions with another student's. Examples:

*'I like **Logger Lover** best.'*
'I like the tune.'
'I think the words are silly.'
'I can't stand it.'
'I don't like the singer's voice.'

Unit 25: Lesson B

Students continue to practise talking about preferences. They study a song.

Principal structures: *How about...?*; *What about...?*; *Why don't...?*; interrogative *which* and *what*; *the one/ones.*

Words and expressions to learn: *tune*; *voice*; *verse*; *concert*; *stairs*; *folk (music)*; *mad (about)*; *sentimental*; *lonely*; *then (= in that case)*; *what's on*; *Here we are. (= Here it is.)*; *quite a*; *otherwise*; *What about...?*; *plenty of.*

Phonology: pronunciation of vowel + *r* combinations; rising intonation signalling a question.

Language notes and possible problems

1. Songs In Exercise 2 students listen to three songs; they choose a song to study in depth in Exercise 3. You may want to choose three songs that are more suitable for your students, if you think they will not like any of those chosen for the book.

2. *Which* and *what* The rules for distinguishing interrogative ***which*** and ***what*** are very complicated. For the purposes of Exercise 5, students simply need to learn that *which* is usually used when we are selecting between a small number of alternatives (e.g. ***Which*** *of the three songs do you prefer?*), while *what* is used when the choice is wider (e.g. ***What*** *sort of music do you like?*).

If you are short of time

You can leave out Exercise 7 if pronunciation is not a priority for your students; you can shorten Exercise 4 by simply letting students listen to the song they have chosen again, without studying it.

Optional extra materials

Recordings and copies of words of songs, if you want to replace the songs in Exercises 2 to 4 with something else. Extra cassette players, if you want the students to work in groups for Exercise 4.

1 Dialogue

- Give students a few minutes to try and put the words in the correct blanks.
- Let them compare answers before playing the recording through once without stopping.
- Ask them if they want you to play the recording again before checking the answers.

Answers: then, about, Let's, one, but, for, at, don't

- Call for questions on any points that the students do not understand. If the following do not come up in the question period, you may want to point them out:
  – *Then* in the first sentence means *in that case.*
  – *Here we are* in this situation means *Here it is.*
  – *Quite a* means *a very big.*
- Then get each student to choose four or more useful words or expressions from the dialogue and write them down. Walk round while they are working to give any help that is needed.

- Practice Book Exercise 3 revises the vocabulary from this exercise.

2 Reacting to songs

- Get students to copy the table, and explain how they are to fill it in.
- Then play the three songs through without stopping.
- After going over the example sentences with them, and getting two or three students to tell the class some of their reactions, put the students into pairs to compare reactions.

3 Choosing a song

- Divide the class into groups of three to five.
- Each group must decide which song they would like to hear again. They can look at the words on pages 158–159. Remind them to try and use some of the words and expressions they wrote down in Exercise 1.
- Walk round while they are working to give any help that is needed.

4 Studying a song

- If you have access to a number of cassette players and sufficient copies of the cassette, you may want to let the groups from Exercise 3 each work on the song they have chosen.
- Otherwise get the groups to report on their choices, and decide which of the songs is most popular.
- The song(s) should be played again while students follow in their books.
- Students can ask you or use their dictionaries for help with unfamiliar words.
- Depending on the song, students may want to sing along with the recording when they have understood everything.
- Some notes on the songs:
  The Riddle Song is a traditional American folk song. The word *pipping* in the last verse refers to the 'peep-peep-peep' sound that young chicks make. Presumably the soft cartilage of young chicks was not considered as bone.
  Logger Lover is an American or Canadian song, here in an adapted version. A *logger* is a man who cuts down trees for a living; a *mackinaw* is a sort of heavy jacket.
  What Did You Learn in School Today? is a highly ironical modern song by the American singer Tom Paxton. Reference is made in the second verse to the fact that capital punishment still exists in the United States.

5 *Which* or *what*

- Discuss the answers to the first two questions.
- See if students can work out the difference between *which* and *what*; if they cannot state the difference clearly themselves, explain it to them (see *Language notes*).
- Carry on with the exercise, orally or in writing, as you prefer.
- Practice Book Exercise 1 gives more work on *which* and *what*.

6 *One/ones*

- Get students to do the exercise individually, and then to compare answers with each other before checking with you.
- Point out that *one/ones* is used somewhat as if it were a noun: it can be used with articles and other determiners; it can be preceded by an adjective or followed by a modifying phrase.
- Practice Book Exercise 2 gives more work on this point.

7 Pronunciation: vowel + *r*

- Play or say the words in each group and get students to imitate them.
- Make sure they realise that all the words in each group are pronounced with the same vowel.
- Some students may need to practise the distinction between /eə/ (group 3) and /ɪə/ (group 4).
- Note that spelling is not a good guide to pronunciation in the last three groups: *ere* can be /eə/, /ɪə/, or /ɜ:/; *ear* is usually /ɪə/, but can also be /ɜ:/; *or* is sometimes /ɜ:/.

8 Intonation

- A rising intonation can show that a word or expression is used interrogatively.
- If students listen carefully to the recording, they should be able to add question marks to the conversation, at which point it will start to make sense.

Tapescript for Exercise 8

1. PETER: John?
2. JOHN: Peter.
3. PETER: Tired?
4. JOHN: Tired.
   Thirsty.
6. PETER: Drink?
7. JOHN: Beer.
8. PETER: Music?
9. JOHN: Yes.
10. PETER: Good day?
11. JOHN: Terrible.
12. PETER: Problems?
13. JOHN: You know Jake?
14. PETER: Jake?
15. JOHN: Jake Lewis.
16. Friend of Janet's.
17. PETER: Well?
18. JOHN: His wife.
19. PETER: Mary?
20. JOHN: Mary.
21. PETER: Yes?
22. JOHN: More beer.
23. PETER: Yes?
24. JOHN: She's mad.
25. PETER: Mad?
26. JOHN: Mad.
27. Listen...

Summary

- Tell students to look over the Summary and learn the new vocabulary.

Practice Book

- Tell students which exercises you want them to do.

3 Work in groups. Decide on one of the three songs that you would like to hear again. Speak English! You can use some of the words and expressions from Exercise 1.

4 Listen to one of the songs again. Study the words; use a dictionary or ask questions. (The words are on pages 158–159.)

5 Grammar. Put in *which* or *what*.

1. .... of the three songs do you prefer?
2. .... sort of music do you like?
3. .... time is the concert?
4. We can listen to the record now or after dinner – .... do you prefer?
5. ....'s your favourite sort of music?
6. If you could play the piano, the violin or the trumpet, ... instrument would you choose?
7. 'Your sister came and borrowed your new record.' '............ sister – Liz or Judy?'

Ewan MacColl

6 Match the questions and the answers. Some answers can go with more than one question.

Which guitar is yours?
Which seats are ours?
Which room do you practise in?
Which is your favourite song?
Which record shall I put on?
What sort of songs do you like?

Sentimental ones.
The one by the stairs.
The new one.
The biggest one.
The one about being lonely.
The ones near the front.

7 Pronunciation. Say these words.

1. guitar Mozart Parton mark start
2. your record sort four more born
3. stairs compare where there share
4. here near hear beer we're ear
5. word work world heard learn early certain hers weren't bird shirt skirt girl turn fur

8 Write down this conversation. Listen to the recording and decide where to put the question-marks (?).

1. John.
2. Peter.
3. Tired.
4. Tired.
5. Thirsty.
6. Drink.
7. Beer.
8. Music.
9. Yes.
10. Good day.
11. Terrible.
12. Problems.
13. You know Jake.
14. Jake.
15. Jake Lewis.
16. Friend of Janet's.
17. Well.
18. His wife.
19. Mary.
20. Mary.
21. Yes.
22. More beer.
23. Yes.
24. She's mad.
25. Mad.
26. Mad.
27. Listen...

Different kinds

A Animals and man

1 Do you know the names of some of these?
Work in groups, and try to match as many of
the words and pictures as possible.

backbone bat dinosaur dog eagle frog insects shark shell skeleton snake tiger trout whale

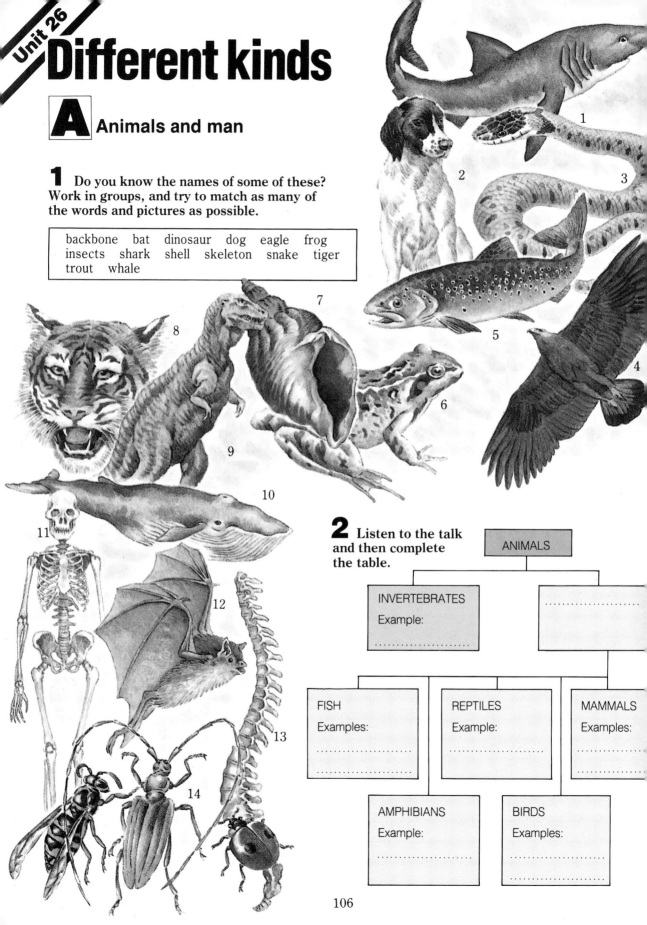

2 Listen to the talk and then complete the table.

ANIMALS

INVERTEBRATES

Example:

....

....

FISH

Examples:

....

....

REPTILES

Example:

....

MAMMALS

Examples:

....

....

AMPHIBIANS

Example:

....

BIRDS

Examples:

....

....

Unit 26: Lesson A

Students learn the language of classification by studying the structure of the animal kingdom.
Principal structures: *although*-clauses.
Words and expressions to learn: *insect; skeleton; backbone; belong; typical; related to; divided into; except for; in many ways.*

Language notes and possible problems

1. Vocabulary It is important for students to understand that their task is to learn the language of classification, not the names of the different classes and kinds of animals. Students who are interested can of course do so, but make it clear that they don't have to memorise words like *mammal* or *trout* unless they particularly want to.

2. Although Students whose languages are very different from English may have difficulty in constructing complex sentences with subordinate clauses, especially when the conjunction comes at the beginning of the sentence. Look out for mistakes like **Although she was tired, but she went out.*

3. Pronunciation of although Students may have difficulty in saying the word correctly, and in distinguishing it from *also*. Make sure they realise where the stress comes in each word: *although* is pronounced /ɔːlˈðəʊ/; *also* is /ˈɔːlsəʊ/.

If you are short of time

Exercises 3–5 can be done for homework. Exercise 4 can be dropped if your students find it easy to make sentences with *although*.

1 Preteaching (matching exercise)

● This exercise helps students to get used to some of the words that will come up in Exercise 2.
● Let them try the exercise on their own first; then get them to work in groups pooling their knowledge.
● Finally, discuss the answers with the whole class, and practise the pronunciation of the new words.

2 Listening practice

● Play the recording through once, without stopping and without giving any explanations.
● See if students can fill in some of the spaces in the table.
● Play the recording again (twice if necessary), and get students to try to complete the table.
● Let them compare notes and then tell them the answers.
● Answer questions and explain problems.

Answers to Exercise 2

Example of invertebrates: *insects.*
Right-hand main heading: *vertebrates.*
Examples of fish: *trout, shark.*
Example of reptile: *snake.*
Examples of mammals: *bat, whale.*
Example of amphibian: *frog.*
Examples of birds: *eagle, duck.*
(Students may of course think of other examples of their own.)

Tapescript for Exercise 2

There are many different kinds of animals in the world. About 95% of them are invertebrate – that is to say, they do not have internal skeletons with backbones. Many invertebrates have shells; others have external skeletons. So these invertebrates are soft inside and hard outside. Invertebrates include insects, which make up 80% of all the animals in the world. We know of about one million different kinds of insects, and scientists think that there may be the same number still waiting to be discovered.

About 5% of the world's animals are vertebrates. Vertebrates are soft outside and hard inside: they have internal skeletons with backbones. The main groups of vertebrates are fish, amphibians, reptiles, birds and mammals. Fish – which live in water – are the largest group. Examples of two kinds of fish are trout and sharks. Not all vertebrates that live in water are fish. Whales, for instance, are mammals, although they look very like fish. Amphibians live between land and water – a frog is a typical amphibian. Reptiles – for example snakes – are cold-blooded animals which live on land. For 160 million years large reptiles – dinosaurs – were the most important animals on the earth. Birds are like reptiles in many ways, but they are warm-blooded. They are the only vertebrates which can fly, except for bats. (Although they look rather like birds, bats are actually mammals.) There are big differences between different kinds of birds; compare an eagle with a duck, for example.

Mammals are warm-blooded, like birds. But unlike birds, mammals do not lay eggs. They grow their babies inside them, and when the babies are born, their mothers feed them on milk.

3 Vocabulary

● This exercise helps students to activate some of the 'classifying' vocabulary that has been presented. It is probably best to ask students to write some of the answers. The rest can be done orally.

4 *Although*

● Look through the examples, and make sure students understand how *although* is used (especially if they do not have a conjunction in their language(s) which is used in the same way).

● Practise the pronunciation of *although* if necessary.

● Ask students to write the answers to the first two questions, and check to see whether everybody has got them right.

● Then continue orally or in writing, as you prefer.

● Further work on *although* is given in the Practice Book.

5 Building up a text

● This exercise gives more practice in the use of 'classifying' language. At the same time, students try to solve some of the problems involved in putting sentences together into a coherent text.

● The exercise can be done either individually or in groups.

● Students must start by choosing a subject. If anybody 'can't think of anything', make some suggestions (for example cars, houses, people, women, men, teachers, vegetables, jobs, computers).

● You will probably need to walk round helping students with vocabulary, and making sure that their sentences fit together sensibly.

Summary

● Remind students to look over the Summary and learn the new material.

Practice Book

● Tell students which exercises you want them to do.

3 Complete the sentences with words and expressions from the box.

all	although	are related	be divided	belong	different
except for	for example	in many ways	kinds	main	most
only	or	others	several	typical	

1. There are two .... of bank account: current and deposit.
2. Chinese looks like Japanese, but actually the two languages are very ....
3. British and American people are like each other ....
4. Some birds – .... robins – eat insects.
5. .... bats can fly, they are not birds.
6. Dogs can .... into two kinds: those that .... to wolves and those that are more like jackals.
7. Spaghetti is a .... Italian food.
8. Not .... people who live in the United States speak English.
9. February is the .... month that has 28 days.
10. Cows .... to a group of mammals called herbivores, ... grass-eaters.
11. .... birds can fly.
12. There are .... different kinds of bicycles.
13. All European languages belong to the same family .... Finnish, Hungarian, Basque and one or two ....

4 Make sentences with *although*. Examples:

Whales look like fish, but they are mammals.
'*Although whales look like fish, they are mammals.*'

Bats can fly, but they are not birds.
'*Although bats can fly, they are not birds.*'

1. She's a famous actress, but she's very shy.
2. I understand your feelings, but I don't agree with you.
3. It was very late, but we went out.
4. I like my work, but I prefer doing nothing.
5. China, Russia, and Cuba are all communist countries, but their systems of government are very different.
6. It was raining, but we decided to go for a walk.

5 Complete four or more of these sentences and put them together to make a text. (You can change the order of the sentences, and you can make other small changes if you like.)

1. There are .... kinds of ....
2. Most of them are ...., but some are ....
3. .... look like ...., but actually they are very different.
4. .... is a typical ....
5. .... belong to a group of .... called ....
6. The difference between .... and .... is that .... is/are ...., while .... is/are ....
7. .... is/are like .... in many ways.
8. .... is/are not at all like ....
9. All .... are ...., except for ....
10. Most .... can ....
11. .... is/are like ...., because ....
12. .... is/are like ...., although ....

B It's a good one

1 Listen to the conversation. It is about one of the things in the box. Each time the conversation stops, say what you think. Examples:

'It might be a baby.'
'It could be a fridge.'
'It can't be a piano.'
'It must be a tree.'

baby	dog	canary	house	garden
flower	tree	car	statue	bookcase
piano	wardrobe	electric typewriter		
table	fridge	piece of beef		

2 Make up similar conversations in groups. See if the other students can work out what you are talking about.

3 Stress. Look at the pictures and listen to the sentences. There are some mistakes in the sentences. Can you correct them? Make sure you use the right stress. Example:

'It's ten past two.'
'No, it isn't. It's ten past **three**.'

Unit 26: Lesson B

Students practise describing, classifying and contrasting; they revise some common vocabulary areas.

Principal structures: revision of modals *might*, *could*, *can't* and *must* (used to express degrees of certainty); revision of *a...one*.

Words and expressions to learn: *bookcase; wardrobe; mouse; camel; lion; cow; India; China; France; Egypt; Israel; strawberry; grape; peach; armchair.*

Phonology: contrastive stress; weak and strong forms.

Language notes and possible problems

Weak and strong forms Students have already done a little work on the weak and strong forms of some words. When they do Exercise 4 you may like to tell them a little more about weak and strong forms. There are quite a number of words – about fifty – which have two different pronunciations, depending on whether they are stressed or not. They are 'grammatical' words: pronouns, prepositions, auxiliary verbs and conjunctions. Most often they are unstressed, and so the 'weak form' is much more common than the 'strong form'. Most students tend to overuse the strong form, which is pronounced with the written vowel. (Weak forms usually have /ə/ or no vowel at all.)

Examples of words with weak and strong forms:

must (/məst, ms/; /mʌst/)
can (/kən, kn/; /kæn/)
have (/həv, əv/; /hæv/)
was (/wəz, wz/; /wɒz/)
that (/ð(ə)t/; /ðæt/)
than (/ð(ə)n/; /ðæn/)
and (/ənd, ən, n/; /ænd/)
but (/bət/; /bʌt/)
am (/(ə)m/; /æm/)
are (/ə(r)/; /ɑː(r)/)
us (/əs/; /ʌs/)
them (/ð(ə)m/; /ðem/)
from (/fr(ə)m/; /frɒm/)
for (/fə(r)/; /fɔː(r)/)

If you are short of time

Drop Exercises 5 and 6; drop Exercise 3 or Exercise 4 if pronunciation is not a high priority.

Optional extra materials

You may like to bring pictures of objects which students don't know the names of, to supplement or replace the illustration to Exercise 7. (See *Alternative to Exercise 7*.)

1 'Mystery conversation'

- Go over the instructions and the words in the box.
- Play the first section of the recording (a 'bleep' will tell you when to stop).
- Ask students what they can say about the mystery object. (For instance, it can't be a baby because one of the speakers says it's expensive.)

- Play the next section of the recording and ask students what they can say about the thing now.
- Continue in the same way (there are six sections).
- By the end of the fifth section, students may already have realised that the thing in question is a piano. The sixth section will make this clear.

Tapescript for Exercise 1: see page 183

2 Students' conversations

- Ask students to work in groups of three or four.
- Give them a quarter of an hour or so to prepare 'mystery conversations' like the one in Exercise 1.
- Encourage students to use some of the key expressions from the dialogue. Examples:

It's a good one.   Do you think so?   I hope so.
Where shall we put it?   It'll look better in/by/on...
Maybe you're right.   That's why I...   one with...
what-do-you-call-it   what-do-you-call-them
I'm surprised...   They don't make them...
It's nice to look at, isn't it?   lots of room

- When groups are ready, let them perform their conversations, and ask other groups to guess what the object in question is.
- You may like to record the conversations – if so, warn the students in advance.

3 Contrastive stress

- Go over the example. Make sure students remember how to give special stress to words. If necessary, remind them that this stress can show a contrast (for instance, between what somebody believes and what is actually true).
- Play the recording, stopping after each sentence and getting the answer first from volunteers, then from the whole class in chorus or individually.

Tapescript and possible answers to Exercise 3

1. She's got two children.
   ('No, she hasn't. She's got *three* children.')
2. He came by car.
   ('No, he didn't. He came by *bus*.')
3. He's eating too much.
   ('No, he isn't. He's *drinking* too much.')
4. There's a dog sitting on the wall.
   ('No, there isn't. There's a *cat* sitting on the wall.')
5. She's reading a newspaper.
   ('No, she isn't. She's *buying* a newspaper.')
6. The post office is on fire.
   ('No, it isn't. The *bank*'s on fire.')
7. One person's singing.
   ('*A lot* of people are singing.')
8. She's wearing white gloves.
   ('No. She's *carrying/holding* white gloves.')

108

4 Weak and strong forms

- Go over the introduction and practise the weak and strong pronunciations.
- Ask students about the first sentence.
- Play or say the sentence and let students check their answers.
- Do the same with the second sentence.
- Ask students why they think *must* is weak in the first sentence and strong in the second. (In the first sentence, *must* is next to *go*, which takes the stress; in the second, *must* is the only verb, so it takes the stress.)

Answers to Exercise 4

1. weak   2. strong   3. strong (emphasised)
4. strong (the only verb)   5. weak (*get* is stressed)
6. weak (*swim* is stressed)   7. strong (the only verb)
8. weak (*understand* is stressed)
9. weak (*been* is stressed)
10. strong (not an auxiliary verb here)   11. weak
12. strong   13. weak   14. strong   15. weak
16. strong

5 Which one is different?

(Exercises 5 and 6 are taken from *Discussions that Work*, by Penny Ur, Cambridge University Press 1981, by kind permission of the author and publisher.)
- Students will already be familiar with 'odd one out' exercises. This one is a little more interesting because there is no one 'right answer'.
- Explain the words in the box (or let students use dictionaries).
- Then see if they can find reasons for regarding as many of the animals as possible as the 'odd one out'.

6 Which one is different? (continued)

- Ask students to work in groups. Each group should work on one of the boxes (as in Exercise 5).
- Get each group to explain its decisions to the class.
- If time allows and students are interested, let groups choose a second box and try again.

Optional activity: vocabulary extension

- If there is time, you could use Exercise 6 to launch a vocabulary revision and extension activity.
- Ask students to choose the vocabulary area (from the boxes in Exercise 6) which they would most like to study, and to join together into small groups with other students who have chosen the same area.
- Tell students to see how many words they can add to the list in the box, by pooling their knowledge, consulting you or other groups, (e.g. *What's the English for* Lisboa?), or using dictionaries.

7 Paraphrase strategies

- This exercise gives students more practice in asking for things whose names they do not know.
- Before starting, look back at lesson 5A Exercise 5, which contains key structures and vocabulary for this activity. These can be put on the board.
- Each student should come out in front of the class and ask for one of the objects illustrated, without saying its name or using his or her hands. (Tell students to put their hands in their pockets or behind their backs.) The class should note the number of the object they think the student wants.

- When the student has finished, ask the class what number they have noted. Find out if they were right.
- After the exercise, students may want to know the names of some of the objects. They are:
1. windscreen wiper   2. rake   3. compass
4. scales   5. lampshade   6. flower pot   7. comb
8. bicycle saddle   9. crutch   10. birdcage
11. clothes pegs   12. mousetrap   13. shoelace
14. frying pan   15. brick   16. magnifying glass
17. binoculars   18. wheelbrace   19. hammer
20. pliers   21. screwdriver   22. cigarette holder
23. harmonica   24. axe   25. garden shears
26. roller skates   27. insecticide

Alternative to Exercise 7

- The exercise can be done with pictures cut out of magazines (and perhaps mounted on cards).
- Give each student in turn a picture and tell him or her to come out and ask for it, as in Exercise 7.

- The class should draw the object the student is asking for, or write the name in their own language.
- When the student has finished, show the picture.

Summary

- Remind students to look at the Summary and learn the new material.

Practice Book

- Tell students which exercises you want them to do.

4 Weak and strong forms. Some words have two pronunciations: a 'weak form' and a 'strong form'. Examples:

	WEAK FORM	STRONG FORM
must	/ms, məst/	/mʌst/
can	/kn, kən/	/kæn/
have	/(h)əv/	/hæv/
was	/w(ə)z/	/wɒz/

Which pronunciations do you think *must, can, have* and *was* have in these sentences?

1. I must go soon.
2. Oh, must you?
3. I really *must* stop smoking soon.
4. Yes, you must.
5. We must get some more milk.
6. I can swim, but not very well.
7. Yes, I can.
8. Nobody can understand what he says.
9. Where have you been?
10. What time do you have breakfast?
11. We've been talking about you.
12. Oh, have you?
13. I was late for work this morning.
14. That *was* nice – thank you very much.
15. Sally was here this afternoon.
16. Oh, was she?

5 Which one is different? Can you find a reason why one of the words in the box is different from all the others? Example:

'*A cow is the only one that has horns.*'
'*We get milk from a cow, but not from the others.*'

Try to find reasons like these for *each* of the words.

| horse   cat   mouse   camel   lion   cow |

6 Now do the same for one of these boxes.

| India   China   the USA   France   Egypt   Israel |

| apple   orange   strawberry   banana   grape   peach |

| fridge   piano   armchair   car   bus   table |

| nose   ear   arm   hand   mouth   foot |

| London   Paris   Copenhagen   Peking   Rio |

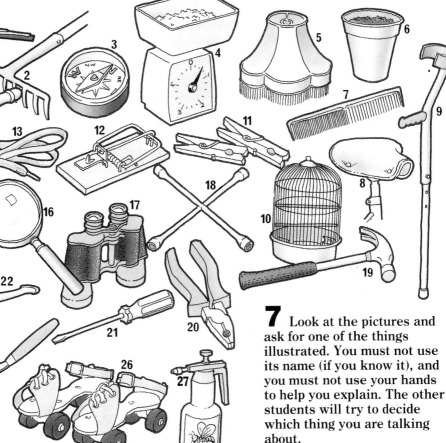

7 Look at the pictures and ask for one of the things illustrated. You must not use its name (if you know it), and you must not use your hands to help you explain. The other students will try to decide which thing you are talking about.

Changes

A As time goes by

Sophia Loren

Yehudi Menuhin

1 Which child became which adult? Try and match the pictures.

1

2

3

Margaret Thatcher

4

King Juan Carlos of Spain

2 Look at the pictures below, taken a few years ago. How has each person changed? Use some expressions from the box.

gained/lost weight	gone grey/bald
got some wrinkles	grown a beard/moustache
started wearing...	let his/her hair grow
cut/dyed his/her hair	become famous
got more/less popular/serious/etc.	

3 How have you changed in the past ten years? Write two sentences on a piece of paper for the teacher to read to the class.

4 Work in groups. Choose one stage of life (childhood, adolescence, young adulthood, middle age, old age). Work together to decide on a list of advantages and disadvantages of the stage of life you have chosen.

Unit 27: Lesson A

Students learn to talk about how time changes people and things.

Principal structures: present perfect; *get +* adjective; *get +* past participle.

Words and expressions to learn: *wrinkle* (noun); *beard; moustache; childhood; adolescence; break; rust; wear (down); crack; gain/lose weight; bald; go grey/bald; middle age; old age.*

Language notes and possible problems

Get and go The use of these words to talk about change is idiomatic in English; you will want to point out that *get* is used with most adjectives (e.g. *get more popular, get old*), but *go* is used with colours and in many cases where people or things change for the worse (e.g. *go grey, go bald, go rusty*).

If you are short of time
Leave out Exercise 8.

1 Sensitisation: matching
● This exercise will get students thinking about ageing and its effects.
● Once you have made clear what the task is, give the students a minute or two to work individually; then let them compare their answers with one another before checking with you.

Answers: 1. King Juan Carlos of Spain
2. Margaret Thatcher 3. Sophia Loren
4. Yehudi Menuhin

2 Changes in people
● Put the students into groups of three or four.
● Go over the expressions in the box and make sure the students understand them.
● Each group should then write at least two sentences about how each of the people has changed between the pictures in this exercise and the pictures in Exercise 1.
● (If, by unfortunate chance, one or more of these people has died since this book was published, make sure that the students use the past simple rather than the present perfect for these cases.)
● Walk around while the groups are working to give any help that is needed.
● When they have finished, let each group read its sentences to the rest of the class.
● You may want to put a few sample sentences on the board, or let each group put one sentence on the board.

3 Personalisation
● Ask each student to write two sentences on a piece of paper, describing how he or she has changed in the past ten years (or less if your students are all in their teens).
● Collect the pieces of paper, shuffle them, and read them out to the class without saying the names; number them as you go.
● The students should write down the numbers and who they think each pair of sentences was written by.

● When you have finished, go through the numbers again and get the students to 'claim' their sentences.

4 Advantages and disadvantages
● Put the students into groups of about four or five.
● Explain the meanings of the terms for the five stages of life.
● Let each group choose one stage; you may want to make sure that the groups choose different stages.
● Depending on the fluency of the class (or group), give them a certain number of points to write down – say three advantages and three disadvantages for a slower class, five of each for a faster one.
● Walk round while they are working to give any help with the language that they may need, but make sure you leave the task of deciding on advantages and disadvantages to the students.
● When the groups have finished, let them read their lists to one another.

5 Things age: introduction

- In this exercise, students listen to someone talking about how an old house ages.
- Look at the picture of the house with them, giving any explanations that are necessary.
- Get them to write down the labels from the picture on a separate piece of paper.
- Ask them to put their pens down; play the recording through once without stopping.
- Then tell them to listen while you play it again; they should try to write down the verb that is connected with each of the words or expressions on their lists.
- If several students have not succeeded in noting the verbs, you may want to play the recording again, with pauses.
- Let students compare answers with one another before checking with you.
- You may want to play the recording a last time so the students can hear the answers again.

Tapescript and answers to Exercise 5

An old house changes all the time. A *timber frame house* like mine *moves*, slowly and naturally, with the movement of the ground over the years. And as time goes by the *wooden beams get harder and harder*, almost like metal. *Steps* and floors *are slowly worn down* by people's feet, and *banisters are polished* by all the hands that slide over them. Of course, some of the changes have to be taken care of; *tiles fall off* the roof and *get broken*, the *paint cracks and peels*. *Pipes can begin to rust* and bricks to crumble if they aren't looked after properly. So living in an old house is like living with another person – it gives you shelter and warmth, but you have to be aware of its needs too.

6 Vocabulary practice

- This exercise practises some of the vocabulary from Exercise 5, as well as revising the form *get* + past participle.
- Go over the example with the students, and then put them into pairs to write sentences for the other situations.
- Walk round while they are working to give any language help that is needed.

Possible answers to Exercise 6

2. It might get rusty. (*or* It might rust.)
3. It might get broken. (*or* It might break.)
4. It might burn.
5. It might get (very) dirty. (*or* It might go grey.)
6. It might get polished. (*or* It might get dirty.)
7. It might crack.
8. It might fall off.

7 Changes in a village: listening

- Explain to the students that they are going to hear a man who has lived in the same village all his life. He is talking about some of the changes in the village.
- Go over the statements with the students, and make sure they understand what their task is.
- Play the recording through without stopping, more than once if necessary, while the students try to answer the questions.
- Let them compare answers with each other before checking with you.

Tapescript for Exercise 7

Most of the people, you see, at that time, before the First World War, were engaged in the, er, farming, with a smaller percentage, um, with the racing stables. They were the two main people, you see, with by far the greater number on the er, farm, and, er, after the First War, you see, quite a few of the fellows went into the army, and they came back, and, er, course they didn't like to settle down to village life, they didn't like to settle down to the discipline which the old farmer was trying to er, re-establish, you see? And there was one occasion where the er, I think I may have told you before, where four or five of them wanted to go to St Giles's far, fair, in September, and er, they asked for the day off, and he said, oh, no, they couldn't go, he hadn't got his harvest in, you know, he wouldn't allow that sort of thing. And em, they said well, they, they were going, and he said, 'Well, if you do, you'll have to find a job somewhere else,' which of course would have been curtains for them years before, because he s-, he, er, had all the houses and all the jobs and all the rest of it, but of course when they came back and they got the sack, they found a job down at the er, er, RAF depot at Milton, you see. And being as they were ex-servicemen, they, er, they walked straight in, and of course a lot of them, well, they all of them said it was the best day's work they did. And from that day, I think, there was a slight drift away from the farm, and, er, things were never *quite* the same.

8 Class survey

- Go over the questions with the students to make sure they understand them.
- Then divide the questions up, so that each question is being asked by at least one student.
- Get each student to ask his or her question of as many people as possible (by getting up and walking round the classroom if this is possible).
- Students should then report the results of their survey to the class.

Summary

- Remind students to look at the Summary and learn the new words.

Practice Book

- Tell students which exercises you want them to do.

Timber frame house

tile

paint

pipe

beam

steps   banister

---

5 Look at the picture with your teacher. Then listen to the recording and write down what happens to each of these: timber frame house, beams, steps, banisters, tiles, paint, pipes.

6 What might happen to these things? Use *get* in some of your answers.

1. A flower that no one waters
   It might die.
2. A car that is never put in a garage
3. A chair dropped from a second-floor window
4. Some food forgotten on a hot cooker
5. A white house in a polluted city
6. A door handle that's used hundreds of times a day
7. A plate put on a hot cooker
8. A book forgotten on the roof of a car

7 You will hear a man talking about a big change in his village. Are these sentences true (T), false (F), or does the man not say (DS)?

1. Most of the people in the village worked in the racing stables before the First World War.
2. Some of the young men from the village went into the army during the Second World War.
3. Some of the young men wanted to go to St Giles' Fair.
4. The farmer told them they couldn't go.
5. The young men agreed not to go.
6. The farmer owned houses in the village.
7. Later the young men found jobs at Blewbury.
8. The young men were happy with their new jobs.
9. After that things were the same in the village once again.

8 Class survey. Choose a question to ask the other members of the class.

1. Has your house or flat changed, or have you changed it, in any way since you first lived there? Explain.
2. Has your neighbourhood changed in any noticeable way since you first lived there? If so, in what way?
3. Is transport in your area better or worse than it was 15 years ago?
4. Is your neighbourhood prettier or uglier than it was when you first lived there? Why?
5. What do you think is the biggest change in your country since your grandparents' time?
6. Name some ways in which you think your grandparents' life was better than yours is.
7. Name some ways in which your life is better than your grandparents' was.

B If he'd been bad at maths, ...

1 On February 6, 1944, Mark Perkins arrived in Switzerland. But if things had been different, ... Look at the diagram (the path of Mark's life is marked in grey) and complete these sentences.

1. He would have studied . . . if he'd been bad at maths.
2. If he had studied literature, he'd have become a . . .
3. If his parents had been well off, he . . . to university.
4. If . . . university, . . .
5. He wouldn't have worked in a bank if his parents . . . well off.
6. If the war hadn't started, he . . . joined the army.

Now make some more sentences about how Mark's life would have been different if . . .

PRISONER UNTIL END OF WAR

NOT ESCAPE

NOT SPEAK ITALIAN

NOT FIND HELP

Caught!

ESCAPE

SPEAK ITALIAN

FIND HELP

GET TO SWITZERLAND

PRISONER OF WAR

ARMY IN ITALY

HURT WHILE FIGHTING

WORLD WAR II

ARMY IN AFRICA

MOVE TO EDINBURGH

LEARN ITALIAN

FALL IN LOVE WITH ITALIAN GIRL

FALL IN LOVE WITH SCOTTISH GIRL

HOLIDAY IN ITALY

HOLIDAY IN SCOTLAND

DO RESEARCH

WORK IN BANK

STUDY PHYSICS

$e=mc^2$

BECOME A JOURNALIST

PARENTS WELL OFF

GO TO UNIVERSITY

STUDY LITERATURE

PARENTS WORKING CLASS

STUDY MATHS

BAD AT MATHS

GOOD AT MATHS

Unit 27: Lesson B

Students learn to talk about hypothetical situations in the past.

Principal structures: affirmative and negative forms of past conditional.

Words and expressions to learn: *literature; physics; research; prisoner; sausage; stand; chip; pavement; escape; bite* (verb); *faint; feel sorry for; well off; working class; wild.*

Phonology: stress and rhythm in past conditional sentences; pronunciation of unstressed *a, e, i* and *o* in initial position.

Language notes and possible problems

1. Past conditional: form The concept behind this structure should not be difficult for most students, but the form may present difficulties for students from some language backgrounds. You may have to watch out for mistakes like **If he would have come, I would...*

2. Past conditional: pronunciation Sentences containing the past conditional can be difficult to pronounce for many students; practice with the stress and rhythm of the model sentences is important in the initial stages.

If you are short of time

Leave out Exercise 3; if pronunciation is not a high priority for your students, leave out Exercises 5 and 6.

1 Mark Perkins' life

- Ask the students to look at the diagram of Mark Perkins' life. Make sure they understand that the shaded line is the path his life took, and the unshaded parts of the diagram are possibilities that did not happen.
- Encourage them to use their dictionaries or consult you to find out the meanings of any new words.
- Then ask them to work individually trying to finish the gapped sentences in the book.
- Let them compare notes before checking with you.
- When you go over the sentences with them, work on the stress and rhythm.
- Then ask each student to write down at least one other sentence about Mark Perkins' life beginning with *If...*
- Point out the fact that the *if*-clause can come at the beginning or the end of the sentence; it should be followed by a comma if it comes at the beginning. Point out that both *would* and *had* can be contracted to *'d.*
- Get the students to form groups of three or four to compare sentences and see if they can write any other sentences.
- Walk round while they are working to give any help that is needed.
- When they have finished, ask each group to read out one or more of its sentences. Pay attention to stress and rhythm.
- Exercise 3 in the Practice Book revises stress in past conditional sentences.

2 Personalisation

- You may want to begin this exercise by giving your own *if*-sentence about your past life, and explaining it in a few words.
- Then ask each student to write an *if*-sentence about his or her past. Remind them about punctuation.
- Divide the class into groups of three or four. Each student should read his or her sentence to the others and explain it.
- Exercise 1 in the Practice Book revises the past conditional.

3 Reading: prediction

- Get the students to work individually or in small groups trying to decide which word goes into each blank. They can use their dictionaries or consult you about difficult words.
- Walk round while they are working to give any help that is needed.
- If they have worked individually, let them compare answers before checking with you.
- Exercise 2 in the Practice Book revises the vocabulary from this lesson.

Answers to Exercise 3
EXPENSIVE KINDNESS
A West German woman's *love* for cats has brought her an *angry* cat and a bill for £23,000.

The story, told by German *police*, began when the 56-year-old woman from Wuppertal *lost* her cat and *put* an advertisement in the *local* paper.

A man *phoned* her to say he had found the *animal*, but in fact it was not hers. However, she felt sorry for the cat, which must have been a stray, and decided to *adopt* it.

On the way home in her *car*, the cat 'suddenly went wild' and bit and scratched her *arm*. This caused the car to *turn* off the road and crash into a parked car, bringing down a sausage stand and a neighbouring *fish* and chip stand.

Boiling *oil* burnt the arms of a 44-year-old woman selling *fish* and chips, and a 21-year-old woman who was waiting for her chips fainted and *hurt* herself falling to the pavement.

4 More practice with negative conditionals

- Ask the students to look back at the story about the German woman and the cat, and to volunteer sentences like the model.
- This should elicit quite a few negative sentences.
- Work on stress and rhythm.

5 Unstressed initial vowels

- Get the students to copy the list and then work individually, marking the stresses in the four lists of words.
- Get them to compare answers before checking with you.
- Ask them if they can say anything about the stress in these words; they should be able to see that all the words are stressed on the second syllable.
- Then ask them to mark the initial unstressed syllables, with a circle around the vowels pronounced /ə/, and a square around the vowels pronounced /ɪ/. Let them compare answers in groups.
- Then play the recording or read the lists yourself to give them a chance to modify their answers before checking with you.

- Ask them if they can make any rules about the pronunciation of the first vowel in a word where the second syllable is stressed.
- They should come up with the rule that *a* and *o* in this position are pronounced /ə/, and *e* and *i* in this position are pronounced /ɪ/.
- You may want to say that there are a few exceptions to this rule.

Answers to Exercise 5
1. about advertisement apply material
2. conditions society protection tobacco
3. besides emergency remember example
4. invent mistake discover impossible

6 Pronunciation: applying the rules

- Put the students in pairs or small groups. Each student in turn should pronounce a word for the other(s), who will check on him or her.
- Alternatively, tell the students that they can volunteer to say words and you will say them after them, without indicating whether their pronunciation is acceptable or not; they can repeat the word for you to echo until they are satisfied with their own pronunciation.

7 Inventing a story

- Ask the students to look at the Mark Perkins diagram again.
- There are five hypothetical paths that can be continued.
- Put the students into groups of three or four and ask them to choose a path and invent a continuation for it.
- They can follow a straight line or make branching paths, as they like.
- Walk round while they are working to give any help that is needed.
- When they have finished, get each group to present their story to the class, saying what would have happened if things had been different. Make sure they use *if*.

Summary
- Make sure students look at the Summary and learn the new words.

Practice Book
- Tell students which exercises you want them to do.

2 Write an *if* sentence about your own past. Then read and explain it to a few other students.

3 Put a word from the box into each blank in the text.

> adopt angry animal arm car fish fish hurt
> local lost love oil phoned police put turn

EXPENSIVE KINDNESS

A West German woman's .... for cats has brought her an .... cat and a bill for £23,000.

The story, told by German ...., began when the 56-year-old woman from Wuppertal .... her cat and .... an advertisement in the .... paper.

A man .... her to say he had found the ...., but in fact it was not hers. However, she felt sorry for the cat, which must have been a stray, and decided to .... it.

On the way home in her ...., the cat 'suddenly went wild' and bit and scratched her .... This caused the car to .... off the road and crash into a parked car, bringing down a sausage stand and a neighbouring .... and chip stand.

Boiling .... burnt the arms of a 44-year-old woman selling .... and chips, and a 21-year-old woman who was waiting for her chips fainted and .... herself falling to the pavement.

(from an article by Anna Tomforde in the *Guardian* – adapted)

4 *The woman's arm wouldn't have been burnt if the car hadn't crashed.* Make some more sentences about what wouldn't have happened.

5 Copy this list and mark the stresses in the words like this: <u>above</u> in<u>stead</u>

1. about   advertisement   apply   material
2. conditions   society   protection   tobacco
3. besides   emergency   remember   example
4. invent   mistake   discover   impossible

What can you say about the stress in all of the words?

Now look at the first syllable of each word. Put a circle ○ around the vowels pronounced /ə/ and a square □ around the vowels pronounced /ɪ/ (for example, ⓐbove; ⬜nstead). Listen to the tape or your teacher to check the answers.

6 Pronounce these words.

continue   deliver   abroad   banana   insurance
election   policewoman   repair   intelligence
Olympic   agreement   explain   disgusting

7 Work in groups. Invent the continuation of a path Mark Perkins didn't take. Then tell the rest of the class about it. Use *if*.

Health

A Taking regular exercise

1 Here are some things you can do to take care of your health. Which two do you think are the most important?

   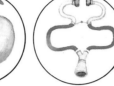  

Not smoking   Taking regular exercise   Eating good quality food   Having regular check-ups   Dieting to keep your weight down   Not drinking alcohol

Now complete one of these sentences; write the sentence down and hand it to the teacher. The other students will try to guess which sentence is yours.

1. ... is the most important thing you can do to take care of your health because ...
2. The things I do to take care of my health are: ...
3. I think that ... is more important for your health than ... because ...

2 Read the story without a dictionary. Don't worry if you don't understand everything. Try to write titles for the pictures with blanks.

Debra Levy is a student at Oxford Polytechnic. A year ago she was extremely thin, got headaches, couldn't concentrate, forgot things. Her face was spotty; her stomach was almost always upset; she couldn't sleep. For
5 a long time, no one could help her. Her doctor used to give her sleeping pills, but each new kind only worked for a short while.

    Then, after talking to a friend with similar problems, Debra began to think she might be allergic to foods and
10 chemicals. She went to see a specialist. The specialist tested her and found out that she was allergic to things she ate, breathed and touched.

    Now Debra is much better. She takes medicine, but she also has to avoid some of the things that make her ill.

Things like chlorine in drinking water, fumes from cars and chemicals in food all hurt her. So she has to drink bottled water, use a special air filter, and avoid tinned or packaged food. Fortunately she shares a house with other women who understand her problem, and they share the cooking and shopping for her diet.

    Debra will finish her studies this year and begin looking for a job. But she is worried that this will be difficult. Most of the jobs that interest her are in London; but she cannot live there because of the polluted air. So learning what was causing her problems has complicated her life, but she sleeps well and is healthy most of the time now.

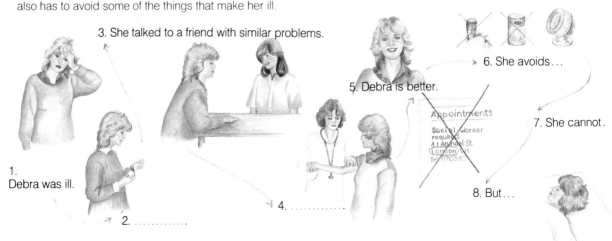

1. Debra was ill.
2. ....
3. She talked to a friend with similar problems.
4. ....
5. Debra is better.
6. She avoids ...
7. She cannot .
8. But ...

Unit 28: Lesson A

Students learn more ways of talking about health and fitness.

Principal structures: *-ing* form as subject or complement; subject and object relative clauses; verbs with two objects.

Words and expressions to learn: *exercise* (noun); *quality*; *headache*; *while* (noun); (*a good*) *example*; *present* (noun); *diet* (verb); *keep*; *concentrate*; *avoid*; *pollute*; *complicate*; *promise*; *heart attack*; *horrible*.

are necessary to their understanding of the text. Do not give them the meanings if the words can be guessed from context or are peripheral to the main story line.
● When most students have finished, let them compare answers with one another before checking with you.

Possible answers to Exercise 2
2. Her doctor gave her sleeping pills.
4. She went to see a specialist.
6. She avoids some of the things that make her ill.
7. She cannot live in London.
8. But she sleeps well and is healthy.

Language notes and possible problems

1. Gerund as subject or complement Some students may have difficulty in learning to use the *-ing* form (and not the infinitive, for example) in these cases, because of interference from their own language. You may want to give them extra practice.

2. Relative clauses People from some language groups may tend to make mistakes like *A friend who she lives near me...* You may want to watch out for these and give extra help if needed.

If you are short of time

Leave out Exercise 3; if your students have no problems with relative clauses, leave out Exercise 4.

1 Staying healthy

Let students look at the pictures and make sure they understand each of the phrases.
● Then ask them to work individually to decide which two things are the most important in taking care of your health.
● Ask for a volunteer to come to the board and keep score. He or she should write up the six phrases – or key words from each.
● In turn, each student should call out the two things he or she has chosen so the scorekeeper can mark up points under those headings.
● Make sure students use the *-ing* form when they are calling out their answers.
● Then ask students each to write down and complete one of the three sentences on a small piece of paper.
● Collect the pieces of paper, shuffle them, and read them out to the class, giving them numbers as you go.
● Students should write down the numbers and their guesses about who wrote each sentence.
● Afterwards, read the sentences again and let each student 'claim' his or her sentence.
● There is work on *-ing* forms in Practice Book Exercise 1.

2 Reading: getting the overall picture

● Ask students to look at the picture story that goes with the text, to get an idea of what the story is about.
● Then ask them to read the text, only trying to understand enough to write titles for the pictures with blanks.
● They should not use their dictionaries, but you may want to let them ask you about difficult words they feel

114

3 Guessing unknown words

- Make sure students understand the task, and then let them work individually for a few minutes.
- They can compare answers in small groups before checking with you.
- In cases where several students have had difficulty, you may want to help them see the clues in the text that point towards the meaning of the word.
- There is work on guessing unknown words in Practice Book Exercise 7.

4 Relative clauses (revision)

- Go over the examples with the students.
- See if they can tell you why there is no relative pronoun in the third example.
- Then let them work individually to answer the questions. You may want them to hand in their answers so that you can be sure that everyone has grasped the point.
- Let them compare answers with one another before checking with you.
- There is work on relative clauses in Practice Book Exercise 2.

Answers to Exercise 4

1. The pills her doctor gave her (*or* . . . used to give her)
2. A friend who had similar problems
3. The specialist who tested her (*or* . . . who she went to see)
4. The things that make her ill
5. Because the jobs that interest her are there

5 Advice to a friend

- Introduce the situation. Ask each student to think of a specific person who is close to them – friend or relative – and who has been told by the doctor to get more exercise.
- Then go over the list of suggestions with the students. Explain that they must choose two or three of the suggestions that they think might work for the person they have chosen. They should try to think of one other suggestion of their own.
- When they have finished this, get them to tell one another which options they have chosen and why.
- The best way to do this is as a walk-round activity, so that each student explains his or her choice to several other students.
- Stop them after a few minutes, when you feel they have had enough practice.
- Then you may want to point out how the verbs in the list of suggestions are constructed, and ask them if they can think of any other verbs that take two objects (there is a list in the Summary).
- There is work on verbs with two objects in Practice Book Exercise 3.
- Some of the vocabulary from this lesson is revised in Practice Book Exercise 4.

Summary

- Remind students to look at the Summary and learn the new words.

Practice Book

- Tell students which exercises you want them to do.

3 Reading skills: guessing unknown words. Match each of the words and expressions from the text (in column A) with its probable meaning in column B. The words are numbered with the lines where they come in the text.

	A		B
3	concentrate		took in through the nose
9	allergic to		think hard about one thing
10	specialist		made ill by
12	breathed		dirty
14	avoid		dirty gas caused by burning
15	fumes		made more difficult
24	polluted		stay away from
25	complicated		doctor with special knowledge

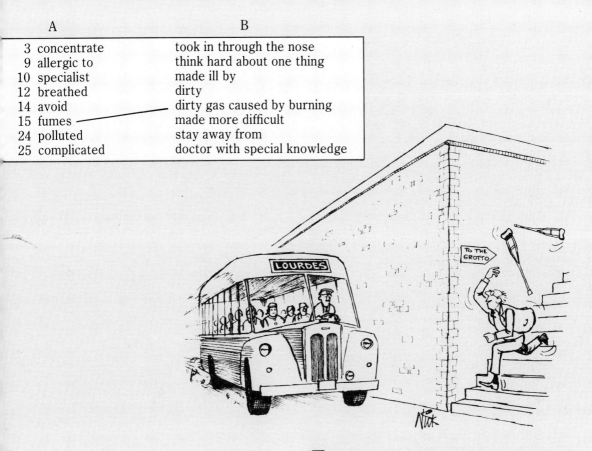

4 Look at these sentences.

She shares a house with other women who understand her problem.

She has to avoid some of the things that make her ill.

She was allergic to things she ate, breathed and touched.

Now complete the answers to these questions about the text.

1. What only worked for a short while? (The pills her...)
2. Who made Debra think she might have allergies? (A friend who...)
3. Who found out she was allergic to things she ate, breathed and touched? (The specialist who...)
4. What does she have to avoid? (The things that...)
5. Why would she like to live in London? (Because the jobs that...)

5 Think of a middle-aged person you know well (wife/husband/mother/father/friend/etc.). Imagine the doctor has told him/her to get more exercise, because of the risk of heart trouble. But he/she isn't doing anything about it. What would you do to encourage him/her? Choose two or three of the suggestions below. Add your own suggestion if you like. Then explain to other students what you would do and why.

WOULD YOU:
- buy him/her a book on exercise?
- give him/her an exercise bicycle?
- tell him/her horrible stories about middle-aged people who have heart attacks?
- ask a health club to send him/her an advertisement?
- show him/her a good example by exercising more yourself?
- promise him/her a present if he/she exercises regularly?

B Where does it hurt?

"I wish you'd called me sooner, Mrs. Moodie."

1 Read the dialogues below while you listen to the recording. Listen for the differences.

(D = doctor; P = patient)

A

D: Where does it hurt?
P: Just here, doctor.
D: Mm. And is that all the time?
P: No. Only when I walk, or when I'm going downstairs. Sometimes when I carry things.
D: When you carry things. Big things?
P: Yes.
D: I see. Now I want you to stand up...

B

D: How often do you get them?
P: Oh, three or four times a week.
D: Three or four times a week. I see. Are they very bad?
P: Oh, yes. They stop me driving. Sometimes I can hardly see, you know.
D: Yes. Do you often get colds?

C

P: It's a really bad cough. It's really bad.
D: Does it hurt when you talk?
P: If I talk a lot, yes.
D: I see. Well I'll just have a look at your chest. Do you drink?

"It's a pity you haven't got appendicitis – I'm rather good at that."

Now listen to these conversations and try to write down the words that go in the blanks.

D

P: It's a really bad pain, doctor. .... here.
D: Which side?
P: .... side.
D: How long has this been going on? When did it start?
P: .... morning, doctor. I thought perhaps it was indigestion, but it's too .... for that.
D: .... Now just .... down here. That's right. Now .... exactly does it hurt? Is it here?
P: Ooh! Yes!

E

D: Good morning, ... Palmer. What's the ....?
P: Well, I've got a .... sore throat, ...
D: .... How long have you had it?
P: Oh, about .... It's .... very painful. It's difficult to ....

F

P: It's every .... about the same time, doctor. Stuffed-up nose, my .... itch, and feel sort of .... the whole time.
P: Is it .... when you're inside or outside?
P: When I'm in the ....

G

P: I get this .... when I bend ...., doctor. Just here.
D: I see. Take your .... off.

2 Copy this list, and then close your book. Find out what each of the words or expressions means, by using a dictionary or asking your teacher. Then listen to the conversations again. Which patient has which problem?

headaches   bronchitis   back trouble
appendicitis   a pulled muscle
hay fever   tonsilitis

Unit 28: Lesson B

Students **learn** to talk about illnesses and to understand what doctors say to them.
Principal structures: frequency adverbs; adverbials of frequency; reporting orders and advice.
Words and expressions to learn: *patient* (noun); *chest; pain; muscle; operation; injection; tablet; stand up; lie down; itch; bend over; advise; painful; How often...?; back trouble; hay fever; sore throat.*
Phonology: assimilation of consonants and linking.

Language notes and possible problems

1. Position of frequency adverbs and adverbials

This is liable to cause trouble for students whose own languages have different rules about the placing of adverbs and adverbials. The basic rules for English are outlined in the Summary, which you may want to go over more carefully than usual with your students. Exercise 1 in the Practice Book gives work on this point.

2. Reporting advice and orders You may want to point out that 'tell' has different meanings in sentences like *He told me to take a deep breath* and sentences like '*You should be more careful,' John told Simon*. In the first case, *told* means *ordered*; in the second it means *said to*, and to report the sentence we could say *John advised Simon to be more careful*.

3. Vocabulary load There is quite a lot of new vocabulary in this lesson. Tell students they are not expected to learn all the new words (see Exercise 6 and the Summary).

4. Consonant assimilation If you think your students will tend to avoid assimilation of consonants that come together in Exercise 4, you may want to point out what happens in each case (see Exercise notes).

If you are short of time

You can leave out Exercise 5; if pronunciation is not a high priority for your students, you can leave out Exercise 4.

1 In the doctor's surgery: listening

- For the first three dialogues, ask the students to listen to the recording and try and write down the differences between the version in their books and the version on the recording.
- Point out that neither version is more correct than the other.
- You may want to play the recording a second time.
- Let students compare answers before checking the differences with you.
- For the last four dialogues, put the students into pairs and get them to try and guess what might go into the blanks.
- Go over the dialogues with them, asking for their answers; make sure you accept any answer that is appropriate, not just the ones in the recording.
- Then let them listen to the recording to find out what was meant to be in the blanks.
- You may want to play the dialogues more than once.

- Answer any questions students may have about the meaning of words and expressions in the dialogues.

Tapescript and answers to Exercise 1: see page 184

2 Which illness?

- Ask students to close their books. Write the names of the illnesses on the board.
- Let students look them up in their dictionaries, or explain the meanings if you prefer.
- Practise the pronunciation carefully (there are several difficulties). Make sure students know how to say the ending *-itis* (/aɪtəs/).
- Then play the recording through without stopping, more than once if necessary, while students note down which problem corresponds to each dialogue.
- Let them compare notes before checking with you.

Answers: A back trouble (*or* a pulled muscle) B headaches   C bronchitis   D appendicitis   E tonsilitis F hay fever   G a pulled muscle (*or* back trouble)

3 *Tell* and *advise*

- Explain the examples to the students.
- Then put them into groups of three or four and ask them to do the exercise.
- They should use their dictionaries to find out the meanings of the new words in the box.
- Walk round while they are working to give any help that is needed.
- When they have finished, let them read their sentences to the class. You may want to put a few sentences on the board.
- Practice Book Exercise 2 gives more work on this point.

4 Pronunciation: linking and assimilation

- Let students try the sentences without the recording first of all.
- Then play the recording sentence by sentence, giving the students plenty of practice on each one.
- Pay special attention to the marked links.

Tapescript for Exercise 4

Where does it hurt? (No gap before *it*; the *t* of *it* merges with the *h* of *hurt*.)
Only when I run. (No gap before *I*.)
I want you to stand up.
How often do you get them? (*do you* becomes /dju:/ or /dʒu:/; the final *t* in *get* is 'unexploded'.)
They stop me working. (The *p* in *stop* is unexploded.)
Sometimes I can hardly see.
Do you ever get hay fever?
It's a really bad cough. (Unexploded *d*.)
It's a really bad pain. (Unexploded *d*.)
This side. (One long *s*.)
Just lie down here. (The *t* of *just* merges with the *l* of *lie*.)
It's difficult to eat.
It's every year about the same time.
I get this pain.

5 A and B types

- This exercise provides some practice with frequency adverbs.
- Put students in pairs to ask one another the questions and note the answers. Walk round while they are working to give any help that is needed.
- The questions are based on some studies that show that certain personality types are more likely to have heart attacks than others, due to the amount of stress they put on themselves.
- If anyone answered 'Yes' to five or more of the questions, he or she is probably a 'Type A' person and may have a higher risk of a heart attack.
- Then put the students into groups of three or four and ask them to imagine that they work for an insurance company. Their job is to produce a questionnaire of about ten questions for people who want to buy life insurance.
- They should try to ask questions about people's health, family history, and habits (e.g. dangerous sports) that will 'weed out' people who stand a higher than normal risk of dying early.
- Walk round while they are working to help where needed.

- When the groups have finished, they can compare questionnaires; in a competitive class, they may want to vote for the best questionnaire.

6 Students choose language items to learn

- Let the students work individually on this exercise, noting five or more useful expressions to learn from Exercise 1.
- Then they can compare their lists with one another.

7 Doctor-patient conversations

- Get students to work in pairs. One in each pair is a doctor, the other is a patient.
- They should prepare conversations similar to the dialogues in Exercise 1, using plenty of the items they noted in Exercise 6 and making sure they include at least two of the frequency adverbs/adverbials from the list.
- Let them know if you are going to tape-record or video-record the conversations.
- Go round helping with vocabulary and pronunciation, and correcting mistakes if necessary.
- When students are ready, listen to them practise and then let them perform their conversations for the class.
- Don't correct while they are performing, but note serious mistakes for treatment later.
- Exercises 3 and 4 in the Practice Book give more vocabulary revision on the items from this lesson.

Summary

- You may want to go over the first part of the Summary with the students to make sure they understand the points there. Remind them to learn the words and expressions in the list.

Practice Book

- Tell students which exercises you want them to do.

3 Here are some more things the doctor said.

A Don't carry heavy things for a while.
B I think you should make an appointment at the
Eye Hospital.

And here is what the patients told their families.

A He told me not to carry heavy things.
B He advised me to make an appointment at the
Eye Hospital.

What do you think the doctor told the other patients? Work in groups to decide, and report to the class. You can use words from the box below, or ask your teacher for help. Begin your sentences like this:

We think the doctor told/advised patient C . . .'

to have: an operation	some physiotherapy	
some tests	a rest	an injection
to take: some tablets	some medicine	
some syrup	some vitamins	
to wear: a bandage		
to do: some exercises		

4 Pronunciation. Say these sentences. Don't separate the words.

Where does it hurt?
Only when I run.
I want you to stand up.
How often do you get them?
They stop me working.
Sometimes I can hardly see.
Do you ever get hay fever?
It's a really bad cough.
It's a really bad pain.
This side.
Just lie down here.
It's difficult to eat.
It's every year about the same time.
I get this pain.

"All right, all right, we'll do it your way, but I still say the appendix is on the right."

5 Are you likely to have a heart attack? Work with a partner: ask each other the questions below, and note down the answers. Then your teacher will tell you how to score the questionnaire.

1. Do you usually eat very quickly?
2. Do you sometimes do more than one thing at a time – for example, boil water for your morning coffee while getting dressed?
3. Do you ever have trouble finding time to get your hair cut or styled?
4. Are you often in a hurry?
5. Is success in your work very important to you?
6. Do you get upset if you have to wait in a queue?
7. Is finishing a job you've started very important to you?

Now imagine you are working for an insurance company. Your job is to make up a questionnaire for people who want life insurance. You don't want to give insurance to anyone who is likely to die very soon!

6 Look back at the dialogues in Exercise 1 and note down five or more useful expressions to learn. Compare your list with those of the students sitting near you.

7 Work in pairs. Prepare a conversation between a doctor and a patient. Use at least two of these words or expressions in the conversation. You can ask your teacher for help with other words.

often   usually   sometimes   never
always   every year/week/etc.
two or three times a . . .   all the time
the whole time

Heads

A   What sort of brain have you got?

1 Listen to the recording. There are ten pieces of conversation. Which of these words goes with which piece? (There may be more than one answer.)

analysing   calculating   classifying
drawing logical conclusions   forgetting
idea   imagination   making decisions
memory   planning

2 What sort of intelligence have you got? Give yourself marks from 1 to 5 for each of the following mental abilities. (1 = very bad   2 = poor   3 = average   4 = good   5 = very good) Which of these abilities do you think are most important? Can you think of any others?

– mathematical ability
– artistic ability
– memory
– imagination
– sense of humour
– decisiveness
– planning ability

– quick thinking
– ability to analyse problems
– logical thinking
– ability to deal with large numbers of facts
– ability to learn new things
– practical common sense

3 Stress. Say these words.

analyse   **classify**   **mem**ory   **prob**lem   **log**ical
practical   **hum**our

for**get**   i**dea**   in**tel**ligence   de**ci**sion
con**clu**sion   mathe**mat**ical   ar**tis**tic   a**bil**ity

imagi**na**tion

4 Do you wish you had a better brain? Which abilities would you like to improve?
Examples:

'I wish I had more artistic ability.'
'I wish I could remember people's names.'
'I wish I was better at making decisions.'

Unit 29: Lesson A

Students learn to talk about mental faculties.
Principal structures: *I wish* + past verb.
Words and expressions to learn: *brain; imagination; ability; fact; common sense; sense of humour; zoo; make decisions; plan; deal with; test; practical.*
Phonology: word stress.

Language notes and possible problems

1. Wish In Exercise 4, students may have difficulty in getting used to the structure after *I wish* (past verb to talk about a wish for the present). Point out that we often use a past verb in English to talk about an imaginary present situation (for example, after *if*).

2. Vocabulary This lesson introduces quite a number of new abstract words. These will be easy for speakers of European languages, who will find that many of the words are similar to their mother-tongue equivalents. Other students will probably find the lesson rather hard work; make it clear that they are not expected to remember all the new words at this stage (see Summary).

3. Talking about oneself Exercise 2 asks students to assess their own abilities. In some cultures it is 'not done' to talk about oneself in this way. If there is a problem of this kind, students can be asked to talk about the abilities of somebody else they know; or the exercise can be dropped.

If you are short of time

Drop Exercises 5 and/or 6; drop Exercise 3 if pronunciation is not a high priority.

1 Matching words and functions

● Look at the vocabulary with the students first of all. See how many of the words they know already and explain the others or let them look them up. Practise the pronunciation.
● See if they can give you examples to illustrate the meaning of the various words.
● Then tell the students to write the letters A to J on a piece of paper, with a space opposite each one.
● Play the first extract and ask students which they think is the right word for it. They will probably say *forgetting* or *memory*.
● Discuss which one is best, and tell them to write it opposite A.
● Then play the rest of the extracts, stopping for a few moments after each one to give students time to write their answers.
● Play the recording through once or twice more if necessary.
● Then let students compare notes before discussing the answers with them.

Answers to Exercise 1
A forgetting (*or* memory)   B imagination
C classifying   D planning   E memory
F making decisions   G analysing   H calculating
I idea   J drawing logical conclusions

Tapescript for Exercise 1: see next page (page 119)

2 What sort of intelligence?

● Go through the list of qualities explaining any difficulties.
● Practise the pronunciation of the words, paying special attention to stress.
● As you go through, ask students to say whether they think they are good or bad at the various things. Say something about yourself.
● When they have understood everything, get them to mark themselves from 1 to 5 for each quality.
● Then invite them to compare notes with other students and discuss their strengths and weaknesses.
● Finally, discuss the relative importance of the various qualities: ask students which three they would most like to have in a high degree.
● If students are interested, they could go on to discuss which qualities are important for people in various jobs (scientist, politician, teacher, . . .).

Alternative to Exercise 2
● Tell students to work in pairs, preferably with people they know well.
● Ask them to write down the list of qualities and give marks both to themselves and to their partners.
● When they have done this, they should exchange papers and see whether their partners' opinion of them corresponds to their own opinion.
● Another variant (if you have the courage) is to ask the class to write down marks for you.

3 Word stress

● Students should already have practised stressing these words correctly while doing Exercises 1 and 2. This exercise gives more practice if it is needed.
● Let students try the words individually and in chorus; the recording can be used as a guide if desired.

4 I wish...

● Get students to make at least one written and one spoken sentence.
● They will probably need help to express their wishes in the most natural form, since the sentence patterns vary according to the nouns and verbs being used.
● As an additional exercise, get students to make wishes about other people (e.g. *I wish my children had more common sense*).

5 Logic test

● Some students like this kind of thing; others hate it (and should not be made to do the exercise against their will).
● The exercise can be done individually (with students comparing notes afterwards) or by group discussion.
● If students are sufficiently interested, they could be invited to make up their own logic problems.

Answers to Exercise 5

1. T 2. F 3. F (the secretary may be a man)
4. T 5a. T 5b. T 5c. F (most of the information in 5 is irrelevant)

6 Memory test

● Try to organise this so that no students look at the test until the beginning of the two-minute period.
● When they have finished, answer any questions about the vocabulary.
● Ask whether students found it easier to remember words they knew well.
● It might be interesting to try the exercise again with words in the students' own language(s), to see how much better they do.

7 Zoo problem

(This exercise is taken from *Discussions that Work* by Penny Ur, Cambridge University Press 1981, by kind permission of the author and publisher.)
● Give students a few minutes to study the plan and look up the names of the animals in their dictionaries.
● Go through the information and make sure students understand what problems the zoo is faced with.
● Then get students to work in groups of three or four. Tell them that each group is a committee responsible for reorganising the zoo so as to solve as many of the problems as possible.
● Give them 15 or 20 minutes to work out their solutions; then let groups compare notes.
● If time allows, you can have a general class discussion about the various solutions. (There is of course no one right answer.)

Summary

● Remind students to look over the Summary and learn the new material.

Practice Book

● Tell students which exercises you want them to do.

Tapescript for Exercise 1

A. There are three things I can never remember: names, faces, and I've forgotten the other.
B. You know, it must be nice to be a cat. If I was a cat, I'd sleep all day...
C. 'We'd like to buy a lawnmower.'
   'Oh yes. Well, which kind would you like? You know there are basically two types of lawnmower, don't you?...'
D. 'Where shall we go for our holidays this year?' 'I thought it would be nice to spend a week camping in Italy.'
   'OK. Let's do that first, and then drive down to Naples and see Bill and Fiona.'
E. I'll never forget the day I met her. June the 14th, 1978. About half past two in the afternoon. I was standing outside the bank. It was raining...

F. 'What shall we do? Shall we go in two cars?'
   'Yes. John and Peter come with me in the Ford, and you three go in Ann's car. You follow me. If you get lost, go to the church and we'll pick you up there.'
G. Money isn't the problem. The real problem is time. It's essential to finish the first part of the work before John goes to Brazil. Otherwise everything's going to be late and we'll lose a year's sales. Do you see what I mean?
H. 'What's thirty-seven and twenty-six and fourteen and a hundred and eighty-seven?' 'Two hundred and sixty-four.'
I. 'What shall we have for supper?'
   'I don't know.'
   'Nor do I.'
   'I know! Let's have Spanish omelettes. We haven't had those for ages.'
   'Yes – great!'
J. 'Somebody phoned while you were out.'
   'Who was it?'
   'I don't know. A woman. Young. American, I think.'
   'Oh, yes. It must have been Elaine.'

5 Logic test. Put 'T' if the argument is a good logical one which leads to a true conclusion. Put 'F' if the argument is illogical and leads to a false conclusion.

1. I am taller than John. John is taller than Kim. Therefore I am taller than Kim. _T_
2. My brother lives in France. People who live in France often drink wine. Therefore my brother often drinks wine. _F_
3. My secretary is not old enough to vote. My secretary has beautiful hair. Therefore my secretary is a girl under 18.
4. The person who telephoned was drunk. He had an Irish accent. He said he was an old friend of my wife's. My wife's only Irish friend doesn't drink. Therefore the person who phoned was lying.
5. All North Fantasians have blue eyes. My Fantasian friend Eric Dogwesk is good at smashball. Smashball players often eat cucumbers. All South Fantasians have green eyes. All tall strong Fantasians are good at smashball. Eric Dogwesk has green eyes and hates cucumbers. All blue-eyed Fantasians are tall and strong. All smashball players sing sentimental songs in the bath. All green-eyed Fantasians are short and fat. Therefore:
   a. Eric Dogwesk sings in the bath.
   b. Eric Dogwesk is not a North Fantasian.
   c. Eric Dogwesk is strong and tall.

6 Memory test. Turn to page 159. You will see a square with twenty words in it. Study them for exactly two minutes. Then close your book and see how many of them you can write down.

7 Are you good at organising? Study the plan and the information. Then work in groups and find a good way of reorganising the zoo.

INFORMATION

1. The giraffe is going to have a baby soon, so it must be put somewhere quiet.
2. One of the lions has died; the other should move to a smaller enclosure.
3. Small children are frightened by seeing the crocodiles as they come in.
4. The zoo has been given a new panda.
5. The monkeys are very noisy.
6. The camel is rather smelly.
7. All the enclosures should be filled.
8. Harmless animals should not be put next to predators (animals which are their natural enemies and might frighten them).
9. The zoo has enough money to buy two wolves or four flamingoes or a pair of small deer.

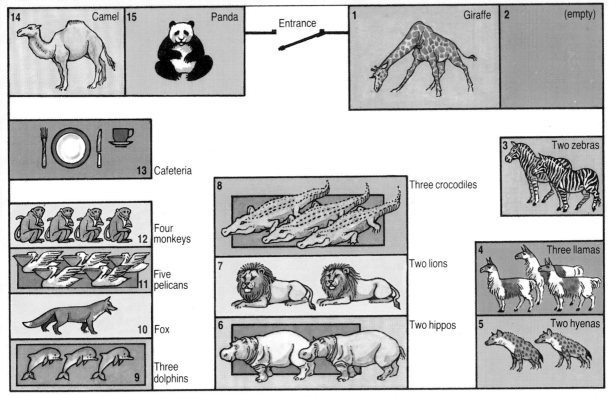

14 Camel | 15 Panda | Entrance | 1 Giraffe | 2 (empty)
13 Cafeteria | 3 Two zebras
12 Four monkeys | 8 Three crocodiles
11 Five pelicans | 7 Two lions | 4 Three llamas
10 Fox | 6 Two hippos | 5 Two hyenas
9 Three dolphins

B Take your choice

Choose one or more of these activities.
For the first six, you will need to use your
memory; for the others, your imagination.

1 Listen to the story and write down what
you can remember. You will need these names.

Pythias   Marseilles   Gibraltar
Mediterranean   Atlantic

2 The teacher will show
you twenty objects for one
minute and then put
them away. See if
you can remember
all of them.

3 Stand with some other students in two
lines, facing each other. Observe the students
in the other line for one minute. Then go away
and (without looking at them) see if you can
remember and write down what everybody was
wearing. Work together with the other
students in your line.

4 Work with a partner.
Both of you look very
carefully at the room (and the
people and things in it) for one
minute. Then one of you
closes his or her eyes, while
the other asks questions
about the room.

5 Listen to the recorded
sounds. Then try to write
down everything you heard in
the correct order.

6 Listen to the story about
the lift, and see if you can
answer the question at the end.

Unit 29: Lesson B

Students are given a choice of fluency-practice activities based on memory and imagination.
Structures: various structures are revised, depending on the choice of activities.
Words and expressions to learn: determined by the students' choice of activities (note that there is no Summary for this lesson).

Materials required
Exercise 2: 20 objects of which students know the English names (see exercise instructions).
Exercise 11: a collection of everyday objects (see exercise instructions).

Note
The lesson contains a choice of 13 different activities. Ideally students should be able to choose their activities individually, with students who have made the same choice working together in groups at the same time (as far as it is feasible to organise this).

1 Recalling a text

- Play the recording twice without stopping or giving any explanations; students can make notes.
- Tell students to write down what they remember.
- They don't have to recall the exact words, of course, but neither should they make an effort to avoid the original words if they do remember them.

Tapescript for Exercise 1
The first person who travelled to the far north and wrote about his experiences was a man called Pythias. He came from Marseilles, in the South of France, and lived about 2,200 years ago. At that time people thought that Gibraltar (where the Mediterranean Sea joins the Atlantic) was the edge of the world. Pythias didn't believe this. He sailed to Gibraltar, turned right, and went straight on. In his story, he says that after he and his companions had sailed north for a long time, they came to a place where even in summer there is ice and snow. There were white mountains that moved in the sea and shone in the sun like diamonds. He saw birds that dived and swam under water, and a great animal with a white coat that walked on the ice, roaring like a lion. The sun never set, and they lost count of the days and nights. At the end of the journey there was less ice, and they came to a land rising out of the clouds which they called 'Thule'. When Pythias returned and wrote about his journey, nobody believed him, and he was called 'Pythias the liar'.

2 Remembering objects
- All the objects should be things whose names the students know – and can benefit from revising.
- Suggestions: pen, pencil, watch, glasses, handbag, chequebook, spoon, photo, ring, cassette, shoe, flower, mushroom, book, (toy) car, ticket, toothbrush, wallet, newspaper, envelope.
- Students should not make notes while observing.

3 Observing other students
(Note that this activity has already been suggested as an option in Unit 1, Lesson B.)

- It is best if you can use two rooms, or one room and a corridor.
- Get students in two lines observing each other (between four and eight in each line). In a large class, have two pairs of lines.
- Give students a minute or more to observe; then send one group to another room (or to the other end of the classroom).
- Each group has to recall what the people opposite were wearing, and in what order they were standing.
- One student in each group acts as secretary, noting everything that is remembered.
- When students are ready, tell the people in each group to exchange some articles of clothing and/or jewellery.
- Students then form the two lines again, but do not stand in the same order.
- Their job is to get everything as it was before, taking turns to give instructions.
- Put some model sentences on the board. Examples:
  Maria, go and stand next to Bill.
  Alex, go and stand between Paul and Alice.
  Joe, take off that watch and give it back to Ann.
  Rosa, get your necklace back from John.

(With acknowledgements to Maley and Duff, *Drama Techniques in Language Learning*, Cambridge University Press 1978, 1982.)

4 Observing the room
- Students take turns to question and be questioned.
- Useful sentence patterns:
  Is there a . . . ?
  How many . . . are there?
  Where is the . . . ?
- Alternatively, get students to look out of the window and then question each other about what they saw.

5 Recorded sounds
- Students will hear the following:
a clock ticking, a typewriter, a phone ringing, a voice saying 'Hello', a voice saying 'Yes', a voice saying 'Goodbye', a phone being put down, a cat miaowing, footsteps, a door opening, somebody dropping something, a voice saying 'Damn!', a cat miaowing, a door closing, footsteps, a radio, a car starting.

6 The liftboy
- Tell students they are going to hear a story about a liftboy (pre-teach this word).
- Explain that they must do their best to remember everything they hear. (Most of the details in the story are irrelevant, but don't tell students this.)
- The question at the end is 'What is the name of the liftboy?' Unless students remember the first sentence ('Imagine you're a liftboy'), they will probably insist that they have not been told the answer.

There is no tapescript for Exercise 6.

7 Miming a machine
- This is a useful (but time-consuming) way of revising the names of common machines.
- Volunteers take it in turn to mime a machine.
- The others try to write down the name of the machine.

8 Three lies
- Demonstrate yourself first. Include some unlikely (but true) facts as well as three lies.
- Then ask for volunteers to carry on.
- In a fluent class the exercise can be done in groups.

9 Travel agents
- Spend ten to fifteen minutes preparing. Travel agents should decide how to make their holidays sound attractive; the others decide what questions they will want to ask.
- Help with words and expressions where necessary.
- Each travel agent should sell a different holiday; students go to each agent before making a decision.
- In a large class, students can go round in pairs.
- Possible holidays: the four mentioned in the Student's Book; the North Cape (in northern Norway) in December; a tour of British prisons; the Birmingham canals; Scottish coal mines; a working holiday in a bicycle factory; a walking holiday across Australia.

10 Candidates for an award
- Give the class a quarter of an hour to prepare.
- Let the committee interview the candidates in turn.
- After the interviews, let the committee discuss in another room if possible.
- When they come back, they must announce their decision and give reasons.
- In a small class, leave out the candidates' families.

11 Visitors from space
- This can be done in groups, with each group being given the same (or different) objects.
- Give students ten to fifteen minutes to decide what the objects are (assuming they are visitors from space who know nothing of our civilisation).
- Then let each group announce their conclusions.
- Suggestions: toilet roll, light bulb, clothes peg, shoe, guitar, comb, camera, stamp, bra, tie, spoon.

12 Updated fairy story
- This works best if students are all from similar cultural backgrounds and know the same stories.
- Discuss how it would be possible to modernise a well-known fairy story. (For instance, 'Cinderella' could become 'Cinderello' – a non-sexist story with all the roles reversed. Giants can become policemen. Fairy godmothers can be politicians.)
- Give students 20 minutes to plan their stories in groups of six to eight.
- Tell them to distribute the roles and dramatise the stories. Warn them if you will be recording them.
- Let them rehearse and then perform for the class.

13 Class story
- This is an easy and popular exercise.

- You may like to record the story and play it back to the class when you have finished.

Summary
- There is no Summary for this lesson. Tell students to learn any useful vocabulary that has come up.

Practice Book
- Tell students which exercises you want them to do.

7 Mime a machine. See if the other students can write down the name of your machine.

8 Tell the class something about yourself (family, childhood, school, . . .), but put in three lies. See if the other students can guess which are the lies.

9 Six of the students are travel agents. They will try to sell holidays in Greenland, Siberia, the Sahara Desert in August, Manchester in November, and similar places. The other students will go round making enquiries about holidays. See which agent does the best job of selling.

10 A rich woman has offered £10,000 to pay one person to spend a year doing as much good as possible to the world's people. Three students are the committee who have to decide who will get the prize. The other students work in groups of three or four; in each group, one student is a candidate for the prize, and the others are their families who help them prepare for the interview. After fifteen minutes' preparation, the committee interviews each candidate in turn.

11 You have just arrived in a spaceship from a distant world. You are studying the earth's civilisation, but you don't know much about it yet. The teacher will give you some everyday things: try to decide what they are for.

12 Work with some other students and prepare a modern version of a fairy story.

13 Make up a class story. One person starts, the next person continues, and so on in turn. Here is a possible beginning:

'*Mary was walking home late at night...*'

121

Work

A Working makes me think

In Japan, teachers earn far less than factory
   workers.
In Denmark, teachers are among the best-paid
   workers.
A New York dustman makes three times as much
   as an Indian army general.
A German bus driver gets twice the pay of a British
   bus driver.
In China, university professors earn as much as
   government ministers.
Chinese journalists are the worst-paid journalists in
   the world.

1 In your country, which of the following
people are well paid? Which ones earn average
wages? Which ones are badly paid? Make three
lists on a piece of paper. Then try to arrange
each list in order of earnings.

bus driver   company director   dustman
factory worker   farm worker   army general
government minister   nurse
primary-school teacher   housewife
university professor

2 In your opinion, which of
the people in Exercise 1
should be paid most? Which
should be paid least? Should
any of the others be better
paid, or worse paid, than they
are? Compare your opinion
with two other people's and
report to the class.

3 Copy the list below. Then you will hear
four people: John (who works with racehorses)
Jane (a part-time legal secretary), Keith (a
printer's reader) and Sue (a nurse). Write down
what they like and dislike about their jobs.

WHO DISLIKES:
the routine of the job?
not having enough time to do the job well?
the old-fashioned way of working?

WHO LIKES:
the contact with people?
having to think?
travelling?
the job itself?

Unit 30: Lesson A

Students learn to say more about work and people's attitude to it.
Principal structures: adverbs of manner with past participles (*well paid, badly paid*); *should* + passive infinitive (*should be paid*).
Words and expressions to learn: *factory; dustman; army; pay; professor; journalist; farm; routine; contact; security; pension; promotion; responsibility; freedom; primary school; have* (something) *in common; retire.*
Phonology: pronunciations of the letter *u*.

Language notes and possible problems

1. Adverbs with past participles Students should note the word order in expressions like *well paid, badly paid*. These expressions can be adjectival rather than verbal (as in *a well-paid job* or *the best-paid workers*) and then they are generally written with a hyphen.

2. *Should* + passive infinitive Students may have a little difficulty with the structure *should be paid* in Exercise 2. Make sure they practise it enough.

3. Pronunciations of *u* Generally, the letter *u* is pronounced /ʌ/ in English if it is followed by only one consonant at the end of a word; or if it is followed by two consonants. If it is followed by *r* it is pronounced /ɜ:/. Otherwise it is usually pronounced /ju:/, except after *r*, and sometimes *s* and *l*, when it is pronounced /u:/.

There is a slight variation in usage here, and we have chosen to follow the usage of the standard dictionaries. This usage is also the more common one, and fortunately more regular: /u:/ after initial *r*, *s* and *l*. If this is not your own usage (if you say /su:pə(r)/ but /sju:t/, for example) you may want to modify Exercise 5; or you may decide to give your students an easy rule, and use the recording instead of reading the models in this exercise.

If you are short of time
You can give Exercise 4 for homework.

1 Comparative earnings
● Look through the text about comparative earnings.
● Explain any difficulties and practise the pronunciation of the new words.
● Note that *professor* is a 'false friend' for some students (similar words in many European languages simply mean 'teacher' or 'secondary-school teacher') and you may have to point out that the English word refers to a senior university teacher.
● Ask students for their reactions.
● Go over the list of professions with the students, making sure they understand them.
● Then ask each student to put the professions from the list into three groups, according to whether the people are well paid, earn average wages, or are badly paid in the student's country.
● They should try to arrange each list in order of earnings.
● There may be some discussion about how to compute a housewife's earnings; you can decide whether this will be an interesting or acrimonious discussion in your own class.
● While the students are working, write some phrases on the board that they can use in talking about their answers, e.g. *far less than; among the best-paid workers; twice as much as; worst-paid workers; better paid than . . .*
● Then ask each student to volunteer one sentence about his or her list, trying to use one of the phrases from the board. You may want to allow other students to challenge an assertion as it is made.

2 Changing things
● Let students do this individually first of all.
● Then get them to form groups of three or four and exchange views. Encourage them to discuss in English; help with vocabulary where necessary.
● Each group should then report to the class on the two most important points in their discussion.
● This may lead to a whole-class discussion of the topic if you allow other class members to comment on each group's report.

3 Listening: people's attitude to jobs
● Go over the list of questions with the students, making any explanations that are necessary (you may have to explain *routine*).
● Then ask students to copy the questions onto a piece of paper so that they can write down the answers as they hear them.
● Tell them that they will hear four people talk about their work. Point out what each person's job is (as noted in the rubric).
● Tell the students that some of the questions may have more than one answer.
● Then play the recording, more than once if necessary, while students try to write the answers.

Answers to Exercise 3
John, Jane and Sue don't like the routine of their jobs.
Keith doesn't like not having enough time for his job.
Sue doesn't like the old-fashioned way of working.
Sue likes the contact with people.
Jane likes having to think.
John likes travelling.
Keith likes the job itself.

Tapescript for Exercise 3: see page 184

4 Completing a text

• Note that many of the blanks in the text can be filled in more than one way.

• A good way to approach this exercise is to go through it with the whole class, discussing the possible ways of completing each blank.

• Alternatively, you can divide the text into parts and let different groups work on each part, trying to see how many possibilities they can come up with for each blank. Each group then presents its part of the text to the class.

Possible answers to Exercise 4
(Students may come up with other plausible answers for some of the blanks.)

Alan is *a* commercial traveller. He works for a firm *that / which* manufactures and sells different kinds of industrial glue. He *spends* most of his time travelling, visiting customers and possible customers in various *parts / regions / areas* of the country.

Alan doesn't *like* his job much, and he is unhappy for several reasons. First of all, he *dislikes / hates* living out of suitcases. When he was younger he *liked / loved* the travelling, but now he is tired of *going / moving* from one hotel room to another, spending his life visiting factories in small industrial towns. And he doesn't enjoy *being / speaking* with the people he meets. He gets on well enough with them, but he doesn't *think / feel* they have very much in common. Alan's interested in literature and politics. Most of the *factory* managers he meets just seem to be *interested* in talking about work and golf. Alan doesn't find glue very interesting – in fact, he would be *happy / delighted / pleased* if he never *saw* a tube of glue again in his whole life.

Although the *pay / money* and the conditions are good, and his firm treats him well, Alan would very much like to *leave / change* his job. He *wants / would like / would love* to stay in one place and see more of his *wife* and children. Unfortunately he doesn't have much choice; it isn't easy to find *work / jobs* these days, and Alan is fortunate to be employed. Still, he can't wait to retire. He knows he is lucky in many *ways*, but sometimes he *feels / is* so unhappy that he wants to scream.

5 Pronunciations of the letter *u*

• Read or play list number 1 while the students listen. (See *Language notes*.)

• Ask the students to form groups of three or four and try to write a rule for this pronunciation of the letter *u*.

• Then let the different groups compare rules and decide which group has come up with the best rule.

• Follow the same procedure for lists 2, 3 and 4.

• Then get the students to decide which words in the box go in groups 1, 2, 3 and 4.

• Go over the common exceptions and get the students to practise them.

Answers, and possible rules for Exercise 5
(These rules only apply in stressed syllables.)
1. /ʌ/: *u* followed by only one consonant at the end of the word; or *u* followed by two consonants. (*jump, hut, butter, customs, run*)
2. /juː/: in most other cases. (*introduce, stupid, universe, amused, use*)
3. But /uː/ in other cases after initial *r*, *s*, or *l*. (*fruit, suit, true*)
4. And /ɜː/ when *u* is followed by *r* plus consonant. (*burglary, burn, purpose*)

6 What's important in a job?

• Go over the list of words and expressions with the students, explaining any problems and practising the pronunciation.

• Then ask students to spend five or ten minutes working individually, deciding which of the items matter most to them, and making a list of the four most important things and the one least important thing.

• When they have done this, each student should try and find someone else whose answer is as close to his or hers as possible (ideally by getting up and walking around the room).

7 Present activity: likes and dislikes

• Each student should write at least one positive thing and one negative thing about his or her job or activity.

• Collect the papers, shuffle them and read them to the class, numbering them as you go.

• Students should write down each number and their guesses as to who wrote it.

• When you have finished, read the sentences again for each student to 'claim' his or her sentences.

Summary
• Remind students to look over the Summary and learn the new words.

Practice Book
• Tell students which exercises you want them to do.

4 Read this text and try to put in the missing words and expressions.

Alan is .... commercial traveller. He works for a firm .... manufactures and sells different kinds of industrial glue. He .... most of his time travelling, visiting customers and possible customers in various .... of the country.

Alan doesn't .... his job much, and he is unhappy for several reasons. First of all, he .... living out of suitcases. When he was younger he .... the travelling, but now he is tired of .... from one hotel room to another, spending his life visiting factories in small industrial towns. And he doesn't enjoy .... with the people he meets. He gets on well enough with them, but he doesn't .... they have very much in common. Alan's interested in literature and politics. Most of the .... managers he meets just seem to be .... in talking about work and golf. Alan doesn't find glue very interesting – in fact, he would be .... if he never .... a tube of glue again in his whole life.

Although the .... and the conditions are good, and his firm treats him well, Alan would very much like to .... his job. He .... to stay in one place and see more of his .... and children. Unfortunately he doesn't have much choice; it isn't easy to find .... these days, and Alan is fortunate to be employed. Still, he can't wait to retire. He knows he is lucky in many ...., but sometimes he .... so unhappy that he wants to scream.

5 Pronouncing the letter *u*. Listen to the pronunciation of each group of words and try to make a rule. After you have worked out all the rules, say which group each of the words in the box belongs to.

1. bus cut drug much dustman under
2. university music tune produce fuel
   cure communicate
3. rule ruin suitcase superstition blue
   glue
4. nurse turn church

burglary introduce stupid jump universe
hut butter fruit suit amused burn
customs use true computer purpose run

Notice these common exceptions:

put pull push busy business truth

And of course, *u* is usually pronounced /ə/ when it is not in a stressed syllable, as in these words:

figure literature
(and other words ending in *-ure*)
suppose surprise until industry
fortunate(ly) unfortunate(ly)

6 Which of these things do you think are most important in a job? Choose the four most important and the one least important thing. Then try to find someone else in the class who has made the same choice as you.

working with nice people   security
good holidays   good pay   short hours
getting on with your boss   travelling
comfortable working conditions   a good pension
interesting work   the chance of promotion
responsibility   freedom

7 Write one or two things you like and one or two things you don't like about your present job or activity. The teacher will read everyone's likes and dislikes to the class. Try to guess who has written what.

B Do you have to work long hours?

1 Work in pairs. One of you chooses a job from this list (without telling his or her partner).

architect   businessman or businesswoman
coal miner   doctor   electrician
housewife   lorry driver   photographer
pilot   shop assistant   teacher

The other asks the following questions, and then tries to guess his/her partner's job.

Do you have to get up early?
Do you have to get your hands dirty?
Do you have to travel?
Do you have to think a lot?
Did you have to study for a long time to learn the job?
Do you have to work long hours?
Do you have to handle money?
Do you work with people or alone?
Do you have to write letters?
Do you have much responsibility?

2 Listen to the recording. You will hear a person speaking on the telephone from a factory. Answer these questions.

1. Who is speaking?
   a. the managing director
   b. the managing director's secretary
   c. the accountant
   d. the sales manager
   e. the personnel manager
2. Who is he speaking to?
   a. one of the directors
   b. his wife
   c. his secretary
   d. a customer
   e. an advertising agency
   f. a journalist
3. What do they make in the factory?
   a. shoe polish
   b. typewriters
   c. knives
   d. washing machines
   e. chairs
   f. electric heaters
   g. bicycles

My dad works at being a striker and when I grow up I shall work there as well

George aged 6

A prime minister is so busy he doesn't have time to think

Bruce aged 8

When you grow up and get a job the politicians make you pay for their taxis.

John aged 8

3 Pronunciation of *au* and *ou*. Say these words after the recording or your teacher. Can you write the rules for *ou*?

1. /ɔː/ automatic cause daughter
   fault authority dinosaur
2. /aʊ/ without housewife hours sound
   bound accountant
3. /ɔː/ pour your four course
4. /ə/ unconscious previous serious
   colour neighbour favour

Exceptions: aunt laugh draughtsman
because
should could would
trouble double couple cousin enough
you through group
although
cough
journalist

Unit 30: Lesson B

Students continue to practise talking about work.
Principal structure: *have to.*
Words and expressions to learn: *team; heater; handle* (verb); *design* (verb); *waste; check; frustrate; work long hours; mad; especially; on (your) own;* some names of professions as chosen by students.
Phonology: pronunciations of *au* and *ou.*

Language notes and possible problems

1. Have (got) to This verb has two sets of forms:
a. *I've got to   Have you got to?   I haven't got to*
b. *I have to   Do you have to?   I don't have to*
The second set of forms is used when we are talking about habits, repetitions or general cases (as in Exercise 1). In other cases, both sets of forms are common in British English.

2. Vocabulary Two lexical fields are touched on in this lesson: the names of professions and jobs, and the names of the various positions in a company organisation. Point out to students that they need only choose five of these from the list in the Summary to learn. But students who are more interested might want to explore one or both of these fields further with dictionaries, checking their findings with you.

Materials needed
Cards or slips of paper with names of jobs for Exercise 5.

If you are short of time
You can leave out Exercise 2; if pronunciation is not a high priority for your students, you can leave out Exercise 3.

1 Guessing game
● Go over the list of jobs and the questions, giving any explanations that are necessary.
● Practise the pronunciation. Make sure students can say the questions reasonably fluently.
● Then ask students to work in pairs. Each one in turn chooses a job; his or her partner tries to work out what it is by asking the questions.
● Pairs who finish quickly can choose new jobs.
● Practice Book Exercise 1 gives more revision of *have to.*

2 Mystery conversation
● Go over the instructions and the questions and make sure students understand everything.
● Then play the recording once and ask students to write down who they think is speaking and what they think the factory makes.
● Play the recording a second time if necessary.

Answer: The managing director is speaking, and the factory makes knives – with wooden handles in this case.

Tapescript for Exercise 2
I'm sorry. I'm afraid they're not ready yet.
... Yes, I know we promised them for May 15th.
... Yes, Mr Wallace, I know it's July now.
... Well, we've had such a lot of problems.

... Two strikes. And our suppliers ran out of steel in April.
... Yes, that's right.
... No, we couldn't. Everybody's short of top-quality steel at the moment.
... I don't know why, Mr Wallace. Ask the government. Then half my workforce was off sick in May.
... I can't help it, Mr Wallace. It's the weather. Three feet of snow on the first of May – it's not surprising. Then I lost my production manager. He went to America.
... More money, I suppose. I'd go too if I could. And there's a shortage of wood at the moment. Shortage of everything.
... Next week. By the end of next week. I promise.
... Yes, I know that's what I said last time.
... Goodbye.

3 Pronunciation of *au* and *ou*
● Get the students to pronounce the words in the four numbered lists after you or the recording.
● Some students may have a tendency to mispronounce *au* (as /aʊ/, for example), so you may want to watch out for this.
● Then ask the students to work in groups to write the rules for the three pronunciations of *ou* (usually /aʊ/; /ɔ:/ before *r*; /ə/ in unstressed *-ous* and *our*).
● Go over the common exceptions with the students.
● Then ask them if they can think of any other words with *au* or *ou.*

4 Dialogue: gap-filling

- Put students in pairs or groups of three to try and put one of the words or expressions into each gap in the dialogue.
- Encourage them to use their dictionaries to look up new words, and only to ask you if they are in doubt.
- Walk round while they are working to give any help that is needed.
- When they have finished, play the recording, more than once if necessary, so that they can check their answers.

Tapescript and answers for Exercise 4

KATE: What do you do, *exactly*?

PETER: I'm a mechanical engineer. Right now I'm designing a robot to *move* heavy things.

KATE: That sounds *exciting*. Do you work *on your own* or are you part of a team?

PETER: I'm the *only* engineer. I should have a technician *working* with me, but I don't, so I waste a lot of my time.

KATE: *You mean* you have to go and check that they're actually building the thing the way it's supposed to be built?

PETER: Yeah. It gets *a bit* frustrating at times. I do have a French draughtsman who works for me. He's a very good draughtsman, but not easy to *get on* with. Well, I don't think so, anyway.

KATE: Doesn't *sound like* a lot of fun.

PETER: Oh, the job *itself* is fun. I guess there are bound to be some problems when you have a lot of *different* nationalities working on the same project. *Especially* when the other European engineers get paid much more than we do.

KATE: *Really*? That's *terrible*!

PETER: I know, I know. Sometimes I think I'm mad to keep at it. But when that's what you love *doing*, you just can't stop and do *something else*.

5 Students' conversations

- Give each student a piece of paper or card with the name of a job on it. (For suggestions, see below. Of course, you will want to be careful about students' individual and cultural susceptibilities here; some students may think it great fun to get 'dustman', but others may feel demeaned by it.)
- Put the students in pairs and ask them to prepare party conversations about their new jobs, using five or more words or expressions from the dialogue in Exercise 4.
- Walk round while they are working to give any help that is needed.
- You can then ask students to perform their conversations for a group or the whole class; or you can get them to tape-record or video-record them (in which case you should let them know in advance that this is what you are going to do).
- Or, if you feel your class can manage it, do an improvisation: when the pairs have finished their prepared conversations, ask everyone in the class to stand up and pretend they are at a party.
- They should keep pretending they have the jobs you have given them, choose new partners and start talking to one other, imagining they are strangers.
- When one conversation is coming to an end, the students can move off (as one does at a party) and join

other students or groups, starting up new conversations.

Suggested jobs for Exercise 5
The King's or Queen's dog's doctor
The first astronaut on the planet Mars
A dustman or -woman   A window cleaner
An astrologer   A millionaire businessman or -woman
A racing driver   A newspaper seller   A pig-farmer
A vacuum-cleaner salesman or -woman   A zoo-keeper
A general   A fortune-teller   A gambler   A burglar
A police inspector   A ballet dancer   A deep-sea diver
A designer of women's underwear   A tax inspector

Summary
- Remind students to look over the Summary and learn the new words.

Practice Book
- Tell students which exercises you want them to do.

4 Try and fill the gaps with words and expressions from the box.

a bit	different	doing	Especially	exactly	exciting
get on	itself	move	only	on your own	Really
something else	sound like	terrible	working	You mean	

KATE: What do you do, ...?
PETER: I'm a mechanical engineer. Right now I'm designing a robot to .... heavy things.
KATE: That sounds .... Do you work .... or are you part of a team?
PETER: I'm the .... engineer. I should have a technician .... with me, but I don't, so I waste a lot of my time.
KATE: .... you have to go and check that they're actually building the thing the way it's supposed to be built?
PETER: Yeah. It gets .... frustrating at times. I do have a French draughtsman who works for me. He's a very good draughtsman, but not easy to .... with. Well, I don't think so, anyway.
KATE: Doesn't .... a lot of fun.
PETER: Oh, the job .... is fun. I guess there are bound to be some problems when you have a lot of .... nationalities working on the same project. .... when the other European engineers get paid much more than we do.
KATE: ....? That's ....!
PETER: I know, I know. Sometimes I think I'm mad to keep at it. But when that's what you love ...., you just can't stop and do ....

5 The teacher will give you a new job. Work with another student and prepare a 'party' conversation about your work. Try to use at least five words or expressions from Exercise 4.

Travel

A Where are they?

1 Put in the right word.

THIS		THAT
THESE		THOSE
HERE		THERE
COME		GO

1. I'd like to *come / go* away for a holiday again soon.
2. You must *come / go* and see us again one of these days.
3. Let's all *come / go* and see Harry this weekend.
4. I've found something very strange. *Come / Go* and have a look.
5. I'm afraid Mrs Barnes is busy just now. Could you *come / go* back tomorrow morning?
6. 'Newport 361428.' 'Hello, Is Helen *here / there?*' 'I'm sorry. She's not *here / there* just now.'
7. 'Moreton 71438.' 'Hello, *this / that* is Judith. Is *this / that* Phil?'
8. 'Do you know Africa?' 'No, I've never been *here / there.*'
9. '*This / That* is a nice place. I like it.'
10. 'I'm glad you like it. So do I. Have you been *here / there* before?'
11. 'No, *this / that* is my first visit.'
12. 'Have you seen *this / that?*' 'What?' 'In *this / that* morning's paper. Look!'
13. I'll never forget *this / that* morning, 20 years ago, when I first saw Mrs Newton.
14. Listen to *this / that.* You'll enjoy it. It's a great piece of music.
15. Who's *this / that* over there?
16. Jane, I'd like you to meet Peter. Peter, *this / that* is my friend Jane.
17. 'How's your lunch?' 'OK, but I don't like *these / those* potatoes much.'
18. Who were *these / those* people you were with last night?
19. Do you remember *these / those* cheese pies we used to buy in Parikia?
20. 'How do you like *these / those* trousers?' 'They really suit you.'

2 Match the words and the pictures. (There are too many words.)

> tube take-off check-in taxi garage
> speeding bank petrol station landing
> delay package tour enquiry
> compartment waiting roundabout
> luxury hotel accident giving directions

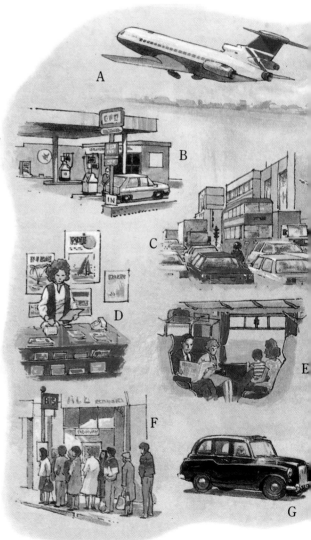

Unit 31: Lesson A

Students learn the language appropriate to a choice of 'travel' situations.
Structures: the contrast between *come* and *go*, *here* and *there*, *this/these* and *that/those*.
Words and expressions to learn: *tube*; *take-off*; *garage*; *petrol station*; *enquiry*; *compartment*; *roundabout*; *speed* (verb); *land*; *delay*; other vocabulary selected by students.
Phonology: /ə/ in unstressed syllables.

Language notes and possible problems

1. *Come/go*, *this/that*, *these/those*, *here/there* These contrasts are difficult for many students. In some languages there may be only one word in current use corresponding to one of the English pairs; or there may be three; or there may be two words with a slightly different range of use from the English words (so that a given word sometimes corresponds to *come* and sometimes to *go*, for instance).

The rules for the use of the English words are not simple (especially in the case of *come* and *go*). At this stage, however, it is enough if students learn that *come*, *here*, and *this/these* relate to the speaker's position (a movement towards that position, or nearness to it, or something of the kind), while *go*, *there* and *that/those* relate to movements and positions of other types. *This/these* can also refer to time: they are used to talk about what is going on at the moment, or what is about to happen.

There is a related difference between *bring* and *take* (not practised here).

2. *Garage* Note that this word can be used to mean three different things: a place to keep a car under cover (already learnt); a repair workshop (taught here); and (in some people's usage) a petrol station.

1 *Come/go*, *here/there* etc.

● Work through the exercise, varying the approach (pick on individuals to answer some questions, call for volunteers for others, get everybody to write others).
● As you go through, see if students can work out the rules governing the use of these words.
● Explain if necessary (see *Language notes*).

Answers to Exercise 1

1. go 2. come 3. go 4. Come 5. come
6. there; here 7. this; that 8. there 9. This
10. here 11. this 12. this; this 13. that 14. this
15. that 16. this 17. these 18. those 19. those
20. these

2 Matching words and pictures

● Ask students to do this individually first of all; then let them compare notes.
● Go over the answers with them and practise the pronunciation of the new words.

Answers to Exercise 2

A. take-off B. petrol station C. delay
D. package tour E. compartment F. waiting
G. taxi H. garage I. check-in J. tube K. accident
L. giving directions M. enquiry N. speeding
(There are no pictures corresponding to *landing*, *bank*, *roundabout* or *luxury hotel*.)

3 /ə/

- Give students some time to try to decide how the first four words are pronounced.
- Then discuss the answers and practise saying the words.
- Next, ask students to try to decide which five words in the next group are pronounced with /ə/.
- Let them compare notes.
- Play the recording (or say the words) and see if they want to change any of their answers.
- Give them the answers and practise saying the words.
- Remind them that unstressed *a*, *o* and *u* are usually pronounced /ə/, whereas unstressed *e* is usually pronounced /ɪ/ (as in *remind*, *women* and *decide*).

Answers to Exercise 3

/ə/	other vowels
forget /fəˈget/	remind /rɪˈmaɪnd/
afraid /əˈfreɪd/	minute /ˈmɪnɪt/
until /ənˈtɪl/	women /ˈwɪmɪn/
comfortable /ˈkʌmftəbl/	decide /dɪˈsaɪd/
Europe /ˈjuərəp/	business /ˈbɪznɪs/

4 Matching conversations and pictures

- Play the recording without stopping first of all.
- Then play it again while students note their answers.
- Play it a third time as an additional check if necessary.
- Discuss the answers.

Tapescript and answers to Exercise 4

1. . . . or you can have three weeks in Cairo, return air fare, hotel room and full board, and a choice of excursions, for £542 inclusive. (*travel agent*)
2. What time is the next train to Godalming? (*station enquiry office*)
3. First on the right, second on the left. You can't miss it. (*giving directions*)
4. How long do you want to leave it for? (*left luggage office, not illustrated*)
5. Do you mind if I open a window? (*railway compartment*)
6. You go back down the road and stop the traffic. I'll phone for an ambulance. (*accident*)
7. 'How often are they supposed to run?' 'Every ten minutes.' 'The last one didn't stop, you know. It just went straight on.' (*bus stop*)
8. Change at Piccadilly Circus and take the Bakerloo Line. (*tube*)
9. Have you got any hand baggage? (*check-in*)
10. 'Do you know what speed you were doing, sir?' 'Er, about 40.' 'You were doing 55, sir. Have you been drinking?' (*speeding*)
11. Fill up with four star, please. And could you check the oil and the tyre pressures? (*petrol station*)
12. Hello, darling. I'm going to be a bit late, I'm afraid. There's a traffic jam a mile long. (*traffic jam*)
13. We shall shortly be taking off on our flight to Rome. Please observe the no-smoking sign and ensure that your seat belt is fastened and your seat back is in the upright position. (*plane taking off*)
14. Could you take me to Victoria, please? (*taxi*)
15. It's making a funny noise, and it's very difficult to start from cold. And I think the brakes need checking. And it needs a service. (*garage*)

5 Listening for the exact words

- Ask students to choose one of the fragments of conversation that they have just heard to study. If they can't make up their minds, choose one for them.
- Ask what they can remember of what they heard.
- Play the fragment again and see if they can write down exactly what they hear.
- Play the fragment several times if necessary until they have got as close as they are going to to the exact words.
- Then write the fragment on the board for them.
- Explain any difficulties.
- If students like the exercise, it can be repeated with another fragment.

6 Students' conversations

- Ask students to choose a situation that they would like to study in detail from a language point of view.
- Then get students to join into pairs, according to their first choice of situation as far as possible. (Groups of three are also feasible.)
- Each pair should look over the vocabulary list corresponding to their choice of situation (unless they have chosen one that is not illustrated) and ask whatever questions they want to. You will need to go round from group to group while this is going on.
- When students have understood the new words and expressions, they should prepare a simple conversation practising some of what they have learnt.
- Get them to practise their conversations; listen to them and make corrections if necessary (but don't over-correct).
- You may like to tape-record or video-record the conversations. If so, warn the students in advance.

Summary

- Go over the Summary with the students and remind them to learn the new vocabulary.

Practice Book

- Tell students which exercises you want them to do.

3 The vowel /ə/ comes five times in these four words. Can you decide where? Where are the words stressed? Can you pronounce them?

picture   compartment   roundabout   luxury

Five of these words contain /ə/. Which ones? Can you say them?

remind   forget   afraid   minute   women
until   decide   business   comfortable   Europe

4 Look at the pictures again and listen to the pieces of conversation. Which one goes with which picture? (There is one piece too many.)

5 Listen to one of the pieces of conversation again. Try to remember exactly what was said. Can you write it down?

6 Work with another student. Prepare and practise a conversation for one of these situations (or a different one if you prefer):

– having a car repaired
– asking/giving directions
– an enquiry about air travel
– a train enquiry
– being stopped by police.

Some useful words and expressions:

CAR REPAIRS
steering   brakes   engine   plugs   starting
backfire   exhaust   silencer   tyres
puncture   windscreen wipers   wiper motor
check the brakes/steering/plugs/...
tighten the brakes/steering
change the plugs/oil/...
rust   service

GIVING DIRECTIONS
straight ahead   turn right/left at...
take the first/second on the left/right
first right, second left
keep straight on for about 500 yards
crossroads   traffic lights   fork   T-junction
you come to a T-junction

AIRPORT ENQUIRY
flight number   check-in   delay
standby   take-off   land   boarding card
smoking/non-smoking   stop over   fare
one way   round trip   hand baggage
insurance   ticket   make a reservation

TRAIN ENQUIRY
What time...?   the next train for...
Which platform...?   single   return
day return   direct   change   fast train
leave   arrive at   first class   second class
fare   ticket   seat reservation

STOPPED BY POLICE
What speed were you doing?
How fast were you going?
Is this your vehicle?
overtake   lights   traffic lights   stop sign
speed limit   speeding   driving licence
registration book
certificate of insurance
Have you been drinking?
Blow into this.

B Who has the right of way?

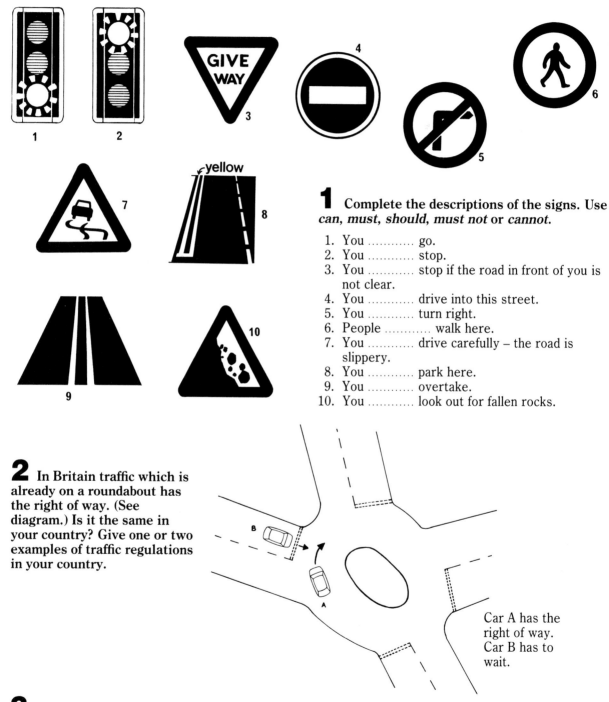

1 Complete the descriptions of the signs. Use *can, must, should, must not* or *cannot*.

1. You .... go.
2. You .... stop.
3. You .... stop if the road in front of you is not clear.
4. You .... drive into this street.
5. You .... turn right.
6. People .... walk here.
7. You .... drive carefully – the road is slippery.
8. You .... park here.
9. You .... overtake.
10. You .... look out for fallen rocks.

2 In Britain traffic which is already on a roundabout has the right of way. (See diagram.) Is it the same in your country? Give one or two examples of traffic regulations in your country.

Car A has the right of way. Car B has to wait.

3 Make up some traffic regulations for Fantasia (a strange country where everything is different). Example:

'You must not drive at over 30mph on Sundays.'

128

Unit 31: Lesson B

Students learn some language relating to road traffic; they practise expressing concepts of obligation.

Principal structures: modals of obligation (*must, must not, can, cannot, should*).

Words and expressions to learn: (*road*) *sign; traffic; pedestrian; pedestrian crossing; junction; the right of way; diagram; regulation; overtake; park; approach; clear; slippery; in the opposite direction.*

Phonology: /θ/ and /ð/.

Language notes and possible problems

1. Modals of obligation Discussion of traffic regulations gives students a chance to revise the use of *must, can* etc. You may want to remind students about the grammatical features of modal verbs (no third-person *-s; do* not used in questions and negatives; following infinitive does not have *to*).

2. *Must not* This expression may be misunderstood by some students. Make sure they realise it means *is forbidden to* and not *is not obliged to.*

3. *Must not* and *cannot* In contexts such as traffic regulations, *must not* and *cannot* have very similar meanings. If students ask about the difference, you can say that *must not* is 'stronger'. Remind students that *cannot* is written as one word.

4. *Should* (*not*) and *must* (*not*) The difference is neatly illustrated here. In this context, things that you should do are not generally legal obligations; things that you must do are. (See examples in Exercise 1.)

5. /θ/ and /ð/. While doing Exercise 5, you may like to remind students that very few words begin with /ð/. The ones that do are the 'grammatical' words *the, this, that, these, those, they, them, then, there, though, thus, than,* and *therefore.*

If you are short of time

Drop Exercises 2 and 3; drop Exercise 5 if pronunciation is not an important priority.

1 Road signs; modal verbs

● This can be done individually or by class discussion, as you wish.

● Explain any problems of vocabulary as you go through.

Answers to Exercise 1

1. can / must   2. must   3. must   4. must not / cannot
5. must not / cannot   6. must not / cannot   7. should
8. must not / cannot   9. must not / cannot   10. should

2 Traffic regulations

● Explain the meaning of *right of way.*

● Ask students whether the regulations for roundabouts are the same or different in their country.

● Get them to write one or two sentences describing traffic regulations.

3 Traffic regulations for Fantasia

● This is best done in groups.

● See which group can make up the craziest regulations.

● Help with vocabulary if necessary.

● When students are ready, let groups tell each other their regulations.

4 Newspaper report

• This is an authentic report, unedited. The exercises based on it are by Ruth Gairns and Stuart Redman, and are reproduced by permission.

• Students will not understand everything, but they should be able to answer the question if they read carefully.

• Give them a few minutes to read the report (without dictionaries).

• Ask them to decide which map is the right one (it is the first), and let them compare notes.

• See if they can explain their reasons for choosing one or other map.

• Don't explain the difficult words (students have to guess what they mean in Exercise 8).

5 Pronunciation of *th*

• Give students a minute or two to try to answer the question.

• The 'odd word out' is *third* (/θɜːd/); all the others are pronounced with /ð/.

• Use the recording to demonstrate if you wish.

• See *Language notes* for a list of words which begin with /ð/. Other common words containing /ð/ include *other, mother, brother, father, together, although, with.*

6 Guessing words

• Make sure students know what they are supposed to do.

• Although they are not very likely to know these words, they should be able to get a good idea of their meanings, without asking questions or looking them up, just by seeing how they are used in the text.

• Some students are not very good at contextual guessing of this kind, while others find it easy.

• When students have decided what they think the words mean, ask them to try to explain their ideas to each other.

• Finally, get volunteers to tell you their interpretations. (Let them explain in any way they like: with gestures, translations, synonyms or whatever.)

7 Drawing what happened

• Give students five minutes or so to read the text and do their drawings.

• Then get them to work in groups exchanging drawings and discussing their different interpretations.

8 Pair-work: accounts and drawings

• Students will probably need a quarter of an hour or so to write their accounts.

• Help with vocabulary if necessary, but discourage students from using difficult words which their partners will not understand.

• When they are ready, get them to work in pairs, taking turns to read their descriptions to their partners. Partners have to draw the accident without looking at the text.

Summary

• Tell students to look at the Summary and learn the new material.

Practice Book

• Tell students which exercises you want them to do.

Read the newspaper report. Then look at the two maps and choose the map which corresponds to the report. Find on the map: a roundabout, a pedestrian crossing, a junction.

Smash girl in a tizzy

MOTORIST Lesley Aston doesn't remember much about her trip home from work.

But villagers at Studley, Warwicks, will never forget it.

First, her Austin 1300 rammed the back of another car waiting at a junction.

She drove off without stopping, overtook cars waiting at a pedestrian crossing and swung into a roundabout on the wrong side.

Then 20-year-old Lesley crashed head-on into a second car, swerved into a third and careered into a brick wall before coming to rest on a garage forecourt.

She later told police that she had only vague memories of what had happened, magistrates were told yesterday at Alchester, Warwicks.

Lesley, of Hewell Road, Redditch, Worcs, was fined £150 for reckless driving and failing to stop after an accident or report it.

5 The following words spelt with *th* come in the text.

the   another   without   then   third   that

In one of the words, *th* is not pronounced the same as in the others. Which one? Can you find more words to illustrate each pronunciation of *th*?

6 Read the article again and try to guess the meaning of the following words and expressions.

trip   rammed   head-on   vague   fined
reckless   failing to stop

Lesley's car

* Crash

garage

Lesley's car

* Crash

7 Read the following account of an accident and draw what happened.

Car A tried to overtake car B approaching a road junction. Car C, which was coming in the opposite direction, swerved to avoid car A and crashed into a tree on the corner of the junction.

8 Write an account of an accident. Read it to another student: he or she must try to draw what happened.

129

Revision and fluency practice

A She sounds surprised

1 Listen and say how the people sound. You can use some of the adjectives in the box. Example:

1. 'She sounds surprised.'

afraid	amused	angry	cross	pleased
relaxed	sad	surprised	upset	worried

2 Listen to the recording and answer the questions.

3 How many of the questions can you remember? Example:

'She asked what I was thinking about.'

4 Here are some true sentences about one person's life. Can you complete them correctly?

1. He *would have been* happier at school if he *had been* good at sport. (be; be)
2. If his French lessons at school .... more interesting, he wouldn't have studied German. (be)
3. If he hadn't specialised in languages, he .... mathematics. (do)
4. When he was 24, he was seriously ill: if he hadn't been sent to a very good hospital, he .... (die)
5. He wouldn't have become a teacher if he .... a particular man. (not meet)
6. If he hadn't met a particular woman, he .... to live abroad. (not go)
7. If he .... less hard, he .... himself more. (work; enjoy)
8. He would not have been so happy if he .... a very good family life. (not have)

5 Can you make some true sentences about your life, like the ones in Exercise 4?

6 Revision of tenses. Complete the sentences with the correct verb forms.

1. 'Have you got a light?' 'Sorry, I .... n't ....' (smoke)
2. I .... in this country since January, but I still can't speak the language very well. (be)
3. Yesterday evening the telephone .... three times while I .... a bath. (ring; have)
4. After talking to her for a few minutes, I realised that I .... her before. (meet)
5. 'There's the doorbell.' 'I .... it.' (answer)
6. 'What's the weather like?' 'It .... again.' (rain)
7. How long .... you .... Susan? (know)
8. When .... the next train .... for Liverpool? (leave)

7 Make some bets. You can bet about the results of arm-wrestling contests; about tomorrow's weather; about tomorrow's newspaper headlines; or about anything else you like. Examples:

'I bet you a franc I can beat you at arm-wrestling.' 'OK.'

'I bet you 2p Peter'll win.' '4p.'

'I bet you there'll be something about the strike in tomorrow's newspaper.' 'I'm not betting.'

'I bet it rains tonight.' 'How much?'

Unit 32: Lesson A

Students practise listening and speaking, and revise several points of grammar and vocabulary.
Principal structures: reported questions; past conditionals; revision of tenses; expression of future; *sound* + adjective; *find* + object + adjective; *make* + object + adjective.
Words and expressions to learn: *doorbell*; *newspaper headline*; *reaction*; *result*; *specialise (in)*; *bet*; *beat*; *seriously ill*.

Language notes and possible problems

1. Gambling and competition Some students or teachers may have strong religious or moral objections to gambling, or to contests of strength. If this is the case in your class, you may wish to omit Exercise 7.

2. Bet Note that *bet* can be followed by a present tense to refer to the future (like *hope*). Example: *I bet it rains tonight* (*I bet it'll rain* is also possible).

3. Win and beat Note that students are liable to confuse these two words.

If you are short of time

Just do the exercises which are most useful for your students.

Materials required

Exercise 7: money (real or imitation) for betting.
Exercise 8: your choice of cartoons to supplement or replace the ones in the book.

1 How do the people sound?

● Make sure the students remember the meanings of all the adjectives in the box.
● Ask them to write the numbers 1 to 8 on a piece of paper.
● Tell them they will hear eight people, and must decide how each one is feeling.
● Play the recording through once, pausing briefly after each item.
● Then play it straight through again.
● Students may want to listen a third time if they are not sure of all the answers.

Tapescript and answers to Exercise 1
1. Oh my goodness! I wasn't expecting you! (*surprised*)
2. Ah, this is nice. (*relaxed/pleased*)
3. That was a cross thing for her to do. (*cross*)
4. (Laughter) (*amused*)
5. You stupid idiot! (*angry*)
6. It's dreadful – I don't know what to do. (*sad/upset*)
7. It's coming closer! (*afraid*)
8. Where can he be? He should be here by now. (*worried*)

2 Answering the recording

● Play the recording, stopping after each question for students to answer.
● Get them to write some of the answers.
● Play the recording more than once if students find the exercise difficult.

Tapescript for Exercise 2
What are you thinking about?
Where do you live?
What's your phone number?
How do you spell your surname?
What's the date?
Are you comfortable?
Are you hungry?
What sort of films do you like?
How long have you been learning English?
Have you ever been to New York?
What do you think of the British Prime Minister?
What do you think of the President of the USA?
Do you like fish?
Are you smoking?
Do you smoke?

3 Reporting questions
● The purpose of this exercise is to help students revise reported speech constructions. Explain that they are to begin all their answers with *She asked...*
Students will need to concentrate if they are to get the tenses right: the use of past tenses will probably seem strange to them in some cases.
● First of all, see how many of the questions students can recall spontaneously.
● Then play the recording again, stopping so that they can report the questions.

Answers to Exercise 3
She asked what I was thinking about.
She asked where I lived.
She asked what my phone number was.
She asked how I spelt my surname.
She asked what the date was.
She asked if I was comfortable.
She asked if I was hungry.
She asked what sort of films I liked.
She asked how long I had been learning English.
She asked if I had ever been to New York.
She asked what I thought of the British Prime Minister.
She asked what I thought of the President of the USA.
She asked if I liked fish.
She asked if I was smoking.
She asked if I smoked.

4 Past conditional
● You may want to get students to write the answers to most of these, so as to be sure that everybody has a good grasp of the structure.

Answers to Exercise 4
2. had been 3. would have done 4. would have died
5. hadn't met 6. wouldn't have gone
7. had worked; would have enjoyed 8. had not had

Notes for Exercises 5–8: see next page (page 131)

5 Personalisation: students' lives

- Give students a few minutes to think of 'turning points' in their lives, like the ones described in Exercise 4.
- Let them write down their sentences before they say them if this will help.
- You may need to supply vocabulary.

6 Revision of tenses

- Get students to write down the answers; then discuss them.

Answers to Exercise 6
1. do(n't) smoke   2. have/'ve been
3. rang; was having   4. had met   5. will/'ll answer
6. is/'s raining   7. have...known   8. does...leave

7 Betting

- Decide whether you want students to bet with real money or not.
- If not, you can prepare imitation money (pound notes, five-pound notes, ten-pound notes etc. on slips of paper); or use Monopoly money; or use matches.
- Ask for volunteers for arm-wrestling contests.
- Get the volunteers to bet on themselves, and invite other students to bet on the results (using the structures given in the examples).
- Students should write out their bets.
- After a few arm-wrestling contests, find some other things to bet on – for instance, tomorrow's weather or newspaper headlines.
- Record students' bets and settle up in the next lesson.

8 Reacting to cartoons

- This is a free conversation exercise which can generate practice of a large number of structures that have been studied.
- Encourage students to use the structures *It makes me...* and *I find it...*
- Students will probably need help with vocabulary.
- Note that students from non-European cultural backgrounds may find European humour difficult.
- You may wish to bring in other cartoons to supplement or replace the ones in the book.

Summary

- Tell students to look over the Summary and learn the new vocabulary.

Practice Book

- There is no Practice Book work for this unit.
- Students should spend their spare time preparing for the Test which follows the unit.

8 Look at the cartoons and talk about your reactions. Which ones do you find funny? Which ones don't make you laugh? Are there any that you can't understand? Discuss your reactions with other students.

"Oh dear, I can never remember who has right of way."

"Do you mind? I happen to be next."

"For heaven's sake, start smoking again!"

"Could you help me for a moment, Henry dear – I'm having a bit of trouble with my zip."

WHEN LIGHT FLASHES
REMOVE CLOTHES

131

B | A shock

Work in groups of four, five, or six.
Each group is to prepare, practise and perform a short sketch.
The subject of the sketch is 'a shock'.
It is up to you to decide what sort of shock this is, what you do
about it, what sort of person each of you is, etc.
Besides the shock, you must also bring into your sketch at least
three of the following:
– a story
– travel
– illness
– a song
– authority
– electricity
– a suggestion
– an offer
– a meal
– a bet
– money
– imagination
– something very big
– something very small

132

Sketch
- You should allow plenty of time for this sketch.
- Ideally, students should re-use a lot of the language that they have learnt during the course.
- Detailed instructions are unnecessary: students should be thoroughly familiar with the technique of preparing and performing sketches by this time.
- You may need to put a little pressure on groups that find it difficult to make decisions at the beginning. If necessary, make up their minds for them.
- Stress that this is a *revision* sketch. Students should be looking back through their books to remind themselves of useful language for the topics they have chosen. Discourage them from incorporating too much new language.
- If possible, get students to learn their parts by heart before they perform.
- Warn them in advance if you are going to tape- or video-record them. This will give them an incentive to reach a high standard.

Summary
There is no summary for this lesson.

NOW DO REVISION TEST THREE
(See page 172 and the Test Book.)

Unit 1: Lesson A

Grammar and structures

Introductions

Professor Andrews, this is Dr Baxter.
I'd like to introduce...
May I introduce myself?
Aren't you Henry Pollard?

'How do you do?' 'How do you do?'
I'm glad to meet you.
I've heard so much about you.
Nice to see you again.
I didn't catch your name.

Simple present tense

I work	do I work?
you work	do you work?
he/she/it works	does he/she/it work?
we work	do we work?
they work	do they work?

I do not (don't) work
you do not (don't) work
he/she/it does not (doesn't) work
we do not (don't) work
they do not (don't) work

Spelling:

he works   he stops   he starts   he likes
he wishes   he watches   he misses
he tries   he studies

Simple present tense: questions

    1   2   3
Where do you live?
    1   2   3
Where does your father live?
    (**NOT** Where does live...)

Other structures

Where are you **from**?
What nationality **are** you?
What kind of books do you like?
Can you play **the** piano?
    (**NOT** Can you play piano?)
What do you like **doing** in your spare time?

What does your father look **like**?
What is your mother **like**?

Asking for help in class

How do you say...?
What's the English for...?
How do you pronounce...?
How do you spell...?
What does...mean?
    (**NOT** What means...?)
Is this correct: '...'?

Words and expressions to learn

kind /kaɪnd/
spare time /'speə 'taɪm/
football match /'fʊtbɔːl 'mætʃ/
classical music /'klæsɪkl 'mjuːzɪk/
answer /'ɑːnsə(r)/
work /wɜːk/
introduce /ɪntrə'djuːs/
interest /'ɪntrəst/
travel /'trævl/
find out (found, found)
    /'faɪnd 'aʊt (faʊnd)/
go out (went, gone out)
    /'gəʊ 'aʊt (went, gɒn)/
cheerful /'tʃɪəfl/
glad /glæd/
whereabouts /weərə'baʊts/
so much /'səʊ 'mʌtʃ/

Revision vocabulary: do you know these words?

nationality /næʃə'næləti/
sport /spɔːt/
novel /'nɒvl/
flat /flæt/
first name /'fɜːst 'neɪm/
Christian name /'krɪstʃən 'neɪm/
surname /'sɜːneɪm/
Mr /'mɪstə(r)/
Mrs /'mɪsɪz/
Miss /mɪs/
Ms /mɪz, məz/

Unit 1: Lesson B

Grammar and structures

Have got

I have got (I've got)
you have got (you've got)
he/she/it has got (he's/she's/it's got)
we have got (we've got)
they have got (they've got)

have I got?
have you got?
has he/she/it got?
have we got?
have they got?

I have not (haven't) got
you have not (haven't) got
he/she/it has not (hasn't) got
we have not (haven't) got
they have not (haven't) got

We use *have got* in informal English to talk about possession and similar ideas, especially in the present tense. It means the same as *have*.

I've got a small flat in the city centre.
Have you **got** today's newspaper?
My sister **hasn't got** any children.

Be and *have*

'How old are you?' '**I'm** thirty-five.'
    (**NOT** I have thirty-five.')
I'm thirsty. **I'm** hungry. **I'm** hot. **I'm** cold.
What colour **is** your car?

Position of adverbs

Don't put an adverb between a verb and its object.

I **very much** like dancing.
    OR: I like dancing **very much.**
    (**NOT** I like very much dancing.)
I **often** read thrillers.
    (**NOT** I read often thrillers.)
I **never** get headaches.
    (**NOT** I get never headaches.)
You speak English **very well.**
    (**NOT** You speak very well English.)

Like ... ing

I **like** dancing.
Do you **like** cooking?

Articles

Jane is **a** secretary. (**NOT** Jane is secret
I like dogs. (**NOT** I like the dogs.)

Words and expressions to learn

nurse /nɜːs/
secretary /'sekrətri/
policewoman /pə'liːswʊmən/
T-shirt /'tiːʃɜːt/
ear-ring /'ɪərɪŋ/
history /'hɪstəri/
newspaper /'njuːspeɪpə(r)/
thriller /'θrɪlə(r)/
chocolate /'tʃɒklət/

wear (wore, worn)
/weə(r) (wɔː(r), wɔːn)/
mend /mend/
part-time /'pɑːt 'taɪm/
slim /slɪm/
striped /straɪpt/
least /liːst/
I don't mind /aɪ 'dəʊnt 'maɪnd/

Revision vocabulary: do you know these words?

clothes /kləʊðz/
shirt /ʃɜːt/
blouse /blaʊz/
sweater /'swetə(r)/
trousers /'traʊzəz/
jeans /dʒiːnz/
skirt /skɜːt/
age /eɪdʒ/
job /dʒɒb/
height /haɪt/
daughter /'dɔːtə(r)/
dog /dɒg/
baby /'beɪbi/

meet (met, met) /miːt (met)/
dance /dɑːns/
cook /kʊk/
shop /ʃɒp/
married /'mærɪd/
intelligent /ɪn'telɪdʒənt/
interesting /'ɪntrəstɪŋ/
light /laɪt/
dark /dɑːk/
I can't stand /aɪ 'kɑːnt 'stænd/

Unit 2: Lesson A

Grammar and structures

Present progressive tense

I am (I'm) working
you are (you're) working
he/she/it is (he's/she's/it's) working
we are (we're) working
they are (they're) working

am I working?
are you working?
is he/she/it working?
are we working?
are they working?

I am (I'm) not working
you are not (aren't) working
he/she/it is not (isn't) working
we are not (aren't) working
they are not (aren't) working

We use this tense to talk about things that are happening at the moment when we are speaking or writing.

I **am going** (I'm going) down to have a word with our visitors.
It **is coming** (It's coming) down very low.
Three strange things **are getting** out.

Present progressive questions

      1   2   3
What **are** you **doing**?
      1   2   3
What **are** the President and his wife **doing**?
  (NOT ~~What are doing...?~~)
      1   2   3
Are you **enjoying** your meal?

Spelling of -ing forms

look   looking
open   opening

come   coming } verbs ending in -e
take   taking   }

get   getting } verbs ending in one consonant
stop stopping } + one stressed vowel

lie   lying   } verbs ending in -ie
die   dying   }

Words and expressions to learn

light /laɪt/
sky /skaɪ/
machine /mə'ʃiːn/
suit /suːt/
field /fiːld/
visitor /'vɪzɪtə(r)/
gun /gʌn/
strange /streɪndʒ/
round /raʊnd/

Revision vocabulary: do you know these words?

picture /'pɪktʃə(r)/
top /tɒp/
remember /rɪ'membə(r)/
listen /'lɪsn/
square /skweə(r)/
across /ə'krɒs/
inside /ɪn'saɪd/

Unit 2: Lesson B

Grammar and structures

The two present tenses

We use the *simple present tense* to talk about 'general time': permanent states and repeated actions.

Our light **comes** from the sun.
They usually **walk** to work.
Do you ever **drink** beer?

We use the *present progressive tense* to talk about things which are happening at or around the present moment.

The light **is coming** from a strange machine.
They **are walking** across the field.
What **are** you **drinking**?

Other structures

Do you **believe in** 'flying saucers'?
I **agree with** you.
I **don't agree with** you.
I **think** (**that**) you're right.

➡

Words and expressions to learn

death /deθ/
a god /ə 'gɒd/
the future /ðə 'fju:tʃə(r)/
experience /ɪk'spɪərɪəns/
belief /bɪ'li:f/
reason /'ri:zn/
expression /ɪk'spreʃn/
nonsense /'nɒnsəns/

rubbish /'rʌbɪʃ/
guess /ges/
choose (chose, chosen) /tʃu:z (tʃəuz, 'tʃəuzn)/
explain /ɪk'spleɪn/
definitely (not) /'defənətli (nɒt)/
yes and no /'jes ən 'nəu/

Revision vocabulary: do you know these words?

life /laɪf/
dream (dreamt, dreamt) /dri:m (dremt)/
dead /ded/
sure /ʃɔ:(r)/
intelligent /ɪn'telɪdʒənt/
somewhere else /'sʌmweər 'els/

Unit 3: Lesson A

Grammar and structures

Simple past tense

I walked
you walked
he/she/it walked
etc.

did I walk?
did you walk?
did he/she/it walk?
etc.

(NOT did I walked?)

I did not (didn't) walk
you did not (didn't) walk
he/she/it did not (didn't) walk
etc.

(NOT I did not walked)

I went
you went
he/she/it went
etc.

did I go?
did you go?
did he/she/it go?
etc.

(NOT did you went?)

I did not (didn't) go
you did not (didn't) go
he/she/it did not (didn't) go
etc.

(NOT you didn't went)

The past of *be*

I was
you were
he/she/it was
we were
they were

was I?
were you?
was he/she/it?
were we?
were they?

I was not (wasn't)
you were not (weren't)
he/she/it was not (wasn't)
we were not (weren't)
they were not (weren't)

Spelling of regular past tenses

work — worked
listen — listened
cook — cooked
play — played

live — lived
love — loved } verbs ending in *-e*
hate — hated

stop — stopped
fit — fitted } verbs ending in one vowel + one consonant

marry — married
study — studied } verbs ending in consonant + *-y*

Irregular verbs

Infinitive	Simple past	Past participle
come /kʌm/	came /keɪm/	come /kʌm/
fall /fɔ:l/	fell /fel/	fallen /'fɔ:lən/
find /faɪnd/	found /faʊnd/	found /faʊnd/
get /get/	got /gɒt/	got /gɒt/
go /gəu/	went /went/	gone /gɒn/
hear /hɪə(r)/	heard /hɜ:d/	heard /hɜ:d/
hit /hɪt/	hit /hɪt/	hit /hɪt/
hurt /hɜ:t/	hurt /hɜ:t/	hurt /hɜ:t/
know /nəu/	knew /nju:/	known /nəun/
learn /lɜ:n/	learnt /lɜ:nt/	learnt /lɜ:nt/
leave /li:v/	left /left/	left /left/
lie /laɪ/	lay /leɪ/	lain /leɪn/
see /si:/	saw /sɔ:/	seen /si:n/
swim /swɪm/	swam /swæm/	swum /swʌm/

Words and expressions to learn

Christmas /'krɪsməs/
Christmas Eve /'krɪsməs 'i:v/
storm /stɔ:m/
bag /bæg/
sweets /swi:ts/
bone /bəun/
knee /ni:/
cut /kʌt/
helicopter /'helɪkɒptə(r)/
call /kɔ:l/
hit (hit, hit) /hɪt/

stay /steɪ/
recognise /'rekəgnaɪz/
deep /di:p/
above /ə'bʌv/
afterwards /'ɑ:ftəwədz/

Revision vocabulary: do you know these words?

town /taun/
seat /si:t/
piece /pi:s/
plane /pleɪn/
plastic /'plæstɪk/
dress /dres/
river /'rɪvə(r)/
village /'vɪlɪdʒ/
glasses /'glɑ:sɪz/
insect /'ɪnsekt/

spend (spent, spent) /spend (spent)/
kill /kɪl/
decide /dɪ'saɪd/
die /daɪ/
arrive /ə'raɪv/
wear (wore, worn) /weə(r) (wɔ:(r), wɔ:n)/
try /traɪ/
short /ʃɔ:t/
dead /ded/
by air /baɪ 'eə(r)/

Unit 3: Lesson B

Grammar and structures

Past progressive tense

| I was working |
| you were working |
| he/she/it was working |
| we were working |
| they were working |

| was I working? |
| were you working? |
| was he/she/it working? |
| were we working? |
| were they working? |

| I was not (wasn't) working |
| you were not (weren't) working |
| he/she/it was not (wasn't) working |
| we were not (weren't) working |
| they were not (weren't) working |

*Just when I **was trying** to finish some work*
*Janet **turned up**.*

*I **was getting** ready to come home*
*and the phone **rang**.*

I **lost** all my money when I **was travelling from Istanbul to Athens**.
The phone rang while I **was having** a bath.

Ellipsis

(I) Had lunch with her.
(It) Sounds like a boring day.
(I) Can't remember.

Words and expressions to learn

darling /'dɑːlɪŋ/
meeting /'miːtɪŋ/
talk /tɔːk/
phone call /'fəʊn kɔːl/
memory /'meməri/
turn up /'tɜːn ʌp/
go on (went, gone) /'gəʊ ɒn (went, gɒn)/
get ready /'get 'redi/
rather /'rɑːðə(r)/

together /tə'geðə(r)/
you know /'juː 'nəʊ/
I see /'aɪ 'siː/
as usual /əz 'juːʒuəl/
round the corner /'raʊnd ðə 'kɔːnə(r)/
sound like /'saʊnd 'laɪk/
not really /'nɒt 'rɪəli/
I can't remember /aɪ 'kɑːnt rɪ'membə(r)/

Revision vocabulary: do you know these words?

letter /'letə(r)/
office /'ɒfɪs/
pub /pʌb/
pint /paɪnt/
journey /'dʒɜːni/
try /traɪ/
finish /'fɪnɪʃ/
ring (rang, rung) /rɪŋ (ræŋ, rʌŋ)/

Unit 4: Lesson A

Grammar and structures

Comparative and superlative adjectives

Short adjectives (one syllable) add -er, -est.
old older oldest

Short adjectives ending in -e add -r, -st.
late later latest

Short adjectives with one vowel and one consonant double the consonant.
big bigger biggest

Adjectives with two syllables ending in -y change y to i and add -er, -est.
happy happier happiest

Other adjectives with two or more syllables usually add more, most.
boring **more** boring **most** boring
expensive **more** expensive
most expensive

(See diagram, Practice Book page 18.)

Irregular comparatives and superlatives

good	better	best
bad	worse	worst
much	more	most
little	less	least

Comparatives and superlatives in sentences

A car is heavier **than** a bicycle.
It has got **more** wheels than a bicycle.
  (**NOT** ___ more of wheels...)
A car is not **as** fast **as** a plane.
It has not got **as many** wheels as a plane.
A car does not cost **as much** as a plane.
  (**OR**: A car costs **less** than a plane.)
It is not **nearly** as heavy as a plane.
It costs **much/far** more than a bicycle.
A pram is **a bit** heavier than a bicycle.

A plane is **the heaviest** of the vehicles.

Words and expressions to learn

difference /'dɪfrəns/
wheel /wiːl/
vehicle /'vɪəkl/
ship /ʃɪp/
lorry /'lɒri/
pram /præm/
horse /hɔːs/
bird /bɜːd/
piano /pi'ænəʊ/
violin /vaɪə'lɪn/
trumpet /'trʌmpɪt/
cottage /'kɒtɪdʒ/
intelligence /ɪn'telɪdʒəns/
free time /'friː 'taɪm/
top speed /'tɒp 'spiːd/

Revision vocabulary: do you know these words?

tall /tɔːl/
short /ʃɔːt/
long /lɒŋ/
old /əʊld/
young /jʌŋ/
small /smɔːl/
important /ɪm'pɔːtənt/
interesting /'ɪntrəstɪŋ/
beautiful /'bjuːtɪfl/
difficult /'dɪfɪkʊlt/

Unit 4: Lesson B

Grammar and structures

The same

Her eyes are **the same** colour **as** mine.

Both

ONE-WORD VERBS
We **both speak** Chinese.
My sister and I **both like** music.

TWO-WORD VERBS
We **were both born** in September.
They **have both studied** in the USA.
Anne and Peter **can both sing** very well.

AM/ARE/IS/WAS/WERE
We **are both** fair-haired.
The two children **were both** very hungry.

Both/neither of us

Both of us like dancing.
Neither of us can swim.

Relative pronouns: *who*

Ann is a dark-haired woman **who** is rather shy.
Find somebody **who** speaks Chinese.

Compound adjectives

a **blue-eyed** girl
a **brown-haired** man
a **left-handed** child
a **long-sleeved** pullover

Do

She sings better than I **do**.
He likes golf, but I **don't**.

Like + -ing

I like ski**ing**.
Do you like danc**ing**?

Words and expressions to learn

fish /fɪʃ/
maths /mæθs/
company /'kʌmpəni/
director /də'rektə(r)/
pop music /'pɒp 'mju:zɪk/
interest /'ɪntrəst/
party /'pɑ:ti/
computer /kəm'pju:tə(r)/

hate /heɪt/
dark-haired /'dɑ:k 'heəd/
fair-haired /'feə 'heəd/
similar /'sɪmələ(r)/
left-handed /'left 'hændɪd/
right-handed /'raɪt 'hændɪd/
broad-shouldered /'brɔ:d 'ʃəʊldəd/
neither /'naɪðə(r)/
quite /kwaɪt/
I would rather not answer.
  /aɪ wʊd 'rɑ:ðə nɒt 'ɑ:nsə/

Revision vocabulary: do you know these words?

a cold /ə 'kəʊld/
a headache /ə 'hedeɪk/
dream /dri:m/
swim (swam, swum)
  /swɪm (swæm, swʌm)/
enjoy /ɪn'dʒɔɪ/
look like /'lʊk 'laɪk/
rather /'rɑ:ðə(r)/
shy /ʃaɪ/
alone /ə'ləʊn/
not...at all /'nɒt ət 'ɔ:l/
Do you mind if...? /dju: 'maɪnd ɪf/
That's all right. /'ðæts 'ɔ:l 'raɪt/

Unit 5: Lesson A

Grammar and structures

You buy meat **at a butcher's**.

a thing **with** a hole / **with** a handle
a thing / some stuff **for...ing**

Words and expressions to learn

soap /səʊp/
stamp /stæmp/
film (for a camera) /fɪlm/
tool /tu:l/
stuff /stʌf/
liquid /'lɪkwɪd/
powder /'paʊdə(r)/
material /mə'tɪərɪəl/
hole /həʊl/
wood /wʊd/
guarantee /gærən'ti:/
make /meɪk/
cut (cut, cut) /kʌt/

deliver /dɪ'lɪvə(r)/
round /raʊnd/
Can I look round? /'kæn aɪ lʊk 'raʊnd/
I'm being served. /aɪm 'bi:ɪŋ 'sɜ:vd/
I'm looking for... /aɪm 'lʊkɪŋ fə(r)/
That's all. /'ðæts 'ɔ:l/
I'm afraid not. /aɪm ə'freɪd 'nɒt/
Anything else? /'eniθɪŋ 'els/

Unit 5: Lesson B

Grammar and structures

Infinitive with and without *to*

Can you **tell** me the way to...?
  (**NOT** ~~Can you to tell me...?~~)
Could I **borrow** your bicycle?
  (**NOT** ~~Could I to borrow...?~~)
Shall I **help** you?
  (**NOT** ~~Shall I to help you?~~)
I'll **go** and get it.
  (**NOT** ~~I'll to go...~~)

I would like **to go** out tonight.
  (**NOT** ~~I would like go...~~)
I hope **to see** you again soon.
  (**NOT** ~~I hope see you...~~)
It's nice **to see** you again.
  (**NOT** ~~It's nice see you again.~~)

'Why don't you borrow something of mine?
  Would you like **to**?' 'Yes, I'd love **to**.'

Suggestions

What about your blue dress?
Why don't you borrow something of mine?

Words and expressions to learn

silk /sɪlk/
birthday party /'bɜ:θdeɪ 'pɑ:ti/
change /tʃeɪndʒ/
iron (clothes) /'aɪən/
come round (to visit) (came, come) /'kʌm 'raʊnd (keɪm, kʌm)/
have a look /'hæv ə 'lʊk/
give somebody a hand (gave, given) /'gɪv 'sʌmbədi ə 'hænd (geɪv, 'gɪvn)/
put something back (put, put) /'pʊt 'sʌmθɪŋ 'bæk/
wait a second /'weɪt ə 'sekənd/
one of these days /'wʌn əv 'ði:z 'deɪz/
Have you got the time? /'hæv ju: 'gɒt ðə 'taɪm/
in a hurry /ɪn ə 'hʌri/
That's very kind of you. /'ðæts 'veri 'kaɪnd əv 'ju:/
I'm a stranger here myself. /aɪm ə 'streɪndʒə 'hɪə maɪ'self/

138

Unit 6: Lesson A

Grammar and structures

Will and *is going to*

We use *am/are/is going to* when we can already see the future in the present – when future actions are already planned, or are beginning to happen.

We're **going to** buy a new car.
She **is going to** have a baby.
It's **going to** rain.

We use *will* when we predict future actions by thinking, hoping or calculating.

If both parents have blue eyes, their children **will** have blue eyes.
I hope Ann **will** like these flowers.
We'**ll** arrive in Edinburgh at about six o'clock.

May (= 'will perhaps')

If both parents are tall, their children **may** be tall too.
I **may** go to London tomorrow – I'm not sure.
  (NOT I may to go...)
Mary **may** come and see us next week.
  (NOT Mary mays...)

Words and expressions to learn

grandchild /'græntʃaɪld/
ball games /'bɔːl 'geɪmz/
science /'saɪəns/
firm /fɜːm/
(musical) instrument /'ɪnstrəmənt/
colour-blind /'kʌləblaɪnd/
sociable /'səʊʃəbl/
outgoing /'aʊtgəʊɪŋ/
optimistic /ɒptɪ'mɪstɪk/
musical /'mjuːzɪkl/
may /meɪ/
several /'sevrʊl/

Revision vocabulary: do you know these words?

parents /'peərənts/
daughter /'dɔːtə(r)/
son /sʌn/
couple /'kʌpl/
baby /'beɪbi/
computer /kəm'pjuːtə(r)/
bus driver /'bʌs 'draɪvə(r)/
sport /spɔːt/
maths /mæθs/
cheerful /'tʃɪəfʊl/
shy /ʃaɪ/
depressed /dɪ'prest/
certainly /'sɜːtənli/
probably /'prɒbəbli/
what...like? /'wɒt 'laɪk/
the future /ðə 'fjuːtʃə(r)/

Unit 6: Lesson B

Grammar and structures

Present progressive with future meaning

(Used to talk about future actions which are already planned or arranged, especially when we give the time or date.)

My mother'**s coming** down on Thursday.
  (NOT My mother comes down on Thursday.)
I'**m going** to Cardiff on Wednesday.
  (NOT I go to Cardiff on Wednesday.)
I'**m playing** tennis until a quarter past four.

Prepositions of time

at two o'clock
in the afternoon
on Tuesday
on June 17th
I'm playing tennis **until** a quarter past.
I'll ring you back **in** half an hour.
What time does the film start?
  (NOT USUALLY 'At what time...')

Suggestions

How about Thursday?
Shall we say Monday morning?

Would like + infinitive

I'**d like to make** an appointment...
I'**d like you to meet** my mother.
  (NOT I'd like that you meet...)

Take (time)

It'**ll take** a couple of hours at least.
It'**ll take me** a few minutes to shower and get dressed.

This and *that*

'Who's **that**?' '**This** is Audrey.'

Other structures

I wondered if you were free on Thursday.
I thought you said Tuesday.
Could we make it later?
I'll ring you back.

Words and expressions to learn

couple /'kʌpl/
shower /'ʃaʊə(r)/
diary /'daɪəri/
church /tʃɜːtʃ/
cake /keɪk/
wonder /'wʌndə(r)/
fix /fɪks/
manage /'mænɪdʒ/
practise /'præktɪs/
get changed /'get 'tʃeɪndʒd/
confirm /kən'fɜːm/
It depends. /ɪt dɪ'pendz/
Let me see. /'let mi: 'si:/
I'll ring/call you back.
  /aɪl 'rɪŋ/'kɔːl ju: 'bæk/
say,... /seɪ/
not...either /'nɒt 'aɪðə(r)/
my place /'maɪ 'pleɪs/

Revision vocabulary: do you know these words?

appointment /ə'pɔɪntmənt/
sweater /'swetə(r)/
ironing /'aɪənɪŋ/
mend /mend/
clean /kliːn/
try /traɪ/
free /friː/
early /'ɜːli/
difficult /'dɪfɪkʊlt/
I'm afraid (= 'I'm sorry') /aɪm ə'freɪd/

Unit 7: Lesson A

Grammar and structures

Present perfect tense

I have (I've) broken
you have (you've) broken
he/she/it has ('s) broken
we have (we've) broken
they have (they've) broken

have I broken?
have you broken?
has he/she/it broken?
have we broken?
have they broken?

I have not (haven't) broken
you have not (haven't) broken
he/she/it has not (hasn't) broken
we have not (haven't) broken
they have not (haven't) broken

We use this tense to talk about finished actions, when we are talking about an *unfinished* **time period:**

Have you **ever** eaten octopus?
I have **often** dreamt of being rich.
During the last three years, I have travelled 100,000 miles.

We do not use the present perfect tense when we talk about a *finished* **time period.**

When I was a child, I hated maths.
(**NOT** ~~When I was a child, I have hated maths.~~)
I **saw** John **yesterday**.
(**NOT** ~~I have seen John yesterday.~~)

Present perfect, simple past and simple present

Have you ever...?

PAST ------------- NOW ------------- FUTURE

Did you ever...?   *Do you ever...?*

Have you ever eaten octopus?
When you were a child, **did you ever dream** of being someone else?
Do you ever go out by yourself?

Been (past participle of *go*)

Have you ever **been** to Canada?
I've **been** to Hong Kong twice this year.

Go...ing

Do you ever **go walking** in the rain?
When you were a child, did you ever **go camping**?

Words and expressions to learn

song /sɒŋ/
job /dʒɒb/
ankle /'æŋkl/
billion /'bɪljən/
boat /bəʊt/
dollar /'dɒlə(r)/
grammar /'græmə(r)/
ice-cream /'aɪs 'kriːm/
advertisement /əd'vɜːtɪsmənt/
climb /klaɪm/
go camping (went, gone)
 /'gəʊ 'kæmpɪŋ (went, gɒn)/
run away (ran, run)
 /'rʌn ə'weɪ (ræn, rʌn)/
fight (fought, fought) /faɪt (fɔːt) /
past (adjective) /pɑːst/
in hospital /ɪn 'hɒspɪtl/
recently /'riːsəntli/
on one occasion /ɒn 'wʌn ə'keɪʒn/

Unit 7: Lesson B

Grammar and structures

Present perfect for news

Police **have arrested** a man in connection with the murder of Professor Bosk.
President Martin **has arrived** for a state visit.
The Minister for Consumer Affairs **has just announced**...
Listen! Something terrible **has just happened**!

Present perfect for changes

The population **has doubled** since 1900.
There used to be two bridges, but one **has fallen** down.

Present perfect progressive

I have been working
you have been working
he/she/it has been working
we have been working
they have been working

have I been working?
have you been working?
etc.

I have not been working
you have not been working
etc.

PAST ----|----|----|---- NOW _____ FUTURE

It **has been raining** *for four weeks.*

I **have been working** all day.
How long **have you been studying** English?
She **has been talking** on the phone since ten o'clock.
 (**NOT** ~~She is talking... since ten o'clock.~~)

Non-progressive verbs

I've **known** her for six weeks.
 (**NOT** ~~I've been knowing her for six weeks.~~)
 (**NOT** ~~I know her for six weeks.~~)
How long **have you had** that car?
She's **been** in America for three months.

Since and for

I've been here **since April**.
I've been here **for four months**.
(NOT ~~since four months.~~)
They've been talking **since nine
o'clock**.
They've been talking **for three hours**.

Used to

I **used to** play tennis a lot, but now I
play football.
(NOT ~~now I use to play football.~~)
I **didn't use to** like classical music.
Did you use to play with dolls when
you were small?

Pronunciation: / ˈjuːst tə/
(NOT ~~/juːzd tə/~~)

Words and expressions to learn

election /ɪˈlekʃən/
economy /ɪˈkɒnəmi/
president /ˈprezɪdənt/
trip /trɪp/
percentage /pəˈsentɪdʒ/
unemployment /ˌʌnɪmˈplɔɪmənt/
figures /ˈfɪgəz/
minister /ˈmɪnɪstə(r)/
crops /krɒps/
fruit /fruːt/
silver /ˈsɪlvə(r)/
increase /ɪŋˈkriːs/
sign /saɪn/
improve /ɪmˈpruːv/
average /ˈævrɪdʒ/
abroad /əˈbrɔːd/

Revision vocabulary: do you know these words?

vegetable /ˈvedʒtəbl/
price /praɪs/
population /ˌpɒpjəˈleɪʃn/
rise (rose, risen) /raɪz (rəʊz, rɪzn)/
fall (fell, fallen) /fɔːl (fel, fɔːlən)/
win (won, won) /wɪn (wʌn)/
rain /reɪn/

Unit 8: Lesson A

Grammar and structures

Can for possibility

You **can** (/kn/) get free medical care.
(NOT ~~You can to get…~~)
Where **can** you get a good inexpensive meal?

Will and may

Information centres **will** have information about 'bed
and breakfast'.
If 'bed and breakfast' is too expensive, there **may** be a
youth hostel nearby.

Connectors

In towns and cities there are buses, **and** in London
there is…
Fast food shops are cheap, **but** the food is not always
very good.
The underground is not easy to use, **so** you should learn
about it before you use it.
Your country may have an agreement with Britain for
other medical care, **too**; …
There are **also** coaches between some towns and cities;
these are cheaper than trains.
…a post office. Often **it** is inside a small shop.
People sometimes say 'p' instead of 'pence';
for example, 'eighty p'.

Words and expressions to learn

campsite /ˈkæmpsaɪt/
fare /feə/
coach /kəʊtʃ/
distance /ˈdɪstəns/
underground /ˈʌndəgraʊnd/
accident /ˈæksɪdənt/
embassy /ˈembəsi/
consulate /ˈkɒnsələt/
agreement /əˈgriːmənt/
insurance /ɪnˈʃɔːrəns/
foreign /ˈfɒrən/
at least /ət ˈliːst/
free /friː/
for example /fər ɪgˈzɑːmpl/
also /ˈɔːlsəʊ/

Revision vocabulary: do you know these words?

pence /pens/
pound /paʊnd/
hotel /həʊˈtel/
youth hostel /ˈjuːθ ˈhɒstl/
train /treɪn/

bus /bʌs/
family /ˈfæməli/
only /ˈəʊnli/
post office /ˈpəʊst ˈɒfɪs/
stamp /stæmp/
village /ˈvɪlɪdʒ/
town /taʊn/
shop /ʃɒp/
restaurant /ˈrestrənt/
food /fuːd/
meal /miːl/
pub /pʌb/
country /ˈkʌntri/
journey /ˈdʒɜːni/
health /helθ/
change (verb) /tʃeɪndʒ/
stay /steɪ/
help /help/
buy (bought, bought) /baɪ (bɔːt)/
need /niːd/
sometimes /ˈsʌmtaɪmz/
usually /ˈjuːʒəli/
often /ˈɒfn/
always /ˈɔːlweɪz/
cheap /tʃiːp/
expensive /ɪkˈspensɪv/

Unit 8: Lesson B

Grammar and structures

Should and will have to

You **should take** sunglasses.
(NOT ~~You should to take…~~)
You'**ll have to** have a visa.

Words and expressions to learn

operator /ˈɒpəreɪtə(r)/
airline /ˈeəlaɪn/
wallet /ˈwɒlɪt/
passport /ˈpɑːspɔːt/
customs /ˈkʌstəmz/
pickpocket /ˈpɪkpɒkɪt/
competition /ˌkɒmpəˈtɪʃn/
choice /tʃɔɪs/
pick up /ˈpɪk ˈʌp/
cancel /ˈkænsl/
go through customs (went, gone)
/ˈgəʊ ˈθruː ˈkʌstəmz (went, gɒn)/
reverse-charge call /rɪˈvɜːs ˈtʃɑːdʒ ˈkɔːl/
collect call (American) /kəˈlekt ˈkɔːl/

STD code /ˈes ˈtiː ˈdiː ˈkəʊd/
area code (American) /ˈeərɪə ˈkəʊd/
immigration control /ˌɪmɪˈgreɪʃn kənˈtrəʊl/

Revision vocabulary: do you know these words?

likely /ˈlaɪkli/
easy /ˈiːzi/
light /laɪt/
exciting /ɪkˈsaɪtɪŋ/
tired /ˈtaɪəd/
beautiful /ˈbjuːtɪfl/
sunny /ˈsʌni/
comfortable /ˈkʌmftəbl/

141

Unit 9: Lesson A

Grammar and structures

Present perfect and simple past

The present perfect tense is used to tell people about very recent past events which are 'news'. If you find a box of chocolates on your desk you can say:

Someone **has left** me a box of chocolates!
(**NOT** Someone left me...)

The simple past is used to talk about past events which are completely finished, and which are not 'news'. Compare:

My son **has** just **fallen** off a wall. I think he **has broken** his leg.
When I was ten, I **fell** off a wall and **broke** my leg.

Remember: we do not use the present perfect with 'finished-time' words.

Some of the demonstrators **left** home shortly after midnight last night.
(**NOT** ...have left home shortly after midnight...)

There has been

There's **been** an accident.

Words and expressions to learn

fire /'faɪə(r)/
neighbour /'neɪbə(r)/
kitchen /'kɪtʃɪn/
burglary /'bɜ:gləri/
smoke /sməʊk/
window /'wɪndəʊ/
instructions /ɪn'strʌkʃənz/
ambulance /'æmbjʊləns/
emergency /ɪ'mɜ:dʒənsi/
bleed (bled, bled) /bli:d (bled)/
steal (stole, stolen) /sti:l (stəʊl, 'stəʊlən)/
cover /'kʌvə(r)/

Unit 9: Lesson B

Grammar and structures

Make + object + adjective
Chocolate **makes** you fat.

Make + object + infinitive without *to*
Rain **makes** the flowers grow.
(**NOT** ...makes the flowers to grow.)

Making apologies

I'm sorry. I didn't mean to do it.
I didn't mean to.
I was thinking about something else.
I forgot what I was doing.
It was an accident.
I didn't do it on purpose.

Accepting apologies

That's all right.
It doesn't matter.
It wasn't your fault.

Words and expressions to learn

cough /kɒf/
switch /swɪtʃ/
brake /breɪk/
kiss /kɪs/
mean (meant, meant) /mi:n (ment)/
see (saw, seen) (= understand) /si: (sɔ:, si:n)/
burn (burnt, burnt) /bɜ:n (bɜ:nt)/
It doesn't matter. /ɪt 'dʌznt 'mætə(r)/
That's all right. /'ðæts 'ɔ:l 'raɪt/
my/your fault /'maɪ/'jɔ: 'fɔ:lt/
on purpose /ɒn 'pɜ:pəs/
than usual /ðən 'ju:ʒʊəl/

Learn two or more of these:
accelerator /ək'seləreɪtə(r)/
row /raʊ/
control /kən'trəʊl/
sigh /saɪ/

Revision vocabulary: do you know these words?

rain /reɪn/
chocolate /'tʃɒklət/
forget (forgot, forgotten) /fə'get (fə'gɒt, fə'gɒtn)/
jump /dʒʌmp/
get (got, got) /get (gɒt)/
crash /kræʃ/
lorry /'lɒri/
careful /'keəfl/
else /els/
actually /'æktʃəli/
because /bɪ'kɒz/
so /səʊ/

Unit 10: Lesson A

Grammar and structures

If

If you are travelling at 80kph in a car, you can stop safely in 52m.
If your ancestors' language was Choctaw, they lived in America.
If today is your golden wedding anniversary, you have been married for 50 years.

Special case: *if* + present for future idea

If you **see** a black cat you**'ll have** good luck.
(**NOT** If you will see...)
What **will happen if** John **speaks** to the girl?
(**NOT** if John will speak...)

If and *when*

When I go to bed tonight, I'll...
(I *will* go to bed.)
If I go to Scotland, I'll...
(I *may* go to Scotland.)

Negative imperatives; imperatives with *if*

Don't look at the teacher.
If today is Tuesday, **write** the number 12. **If not, don't write** anything.

Words and expressions to learn

score /skɔ:(r)/
wedding /'wedɪŋ/
great-grandparents
  /'greɪt 'grænpeərənts/
century /'sentʃəri/
island /'aɪlənd/
superstition /su:pə'stɪʃn/
luck /lʌk/

shoulder /'ʃəʊldə(r)/
hat /hæt/
New Year /'nju: 'jɪə(r)/
spill (spilt, spilt) /spɪl (spɪlt)/
itch /ɪtʃ/
close /kləʊz/
drunk /drʌŋk/
safely /'seɪfli/

Revision vocabulary:
do you know these words?

language /'læŋgwɪdʒ/
cat /kæt/
wine /waɪn/
salt /sɔ:lt/
umbrella /ʌm'brelə/
mirror /'mɪrə(r)/
travel /'trævl/

throw (threw, thrown)
  /θrəʊ (θru:, θrəʊn)/
open /'əʊpn/
break (broke, broken)
  /breɪk (brəʊk, 'brəʊkn)/
hit (hit, hit) /hɪt/
dark /dɑ:k/

Unit 10: Lesson B

Grammar and structures

Present tense with future meaning

When you **do** this, the cat will run.
  (**NOT** ~~When you will do this,...~~)
As soon as the kettle **is** full, move the fish.
Turn the small wheel **until** the kettle **is** under the tap.

When and *until*

When a melon is ready to eat, the end opposite the
  stem will be fairly soft.
Onions won't make you cry **until** they lose their roots.

Remember: *until* **can also be used with days, dates,
times, etc.**

She'll be there **until** half past six.

Words and expressions to learn

tap /tæp/
tin /tɪn/
fridge /frɪdʒ/
knife (knives) /naɪf (naɪvz)/
butter /'bʌtə(r)/
onion /'ʌnjən/
turn on/off /'tɜ:n 'ɒn/'ɒf/

fill /fɪl/
cry /kraɪ/
full /fʊl/
sharp /ʃɑ:p/
hard /hɑ:d/
last /lɑ:st/

Learn three or more of these:
kettle /'ketl/   peel /pi:l/
string /strɪŋ/   pour /pɔ:(r)/
hook /hʊk/   spring /sprɪŋ/
bell /bel/   tap (verb) /tæp/
stem /stem/   bubble /'bʌbl/
root /ru:t/   shrink (shrank, shrunk)
skin /skɪn/   /ʃrɪŋk (ʃræŋk, ʃrʌŋk)/
needle /'ni:dl/

THERE IS NO SUMMARY FOR UNIT 11, LESSON A

Unit 11: Lesson B

Words and expressions to learn

experience /ɪks'pɪərɪəns/
salary /'sæləri/
interview /'ɪntəvju:/
canteen /kæn'ti:n/
conditions /kən'dɪʃənz/

Managing Director /'mænɪdʒɪŋ də'rektə(r)/
qualifications /kwɒlɪfɪ'keɪʃənz/
advertise /'ædvətaɪz/
apply /ə'plaɪ/
essential /ɪ'senʃʊl/

full-time /'fʊl 'taɪm/
Yours faithfully /'jɔ:z 'feɪθfʊli/
Yours sincerely /'jɔ:z sɪn'sɪəli/
look forward /'lʊk 'fɔ:wəd/
I look forward to hearing from you.
as soon as possible /əz 'su:n əz 'pɒsəbl/

Unit 12: Lesson A

Grammar and structures

Simple present passive

Trees **are transported** to paper mills
  by land or water.
(= Somebody transports trees to
  paper mills...)

Made from and *made into*

Paper **is made from** wood. Wood **is
  made into** paper.

No *the* in generalisations

Paper was invented by the Chinese.
Oil is produced in Texas.
  (**NOT** ~~The oil is produced...~~)

Words and expressions
to learn

industry /'ɪndəstri/
page /peɪdʒ/
adult /'ædʌlt/
dry /draɪ/
use /ju:z/
grow (grew, grown)
  /grəʊ, gru:, grəʊn)/
reach /ri:tʃ/
get to /'get tə/
AD /eɪ 'di:/
by land /baɪ 'lænd/
daily /'deɪli/
serious /'sɪərɪəs/
Muslim /'mʌzlɪm/

Learn five or more of these:
rice /raɪs/
oil /ɔɪl/
coal /kəʊl/
wheat /wi:t/
wool /wʊl/
gold /gəʊld/
chemicals /'kemɪkʊlz/
iron /'aɪən/
steel /sti:l/
plastic /'plæstɪk/
leather /'leðə(r)/
cotton /'kɒtn/
synthetic fibre /sɪn'θetɪk 'faɪbə(r)/
produce (verb) /prə'dju:s/
mine /maɪn/
manufacture /mænjʊ'fæktʃə(r)/
invent /ɪn'vent/

Unit 12: Lesson B

Grammar and structures

Simple past passive

All three **were arrested** the next morning.
The *Communist Manifesto* **was written** by Marx and Engels.
    (**NOT** ___ was writing by...)

With and *by*

He was killed **with** a revolver.
    (= Someone used a revolver to kill him.)
The police think he was killed **by** his wife.
    (= The police think his wife killed him.)
His leg was broken **by** the fall.
    (**NOT** ___ with the fall...)

Words and expressions to learn

stone /stəʊn/
dance /dɑːns/
body (= dead person) /'bɒdi/
thief /θiːf/
business /'bɪznɪs/
invent /ɪn'vent/
direct /dɪ'rekt/
arrest /ə'rest/
sack /sæk/
owe /əʊ/
search /sɜːtʃ/
import /'ɪmpɔːt/
export /'ekspɔːt/
alive /ə'laɪv/
central /'sentrʊl/
earlier /'ɜːlɪə(r)/

Revision vocabulary: do you know these words?

pocket /'pɒkɪt/
cash /kæʃ/
hotel /həʊ'tel/
flat /flæt/
discover /dɪs'kʌvə(r)/
kill /kɪl/
build (built, built) /bɪld (bɪlt)/
win (won, won) /wɪn (wʌn)/
dead /ded/

Unit 13: Lesson A

Words and expressions to learn

hill /hɪl/
valley /'væli/
stream /striːm/
waterfall /'wɔːtəfɔːl/
wood /wʊd/
path /pɑːθ/
lake /leɪk/
town hall /'taʊn 'hɔːl/
college /'kɒlɪdʒ/
park /pɑːk/
central heating /'sentrʊl 'hiːtɪŋ/
through /θruː/
straight ahead /'streɪt ə'hed/

Revision vocabulary: do you know these words?

across /ə'krɒs/
along /ə'lɒŋ/
up /ʌp/
down /daʊn/
north /nɔːθ/
south /saʊθ/
west /west/
east /iːst/
mountain /'maʊntɪn/
island /'aɪlənd/'

river /'rɪvə(r)/
bridge /brɪdʒ/
road /rəʊd/
town /taʊn/
car park /'kɑː 'pɑːk/
post office /'pəʊst 'ɒfɪs/
crossroads /'krɒsrəʊdz/
theatre /'θɪətə(r)/
cinema /'sɪnəmə/
street /striːt/

Unit 13: Lesson B

Grammar and structures

Linking verbs with adjectives

It **looks heavy**.
    (**NOT** It looks heavily.)
It **is heavy**.
It **feels cold**.
It **smells funny**.

Look like, sound like etc.

Your sister **looks like** you.
It **sounds like** a train.

That: relative pronoun

a thing **that** tells you the time
an animal **that** has a very long neck

a thing (that) you sit on
something (that) you read

Prepositions at the end of relative clauses

a thing (that) you sit **on**
a thing (that) you open the door **with**
a thing (that) you drink **out of**

With

an animal **with** a long neck
    (=an animal **that has** a long neck)

You (=*people*)

A watch tells **you** the time.
A key is a thing that **you** open the door with.

Words and expressions to learn

back /bæk/
ice /aɪs/
tongue /tʌŋ/
envelope /'envələʊp/
feel (felt, felt) /fiːl (felt)/
smell (smelt, smelt) /smel (smelt)/
funny (=strange) /'fʌni/

Learn seven or more of these:

lid /lɪd/
calendar /'kælɪndə(r)/
suitcase /'suːtkeɪs/
hairbrush /'heəbrʌʃ/
pillow /'pɪləʊ/
sheet /ʃiːt/
wrist /rɪst/
queue /kjuː/
sandwich /'sænwɪdʒ/
microphone /'maɪkrəfəʊn/
lipstick /'lɪpstɪk/
magazine /mægə'ziːn/
nail /neɪl/
overcoat /'əʊvəkəʊt/
rose /rəʊz/
umbrella /ʌm'brelə/
beer /bɪə(r)/
litre /'liːtə(r)/
oil /ɔɪl/
pig /pɪg/

Revision vocabulary: do you know these words?

top /tɒp/
boat /bəʊt/
gun /gʌn/
ice-cream /'aɪs 'kriːm/
tap /tæp/
church /tʃɜːtʃ/
suit /suːt/
bicycle /'baɪsɪkl/
pint /paɪnt/
sweater /'swetə(r)/
cat /kæt/
sure /ʃɔː(r)/
heavy /'hevi/
pick up /'pɪk 'ʌp/
wear (wore, worn) /weə(r) (wɔː(r), wɔːn)/
liquid /'lɪkwɪd/
alive /ə'laɪv/
useful /'juːsfʊl/
a bit /ə 'bɪt/

Unit 14: Lesson A

Grammar and structures

Would rather

Would you **rather** live in the same town as your parents or not?
(**NOT** ~~Would you rather to live...~~)
I'd rather take my mother on holiday with me.
I'd rather not invite my in-laws to spend a week with us.
Most people **would rather** spend less time working.

Connectors

Kim and May are married, **but** they do not want to have children.
Although they enjoy playing with their nieces and nephews, they do not want to be full-time parents.
There are a lot of couples with young children in their neighbourhood, **so** they often help one another out.
Besides her husband and her children, she **also** shares her home with her mother-in-law, ...
Because Jack is too ill to live alone, he lives with his son Barry.
Barry is getting married soon, **and** Jack will continue to live with the young couple.

Words and expressions to learn

relative /'relətɪv/
aunt /ɑ:nt/
uncle /'ʌŋkl/
niece /ni:s/
nephew /'nefju:/
cousin /'kʌzn/
grandmother /'grænmʌðə(r)/
grandfather /'grænfɑ:ðə(r)/
granddaughter /'grændɔ:tə(r)/
grandson /'grænsʌn/
mother-in-law /'mʌðərɪnlɔ:/
father-in-law /'fɑ:ðərɪnlɔ:/
brother-in-law /'brʌðərɪnlɔ:/
sister-in-law /'sɪstərɪnlɔ:/
parents-in-law /'peərəntsɪnlɔ:/
in-laws /'ɪnlɔ:z/
society /sə'saɪəti/
rule /ru:l/
adopt /ə'dɒpt/
continue /kən'tɪnju:/
universal /ju:nɪ'vɜ:sl/
healthy /'helθi/
proud (of) /praʊd (əv)/
although /ɔ:l'ðəʊ/
besides /bɪ'saɪdz/

Revision vocabulary: do you know these words?

parent /'peərənt/
child (*plural* children) /tʃaɪld ('tʃɪldrən)/
grandparent /'grænpeərənt/
grandchild /'græntʃaɪld/
husband /'hʌzbənd/
wife (*plural* wives) /waɪf (waɪvz)/
daughter /'dɔ:tə(r)/
son /sʌn/

Unit 14: Lesson B

Grammar and structures

Should

Husbands **should do** some of the housework.
(**NOT** ~~Husbands should to do...~~)

Words and expressions to learn

housewife /'haʊswaɪf/
wage /weɪdʒ/
housework /'haʊswɜ:k/
support /sə'pɔ:t/
own /əʊn/
regular /'regjʊlə(r)/
upset /ʌp'set/
special /'speʃl/
free /fri:/
nowadays /'naʊədeɪz/
pocket money /'pɒkɪt 'mʌni/
(fifteen)-year-old /(fɪf'ti:n) jɪər 'əʊld/
You're right. /jɔ: 'raɪt/

Revision vocabulary: do you know these words?

midnight /'mɪdnaɪt/
foot (*plural* feet) /fʊt (fi:t)/
school /sku:l/
disco /'dɪskəʊ/
end /end/
pay /peɪ/
stay /steɪ/
agree /ə'gri:/
think (thought, thought) /θɪŋk (θɔ:t)/
choose (chose; chosen) /tʃu:z (tʃəʊz, 'tʃəʊzn)/
enough /ɪ'nʌf/
true /tru:/
early /'ɜ:li/
late /leɪt/
of course /əv 'kɔ:s/
perhaps /pə'hæps/
it depends /ɪt dɪ'pendz/
definitely /'defənətli/

Unit 15: Lesson A

Grammar and structures

Would like

Would you **like** to have a white Rolls Royce?
No, I **wouldn't**. / Yes, I **would**.
I'd like to be very rich.
Everybody **would like** to speak a lot of languages.

Want

I **wanted to study** Spanish, but my teachers **wanted me to study** Latin.
(**NOT** ~~...my teachers wanted that I study...~~)

Other ways of expressing wishes and hopes

I'm going to try to learn another language before I'm 30.
I **hope to finish** paying for my car by the end of the year.

By

I'll be there **by** three o'clock. (=at or before three, but not later)

Words and expressions to learn

museum /mju:'zi:əm/
the moon /ðə 'mu:n/
Japan /dʒə'pæn/
magazine /mægə'zi:n/
patience /'peɪʃəns/
artist /'ɑ:tɪst/
midday /mɪd'deɪ/
own (verb) /əʊn/
good at /'gʊd ət/
open (adjective) /'əʊpn/
different (= other) /'dɪfrənt/
political /pə'lɪtɪkl/
really /'rɪəli/
again (=as before) /ə'gen/
everyone /'evrɪwʌn/
by (with time expressions) /baɪ/

Unit 15: Lesson B

Grammar and structures

Want + **object** + **infinitive**
They **want him to give** them some water.
(NOT They want that he gives them...)

Wondered if + **past tense**
We **wondered** if we **could** sleep in your barn.
I **wondered** if you **were** free.

Words and expressions to learn

favour /'feɪvə(r)/
Could you do me a favour?
letter /'letə(r)/
post (verb) /pəʊst/
Sure (of course) /ʃɔ:(r)/
well,... /wel/
the thing is,... /ðə 'θɪŋ 'ɪz/
Thanks a lot.

short of money
That's all right.
you see,... /ju: 'si:/
it's like this
We wondered if we could...
Not at all. /nɒt ət 'ɔ:l/
this way

Unit 16: Lesson A

Grammar and structures

Quantities
They spend **too much** on tobacco.
They don't spend **enough** on food.
They spent **less** on clothing than on transport.
They spent **more** on food than on housing.
How much is £6 in your currency?
I've spent **a lot of** money on clothes.
(NOT I've spent much money...)
I haven't spent **much** on furniture.
I spent **a lot** on transport last year.
(NOT I spent much on...)
She must travel **less**.

Saying amounts of money
£5.25 = 'five pounds and twenty-five pence' or
'five (pounds) twenty-five'

No article with general meanings
They spent a lot on **food**. (NOT ... on the food.)
Alcohol and **tobacco** together cost less than half
as much as housing.
(NOT The alcohol and the tobacco...)

Must and *can*
Alice must spend less on clothing.
(NOT Alice must to spend...)
We **can** spend more on entertainment next year.
(NOT We can to spend...)

Use of verb tenses with time expressions
This year I've spent a lot of money on...
Last year I spent a lot on...
Next year I must spend less on...
Next year I can spend more on...

Words and expressions to learn

electricity /ɪlek'trɪsəti/
goods /gʊdz/
transport /'trænspɔ:t/
opinion /ə'pɪnjən/
currency /'kʌrənsi/
budget /'bʌdʒɪt/
rent /rent/
savings /'seɪvɪŋz/
income /'ɪŋkʌm/
earn /ɜ:n/
spend (spent, spent) /spend (spent)/
miscellaneous /mɪsə'leɪnɪəs/
personal /'pɜ:sənʊl/
exchange rate /ɪks'tʃeɪndʒ 'reɪt/

Learn three or more of these:
fuel /'fju:əl/
tobacco /tə'bækəʊ/
clothing /'kləʊðɪŋ/
services /'sɜ:vɪsɪz/
alcohol /'ælkəhɒl/
communication /kəmju:nɪ'keɪʃn/

Unit 16: Lesson B

Grammar and structures

Making proposals
I'll give you twenty-five pounds.
I'll tell you what.

Quantifiers
If you eat **too much** chocolate, you'll get fat.
I've got **too many** books – I don't know where
to put them all.
'You can have it for thirty-five.' 'No, that's still
too much.'

Too... and *not...enough*
It's **too** heavy to carry.
It's **not** big **enough** to hold all my books.

Words and expressions to learn

pound (weight) /paʊnd/
cover /'kʌvə(r)/
drawer /drɔ:(r)/
chest of drawers /'tʃest əv 'drɔ:z/
portable /'pɔ:təbl/
worth /wɜ:θ/
since (=because) /sɪns/
a friend of mine /ə 'frend əv 'maɪn/
can('t) afford /kn ('ka:nt) ə'fɔ:d/
in...condition /ɪn... kən'dɪʃn/
Come on. /'kʌm 'ɒn/
I'll tell you what. /aɪl 'tel ju: 'wɒt/
To tell you the truth,... /tə 'tel ju: ðə 'tru:θ/
Oh, very well. /'əʊ 'veri 'wel/
I'd prefer... /aɪd prɪ'fɜ:(r)/
if you don't mind /ɪf ju: 'dəʊnt 'maɪnd/

Revision vocabulary: do you know these words?

old /əʊld/
fat /fæt/
heavy /'hevi/
strong /strɒŋ/
difficult /'dɪfɪkʊlt/
long /lɒŋ/
small /smɔ:l/

146

Unit 17: Lesson A

Grammar and structures

Time clauses
I usually read for a bit **before I go to sleep**.
Before I go to sleep, I usually read for a bit.
I enjoyed life more **after I left school**.
After I left school, I enjoyed life more.
Give John my love **when you see him**.
When you see John, give him my love.
I'll phone you **as soon as I arrive**.
  (**NOT** ___ as soon as I will arrive.)
As soon as I arrive, I'll phone you.
I'll wait **until you're ready**.

Still, yet and *already*
John's **still** in bed.
He hasn't got up **yet**.
Susan is **already** dressed.

So and *such*
so handsome
such a handsome man
so quiet
such a quiet life
so kind to her
such a kind person
so good
such good bread
so happy
such happy people

Words and expressions to learn
postman /'pəʊstmən/
mat /mæt/
commercial traveller /kə'mɜːʃl 'trævlə(r)/
make a bed /'meɪk ə 'bed/
undress /ʌn'dres/
brush one's teeth /'brʌʃ wʌnz 'tiːθ/
put out (a light) (put, put) /'pʊt 'aʊt/
go to bed (went, gone) /'gəʊ tə 'bed (went, gɒn)/
address (a letter) /ə'dres/
answer (a letter) /'ɑːnsə(r)/
translate /trænz'leɪt/
keep on (kept, kept) (...ing) /'kiːp 'ɒn (kept)/
report /rɪ'pɔːt/
as many as possible /əz 'meni əz 'pɒsəbl/

Unit 17: Lesson B

Grammar and structures

Past perfect tense

I had (I'd) gone
you had (you'd) gone
he/she/it had (he'd/she'd/it'd) gone
we had (we'd) gone
they had (they'd) gone

had I gone?
had you gone?
had he/she/it gone?
had we gone?
had they gone?

I had not (hadn't) gone
you had not (hadn't) gone
he/she/it had not (hadn't) gone
we had not (hadn't) gone
they had not (hadn't) gone

Simple past and past perfect

PAST (THEN):   I **saw** who it was

EARLIER PAST   I **hadn't seen** her for a
(BEFORE THEN):   very long time

PAST: We **talked** about...

EARLIER PAST: ...the hopes we'**d shared**.

Words and expressions to learn
the way (to somewhere) /ðə 'weɪ/
directions /də'rekʃənz/
recognition /rekəg'nɪʃn/
silence /'saɪləns/
ghost /gəʊst/
feelings /'fiːlɪŋz/
the good old days /ðə 'gʊd 'əʊld 'deɪz/
hope /həʊp/
meeting /'miːtɪŋ/
look /lʊk/
realise /'rɪəlaɪz/
lead (led, led) /liːd (led)/
go wrong (went, gone) /'gəʊ 'rɒŋ (went, gɒn)/
reserve /rɪ'zɜːv/
examine /ɪg'zæmɪn/
repair /rɪ'peə(r)/
pleased /pliːzd/

Unit 18: Lesson A

Grammar and structures

Direct speech and reported speech
They thought 'The sun **goes** round the earth'.
They *thought* that the sun *went* round the earth.

  (**NOT** They thought that the sun goes...)
Galileo said, 'Light and heavy things **fall** at the same speed'.
Galileo *said* that light and heavy things *fell* at the same speed.

Reported questions
They wondered **if/whether** Aristotle was right..
Do you know **whether** Britain has a king **or** a queen?
She asked **what my name was**.
  (**NOT** ___ what was my name.)
Do you know **where she lives**?
  (**NOT** ___ where does she live?)

Words and expressions to learn
the blood /ðə 'blʌd/
illness /'ɪlnɪs/
star /stɑː(r)/
scientist /'saɪəntɪst/
religion /rɪ'lɪdʒən/
politics /'pɒlətɪks/
animal /'ænɪml/
war /wɔː(r)/
experiment /ɪks'perɪmənt/
cause /kɔːz/
tell a lie (told, told) /'tel ə 'laɪ (təʊld)/
discover /dɪs'kʌvə(r)/
flat /flæt/
living /'lɪvɪŋ/
equal /'iːkwʊl/
impossible /ɪm'pɒsəbl/

Unit 18: Lesson B

Grammar and structures

Modal verbs: probability and certainty
It **must** be late – it's getting dark.
It **might** be true, but I don't think it is.
She **can't** be English – she's got a French accent.
'Who's at the door?' 'It **could** be the postman.'

Likely
I'm **likely to be** in London next Tuesday. Can I get you anything?
Do you think it**'s likely to rain**?
There is likely to be a meeting on Tuesday.
There are likely to be about 20 people at the meeting.

Say and *tell*
Fred **said** that he was a photographer.
Fred **told Janet** that he was a photographer.
  (NOT Fred told that . . .)
  (NOT Fred said Janet that . . .)

Words and expressions to learn

full name /'fʊl 'neɪm/
profession /prə'feʃn/
poetry /'pəʊətri/
parking place /'pɑːkɪŋ 'pleɪs/
photograph /'fəʊtəgrɑːf/
likely /'laɪkli/
none /nʌn/

Learn some words from the text about the Amazon Forest.

Revision vocabulary: do you know these words?

age /eɪdʒ/
address /ə'dres/
interest /'ɪntrəst/
education /edjʊ'keɪʃn/
qualifications /kwɒlɪfɪ'keɪʃnz/
spring /sprɪŋ/
phone call /'fəʊn 'kɔːl/
election /ɪ'lekʃn/
say (said, said) /seɪ (sed)/
tell (told, told) /tel (təʊld)/
travel /'trævl/
happen /'hæpn/
true /truː/
famous /'feɪməs/
strange /streɪndʒ/
wet /wet/
by (=not later than) /baɪ/

Unit 19: Lesson A

Grammar and structures

Question-tags
You're German, **aren't you?**
You've changed the room round, **haven't you?**
She can speak Arabic, **can't she?**
Your wife smokes, **doesn't she?**
The film started late, **didn't it?**

Place of prepositions in questions
What are you talking **about?**
  (NOT About what are you talking?)
What are you looking **at?**
Who did she go **with?**
Who are you looking **for?**

Words and expressions to learn

sofa /'səʊfə/
coat /kəʊt/
ground /graʊnd/
weekday /'wiːkdeɪ/
a change /ə 'tʃeɪndʒ/
move /muːv/
ask for /'ɑːsk fə(r)/
delicious /dɪ'lɪʃəs/
hard work
somewhere else
I beg your pardon? /aɪ 'beg jə 'pɑːdn/
I should think
How do you mean?

Could you pass me . . .
I've had enough
How stupid of me!

Learn two or more of these:
mustard /'mʌstəd/
meat /miːt/
bean /biːn/
carrot /'kærət/
wine /waɪn/

Unit 19: Lesson B

Grammar and structures

Agreeing and disagreeing with opinions
I like . . .	So do I.
I quite like . . .	I don't.
I really like . . .	I quite like him/her/ it/them.
I like . . . very much.	
I love . . .	I've never heard of him/ her/it/them.

So do I, Neither do I, etc.
'I like traditional jazz.' '**So do I.**'
'I don't like science fiction.' '**Neither do I.**'
'Sarah is tired.' '**So is Sally.**'
'We're not hungry.' '**Neither are we.**'
'I've got a headache.' '**So have I.**'
'They haven't got a car.' '**Neither have we.**'
'Tim saw Ann yesterday.' '**So did I.**'
'I didn't have a holiday last year.' '**Neither did I.**'
'My brother will be 35 next month.' '**So will I!**'
'I won't be here for the meeting.' '**Neither will I.**'
'Tom was fairer when he was a child.' '**So was Ruth.**'
'You weren't here when he came.' '**Neither were you.**'

Words and expressions to learn

sex /seks/
violence /'vaɪələns/
complete /kəm'pliːt/
awful /'ɔːfʊl/
old-fashioned /'əʊld 'fæʃənd/
whose /huːz/
I didn't think much of it.
I couldn't help it.
It's getting late.
We've got a long way to go.
We ought to be on our way.
I suppose
We'd better be going.
enjoy myself/yourself/etc.
Thank you for coming.
I'll give you a ring.
Thank you so much.

Revision vocabulary: do you know these words?

beginning /bɪ'gɪnɪŋ/
middle /'mɪdl/
end /end/
food /fuːd/
coffee /'kɒfi/
die /daɪ/
laugh /lɑːf/
spend (spent, spent) /spend (spent)/
dirty /'dɜːti/
mine /maɪn/
I can't stand . . .
See you next week.

Unit 20: Lesson A

Grammar and structures

Infinitive of purpose
To make tomatoes easier to peel, cover them...
   (NOT ~~For to make...~~)

By...ing
You can clean dirty saucepans **by filling** them with cold water and vinegar and letting them boil for five minutes.

Had better
I **had** (I'**d**) **better** phone my sister.
   (NOT ~~I'd better to phone...~~)
   (NOT ~~I have better...~~)
You **had** (You'**d**) **better** phone your sister. etc.

Had I **better** phone her now?
Had you **better** phone her now? etc.

I **had** (I'**d**) **better not** wait any longer.
   (NOT ~~I hadn't better...~~)
You **had** (you'**d**) **better not** wait any longer. etc.

Words and expressions to learn

finger /'fɪŋgə(r)/
rabbit /'ræbɪt/
saucepan /'sɔ:spən/
dust /dʌst/
rice /raɪs/
scratch /skrætʃ/
luggage /'lʌgɪdʒ/
examination /ɪgzæmɪ'neɪʃn/
peel /pi:l/
rub /rʌb/
shake (shook, shaken)
  /ʃeɪk (ʃʊk, 'ʃeɪkn)/
stick (stuck, stuck) /stɪk (stʌk)/
catch (caught, caught) /kætʃ (kɔ:t)/
empty /'empti/
tight /taɪt/
pregnant /'pregnənt/

Revision vocabulary: do you know these words?

tomato /tə'mɑ:təʊ/
guitar /gɪ'tɑ:(r)/
glass /glɑ:s/
newspaper /'nju:speɪpə(r)/
ear /ɪə(r)/
potato /pə'teɪtəʊ/
apple /'æpl/
beer /bɪə(r)/
yard /jɑ:d/
ring (rang, rung) /rɪŋ (ræŋ, rʌŋ)/
cover /'kʌvə(r)/
wash /wɒʃ/
pick up /'pɪk 'ʌp/
visit /'vɪzɪt/
dirty /'dɜ:ti/
together /tə'geðə(r)/
comfortable /'kʌmftəbl/
wet /wet/

Unit 20: Lesson B

Grammar and structures

Suggestions
If I were you, I'**d** turn it the other way round.
I **think you ought to** turn it upside down.
Why don't you turn it sideways?
Let's help him.

If + 'unreal' conditions
If I **were** you, I'**d** (I **would**) turn it the other way round.
It **would be** much better if he **turned** it back to front.
What **would** you **do** if you **had** this mess in your kitchen?
I **wouldn't do** it like that if I **were** you.
Wouldn't you?

Ought to
You **ought to** turn it upside down.
She **ought to** be able to get one free.
   (NOT ~~She oughts to...~~)

Imperatives + or
Put a blanket underneath it **or** it'll get dirty.
Cover it **or** it'll get wet.

Remember to, forget to
Remember to cover it...
Don't **forget to** tighten all the screws.

Words and expressions to learn

screw /skru:/
law /lɔ:/
drug /drʌg/
give up (gave, given) /'gɪv 'ʌp (geɪv, 'gɪvn)/
seem /si:m/
immediately /ɪ'mi:dɪətli/
back to front /'bæk tə 'frʌnt/
face downwards /'feɪs 'daʊnwədz/
inside out /'ɪnsaɪd 'aʊt/
sideways /'saɪdweɪz/
underneath /ʌndə'ni:θ/
upside down /'ʌpsaɪd 'daʊn/
the other way round /ði 'ʌðə 'weɪ 'raʊnd/
this way /'ðɪs 'weɪ/
I'll think about it. /aɪl 'θɪŋk ə'baʊt ɪt/
It's no trouble. /ɪts 'nəʊ 'trʌbl/

Unit 21: Lesson A

Grammar and structures

Must and mustn't
In Britain you **must** buy a licence if you have a TV.
   (NOT ~~...you must to buy...~~)
You **must** unplug an electrical appliance before you try to repair it.
You **mustn't** touch anything electrical if you are in the bath.

Phrasal verbs
Switch on the radio. **Switch** the radio **on**.
Switch it **on**. (NOT ~~Switch on it.~~)
Turn up the TV. **Turn** the TV **up**.
Turn it **up**. (NOT ~~Turn up it.~~)

Which (of)
Which would you choose?
Which colour would you like?

Which of the things in the picture would you like?
Which of them would you like?

Words and expressions to learn

plug in /'plʌg 'ɪn/
unplug /ʌn'plʌg/
turn up /'tɜ:n 'ʌp/
turn down /'tɜ:n 'daʊn/

Learn some of these:
tape recorder /'teɪp rɪ'kɔ:də(r)/
stereo /'sterɪəʊ/
record player /'rekɔ:d 'pleɪə(r)/
cassette player /kə'set 'pleɪə(r)/
vacuum cleaner /'vækju:əm 'kli:nə(r)/
hair dryer /'heə 'draɪə(r)/
washing machine /'wɒʃɪŋ mə'ʃi:n/

dishwasher /'dɪʃwɒʃə(r)/
mixer /'mɪksə(r)/
dryer /'draɪə(r)/
heater /'hi:tə(r)/
cooker /'kʊkə(r)/
iron /'aɪən/
toaster /'təʊstə(r)/
bulb /bʌlb/

knob /nɒb/
plug /plʌg/
socket /'sɒkɪt/
lead /li:d/
lamp /læmp/
torch /tɔ:tʃ/
battery /'bætri/
wire /'waɪə(r)/

Unit 21: Lesson B

Grammar and structures

Verb + *-ing* form
It's **started making** a funny noise.
It **keeps sticking**.
It won't **stop dripping**.

Won't
It **won't** start.

Words and expressions to learn

flash /flæʃ/
engine /'endʒən/
dial /daɪl/
record /rɪ'kɔ:d/
wind (wound, wound) /waɪnd (waʊnd)/
rewind (rewound, rewound)
  /ri:'waɪnd (ri:'waʊnd)/

flood /flʌd/
keep (kept, kept) /ki:p (kept)/
ring (rang, rung) /rɪŋ (ræŋ, rʌŋ)/
leak /li:k/
properly /'prɒpəli/
take a photo
there's something wrong with...

Unit 22: Lesson A

Spelling and pronunciation

Two syllables, not three: asp(i)rin, bus(i)ness, cam(e)ra, diff(e)rent, ev(e)ning, ev(e)ry, marri(a)ge, med(i)cine.

Three syllables, not four: comf(or)table, secret(a)ry, temp(e)rature, veg(e)table, usu(a)lly.

Silent letters: shou(l)d, cou(l)d, wou(l)d, ca(l)m, wa(l)k, ta(l)k, ha(l)f, i(r)on, i(s)land, lis(t)en, (w)rite, (w)rong, (k)now, (k)nife, (k)nee, (k)nock, (k)nob, dau(gh)ter, hei(gh)t, li(gh)t, mi(gh)t, ri(gh)t, ti(gh)t, strai(gh)t, throu(gh), wei(gh), nei(gh)bour, ou(gh)t, thou(gh)t, g(u)ess, g(u)ide, g(u)itar, (h)our, (h)onest, We(d)n(e)sday, san(d)wich, si(g)n.

gh = /f/   cough, enough, laugh.
ch = /k/   chemist, headache, toothache, stomach, school, scheme.
a = /e/   any, many.
ea = /e/   bread, breakfast, dead, death, head, health, heavy, instead, leather, pleasure, ready, sweater.
ea = /eɪ/   steak, break.
o = /ʌ/   brother, come, company, cover, government, love, money, month, mother, nothing, one, onion, other, some, son, stomach, wonder, worry.
ou = /ʌ/   country, couple, cousin, double, enough, trouble.
u = /ʊ/   butcher, pull, push, put.

All these words are pronounced with /aɪ/: dial, either, neither, buy, height, idea, iron, microphone.

Strange spellings:

area /'eərɪə/
Asia /'eɪʃə/
Australia /ɒs'treɪlɪə/
autumn /'ɔ:təm/
bicycle /'baɪsɪkl/
blood /blʌd/
biscuit /'bɪskɪt/
busy /'bɪzi/

Europe /'jʊərəp/
foreign /'fɒrən/
friend /frend/
fruit /fru:t/
heard /hɜ:d/
heart /hɑ:t/
juice /dʒu:s/
minute /'mɪnɪt/

moustache /mə'stɑ:ʃ/
one /wʌn/
people /'pi:pl/
sandwich /'sænwɪdʒ/
theatre /'θɪətə(r)/
two /tu:/
woman /'wʊmən/
women /'wɪmɪn/

> THERE IS NO SUMMARY FOR
> UNIT 22, LESSON B

Unit 23: Lesson A

Grammar and structures

Let + object + infinitive
I never **let my emotions build up** inside me.
  (**NOT** ~~...let my emotions to build up...~~)
  (**NOT** ~~...let that my emotions build up...~~)

Words and expressions to learn

mood /mu:d/
secret /'si:krɪt/
smile /smaɪl/
frown /fraʊn/
build up (built, built) /bɪld ʌp (bɪlt)/
get over /'get 'əʊvə(r)/
shout /ʃaʊt/
let (let, let) /let/
hide (hid, hidden) /haɪd (hɪd, 'hɪdn)/

afraid /ə'freɪd/
relaxed /rɪ'lækst/
amused /ə'mju:zd/
sad /sæd/
easy-going /'i:zi 'gəʊɪŋ/
good/bad times /'gʊd/'bæd 'taɪmz/

> **Learn two or more of these:**
> emotion /ɪ'məʊʃn/
> express /ɪk'spres/
> emotional /ɪ'məʊʃənl/
> Damn you! /'dæm ju:/
> Oh dear! /'əʊ 'dɪə(r)/
> You're kidding. /jɔ: 'kɪdɪŋ/

Revision vocabulary:
do you know these words?

problem /'prɒbləm/
laugh /lɑ:f/
cry /kraɪ/
upset (upset, upset) /ʌp'set/
share /ʃeə(r)/
feel (felt, felt) /fi:l (felt)/
angry /'æŋgri/
worried /'wʌrɪd/
pleased /pli:zd/
surprised /sə'praɪzd/
calm /kɑ:m/

Unit 23: Lesson B

Grammar and structures

Who as subject and object
Who **loves** John?
Who **does** John **love**?
Who **saw** you?
Who **did** you **see**?
Who's **waiting for** you?
Who **are** you **waiting for**?

Words and expressions to learn
programme /ˈprəʊgræm/
relationship /rɪˈleɪʃənʃɪp/
dislike /dɪsˈlaɪk/
admire /ədˈmaɪə(r)/
grow (grew, grown) (=become) /grəʊ (gru:, grəʊn)/
last /lɑ:st/
get to know /ˈget tə ˈnəʊ/
fond of /ˈfɒnd əv/

close /kləʊs/
lucky /ˈlʌki/
silly /ˈsɪli/
guilty /ˈgɪlti/
whole /həʊl/
strongly /ˈstrɒŋli/
in love /ɪn ˈlʌv/

Unit 24: Lesson A

Grammar and structures

Countable and uncountable nouns

Countable nouns have plurals, and can be used with *a/an*. Examples: road   house   member   cabinet   idea.

Uncountable nouns have no plurals, and cannot be used with *a/an*. Examples: education   power   water   music   meat.

Note that these are uncountable in English:
English   information   luggage   news   travel   hair   weather.

Who and *which*

Who is used for people, and *which* for things.

The President of Fantasia, **who** is paid a very high salary, is elected for life.
San Fantastico, **which** is the capital of Fantasia, is the centre of government.

Words and expressions to learn
authority /ɔ:ˈθɒrəti/
government /ˈgʌvəmənt/
capital /ˈkæpɪtl/
Parliament /ˈpɑ:ləmənt/
power /ˈpaʊə(r)/
MP /ˈemˈpi:/
area /ˈeərɪə/
leader /ˈli:də(r)/
majority /məˈdʒɒrəti/
party /ˈpɑ:ti/
Prime Minister /ˈpraɪm ˈmɪnɪstə(r)/
department /dɪˈpɑ:tmənt/
news /nju:z/
elect /ɪˈlekt/
local /ˈləʊkl/
responsible (for) /rɪˈspɒnsəbl/
main /meɪn/

Unit 24: Lesson B

Grammar and structures

Imperatives
Affirmative imperative: Be careful.
Negative imperative: Don't be silly.
Emphatic imperative: Do be careful.

Reported commands and requests
His mother **told him to tidy up** afterwards.
She **told him not to invite** the Edwards boy.
   (NOT ~~...to not invite...~~)

Question-tags after negative sentences
You're **not** going to invite that Edwards boy, **are you?**
You **won't** play your father's jazz records, **will you?**

Question-tags after imperatives
See that that letter goes today, **will you?**
(More polite: See..., **would you?**)
Don't make too much noise, **will you?**

Words and expressions to learn
carpet /ˈkɑ:pɪt/
jazz /dʒæz/
noise /nɔɪz/
order /ˈɔ:də(r)/
delivery /dɪˈlɪvri/
part /pɑ:t/
invite /ɪnˈvaɪt/
promise /ˈprɒmɪs/

tidy up /ˈtaɪdi ˈʌp/
urgent /ˈɜ:dʒənt/
last time /ˈlɑ:st ˈtaɪm/
I suppose so /aɪ səˈpəʊz səʊ/
see that... /ˈsi: ðət/
exactly /ɪgˈzæktli/
out of the question

Unit 25: Lesson A

Grammar and structures

Word order: Object just after verb
I **like the Hilliard picture** very much.
   (NOT ~~I like very much the Hilliard picture.~~)
I **like the snow picture** best.
I **don't like the picture** of the young man much.
   (NOT ~~I don't like much...~~)

Very and *too*
I think Sylvia von Harden's face is **very** interesting.
I don't like the colours in the picture of the woman; they're **too** strong.

People who do things (*-er*)
A person who **drives** is a **driver**.
A person who **paints** is a **painter**.

Questions ending in *by*
Who was *The Third Man* directed **by?**
   (NOT ~~By who was...~~) (NOT ~~By whom was...~~)

➡

Words and expressions to learn

snow /snəʊ/
leaf (leaves) /li:f (li:vz)/
painting /'peɪntɪŋ/
writer /'raɪtə(r)/

director /dɪ'rektə(r)/
actor /'æktə(r)/
art /ɑ:t/
statue /'stætʃu:/

play /pleɪ/
return (verb) /rɪ'tɜ:n/
modern /'mɒdn/
real /rɪəl/

public /'pʌblɪk/
great /greɪt/
so-called /'səʊ 'kɔ:ld/
work of art /'wɜ:k əv 'ɑ:t/

Unit 25: Lesson B

Grammar and structures

Asking for suggestions
Where **shall** we go, then?

Making suggestions
How about a concert?
What about Stravinsky, then?
Why don't we have a drink somewhere first?

Which and *What*
Which of the three songs do you prefer?
What sort of music do you like?

The one/the ones
'Which record shall I put on?' '**The** new **one**.'
'Which seats are ours?' '**The ones** near the front.

Words and expressions to learn

tune /tju:n/
voice /vɔɪs/
verse /vɜ:s/
concert /'kɒnsət/
stairs /steəz/
folk (music) /fəʊk/
mad (about) /mæd/
sentimental /sentɪ'mentl/
lonely /'ləʊnli/
then /ðen/
what's on /wɒts 'ɒn/
Here we are. (=Here it is.)
  /'hɪə wi 'ɑ:(r)/
quite a /'kwaɪt ə/

otherwise /'ʌðəwaɪz/
What about...? /'wɒt ə'baʊt/
plenty of /'plenti əv/

Revision vocabulary: do you know these words?

choice /tʃɔɪs/
instrument /'ɪnstrəmənt/
music /'mju:zɪk/
piano /pi'ænəʊ/
violin /vaɪə'lɪn/
trumpet /'trʌmpɪt/
guitar /gɪ'tɑ:(r)/

Unit 26: Lesson A

Grammar and structures

Although /ɔ:l'ðəʊ/
Whales are mammals, **although** they look like fish.
Although whales look like fish, they are mammals.
  (**NOT** Although whales look like fish, but they...)

He lost his job **although** he worked well.
Although he worked well, he lost his job.

Words and expressions to learn

insect /'ɪnsekt/
skeleton /'skelɪtn/
backbone /'bækbəʊn/
belong (to) /bɪ'lɒŋ (tə)/
typical /'tɪpɪkl/
related (to) /rɪ'leɪtɪd (tə)/
divided (into) /dɪ'vaɪdɪd ('ɪntə)/
except for /ɪk'sept fə(r)/
in many ways

Revision vocabulary: do you know these words?

dog /dɒg/
animal /'ænɪml/
fish /fɪʃ/
bird /bɜ:d/
kind /kaɪnd/
difference /'dɪfrəns/
group /gru:p/
different /'dɪfrənt/
main /meɪn/

Unit 26: Lesson B

Words and expressions to learn

bookcase /'bʊkkeɪs/
wardrobe /'wɔ:drəʊb/
mouse /maʊs/
camel /'kæml/
lion /'laɪən/

cow /kaʊ/
India /'ɪndɪə/
China /'tʃaɪnə/
France /frɑ:ns/
Egypt /'i:dʒɪpt/

Israel /'ɪzreɪl/
strawberry /'strɔ:bri/
grape /greɪp/
peach /pi:tʃ/
armchair /'ɑ:mtʃeə(r)/

Revision vocabulary: do you know these words?

nose /nəʊz/
ear /ɪə(r)/
arm /ɑ:m/
hand /hænd/
mouth /maʊθ/
foot /fʊt/
mistake /mɪs'teɪk/

Unit 27: Lesson A

Grammar and structures

Get to talk about changes
He**'s got** more popular.
It**'ll get** dirty.

Words and expressions to learn

wrinkle /'rɪŋkl/
beard /bɪəd/
moustache /məs'tɑ:ʃ/
childhood /'tʃaɪldhʊd/
adolescence /ædə'lesəns/
break (broke, broken)
  /breɪk (brəʊk, 'brəʊkn)/
rust /rʌst/
crack /kræk/

wear (down) (wore, worn) /weə(r) (wɔ:(r), wɔ:n)/
gain weight /'geɪn 'weɪt/
lose weight (lost, lost) /'lu:z 'weɪt (lɒst)/
bald /bɔ:ld/
go grey/bald (went, gone)
  /gəʊ 'greɪ/bɔ:ld (went, gɒn)/
middle age /'mɪdl 'eɪdʒ/
old age /'əʊld 'eɪdʒ/

Unit 27: Lesson B

Grammar and structures

Past conditional

If he**'d studied** literature, he **would have become** a journalist.
If his parents **had been** well off, he **wouldn't have worked** in a
  bank.
The woman's arm **wouldn't have been burnt** if the car **hadn't
  crashed.**

Words and expressions to learn

literature /'lɪtrətʃə(r)/
physics /'fɪzɪks/
research /rɪ'sɜːtʃ/
prisoner /'prɪznə(r)/
sausage /'sɒsɪdʒ/
stand /stænd/
chip /tʃɪp/
pavement /'peɪvmənt/

escape /ɪ'skeɪp/
bite (bit, bitten) /baɪt (bɪt, 'bɪtn)/
faint /feɪnt/
feel sorry for (felt, felt) /'fiːl 'sɒri fə(r) (felt)/
well off /'wel 'ɒf/
working class /'wɜːkɪŋ 'klɑːs/
wild /waɪld/

Revision vocabulary: do you know these words?

decide /dɪ'saɪd/
scratch /skrætʃ/
cause /kɔːz/
crash /kræʃ/
boil /bɔɪl/
burn (burnt, burnt) /bɜːn (bɜːnt)/
wait (for) /'weɪt (fə(r))/
hurt (hurt, hurt) /hɜːt/
fall (fell, fallen) /fɔːl (fel, 'fɔːlən)/
angry /'æŋgri/
local /'ləʊkl/
university /juːnɪ'vɜːsɪti/
war /wɔː(r)/
bring (brought, brought) /brɪŋ (brɔːt)/
find (found, found) /faɪnd (faʊnd)/
fall in love

Unit 28: Lesson A

Grammar and structures

-ing forms
Eating good quality food is the most important thing you can
  do...
  (**NOT** ~~To eat good quality food...~~)
The things I do to take care of my health are: **not
  smoking,**...

Relative clauses
A friend **who had similar problems** made her think she
  might have allergies.
  (**NOT** ~~A friend who she had similar problems...~~)
She has to avoid the things **that make her ill.**
  (**NOT** ~~...the things that they make her ill.~~)
The pills **her doctor gave her** only worked for a short
  while.

Verbs with two objects
I would give **him a book** on exercise.
I would tell **her horrible stories**...

Some verbs that can be used with two objects
are:
bring, buy, give, lend, make, owe, promise, read, send,
show, take, tell, write.

Words and expressions to learn

exercise /'eksəsaɪz/
quality /'kwɒləti/
headache /'hedeɪk/
while /waɪl/
(a good) example /ɪg'zɑːmpl/
present /'prezənt/
diet /'daɪət/
keep (kept, kept) /kiːp (kept)/
concentrate /'kɒnsəntreɪt/
avoid /ə'vɔɪd/
pollute /pə'luːt/
complicate /'kɒmplɪkeɪt/
promise /'prɒmɪs/
heart attack /'hɑːt ə'tæk/
horrible /'hɒrəbl/

Revision vocabulary: do you know these words?

health /helθ/
weight /weɪt/
alcohol /'ælkəhɒl/
medicine /'medsən/
chemicals /'kemɪkʊlz/
advertisement /əd'vɜːtɪsmənt/
smoke /sməʊk/

Unit 28: Lesson B

Grammar and structures

Where to put frequency adverbs in a sentence
These adverbs say how often something happens:
usually, sometimes, often, always, ever, never. They
can go in mid-position in a sentence (after auxiliary
verbs and *am, are, is, was* and *were;* before other
verbs).

Do you **sometimes** feel sleepy after eating?
  (**NOT** ~~Do you feel sometimes sleepy...~~)
  (**NOT** ~~Do you feel sleepy after eating sometimes?~~)
She's **always** in a great hurry.
I **often** eat very quickly.

Often, sometimes and *usually* can go at the beginning of
a clause, to make their meaning more important.

Sometimes I get upset if I have to wait in a queue.
  (**NOT** ~~Always I get upset if I...~~)

➡

Where to put adverbial phrases and clauses in a sentence

Adverbial phrases and clauses (like these from the lesson: *every year, three or four times a week, when you walk, the whole time, all the time*) can go at the end of the sentence; or at the beginning of the sentence followed by a comma.

It happens **every year.**
(**NOT** It every year happens.)
The whole time, I feel sort of funny.
(**NOT** The whole time I feel sort of funny.)

Reporting orders and advice

'Now just lie down here.' He **told me to lie** down.

'Don't carry heavy things for a while.'
He **told me not to carry** heavy things for a while.

'I think you should make an appointment at the Eye Hospital.'
He **advised me to make** an appointment at the Eye Hospital.

'You'd better not do any running for a week or so.'
He **advised me not to do** any running for a week or so

Words and expressions to learn

patient /'peɪʃənt/
chest /tʃest/
pain /peɪn/
muscle /'mʌsl/
operation /ɒpə'reɪʃn/
injection /ɪn'dʒekʃən/
tablet /'tæblɪt/
stand up (stood, stood) /'stænd 'ʌp (stʊd)/
lie down (lay, lain) /'laɪ 'daʊn (leɪ, leɪn)/
itch /ɪtʃ/
bend over (bent, bent) /'bend 'əʊvə(r) (bent)/
advise /əd'vaɪz/

painful /'peɪnful/
How often...? /'haʊ 'ɒfn/
back trouble /'bæk 'trʌbl/
hay fever /'heɪ 'fi:və(r)/
sore throat /'sɔ: 'θrəʊt/

Revision vocabulary: do you know these words?

funny (=strange) /'fʌni/
heavy /'hevi/
downstairs /daʊn'steəz/
inside /ɪn'saɪd/
outside /aʊt'saɪd/
hardly /'hɑ:dli/
exactly /ɪg'zæktli/
sometimes /'sʌmtaɪmz/
often /'ɒfn/
...times a week, day, etc.

Unit 29: Lesson A

Grammar and structures

I wish

I wish I **had** more artistic ability.
I wish I **could** remember people's names.
I wish I **was** (*or* **were**) better at making decisions.

THERE IS NO SUMMARY FOR
UNIT 29, LESSON B

Words and expressions to learn

brain /breɪn/
imagination /ɪmædʒə'neɪʃn/
ability /ə'bɪləti/
fact /fækt/
common sense /'kɒmən 'sens/
sense of humour /'sens əv 'hju:mə(r)/
zoo /zu:/
make decisions /'meɪk dɪ'sɪʒənz/
plan /plæn/
deal with (dealt, dealt) /'di:l 'wɪð (delt)/
test /test/
practical /'præktɪkl/

Learn three or more of these

decisiveness /dɪ'saɪsɪvnəs/
logic /'lɒdʒɪk/
argument /'ɑ:gjə:mənt/
quick thinking /'kwɪk 'θɪŋkɪŋ/
analyse /'ænəlaɪz/
calculate /'kælkjəleɪt/
classify /'klæsɪfaɪ/
draw conclusions (drew, drawn) /'drɔ: kən'klu:ʒənz (dru:, drɔ:n)/
reorganise /ri'ɔ:gənaɪz/
mathematical /mæθ'mætɪkl/
artistic /ɑ:'tɪstɪk/
smelly /'smeli/

Unit 30: Lesson A

Grammar and structures

Adverbs with past participles
Government ministers are **well paid.**
Farm workers are **badly paid.**
Housewives are **the worst-paid** workers in the world.

Should with passive infinitive
Nurses **should be paid** more.
Primary school teachers **should be paid** more than bus drivers.

-ing forms
Keith **hates not having** enough time to do his job well.
Jane **likes having** to think.
Working with nice people is very important to me.
Getting on with my boss is one of the most important things in a job for me.

Words and expressions to learn

factory /'fæktri/
dustman /'dʌstmən/
army /'ɑ:mi/
pay /peɪ/
professor /prə'fesə(r)/
journalist /'dʒɜ:nəlɪst/
farm /fɑ:m/
routine /ru:'ti:n/
contact /'kɒntækt/
security /sɪ'kjʊə:rəti/
pension /'penʃən/
promotion /prə'məʊʃn/
responsibility /rɪspɒnsə'bɪləti/
freedom /'fri:dəm/
primary school /'praɪmri 'sku:l/
have (something) in common /'hæv ('sʌmθɪŋ) ɪn 'kɒmən/
retire /rɪ'taɪə(r)/

Unit 30: Lesson B

Grammar and structures

Have to
Do you **have to get up** early?
You mean you **have to go and check**
  that they're actually building the thing?

Words and expressions to learn

team /ti:m/
heater /'hi:tə(r)/
handle /'hændl/
design /dɪ'zaɪn/
waste /weɪst/
check /tʃek/
frustrate /frʌs'treɪt/
work long hours
mad /mæd/
especially /ɪ'speʃli/
on (your) own /'ɒn (jɔ:r) 'əʊn/

Names of professions
Choose five or more of these:
accountant /ə'kaʊntənt/
architect /'ɑ:kɪtekt/
businesswoman /'bɪznɪswʊmən/
coal miner /'kəʊl 'maɪnə(r)/
draughtsman/-woman /'drɑ:ftsmən
  ('drɑ:ftswʊmən)/
electrician /ɪlek'trɪʃn/
(mechanical) engineer /
  (mɪ'kænɪkl) endʒɪ'nɪə(r)/
personnel manager /pɜ:sə'nel 'mænɪdʒə(r)/
photographer /fə'tɒgrəfə(r)/
sales manager /'seɪlz 'mænɪdʒə(r)/
technician /tek'nɪʃn/

Unit 31: Lesson A

Grammar and structures

Come/go; here/there; this/that
Come over **here** and look at **this.**
Go over **there** and look at **that.**

Words and expressions to learn

tube /tju:b/
take-off /'teɪk 'ɒf/
garage /'gærɑ:ʒ/
petrol station /'petrʊl 'steɪʃn/
enquiry /ɪn'kwaɪəri/

compartment /kəm'pɑ:tmənt/
roundabout /'raʊndəbaʊt/
speed /spi:d/
land /lænd/
delay /dɪ'leɪ/

Unit 31: Lesson B

Grammar and structures

Modals of obligation

Must, can and **should** are 'modal' verbs. They have no
-s in the third person singular; questions and
negatives are formed without **do**; and they are followed
by the infinitive without **to.**

She **should** report the accident.
  (**NOT** She shoulds...)
You **must not** drive without lights at night.
  (**NOT** You don't must drive...)
Can you **park** on a single yellow line?
  (**NOT** Do you can...)
You **cannot turn** right here.
  (**NOT** You cannot to turn...)

Words and expressions to learn

(road) sign /saɪn/
traffic /'træfɪk/
pedestrian /pə'destrɪən/
pedestrian crossing /pə'destrɪən 'krɒsɪŋ/
junction /'dʒʌŋkʃən/
the right of way /ðə 'raɪt əv 'weɪ/
diagram /'daɪəgræm/
regulation /regjə'leɪʃn/

overtake (overtook, overtaken)
  /əʊvə'teɪk (əʊvə'tʊk, əʊvə'teɪkn)/
park (verb) /pɑ:k/
approach /ə'prəʊtʃ/
clear /'klɪə(r)/
slippery /'slɪpəri/
in the opposite direction

Unit 32: Lesson A

Grammar and structures

Sound + adjective
She **sounds** surprised.
You **sound** happy.

Find + object + adjective
I don't **find** it funny.
Do you **find** this cartoon silly?

Make + object + infinitive
It **makes** me laugh.

THERE IS NO SUMMARY FOR
UNIT 32, LESSON B

Words and expressions to learn

doorbell /'dɔ:bel/
(newspaper) headline /'hedlaɪn/
reaction /ri'ækʃən/
result /rɪ'zʌlt/
specialise (in) /'speʃəlaɪz/
bet (bet, bet) /bet/
beat (beat, beaten) /bi:t ('bi:tn)/
seriously ill /'sɪərɪəsli 'ɪl/

155

Additional material

Lesson 7A, Exercise 1

Brighton in the Rain

I've never been to Athens and I've never been to Rome
I've only seen the Pyramids in picture books at home
I've never sailed across the sea or been inside a plane
I've always spent my holidays in Brighton in the rain.

I've never eaten foreign food or drunk in a foreign bar
I've never kissed a foreign girl or driven a foreign car
I've never had to find my way in a country I don't know
I've always known just where I am and where I'll never go.

I've read travel books by writers who have been to Pakistan
I've heard people telling stories of adventures in Iran
I've watched TV documentaries about China and Brazil
But I've never been abroad myself; it's making me feel ill.

I've studied several languages like Hindi and Malay
I've learnt lots of useful sentences I've never been able to say
The furthest place I've ever been was to the Isle of Man
And that was full of tourists from Jamaica and Japan.

I've never been to Athens and I've never been to Rome
I've only seen the Pyramids in picture books at home
I've never sailed across the sea or been inside a plane
I've always spent my holidays in Brighton in the rain.

Jonathan Dykes (lyrics)
Robert Campbell (music)

Lesson 9B, Exercise 7

You Made Me Love You

You made me love you
I didn't wanna do it
I didn't wanna do it
You made me love you
And all the time you knew it
I guess you always knew it.
You made me happy, sometimes
You made me glad
But there were times when
You made me feel so sad.

You made me sigh, 'cause
I didn't wanna tell you
I didn't wanna tell you
I think you're grand, that's true,
Yes I do, 'deed I do, you know I do
Gimme, gimme, gimme, gimme
What I cry for
You know you've got the kind of kisses
That I'd die for
You know you made me love you.

(Monaco and McCarthy)

Lesson 10A, Exercise 8

Song for a Rainy Sunday

It's a rainy Sunday morning and I don't know what to do
If I stay in bed all day, I'll only think about you
If I try to study, I won't learn anything new
And if I go for a walk on my own in the park,
I'll probably catch the flu!

I just don't know (He doesn't know)
What to do (What to do)
I just don't know (He doesn't know)
What to do (What to do)

If I stay in bed all day, I'll only think about you
If I try to study, I won't learn anything new
And if I go for a walk on my own in the park,
I'll probably catch the flu – atchoo!

It's nearly Sunday lunchtime and I don't know where to eat
If I walk to the fish and chip shop, I'll only get wet feet
If I stay at home for lunch, I'll have to eat last week's meat
And if I get in my car and drive to the pub, I probably won't
   get a seat

I just don't know (He doesn't know)
Where to eat (Where to eat)
I just don't know (He doesn't know)
Where to eat (Where to eat)

If I walk to the fish and chip shop, I'll only get wet feet
If I stay at home for lunch, I'll have to eat last week's meat
And if I get in my car and drive to the pub, I probably won't
   get a seat

The rain has stopped and I'd like to go out
But I don't know where to go
If I invite you out for a drink, you'll probably say no
If I go to the theatre alone, I won't enjoy the show
And if I stay here at home on my own, I'll be bored and
   miserable, so

I just don't know (He doesn't know)
Where to go (Where to go)
I just don't know (He doesn't know)
Where to go (Where to go)

If I invite you out for a drink, you'll probably say no
If I go to the theatre alone, I won't enjoy the show
And if I stay here at home on my own, I'll be bored and
   miserable, so

I'm going to the theatre but I don't know what to wear
I know if I look through my socks I'll never find a pair
If I put on my new green boots people will probably stare
And if my tie isn't straight and they complain 'cause I'm late,
I'll say, 'Listen, mate: I don't care!'

I just don't care (He doesn't care)
What I wear (Life isn't fair)
I just don't care (He doesn't care)
What I wear (Life isn't fair)

I know if I look through my socks I'll never find a pair
If I put on my new green boots people will probably stare
And if my tie isn't straight and they complain 'cause I'm late,
I'll say, 'Listen, mate: I don't care!'

Jonathan Dykes (lyrics)
Robert Campbell (music)

Lesson 13A, Exercise 10

The Island

Each night I dream of a beautiful island
Surrounded by beaches and covered in flowers.
Butterflies dance through the sweet-smelling meadows
And birds sing their love songs for hours.

Crystal clear water runs down from the mountains
And flows through deep valleys as a sparkling stream.
Gentle sea breezes blow over my island
While sunshine pours over my dream.

Each night I visit the island of my dreams,
Each night I visit the island of my dreams,
I leave the real world behind,
It's somewhere deep in my mind,
Not too easy to find,
The island.

Bright orange squirrels play games in the tree tops
And chase through the branches where nightingales sing.
It looks so peaceful I wish I could take you
To where each night's the first day of spring.

Chorus.

I leave the real world behind,
It's somewhere deep in my mind,
Not too easy to find,
The island.

The island.   The island.

Jonathan Dykes (lyrics)
Robert Campbell (music)

Lesson 14B, Dialogue B

MOTHER: Can I speak to you for a minute, Em?
DAUGHTER: ....
MOTHER: Well, I'm very upset about how late you were
           out last night.
DAUGHTER: ....
MOTHER: I still think that's too late for a fifteen-year-old
           girl who has to go to school the next day.
DAUGHTER: ....
MOTHER: Well, you're not all the other kids. And I'm sure
           some of them have to be in early.
DAUGHTER: ....
MOTHER: Especially on school nights. I don't want you in
           after ten when you've got school the next day.
DAUGHTER: ....
MOTHER: Well, if there's a special night we can talk about
           it before you go. I'm sure we can agree if we
           talk about it.
DAUGHTER: ....
MOTHER: Thanks, darling.

Unit 19 Dialogues

DIALOGUE 1

(The doorbell rings.)

PETER: I'll go.
ANN: OK.

(Peter opens the door.)

PETER: Hello, hello. Nice to see you.
SUE: Hello, Peter. Are we late?
PETER: No, not at all. You're the first, actually.
JOHN: Oh, good. Who else is coming?
PETER: Come in and have a drink. Well, there's Don and
        Emma, Jo and Stephen, and my sister Lucy and her
        new boyfriend. Can't remember his name. Let me
        take your coat. You know Lucy, don't you?
SUE: I think we've met her once.
ANN: Hello, Sue. Hello, John. Lovely to see you. I'm so
        glad you could come. Now, what can I get you to
        drink?

SUE: What have you got?
ANN: Oh, the usual things. Sherry; gin and tonic – I think;
        vodka; I think there's some beer; a glass of
        wine . . . ?
SUE: I'll have a gin and tonic, Ann, please.
JOHN: So will I.
SUE: Doesn't the room look nice, John? You've changed it
        round since we were here last, haven't you? The
        piano was, let me see, yes, the piano was over by
        the window, wasn't it?
PETER: That's right. And we've moved the sofa over there
        and . . .

DIALOGUE 2

JOHN: So you work in a pub.
LUCY: Yes, that's right.
JOHN: What's it like?
LUCY: It's nice. I like it. You meet a lot of interesting
        people. A lot of boring ones too, mind you.
JOHN: I beg your pardon?
LUCY: I said, a lot of boring ones too.
JOHN: Oh, yes. I can imagine. A pub – I should think that's
        hard work, isn't it?
LUCY: Yes and no. It depends.
JOHN: How do you mean?
LUCY: Well, it's hard at weekends. I mean, last Saturday
        night, with both bars full and one barman away ill –
        well, my feet didn't touch the ground. But on
        weekdays it's usually very quiet.
        What about you? What do you do? You're an
        accountant or something, aren't you?
JOHN: I work in a bank.
LUCY: Oh yes, that's right. Ann said. That must be nice.
JOHN: It's all right.
LUCY: But you have to move round from one place to
        another, don't you? I mean, if you get a better job – if
        they make you manager or something – it'll probably
        be in another town, won't it?
JOHN: Yes, probably.
LUCY: I wouldn't like that. I mean, I've got lots of friends
        here. I wouldn't like to move somewhere else.
JOHN: Oh, we like it. We've lived here for, what, six years
        now. We're ready for a change.

DIALOGUE 3

DON: Have you got the salt down your end, Steve?
STEPHEN: What are you looking for?
DON: The salt.
STEPHEN: Salt. Salt. Oh, yes. Here it is. And could you pass
          me the mustard in exchange?
          This is delicious beef, Ann. Who's your butcher?
ANN: Not telling you.
          What are John and Lucy talking about?
JOHN: Work, I'm afraid.
SUE: I thought so. It's all John ever talks about. Work
          and food.
JOHN: Well, there are worse things in life. Especially if
          the food's like this.
ANN: Thank you, John. Would you like some more?
          Have another potato. Some more meat. Some
          beans. A carrot. A piece of bread.
JOHN: No, thanks. That was lovely, but I've had enough.
          Really. I'll have another glass of wine, perhaps.
EMMA: Here you are, John.

          (Crash!)

          Oh, damn! I *am* sorry, Ann. How stupid of me.
ANN: That's all right. It doesn't matter at all. Really.
          They're very cheap glasses.

DIALOGUE 4

ANDY: I didn't like it at all.
EMMA: Oh, I thought it was lovely.
JOHN: It was rubbish. Complete rubbish. Absolute nonsense.
ANN: I didn't think much of it, I must say.
LUCY: I liked it. At the end, when she was dying, I cried. I couldn't help it. I cried and cried.
STEPHEN: Jo said it made her laugh.
JO: No, I didn't. Oh, Steve, you are awful! Really! No, it's just that – I don't know – it didn't say anything to me.
JOHN: I'm afraid I must be very old-fashioned, but I like things to have a beginning, a middle and an end.
STEPHEN: Yes, so do I.
JOHN: And I *don't* like a lot of sex and violence.
EMMA: Oh, I love sex and violence!
ANN: More coffee, anybody?
ANDY: I don't like violence.
EMMA: But listen. Why didn't you like it? I thought it was great. Really.
ANN: So wordy. It was really really boring. They just talked and talked and talked all the time.
STEPHEN: I can't stand –
EMMA: No, look –
LUCY: I don't think –
DON: Three old women sitting around talking for two and a half hours. If that's what you want, you might as well go and spend the evening in the old people's home.
LUCY: It wasn't like that at all.
ANDY: Yes it was.
LUCY: No it wasn't.
ANDY: Yes it was.
ANN : Who wrote it, anyway?
JO: Don't know. What's his name? Fred Walker, something like that.
ANDY: Who's he?
DON: Never heard of him.
STEPHEN: Didn't he write . . .

DIALOGUE 5

DON: Well, I'm afraid it's getting late, and we've got a long way to go.
SUE: So have we. We ought to be on our way, I suppose.
JO: Yes, we'd better be going, too. Thank you so much, Ann. We really enjoyed ourselves. Lovely food, nice people, good talk, . . .
ANN: Well, thank you for coming.
EMMA: You must come over to us soon. When we've finished moving. I'll give you a ring.
JOHN: Now, where's my coat?
PETER: Here it is, John.
JOHN: No, that's not mine. This is mine.
PETER: Oh, sorry. Well, whose is this, then?
ANN: Andy's, I think.
ANDY: Is it old and dirty? Yes, that's mine.
LUCY: Well, bye, Ann, bye, Peter. See you next week.
EVERYBODY: Bye, bye.

Lesson 14B, Dialogue A

MOTHER: ....
DAUGHTER: Sure, Mum, what's the problem?
MOTHER: ....
DAUGHTER: But Mum, I was in by twelve o'clock!
MOTHER: ....
DAUGHTER: Well, I don't think so. All the other kids stay out late.
MOTHER: ....
DAUGHTER: Yeah, some of them do, I suppose.
MOTHER: ....
DAUGHTER: But last night was special. It was the disco at the club.
MOTHER: ....
DAUGHTER: All right, Mum. Perhaps you're right. I'll talk to you about it next time.
MOTHER: ....

Lesson 23B, Exercise 8

Trying to Love Two Women

Trying to love two women
Is like a ball and chain
Trying to love two women
Is like a ball and chain
Sometimes the pleasure
Ain't worth the strain
It's a long old grind
And it tires your mind

Trying to hold two women
Is tearing me apart
Trying to hold two women
Is tearing me apart
One's got my money
And the other's got my heart
It's a long old grind
And it tires your mind

When you try to please two women
You can't please yourself
When you try to please two women
You can't please yourself
Your best is only half good
A man can't stock two shelves
It's a long old grind,
And it tires your mind

(first verse twice)   *(Sonny Throckmorton)*

Lesson 25B, Exercise 2

The Riddle Song

I gave my love a cherry, it had no stone
I gave my love a chicken without a bone
I told my love a story, it had no end
I gave my love a baby with no crying.

How can there be a cherry without a stone?
How can there be a chicken without a bone?
How can there be a story that has no end?
How can there be a baby with no crying?

Well a cherry when it's blooming, it has no stone
A chicken when it's pipping, it has no bone
The story of I love you, it has no end
A baby when it's sleeping has no crying.

The Riddle Song by Harry Robinson and Julie Felix
© 1965, TRO Essex Music Ltd.

Logger Lover

As I walked out one evening
'Twas in a small cafe
A forty-year-old waitress
To me these words did say:

I see that you are a logger
And not just a common bum
For nobody but a logger
Stirs his coffee with his thumb.

My lover, he was a logger
There's none like him today
If you poured whisky upon it
He would eat a bale of hay.

My lover came to see me
'Twas on one winter's day
He held me in his fond embrace
And broke three vertebrae.

He kissed me when he left me
So hard he broke my jaw
And I could not speak to tell him
He'd forgot his mackinaw.

Well, the weather tried to freeze him
It did its level best
At one hundred degrees below zero
Well, he buttoned up his vest.

It froze clear through to China,
It froze to the stars above
At one thousand degrees below zero
It froze my logger love.

And so I lost my lover
To this cafe I did come
And here I wait till someone
Stirs his coffee with his thumb.

(Traditional)

What Did You Learn in School Today?

What did you learn in school today,
Dear little boy of mine?
What did you learn in school today,
Dear little boy of mine?
I learned that Washington never told a lie,
I learned that soldiers seldom die,
I learned that everybody's free,
That's what the teacher said to me,
And that's what I learned in school today,
That's what I learned in school.

What did you learn in school today,
Dear little boy of mine?
What did you learn in school today,
Dear little boy of mine?
I learned that policemen are my friends,
I learned that justice never ends,
I learned that murderers die for their crimes,
Even if we make a mistake sometimes,
And that's what I learned in school today,
That's what I learned in school.

What did you learn in school today,
Dear little boy of mine?
What did you learn in school today,
Dear little boy of mine?

I learned our government must be strong,
It's always right and never wrong,
Our leaders are the finest men,
And we elect them again and again,
And that's what I learned in school today,
That's what I learned in school.

(Tom Paxton)

Memory Test for Lesson 29A, Exercise 6

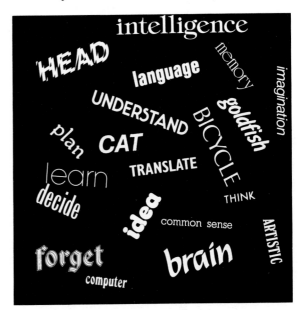

Revision Tests

The Tests on the following pages, which are also available separately in Test Books for students, have three main purposes:

1. To show you and the students whether there are any points that have not been properly learnt, for whatever reason.
2. To identify any students who are having serious difficulty with the course.
3. To motivate the students to look back over the work they have done and do some serious revision, before they move on to the next phase of the course.

It is not intended that students should 'pass' or 'fail' the Tests, and it is not particularly useful to give 'marks', though students ought to be told whether their performance is satisfactory. In principle, most students ought to get most answers right; if this does not happen, efficient learning is not taking place (because of poor motivation, too rapid a pace, absenteeism, failure to do follow-up work outside class, or for some other reason). Of course, nobody can be expected to retain all the material that has been presented, but a student who finds the whole of a Test too difficult may have considerable difficulty coping with the next part of the course, particularly if the main weakness is in the area of vocabulary learning.

The Tests which follow Units 11 and 22 cover most of the grammar that comes in the previous 11 units, and a fair sample of the vocabulary and usage. There are also pronunciation, listening and writing components. The Test which follows Unit 32 covers the same language areas, but includes material from the whole book.

These Tests should each take something between ninety minutes and two hours, depending on the class.

Revision Test One

Grammar and structures

Put in the missing words.

1. .... is your boss like?
2. .... is something wrong with my leg.
3. There .... been an accident – can you phone for an ambulance?
4. I saw her for the first time .... two o'clock .... the afternoon, ... Monday 12 March, 1984.

1. *What*
2. *There*
3. *has*
4. *at; in; on*

Put in *may not, won't, shouldn't* or *can't*.

5. The trains are often late on Saturdays, so I .... arrive on time tomorrow.
6. 'Don't forget to say hello to Jane for me.' 'No, I ....'
7. You .... go swimming there – it's dangerous.
8. 'Is that John?' 'It .... be – he's in Canada.'
9. I .... be in the office tomorrow. I'll tell you later, when I'm quite sure.

5. *may not*
6. *won't*
7. *shouldn't*
8. *can't*
9. *may not*

Put in the correct form of the verb.

10. I like Jane – she makes me .... (*laugh*)
11. Something very strange .... yesterday while we .... breakfast. (*happen; have*)
12. .... you ever .... *Gone with the Wind?* (*see*)
13. I don't want to go for a walk – it .... (*rain*)
14. I'll come and see you if I .... time. (*have*)

10. *laugh*
11. *happened* *were having*
12. *have (you ever) seen*
13. *'s/is raining*
14. *have*

Put in the correct word.

15. I was tired, ... I went to bed. (*so/because*)
16. I'll have some more bread, ... you don't mind. (*if/when*)

15. *so*
16. *if*

17. I've been in this country .... three
    years. *(since/for)*

17. *for*

Put the words in the correct order.

18. people laughing those are why ?

    ....

18. *Why are those people laughing?*

19. my languages very speaks father well three .

    ....

    ....

19. *My father speaks three languages very well.*

20. Scotland are both travelling parents in my .

    ....

    ....

20. *My parents are both travelling in Scotland.*

21. Write the -ing forms.

spell *spelling*

sit ....

make ....

sleep ....

stop ....

hope ....

21. *sitting*

    making

    sleeping

    stopping

    hoping

22. Write the past tenses and past participles.

go *went* *gone*

see ....

bring ....

break ....

drive ....

hear ....

write ....

stop ....

hope ....

rain ....

try ....

play ....

22. *saw, seen*

    brought, brought

    broke, broken

    drove, driven

    heard, heard

    wrote, written

    stopped, stopped

    hoped, hoped

    rained, rained

    tried, tried

    played, played

Vocabulary and language use

1 Write the names of six or more things that you might find in a kitchen.

....   *1. (various possible answers)*

....

2 Write the names of six or more parts of the body (for example: *arm, leg*).

....   *2. (various possible answers)*

....

3 Put in the missing words.

A: .... afternoon. I
   help you?

B: Yes, ... some ....
   for cleaning carpets.

A: Yes, ... course. ....
   you like the large, ..., or small
   size?

B: The large size, please. How .... is
   that?

A: One .... sixty.

3. Good; Can

I'd like (I'm looking for / I need); stuff (liquid / powder)

of; Would

medium

much

pound

4 Put in the missing words.

A: .... to go to the cinema
   tonight?

B: Yes, I .... Did you have a
   special film in mind?

A: Well, there's that new Japanese film at the
   Phoenix. Starts at seven. ....
   .... go there and then
   have a late dinner at the Indian restaurant?

B: Sounds lovely. .... we go
   in my car? And then I can drive you home
   afterwards.

A: Well, that's very ....
   That would be great, if you're sure you

   ....

B: Not at all! I actually like driving at night.

4. Would you like

would ('d love to)

Why don't we (Shall we)

Shall (Why don't)

kind of you (nice of you)

don't mind

Pronunciation

The sound /ə/ comes once in the word *mother*
(/'mʌðə(r)/), twice in the word *America*
(/ə'merɪkə/), and twice in the word
computer (/kəm'pju:tə(r)/).
Which of these words are pronounced with /ə/?

guarantee   paper   coming   machine
football   answer   introduce   woman
belief   rubbish   explain   visitor

guarantee (/gærən'ti:/); paper (/'peɪpə(r)/);
machine (/mə'ʃi:n/); answer (/'ɑ:nsə(r)/);
introduce (/ɪntrə'dju:s/); woman (/'wʊmən/);
visitor (/'vɪzɪtə(r)/)

Listening

Read the questions about some radio
advertisements. Then listen to the
advertisements two or three times and answer
the questions.

📼 Ⓐ

Give the students time to read the questions, and
then play the recording at least twice. Play it a third
time if the students want you to. The information
they must listen for is fairly clear.

1. Dorchester-on-Thames is on a road between
   Oxford and Henley. What's the number of the
   road? ....

   1. A43

2. What's the date of the third Swindon Country
   Music Festival? ....

   2. April 14

3. A woman likes Ariel Automatic washing
   powder. What colour shirts do she and her
   husband wear? ....

   3. white

4. At Swindon Glass, do prices include VAT?
   ....

   4. yes

5. What day is the Fleet Street market on?
   ....

   5. Saturday   ➡

Writing

Describe somebody you know. Write five to ten
sentences.

The most important thing is that students should
communicate successfully. If a student produces a
description which could be understood by an ordinary
British or American reader, then he or she has
completed the task satisfactorily. If the language is
reasonably correct and the description is interesting
and well-constructed, so much the better.

Tapescript for listening test

WOMAN: On the outskirts of Oxford lies Dorchester-on-Thames, a quiet, pretty village.

MAN: That's until Motor Sports Centre arrived. The dealer that covers the complete Mazda range; market leaders in finance and leasing packages, with probably Britain's largest selection of the fabulous RX7. Nobody's beaten their fantastic deals yet. Sales, after-sales, service, courtesy cars, and the best deals ever on Mazda RX7s, cars and commercials.

WOMAN: All at Motor Sports Centre in beautiful Dorchester-on-Thames, on the A43 Oxford to Henley Road. Telephone Oxford 341010.

David Houston has had sixteen number one hits in America. WR have brought him to England to top the bill at the third Swindon Country Music Festival, in the Wyvern Theatre on Sunday, April the 14th.
(*Song*) Your lips are warm and close to mine, I know they taste like warm red wine...
Lee Williams will be presenting WR Country live from the foyer. Then from eight o'clock the concert starts with Tokyo Matsu, and Britain's Hickory Lake and Hamilton's Power. The third Swindon Country Music Festival, at the Wyvern Theatre Sunday, April the 14th. Tickets on sale now.

MAN: Hello there. I got with me, um, Jill Lancashire, and you got a new washing machine, is that right?

WOMAN: Er, I treated myself to a Servis Quartz, and with that came the packet of Ariel Automatic.

MAN: Since you've been using Ariel, you ever been tempted to, sort of, you know, break away and try something else?

WOMAN: I wouldn't dare (*laughter*). My husband's a police motorcyclist, (*Yeah*) and he has a white shirt every day, which gives me lots of dirty collars and cuffs. And I'm a waitress, I have a white shirt every day, ...

MAN: What sort of stains do you tend to get on them?

WOMAN: Um, it depends what the menu of the day is (*laughter*). It's, it's usually gravy and er, sauces. (*Yeah*) I can pick up the shirts and throw them in the machine with Ariel Automatic, and the whole job is done. They come out clean and fresh on a low temperature, time after time.

MAN: Which must be a great relief for you.

WOMAN: It's lovely.

MAN: That's great.

Swindon Glass opens up the doors to a new, larger glazing home improvement showroom. They've a better range, and many special offers. For example, aluminium double-glazed front doors from £147; back doors from £138; and patio doors, with safety glass, from only £197. All prices include VAT. At Swindon Glass, you'll find many other glazing home improvements as well, like sliding wardrobe doors, and room-stretcher mirrors. Come and see for yourself at Swindon Glass, on the Oakus Trading Estate, Swindon.

Shop in Swindon this Saturday and you'll notice a big difference. The Fleet Street Saturday Market is now bigger than ever, with over 200 stalls for you to see. Why walk all over town? Everything's right here in Swindon's only open-air market. You'll find fresh food, household goods, fashions, gifts. With over 200 stalls, the choice is endless. Compare our prices with shops or supermarkets, and we're certain you'll find the Market a real bargain. Enjoy your shopping in the fresh air – come to the Fleet Street Market this Saturday.

Revision Test Two

Grammar and structures

Make 'question-tags'.

Example: It's a nice day, *isn't it?*

1. You're German, ...
2. Philip smokes, ...
3. Ann will be here tomorrow, ...

1. *aren't you?*
2. *doesn't he?*
3. *won't she?*

Put in the right form of the verb.

4. My mother .... in an accident last week. (*hurt*)
5. I .... English since last May. (*study*)
6. I didn't know you .... a doctor. (*be*)
7. If I .... you, I would take a holiday. (*be*)
8. I'm going to London tomorrow .... some shopping. (*do*)
9. Our house .... in 1660. (*build*)
10. Why don't you .... me the truth? (*tell*)
11. Let's .... a party. (*have*)
12. Somebody ought .... Mary. (*help*)

4. *was hurt*
5. *have been studying*
6. *were*
7. *were*
8. *to do*
9. *was built*
10. *tell*
11. *have*
12. *to help*

Put the word in the right place.

Example: She is ⌄at home. (*never*)

13. Do you know what her name? (*is*)
14. Who are you writing? (*to*)
15. I go to Wales. (*often*)

13. *Do you know what her name is?*
14. *Who are you writing to?*
15. *I often go to Wales.*

Put a word in each blank.

16. In winter it .... dark before five o'clock.
17. 'What are you doing this evening?' 'I don't know. I .... go and see Pat.'
18. Get out of my house, ... I'll call the police.
19. I got some money .... selling my car.
20. It .... be better if you came tomorrow.

16. *gets/is*
17. *may/might/should/ought to*
18. *or*
19. *by/for*
20. *would/might*

➡

167

Put in the right preposition.

21. I spend too much money .... beer.

22. .... my opinion, the Conservatives are going to win the election.

23. 'How did you like the film?' 'I didn't think much .... it.'

24. John fell .... a wall and broke his leg.

21. on

22. In

23. of

24. off

Vocabulary and language use

What are the opposites?

Example: easy *difficult* ....

1. plug in ....

2. switch on ....

3. turn up ....

1. unplug

2. switch off

3. turn down

Write some more words in each group.

4. grandfather, aunt, brother

....

....

(at least seven words)

5. hill, valley

....

(at least three words)

6. TV, fridge, toaster

....

....

(at least five words)

4–6. (various possible answers)

Put one or more words in each blank.

7. 'Do you know Corinne?' 'Yes, she's a very good friend of ....'

8. Could you .... me the salt, please?

9. 'Could you do me a ....?' 'It depends. What is it?' 'Type a letter for me.'

10. 'Would you like to buy my car?' 'No, I'm very .... of money just now.'

11. 'Can I talk to you for a minute?' 'Not just now, if you don't mind. I'm .... hurry.'

12. 'Let me help you.' 'That's very .... of you.'

13. 'I'm sorry to .... you, but I .... if you could tell me the way to the station.'

7. mine

8. pass

9. favour

10. short

11. in a

12. nice/kind

13. trouble

wonder/wondered

14. 'Thanks very much.' 'That's ....'

15. I look forward to .... from you.
    Yours sincerely,
    James Parker.

16. 'Is this the right road?' 'Yes, I think
    ....'

17. 'People who drive when they've drunk too
    much should go to prison.' 'No, I ....
    agree.'

18. 'Are you trying to say that I'm stupid?' 'No, of
    course ....'

19. 'What's that noise?' 'It sounds ....
    John's car.'

20. Could you tell me as soon as ....,
    please?

14. *all right / OK*

15. *hearing*

16. *so / it is*

17. *don't*

18. *not / I'm not*

19. *like*

20. *possible*

Pronunciation

Where is the stress?

Examples: me̠dicine   prefe̠r

grandfather   definitely   perhaps

electricity   housework   calendar

magazine   society   museum   Japan

grandfather   definitely   perhaps

electricity   housework   calendar

magazine   society   museum   Japan

Listening

**Read the questions about a radio news
programme. Then listen to the programme too
or three times and write the answers.**

1. Some children were killed. What country was
   this in? ....
   How many children died? Up to ....
   children.

2. Police were looking for a man. They used a
   helicopter, and what else?
   ....

3. A man killed his ex-wife. Who else was in the
   room when he did it? ....
   He killed her because she slept with someone –
   who? ....

4. A Devizes woman has written a book about
   Peru. Where did she find the story?
   ....
   Who went to Peru?
   ....

*Give the students time to read the questions, and
then play the recording twice; play it a third time if
students want you to. The information they must
listen for is fairly clear.*

1. *South Africa*
   up to 40 children

2. *(tracker) dogs*

3. *the children*
   a cousin

4. *in old family letters*
   her grandparents / her grandmother / a brave woman

Writing

Write about a place that you like very much.

The most important thing is that students should communicate successfully. If a student produces a piece of writing which could be understood by an ordinary British or American reader, then he or she has completed the task satisfactorily. If the language is reasonably correct and the passage is interesting and well-constructed, so much the better.

Tapescript for listening test

Up to 40 children are feared dead in South Africa after their double-decker school bus ran out of control and plunged into a reservoir in a Johannesburg suburb. From there, Beatrice Hollier reports:

'Between 30 and 40 schoolchildren are believed to have been killed when the tyre of the bus in which they were travelling burst. The double-decker bus left the road and plunged into a suburban dam. The city's mayor says the Afrikaans children were on their way home from school. Relatives gathered around the dam while police divers began recovering the bodies. The exact number of dead is not known, but at least eight children were rescued by passers-by.

Beatrice Hollier, IRN, Johannesburg.'

A man's still being quizzed by police in Swindon after a chase earlier this afternoon involving a helicopter and tracker dogs. The operation began at the Membury services on the M4. Officers were questioning a man when he ran away across fields. Both Wiltshire and Thames Valley forces were involved in the chase; a man was eventually detained.

A Swindon man has been found guilty of murdering his former wife and jailed for life. A jury took just 50 minutes to record a unanimous verdict on 47-year-old ————— of Ponting Street. Bristol Crown Court heard he stabbed his ex-wife Vicky in front of their two young children, after hearing she'd slept with a cousin.

A Devizes woman has turned a collection of faded family letters into a book on her Edwardian grandparents' missionary trip to Peru. The trip was made at the turn of the century. Jenny Coombes of Roundway Hill Farm sees the publication of her book, *Jessie's Journey*, next month. She says the letters show that her grandmother was a very brave lady.

'When I first typed the letters out, um, I didn't realise the story behind them, and when I discovered it I thought that it ought, is a story that more people could hear about, because she was a brave woman. And I think if people can hear of things like this that used to happen as far, long ago as then, they perhaps can realise that people can still go on being brave now, even though nowadays you can go out and you can do VSO, but in those days, the thing you could do was be a missionary.'

Jenny Coombes of Devizes. Linda Cooch, WR News

Revision Test Three

Grammar and structures

Put in the right form of the verb.

1. I .... for you
   since two o'clock. Where have you been? (*wait*)

2. When I .... home
   yesterday, the children
   .... TV. (*get; watch*)

3. I don't think teachers should
   .... as much as doctors. (*pay*)

4. Do you enjoy ....? (*read*)

5. She's so funny. When she starts talking I can't
   stop .... (*laugh*)

6. My parents wanted me .... a
   lawyer. (*be*)

1. *have been waiting*

2. *got; were watching*

3. *be paid*

4. *reading*

5. *laughing*

6. *to be*

**Put in *may, can, could, can't, must* or *will have
to.***

7. I .... be getting a new
   job. I don't know yet.

8. 'Here's a letter for you.' 'It's from Greece. It
   .... be from Sonia.'

9. 'I'm afraid you've failed your exam.' 'Oh no! I
   .... believe it.'

10. I .... try the exam
    again next year.

11. .... I look round?

12. John said I .... use his
    telephone.

7. *may*

8. *must*

9. *can't*

10. *will have to*

11. *can/could/may*

12. *could*

Put in *of* if necessary.

Examples: a lot .....*of*..... people

        too many .....—..... people

13. some .... my friends

14. all .... us

15. most .... people

16. most .... the people in this room

17. a piece .... bread

18. enough .... sugar

13. *of*

14. *of*

15. *–*

16. *of*

17. *of*

18. *–*

172

Put in _a_ or _the_ if necessary.

Examples: Can you lend me ....._a_..... pen?

What's ....._the_..... time?

I'll see you .....⌐..... next week.

19. .... books are expensive.		_19. –_
20. My sister's .... dentist.		_20. a_
21. Is your father at .... home?		_21. –_
22. Do you play .... football?		_22. –_
23. Could you shut .... door, please?		_23. the_
24. Could you do me .... favour?		_24. a_
25. It's .... long way from my home to my office.		_25. a_

Put in the right word.

26. 'Why did you come ....?' 'To see you.' (_here/there_)

       26. here

27. We're having a party here tonight. Would you like to ....? (_come/go_)

       27. come

28. 'Did you like .... music?' 'Not much.' (_this/that_)

       28. that

29. They're .... nice people that everybody likes them. (_so/such_)

       29. such

30. 'Hasn't Mary got up ....?' 'No, she's .... asleep.' (_still/yet/already_)

       30. yet; still

Vocabulary and language use

Put some more words in these lists.

1. butcher's, bookshop

....

....

(at least five words)

       1–5. (various possible answers)

2. dog, tiger

....

....

(at least seven words)

3. banana, orange

....

(at least three words)

4. doctor, engineer

....

....

(at least four words)

5. steering wheel, brake

....

....

(at least three words)

Put a word in each blank.

6. 'I don't feel well.' 'Why don't you go and lie

.... for a bit?'   6. *down*

7. Teachers .... less money than   7. *earn/get*

   dustmen.

8. 'Are you married?' 'No, I'm not. I'm

   ....'   8. *single/widowed/divorced*

9. The head of the government in Britain is

   called the .... Minister.   9. *Prime*

10. .... me. Can I ask you a question?   10. *Excuse*

11. Do you .... if I close the window?   11. *mind*

12. 'What's the matter with your voice?' 'I've got

    a .... throat.'   12. *sore*

13. 'Can I borrow your car?' 'Yes, I suppose

    ....'   13. *so*

14. 'Hello, Stratford 315 4648.' 'Hello. Could I

    .... to James Brice, please?'   14. *speak*

15. 'Can I borrow your dictionary?' 'I'm

    .... I'm using it right now.'   15. *afraid*

16. 'Where do you want to go this weekend?'

    'How .... Wales?'   16. *about*

17. Please help me. I've got a terrible

    ....   17. *problem*

18. I .... if I could use your telephone.   18. *wondered/wonder*

19. 'I'll give you four pounds.' 'It's worth six.'

    'Oh, come on. Let's .... the   19. *split*

    difference. Five.' 'Oh, well, OK.'

20. There are .... to be about 25 people   20. *likely/going*

    at the party.

Pronunciation

1 Divide these words into five groups according to the pronunciation of the letter *o*. (For example, *not* and *off* go in the same group, but *not* and *note* go in different groups.)

not   off   note   gone   mother   over
stop   come   home   woman   don't   visitor

1. /ɒ/: *not, off, gone, stop*
   /əʊ/: *note, over, home, don't*
   /ʌ/: *mother, come*
   /ʊ/: *woman*
   /ə/: *visitor*

2 Divide these words into five groups according to the pronunciation of the letter *a*.

cat   make   many   after   table   apple
about   any   glass   match   machine

2. /æ/: *cat, apple, match*
   /eɪ/: *make, table*
   /e/: *many, any*
   /ɑː/: *after, glass (southern British English)*
   /ə/: *about, machine*

Listening

🔲 Ⓐ

Read these questions. Then listen to the recording twice and try to answer them.

Give the students time to read the questions. Then play the recording twice; play it a third time if students want you to. The information they must listen for is fairly clear.

1. Who did the woman fight with when she was younger? ....

   1. her brother

2. Who watched the fight?

   ....

   2. other children

3. How long did the children have to fight?

   ....

   ....

   3. until their mother said they could stop

4. What did her brother set fire to?

   ....

   4. a bedroom

5. How many matches did he have to strike?

   ....

   ....

   5. two full boxes of kitchen matches

6. Did this stop him playing with matches?

   ....

   6. yes   ➡

Writing

Write about a journey, or about a time when you were ill.

The most important thing is that students should communicate successfully. If a student produces a piece of writing which could be understood by an ordinary British or American reader, then he or she has completed the task satisfactorily. If the language is reasonably correct and the passage is interesting and well-constructed, so much the better.

Tapescript for listening test

You can be creative about it. I think this was one thing abou
my mother (*Yeah*), she was so good at . . . When we were
teenagers my brother and I used to physically fight quite a
bit. We got into a period where we really were fightin' a lot
and chasin' one another around the house and . . . fightin'.
And she got tired of it and one day she called all the kids tha
we knew in the neighbourhood, and she made, she ma-, she
got 'em, got about ten kids out there, and she made us fight
until she told us we could stop (*general laughter; 'Ah, lovely!'*
'I'll remember that!'). In front of all these kids! And I'll tell
you, we didn't fight for a long time after that!
– Well, mine are like that now.
– Yeah.
Or like, when one of my boys set fire to, one of my brothers
set fire to the bedroom once, 'cause he was just into
matches and all. And she set him out, after that she set him
out on the front walk and she gave him two full boxes of
kitchen matches, and she did not let him get up until he had
one by one struck every (*general laughter*)
– Did it stop him?
And it stopped him, yeah.
– Yeah.

Tapescripts

Lesson 1B, Exercise 1

Keith is 37. He's married, and he's got two children: a boy and a girl. He works as a printer's reader. He's a good-looking man: very tall and quite slim, with light brown hair. He has a soft deep voice. Today he's wearing white trousers and a blue striped T-shirt. He wears an ear-ring in his left ear.

Sue is 33. She's married, and she's got two children: a boy and a girl. She works as a part-time nurse. She's pretty: slim and blonde, not very tall. She has quite a hard voice. Today she's wearing olive green trousers and a shirt of the same colour.

John's 41, but he looks older. He's married with two children: a boy and a girl. He works with racehorses. He's very short, slim and thin-faced – but very strong. He's got dark brown hair. He's the only one of these five people with a northern accent. Today he's wearing black trousers and a blue short-sleeved shirt.

Alexandra is 17. She has just left school. She's not married, and has no children. She wants to be a policewoman. She is not very tall, rather heavily built, and has red hair. Today she is wearing a brown and white sweater and blue jeans.

Jane is 37. She is married with two children: a boy and a girl. She works as a part-time secretary with a firm of solicitors. She's pretty: slim and dark-haired, not very tall. Today she's wearing a grey skirt and a white blouse.

Lesson 1B, Exercise 3

'All right. Keith. How old are you?'
'Thirty-seven.'
'Thirty-seven, yeah? And, erm, you married?'
'Yes.'
'Yeah. Have you got children?'
'Two.'
'Yeah. What are their names?'
'Toby and Lucy.'
'Toby and Lucy. How old are they?'
'One's 11, that's Lucy; and Toby's 13.'
'Yeah. Tell me about your job, Keith.'
'Well, I work at the Oxford University Press. I'm a printer's reader and copy editor.'
'Erm, what sort of hours of work do you have?'
'Erm, 7.30 in the morning – '
'You start work at 7.30?'
'Yes. I start at 7.30 in the morning and finish at 4.15. That's with a 45-minute lunch break.'
'Yeah. Do you like it that way? Do you like starting very early?'
'No, I don't. No.'
'How do you go to work?'
'Er, well, I cycle from here to Didcot station, and then catch the train and – return journey.'
'Tell me one or two things you like doing, and one or two things you don't like doing. What do you like doing? What do you do for enjoyment?'
'Well, I'm quite interested in antiques.'

'Yes.'
'Things I don't like – I don't like decorating. I'm not awfully keen on gardening.'
'OK.'
'What reading – what sort of – what newspaper do you read?'
'*The Times.*'
'*The Times*, yeah.'
'And *The Sunday Times*.'
'Yeah. And what kind of books do you read?'
'Erm – tends to be more along history lines. Not novels, generally, more general history. Local history especially.'
'Yeah, OK. Do you smoke, Keith?'
'No.'
'You drink?'
'Occasionally.'
'Yeah. Do you go to church?'
'Not very often, no.'
'Right. Thank you very much indeed.'

'Sue, how old are you?'
'Thirty-three.'
'Children?'
'Two – a girl who is eight, and a boy who's seven.'
'Yeah.'
'Stephanie and Malcolm.'
'Erm, work, Sue. What do you do?'
'Nursing part-time. 7.30 in the morning till 1.30, or 4.30 till 9.30.'
'How do you get to work?'
'By car.'
'How long does it take?'
'Half an hour.'
'OK. Tell me some things you like doing, Sue.'
'Reading.'
'Mm. What do you read?'
'Erm. Philosophy.'
'Yeah.'
'And, erm, I like Dick Francis and those sort of novels. Erm and the odd historical novel, and your more serious novels as well.'
'What newspaper do you read?'
'Erm, I very rarely read a newspaper, I hate to admit. But if I read one, it's *The Telegraph* or the – I don't know, I find them all pretty difficult to read, newspapers.'
'Do you smoke?'
'No.'
'You drink?'
'Yes.'
'Yeah. Go to church?'
'No.'

'How old are you, John?'
'Forty-one.'
'Yeah. Children?'
'Yeah. Two. John and Debbie.'
'OK.'
'Er, John's 17, Debbie 16.'
'What's your job, John?'
'Well, working with racehorses.'
'What sort of hours of work do you have? When do you start when do you finish?'
'Very easy, actually, for the stable I'm in. We don't start till eight o'clock through the week. Seven o'clock on Monday. Weekends are very good. It's only half an hour morning and afternoon. But normal hours, we'll say from quarter to

eight, eight o'clock till half eleven or twelve. Finish then again, start again at four o'clock till half past five.'
'How do you get to work?'
'By car.'
'Tell me something you like doing, John. What do you like doing?'
'Well, what I like – what I love doing is gardening.'
'Yeah.'
'Anything you don't like doing?'
'Not really.'
'What about reading? What do you like to read?'
'I don't read a lot. I like thrillers. I've got Dick Francis – all them books – I've got the lot. Read every one of them. Terrific. And that's about it. Couldn't get into anything else.'
'You a newspaper reader?'
'Just *The Sun*.'
'Do you smoke, John?'
'I do, yeah.'
'How much?'
'Twenty, twenty-five a day.'
'You drink?'
'Just a little.'
'Go to church?'
'No.'

'Alexandra, how old are you?'
'Seventeen.'
'Children?'
'Er, no.'
'What do you do, Alexandra?'
'Well, I have been doing an A-Level course. But I've rather sort of given up on that. It wasn't very successful. And I don't think I would have passed them. So hopefully I'm going to Abingdon College to do a secretarial course for a year. And then I want to join the police force.'
'Join the police?'
'Yeah.'
'Yeah. Erm – tell me something you like doing – or some things you like doing – what do you enjoy doing?'
'Erm, reading, walking, cycling, erm – actually, most of them are sort of solitary interests. But I also like sort of going out in the evenings and meeting people.'
'What do you read? What sort of thing do you like reading?'
'Well, just about anything I can get my hands on. Erm, I'll just read books and books and books. But not really sort of history or anything like that. Not heavy stuff.'
'Yeah.'
'Do you read a newspaper?'
'Erm, *The Express*.'
'Yeah. You smoke?'
'No.'
'Drink?'
'Yes.'
'Go to church?'
'Erm, well, I haven't for some time.'

'How old are you?'
'Thirty-seven.'
'Yeah. Children?'
'Yes, two. Toby, who's 13, and Lucy, who's 11.'
'Yeah. Job? What do you do?'
'Yes. I work part-time doing secretarial work with solicitors in Wantage.'
'What's part-time? How many hours?'
'Nine till one.'
'Every day?'
'Yeah. Well, five days a week.'
'Yeah. How do you get in there? Do you drive?'
'No. Well, I can, but I don't have a car. So I have to take the bus.'

'What do you like doing?'
'Er, I like gardening. Er, I like reading, er, if I get time.'
'What sort of thing do you read?'
'Things that aren't too heavy. Erm, not science fiction.'
'Don't like science fiction?'
'No.'
'Newspaper?'
'Erm, well, *The Times*.'
'Is there anything you don't like doing?'
'Mending. Darning socks.'
'Do you smoke?'
'No.'
'Drink?'
'A bit.'
'Go to church?'
'Christmas, Easter and Harvest Festival.'

Lesson 4B, Exercise 4

'Well, height, to start with.'
'John is very small, and Keith's very tall.'
'They're both quite slim, though, aren't they?'
'Yeah.'
'Their interests differ, I think, 'cause Keith can't stand gardening, and John says it's one of his main relaxation activities, I think.'
'They've both got two children. A girl and a boy.'
'In the same order.'
'Yes.'
'Keith's hair is darker than John's, isn't it?'
'No.'
'I would have said the other way round.'
'I think John's is darker.'
'John's hair's darker.'
'No, Keith's is sort of gingery, isn't it?'
'And John's is dark brown.'
'Dark brown, yes. And John obviously has some sort of dressing in his hair, whereas Keith doesn't.'
'John's older than Keith.'
'They're both slim, but John has a thinner face.'
'Very thin face, yes.'
'Yes, he's obviously the sort of jockey type look.'
'Keith wears an ear-ring.'
'Yes. Yes, he does. In his left ear.'
'Yes.'
'What are they wearing?'
'Er, Keith is wearing trainers, white trousers, and er –'
'Oh, he's got a blue striped T-shirt on.'
'Yes. Blue striped T-shirt on. John's wearing black cord trousers, black shoes and –'
'You notice a lot, don't you? A blue short-sleeved shirt. A casual-type shirt, I would have said.'
'No necklaces or anything.'
'No.'
'And John's got dark socks as well.'

Lesson 7B, Exercise 1

FBC Radio 2. Here is the news for today, Wednesday 25th April, at eleven a.m.

President and Mrs Martin of Outland have just arrived in Fantasia for a state visit. This is the first official visit by an Outland head of state since the end of the War of Independence in 1954, and it is expected to last three days. The president and her husband were at the airport to welcome President and Mrs Martin, who are old friends of theirs: Mrs Rask and Mrs Martin first met at the 1960

Olympics, in which Mrs Rask won a silver medal for the high jump, and Mrs Martin represented Outland in the 100 metres. Dr Rask has known President Martin since their student days at the University of Goroda.

Dr Rask has just returned from an overseas fact-finding tour. For the last six weeks, he has been visiting Third World countries in his capacity as President of 'Families against Hunger'. Speaking at a press conference shortly after his return, Dr Rask said that increased aid to the Third World was an urgent priority.

Demonstrations are continuing against the proposed dam on the Upper Fant river, and demonstrators have been marching through the Centre of San Fantastico for several hours. Traffic in Wesk Square has been very slow since half past eight this morning, and motorists are advised to avoid the city centre.

The heavy rain which has been falling steadily for the past four weeks has caused widespread flooding. The River Fant has just burst its banks in North Milltown, and parts of the town centre are under water. The bad weather has ruined many vegetable crops, and vegetable prices in San Fantastico have been going up steadily for the last ten days. The Minister for Consumer Affairs has just announced that price controls on vegetables and fruit will come into effect next week.

Foreign exchange. The Fantasian Grotnik has risen to its highest level against the Outland dollar since last July. The Exchange rate is now 1.23 dollars to the Grotnik.

Miners' leaders and Coal Board chiefs have been meeting to discuss the strike since early this morning. There has been no announcement so far, but unofficial sources say that some progress has been made.

The fire which has been burning in Grand South Station for the last three days is now under control. The origin of the fire, which started in the station restaurant on Sunday, is still unknown. Three more firemen were overcome by smoke this morning, and have been taken to hospital.

News has just come in that police have arrested a man in connection with the death of Professor Carpathia Bosk, the well-known sculptor. The man has been charged with first-degree murder, and will appear in court on Tuesday.

And now the weather. Heavy rain will continue in most parts of the country, *(fade)*.

Lesson 10A, Exercise 4

Episode 1
John is having lunch in a restaurant. Suddenly he sees a beautiful girl at the next table. She is *very* beautiful. He wonders whether to speak to her. She smiles at him.
JOHN: Shall I speak to her?

What will happen if John speaks to the girl?

Episode 2
JOHN: Excuse me.
GIRL: Yes?
JOHN: May I join you?
GIRL: Of course.
JOHN: What's your name?
GIRL: Olga. Let's have some champagne. Lots of champagne.

What will happen if John drinks lots of champagne?

Episode 3
JOHN: Waiter! A bottle of champagne, please!
WAITER: Certainly, sir.

JOHN: Waiter! A bottle of champagne, please!
WAITER: Certainly, sir.

JOHN: Waiter! A bottle of champagne, please!
WAITER: *Another* bottle, sir?

OLGA: Darling.
JOHN: Yesh?
OLGA: Let's go to the zoo.
JOHN: The zoo? But I've got to go to work.
OLGA: Work? How boring. We're going to the zoo. I want to see the snakes.

What will happen if John goes to the zoo?

Episode 4
OLGA: Look at those lovely snakes.
JOHN: Be careful. Don't lean over!
OLGA: Oh! I've dropped my bag!
JOHN: Where is it?
OLGA: Down there. By that green snake. Get it for me, darling.
JOHN: What?
OLGA: Do you love me?
JOHN: Er, yes.
OLGA: Then get my bag.

What will happen if John tries to get Olga's bag?

Episode 5
JOHN: All right. I'll get it with my umbrella. Just a moment. Here you are, darling. I've got it. Darling! Where are you? Where's she gone? That's funny. She's gone. And I don't know where she lives, or anything... Perhaps her address is in her bag – I'll have a look. My God! What's this? A revolver! What shall I do? Perhaps I should go to the police.

What will happen if John goes to the police?

Episode 6
John doesn't go to the police. He goes back to his office.
JOHN: Good afternoon, sir.
BOSS: Good evening, Mr Armitage. Do you know what time it is? It's five o'clock.
JOHN: Yes, sir. Well, I met this girl and we went to the zoo and she dropped her bag in the snake-pit and I got it out with my umbrella and she wasn't there any more and there was a revolver in her bag.
BOSS: Girl... zoo... bag... snakes... revolver... That's it! You've gone too far! I'm sorry, Mr Armitage, but you'll have to go.
JOHN: You can't do this to me!
BOSS: Oh yes I can! Get out!
JOHN: Oh no you can't. I've got a revolver!
BOSS: Hey! What are you doing? No! Don't shoot!

What will happen if John shoots his boss?

Episode 7
John shoots his boss. He takes £20,000 out of the office safe, leaves the office and takes a taxi to the airport.
JOHN: First class to San Francisco, please.
CLERK: One way or round trip?
JOHN: One way. What time is the flight?
CLERK: Six-thirty, sir.
JOHN: Good. Time for a drink.

JOHN: A large whisky, please.
John sits down with his whisky. Suddenly he sees a beautiful girl at the next table. She is *very* beautiful. He wonders whether to speak to her. She smiles at him.

What will happen if John speaks to the girl?

Lesson 11A, Exercise 4

The twelve o'clock news. This is Alan King.

Distillers, Britain's biggest Scotch whisky manufacturers, has announced it's to axe 715 jobs and close two of its Scottish plants.

A nineteen-year-old airman has been beaten around the head, kicked and punched in Chippenham. He'd been heading back to camp at Hullavington when three youths attacked him in Malmesbury Road. The airman needed hospital treatment for cuts and bruises. Police said the attack was unprovoked; no money was stolen. They're now appealing for help from the public.

Two women thought to be responsible for widespread credit-card fraud have failed in an attempt to swindle a Chippenham off-licence. Les Skipper reports:
The women, both in their late twenties, tried to use a stolen Access card to buy £34 worth of spirits at Roberts wine merchants in Market Place. When the store assistant decided to check the card, the women made a speedy exit. It's thought they made off in either a white Jaguar car or a blue Hillman estate. One of the women is tall – about six feet; the other is about five feet five. The tall one has dyed blonde hair. They both have London accents.

Residents in the village of Amport, near Amesbury, now have to go to church if they want to buy a stamp. Their new sub-post-office is housed in the local Methodist chapel. Although it's thought to be the only one of its kind in the country, owner Betty Smith says the service she offers is perfectly normal.

Camping equipment's been stolen in a raid near Witney. The break-in was at Cassington caravan park in Eynsham.

Thank you, Linda. The weather. It'll be rather cool and fairly cloudy today, with a few showers, but also some sunny intervals, particularly later this afternoon. The evening will be dry, with a few clear intervals. High temperatures this afternoon around nineteen centigrade, that's sixty-six degrees fahrenheit, and winds will be north-westerly, light or moderate. The outlook for tomorrow and Thursday: rather cloudy at first, with isolated showers, but dry with some sunshine on Thursday, and it will become warmer.

Lesson 12A, Exercise 2

1. Paper was invented by the Greeks.
2. It was invented in the first century.
3. The British learned how to make paper in the 18th century.
4. Paper-making is an unimportant industry in Britain.
5. British paper is imported from South Africa.
6. All British paper is made from wood grown in Great Britain.
7. Trees are usually transported to the paper mills by air.
8. When wood pulp is dried it is made into paper.
9. Four hundred trees are needed to make a typical forty-page newspaper.
10. There may not be enough paper in the year 2000.

Lesson 12B, Exercise 3

JANE: I think, um, that J.F. Kennedy was killed in 1963 by Oswald. 'Course it was never proved.
KATY: OK.
ALEXANDRA: I'm sure radium was discovered by Pierre and Marie Curie.
JOHN: And I'm sure J.F. Kennedy was killed by Oswald in '63. (*laughter*)
SUE: I think, I think *Psycho* was written by Hitchcock. (*Mm. Mumbles.*) I don't know when.
KEITH: I know America was discovered by Columbus in 1492. (*Oh!*)
STEVE: And I know Everest was first climbed by Hillary and Tensing in – (*laughter*)
MIKE: I think, I think *Hamlet* was written by Shakespeare in, er, 1600.
KATY: Well, I know the *Communist Manifesto* was written by Marx and Engels.
STEVE: I think, (*was written*) I think (*by*) paper was discovered by the Chinese in... question mark.
OTHERS: The first century.
SUE: I know *Hamlet* was written by Shakespeare.
RUTH: Ah! but... (*laughter*)
SUE: Some people don't think so. (*Bacon. Bacon. Yes. Ah. Yes. Laughter.*) I think so.
JOHN: Er, another one. 1974 World Cup... I think the 1974 World Cup was won by West Germany.
MIKE: I think the Taj Mahal was built by Shah Jehan.
SUE: I was just gonna say that! (*Mm.*)
KATY: I think TV was invented by Baird (*Baird. Mm. Yes. Mm. Yeah.*) in... 1923? (*Sounds likely. Yeah. Mm, yes.*)
KEITH: Um, I know radium was discovered by Pierre and Marie Curie.
ALEXANDRA: Mm. (*Mm.*) But I didn't get a date.
KEITH: There's no date, I sh...
ALEXANDRA: 1808.
SUE: No.
KEITH: No, hardly.
JANE: 1898, I should think, (*1898.*)...
KEITH: No.
JANE: No? Not 1898?
KEITH: It's, it's, it's twen-, (*1848?*) twentieth century.
JOHN: Twentieth century, yes.
KEITH AND JANE: Twentieth century.
JANE: Well, it's nearly the twentieth century!
KEITH: I should say 'by'. Just finish 'by' the er, ...
SUE: Beethoven wrote the *Pastoral Symphony*, right?
ALEXANDRA: How 'bout '98, 1898? (*Yeah.*) That'll, I think...
MIKE: Can you say it from left to right?
JANE: That's what I said, 1898.
SUE: Sorry.
JANE: Almost, isn't it?
SUE: I think I know the *Pastoral Symphony* (*laughter*) I think the *Pastoral Symphony* was written by Beethoven. I don't know when.

Lesson 14A, Exercise 8

1
JOHN: No, I wou– I wouldn't like to have more. I got two and I think two is, er, just right.
KEITH: I find occasionally I've earn, well, yearnings, should I say, not earnings, (*laughter*) to erm, have, it would be nice to have another baby, (*Hm-hm*) and, but there are occasions again when it's... would be better without any children at all.

SUE: I, I have no yearnings to have more children at all; I'm happy with the two. But like you, there are times when I could do without them. (*laughter*) Very much. (*laughter*)

2

JANE: Send them on their own! (*laughter*)

JOHN: Yeah, I think it'd be a great idea to give them the money and let them have a holiday on their own. (*Mm*)

KEITH: As my parents live separately, it could work out quite expensive. (*laughter*)

SUE: I'd rather give them the money, I think, to have a holiday on their own.

JANE: I don't think my parents would go! (*laughter*)

3

SUE: I'm quite happy with what I've got.

JANE: I always rather fancied an elder brother, but I couldn't arrange it. I thought (*laughter*)

JOHN: Yeah, I think... Yeah, I think our family's about right, but, er, I mean, I hardly ever see them anyway, you know, so... (*Mm*) I would think if I was living up there, and seeing them every day, every night or whatever, might get a bit put out, you know, with being three brothers and two sisters. But I don't know, ah, it's all right as it is.

MIKE: Can I have the same number but change them? (*laughter*)

4

JOHN: Oh, have them when you're young. Get it over with. (*laughter*)

SUE: I think late twenties is a good age.

ALEX: Yeah. (*Mm-hm*) About twenty-seven, twenty-eight (*Mm*), and then that's, you've had your youth and y, and your enjoyment of everything and met lots of young people, and then, (*laughter*), and then settle down.

KEITH: I think it's reasonably nice to have them youngish. (*Yeah*)

JANE: I think you've got to have a bit of experience of life (*Mm*) beforehand. I wouldn't want, I wouldn't have wanted to go straight from school to having children.

MIKE: I had my first children in my mid-twenties and I think I was, I was too young really, wasn't mature enough. And er, now with Mark erm, I feel fine, just, just about the right age to have a child.

SUE: The answer is, I think, not to, well, if there is an answer, is not to have children until you feel you're ready, no matter what anybody says to you.

5

KEITH: I think I'd prefer to have more time at home. My, my day tends to be a twelve-hour day. And part – after that it's sleeping. It seems to be that throughout the week it's getting up, going to work, going to bed; getting up, going to work, you know... (*Mm*) I'd rather see more, I think.

JANE: I think I probably see enough of them.

MIKE: Well I work at home so I, I already see plenty of my family. I'd certainly like to work less.

Lesson 16B, Exercise 6

Lot 99: An old blue and white bowl and cover. Lot 99, there it is, being shown down the bottom, is it? Yes? Don't be shy! There it is. Who'll give me a couple of pounds for it? Two pounds somewhere, for the little blue and white? Two I have. Three somewhere? Three. Four? No? Three with the gentleman down there. Four. Five. Six anywhere now? Five pounds I am bid. Are you all done? (*Hammer*) Name, madam, is...? (*Hunt*) Hunt. Thank you.

Small bedroom chair, Lot 104. There it is being shown, very nice indeed. Who'll give me a couple of pound for it? Nice little chair. Pound, then? Pound on my left. Two anywhere? Two. Three. It's yours in the doorway at three, yes. Four anywhere? Against the lady sat down. Are you all done at three? Finished? (*Hammer*) Name, madam? Holtby. Well, you can't pay yet, there's nobody here, madam.

Portable light, in excellent condition, it says. There we are! Probably don't believe – there's two of those, is there, or one? (*Two.*) Two of 'em, my goodness gracious me. Who'll give me a fiver for 'em, then? Five pounds these two small lights with the glass shades, three then. Nobody want them at three pounds? Three I have. Four. Five anywhere? Four pound I am bid. Five, sat down. Sorry, it's at the front that I saw first. Six anywhere? Five just you at the front. Six anywhere? All done at five? Six. Seven anywhere now? All done at five. (*Hammer*) Crowther.

Two boxes of miscellaneous, 122. Sample being shown. Who'll give me a pound for that lot? One pound I am bid. Two. Three anywhere? Three. Four. Five. Six. Six pound. All done at six? (*Hammer*) Day, is it? Day.

A white chest of drawers. Is that right? Yeah. Yes, it is, it's not a child's teak wardrobe now. It's a white chest of – four drawers, is it, Tony? Who'll give me a pound for it? A chest of four drawers. Down the end. Pound somewhere? Pound. Two somewhere? Nothing wrong with it. One pound I am bid. Two anywhere? Two. Three anywhere now? Are you all done at two? Three. Four anywhere? Three down here. Four anywhere? (*Hammer*) Name, sir? (*Drew*) Drew.

Lesson 19A, Exercise 12

Example: 'It's a nice day,...' '...isn't it?'
1. You work in a bank,...
2. That was a great film,...
3. You've met my sister,...
4. You'll be late,...
5. She had an accident last year,...
6. John speaks German,...
7. You were in England last May,...
8. Susan went to Kenya last month,...
9. You've been painting,...
10. Joe and Lois used to live in France,...

Lesson 21B, Exercise 4

WOMAN: Hello. Can I help you?
MAN: Yeah, I hope so. I've got a problem with a Tower pressure cooker that I bought from you some –
WOMAN: Stainless steel?
MAN: Stainless steel, yeah. What it's –
WOMAN: Automatic, then, isn't it?
MAN: Beg your pardon?
WOMAN: Automatic.
MAN: Uh, what do you mean by automatic?
WOMAN: It releases its pressure itself. Is it – a stainless steel, release its own pres –
MAN: Yes, that's what it, that's what it ought to do, yes, but I'm afraid it's not doing that. We, um, it won't release all the pressure when the, when you finish cooking with it, and we can't get the top off.
WOMAN: How long have you had it?
MAN: 'Bout a year. Now I think it's got a ten-year guarantee, hasn't it?
WOMAN: They, yes, I believe they do. I, I'll have to go across and have another look
MAN: Yeah.
WOMAN: 'cause they
MAN: The problem is that I, I can't find the guarantee certificate.
WOMAN: You've got your receipt?
MAN: We've got the sales receipt, yes. Now
WOMAN: Yes
MAN: uh, can I bring it in to you?
WOMAN: Yes, I'd suggest you bring it back.
MAN: Yeah.
WOMAN: Um, I'll take your name. Just let me get a piece of paper. (*pause*) Right. Your name is...?
MAN: OK. My name is Patterson,
WOMAN: Mr Patterson?
MAN: Yeah.
WOMAN: And the address?
MAN: is Lower Farm Cottages,
WOMAN: Lower Farm
MAN: Cottages
WOMAN: Cottages
MAN: East Hagbourne,
WOMAN: East...Hadley?
MAN: No, *Hagbourne*,
WOMAN: Oh, sorry, East Hagbourne, I know where that is.
MAN: Er, OK. Near Didcot.
WOMAN: I thought you said Hadley.
MAN: (*laugh*)
WOMAN: East Hagbourne, near
MAN: Near Didcot, that's right. Um,
WOMAN: Near Didcot.
MAN: OK, um, I'll
WOMAN: Well if you bring it in, uh, with your receipt,
MAN: Yeah.
WOMAN: I'll show, I'll now talk to my manager about it, and
MAN: Yeah.
WOMAN: um, you've had it a year?
MAN: Had it about a year, yes.
WOMAN: About a year.
MAN: Can't tell you exactly.
WOMAN: And, uh, he'll tell me what to do. He may suggest, uh, just automatically giving you, or they may suggest I have to send it back after what he says.
MAN: Yeah. Yeah. OK.
WOMAN: All right?
MAN: All right. Thank you very much for your help.
WOMAN: I'll put it down in a book, so that if I'm not here,
MAN: Yeah.
WOMAN: somebody will know about it. All right?

MAN: OK. Thanks a lot.
WOMAN: Oh, sorry, which, what make was it, let me write this down, Tow –
MAN: Tower. It's a Tower.
WOMAN: It's a Tower stainless steel.
MAN: That's the one, yeah.
WOMAN: I think they're about £34.
MAN: Yeah, I can't – uh, something like that, yes, I don't remember exactly.
WOMAN: Yes, something like that.
MAN: Mm.
WOMAN: All right, I've got the particulars. Thank you then.
MAN: OK. Thank you.
WOMAN: Bye.
MAN: Bye.

Lesson 24A, Exercises 7–9

The USA – the United States of America – is a federation of fifty states. Forty-eight of these states are in the same general area, between Canada in the north and Mexico in the south. The other two states are geographically separate: Alaska is in the extreme north-west of the American continent, and Hawaii is in the middle of the Pacific Ocean. The federal capital is Washington, south of New York near the east coast.

Washington is the centre of federal government, but each state has its own capital and its own government. State governments have a large amount of power and independence: they make their own laws, and they are also responsible for education, for the state police force, for the prison system, for road-building and many other things.

Federal laws are made by Congress, which is the equivalent of the British Parliament. There are two 'houses': the House of Representatives and the Senate. Each state sends representatives and senators to Congress. Elections to the House of Representatives are held every two years, while senators are elected for a six-year period.
  The President is elected separately, together with the Vice-President. They serve for a term of four years. The President chooses the people who will form his cabinet. These do not have to be elected Congressmen – they can be brought in from outside Congress – but the Senate must agree to their appointment.
  There are two main political parties in the United States: the Democrats and the Republicans. The Democrats are slightly more to the left than the Republicans, but the differences between their policies are not usually very great.
  The United States does not have a separate ceremonial Head of State.

Lesson 26B, Exercise 1

A: It's a good one.
B: Do you think so?
A: Oh, yes.
B: I hope so. It's expensive enough.

A: Where shall we put it?
B: In the living-room, I thought.

A: What, by the window?
B: I think it'll look better by the sofa.
A: Yes, maybe you're right. It's big, isn't it?
B: That's why I got this kind. I wanted a really big one. One with eight what-do-you-call-them, things, you know.

A: Yes. I know. They don't usually have eight, do they?
B: No, not usually.

A: I'm surprised you got a white one.
B: Well, I would have liked a red one, actually. But they don't make them in red.

A: It's nice to look at, isn't it?
B: Lots of room on top.
A: You could put flowers on it.
B: I'd be afraid to do that. I mean, if you knocked them over – suppose you knocked them over, and the water went inside. It'd ruin it.
A: Yes, I suppose it would.

A: Are you going to play it?
B: Oh, yes.
A: Can you play?
B: Well, not yet. But I'm going to take lessons. I expect I'll soon pick it up. My family's very musical, you know. Can you play?
A: Yes, a bit...

(Note: the 'eight what-do-you-call-them' referred to in the third section are octaves – most pianos have seven and a quarter.)

Lesson 28B, Exercise 1

(Answers are in *italics*.)

A

D: Where does it hurt?
P: Just here, doctor.
D: *I see. Does it hurt* all the time?
P: No. Only when I *run*, or when I'm going *up*stairs. Sometimes when I carry things.
D: When you carry things. *Heavy* things?
P: Yes.
D: *Right*. Now I want you to stand up...

B

D: How often do you get them?
P: Oh, *two* or *three* times a week.
D: *Two* or *three* times a week. I see. Are they very bad?
P: Oh, yes. They stop me *working*. Sometimes I can hardly see, you know.
D: Yes. Do you *ever* get *hay fever*?

C

P: It's a really bad cough. It *hurts*.
D: Does it hurt when you *breathe*?
P: If I *breathe deeply*, yes.
D: I see. Well, I'll just have a *listen to* your chest. Do you *smoke*?

D

P: It's a really bad pain, doctor. *Down* here.
D: Which side?
P: *This* side.
D: How long has this been going on? When did it start?
P: *Yesterday* morning, doctor. I thought perhaps it was indigestion, but it's too *bad* for that.
D: *All right*. Now just *lie* down here. That's right. Now *where* exactly does it hurt? Is it here?
P: Ooh! Yes!

E

D: Good morning, *Mrs* Palmer. What's the *problem*?
P: Well, I've got a *bad* sore throat, *doctor*.
D: *Oh, dear*. How long have you had it?
P: Oh, about *a week*. It's *getting* very painful. It's difficult to *eat*.

F

P: It's every *year* about the same time, doctor. Stuffed-up nose, my *eyes* itch, and I feel sort of *funny* the whole time.
D: Is it *worse* when you're inside or outside?
P: When I'm in the *garden*.

G

P: I get this *pain* when I bend *over*, doctor. Just here.
D: I see. Take your *shirt* off.

Lesson 30A, Exercise 3

JOHN: What I like about my work is, I think is getting away from the job itself, well, not the job itself, going racing, travelling, things like that. I *hate* going there, just doing the same thing day in and day out. To me you need the break, and er, the best thing about it is when you go to work without the intentions of going anywhere, and then somebody comes up to you and says, 'You've got an hour to get ready, you're going to France for fifteen days,' or something like that. Terrific. I enjoy that. Love travelling, love travelling.

JANE: Um, I think working makes me think, to use my brain, when I'm at home I tend to run on automatic pilot.

KATY: OK, and s–, one thing you don't like about your work?

JANE: Er, having, having a routine, I suppose. I'd rather be able to do what I want when I want.

KEITH: The thing I don't like about my job is the time. Each job now is becoming tighter and tighter on time to do, and you have less time to do it expertly, as it used to be done in the past. And, er, it's very very difficult to do a job. This is why more mistakes get into books, believe it or not.

KATY: And what do you like about your job?

KEITH: Well, I enjoy the job itself, because of the varied subjects we actually do. And, er, especially things like examination papers. Dictionary work's probably my favourite.

SUE: I like the one-to-one contact with people. And I dislike um, the continuing attachment with the old-fashioned way of nursing, which is, er, 'The nurse knows best.' That's basically it. And I dislike the routine of that old-fashioned idea.

Notes

Acknowledgements

The authors and publishers are grateful to the following copyright owners for permission to reproduce photographs, illustrations, texts and music. Every endeavour has been made to contact copyright owners and apologies are expressed for any omissions.

page 21: Reproduced by permission of Syndication International. page 31: Reproduced by permission of *Punch*. page 39: Reproduced by permission of British Telecom. page 60: *cl* 'My mother said...' from *God Bless Love*, Nanette Newman (Collins, 1972), © Invalid Children's Association, reproduced by kind permission of ICA. *tc, br* 'Dear God...', 'If they don't want...' from *Children's Letters to God* (Fontana, Collins, 1976), reproduced by permission of the Publisher. *cr* 'My mum only likes...' from Extracts from Nanette Newman's Collections of Sayings, by permission of the authors, © reserved. page 61: From Extracts from Nanette Newman's Collection of Sayings, by permission of the authors, © reserved. page 92: *tr* Courtesy of John, Hairdresser, Croydon, *cr* Mobil Oil Company Limited. page 93: *tr* Courtesy of Joan Galleli, The Shirley Poppy. page 96: *b* Reproduced by permission of *Punch*. page 98: From the *Longman Active Study Dictionary of English* edited by Della Summers, Longman 1983. page 102: *tr* Photographie Musée National d'Art Moderne, Centre Georges Pompidou, Paris. *tl* Reproduced by courtesy of the Trustees, The National Gallery, London. *bl* Reproduced by courtesy of the Board of Trustees of the Victoria and Albert Museum. page 104: *l* Courtesy of Gallery Lingard. *r* Reproduced from the poster of the London Mozart Players 1984–1985. *c* Reproduced from London Features International Ltd. page 113: From an article by Anna Tomforde in the *Guardian* – adapted. page 115: Reproduced by permission of *Punch*. page 116: *t* Reproduced by permission of *Punch*. *b* From *Weekend Book of Jokes* 21 (Harmsworth Publications Ltd.), reproduced by permission of Associated Newspapers Plc. page 117: Reproduced by permission of Syndication International. page 124: 'My dad...', 'A prime minister...' 'When you grow up...' Reproduced by permission of Bryan Forbes Ltd. page 128: Nos. 1-7, 10 from *The Highway Code* (Her Majesty's Stationery Office), Reproduced by permission of the Publisher. Colour details: 1. green light showing. Other lights are red (top) and amber (middle). 2. same as (1) except that red light is showing. 3. red triangle, white background, black letters. 4. white circle, red background, white horizontal line. 5. red circle and diagonal, white background, black directional sign. 6. red circle, white background, black man. 7. red triangle, white background, black car and lines. 8. grey road, yellow double lines, white dotted lines. 9. grey road, white lines. 10. red triangle, white background, black rocks. page 131: *tl* McLachlan. *tr, c, bl* Reproduced by permission of *Punch*. *br* Reproduced by permission of Syndication International. page 156: Song *You Made Me Love You*, lyrics: Joe McCarthy, music: James V. Monaco. © 1913 Broadway Music Corp, USA. Sub-published by Francis Day & Hunter Ltd., London WC2H 0LD. Reproduced by permission of EMI Music Publishing Ltd. and International Music Publications. page 158: Song *Trying to Love Two Women*, by Sonny Throckmorton, © Cross Keys Publishing Company Inc., USA. Sub-published by EMI Music Publishing Ltd., London WC2H 0LD. Reproduced by permission of EMI Publishing Ltd. and International Music Publications. page 158: Song *The Riddle Song* by Harry Robinson & Julie Felix, © 1965 TRO Essex Music Ltd., Bury Place, London WC1A 2LA for the World International Copyright secured. All Rights Reserved. page 159: The version of the song *Logger Lover* is by Dick Stephenson and is used with permission. page 159: *What Did You Learn in School Today?*, words and music by Tom Paxton. Reprinted by permission of Harmony Music Limited, 19/20 Poland Street, London W1V 3DD.

The songs *Brighton in the Rain* (Lesson 7A, page 156), *Song for a Rainy Sunday* (Lesson 10A, page 156), *The Island* (Lesson 13A, page 156), *My Old Dad* (Lesson 14A, page 59), *Another Street Incident* (Lesson 17B, page 72), and *A Bigger Heart* (Lesson 22A, page 90) were specially written for *The Cambridge English Course* Book 2 by Jonathan Dykes (lyrics) and Robert Campbell (music). The recorded material for Lesson 11A, Exercise 4 (page 181) and Revision Tests 1 (page 166) and 2 (page 170) is used by kind permission of Wiltshire Radio.

Ace Photo Agency: p92 *l*. BBC Hulton Picture Library: p110 *br*. Camera Press Limited: p110 *tr*, nos. 2, 3, *c* (Margaret Thatcher), *b* (second from *l*). The Daily Telegraph: pages 98 *l*, 122 (teacher, farmer, 3 industrial photos). p50: *tc* Courtesy of Jaakko Poyry (UK) Limited. London Features International Limited: p104 *c*. Monitor Picture Library: p93 *tl, br*. Pictorial Press Limited: p110 *b* (second from *r*). Alan Philip: pages 6–7, 36, 64. The Press Association: p95 *t*. Doc Rowe: p105. Spectrum Colour Library: pages 36–37, 98 *r*. Sporting Pictures UK Limited: p95 *b*. Syndication International Limited: pages 110 *tc, cr*, nos. 1, 4, *bl*, 122 (housewife, nurse). John Topham Picture Library: pages 68, 74–75. p125: © United Kingdom Atomic Energy Authority, used with permission. Reg van Cuÿlenburg: pages 22, 63, 66–67. Catherine Walter: p8. Wiggins Teape Group: p50 *tr, br*. Jason Youé: pages 92 *tr, cr*, 93 *tr, cl, cr*, 125 *t*.

John Craddock: Malcolm Barter, pages 14 *t*, 37 *b*, 38–39, 58, 69 *b*, 78–79, 80–81; Alexa Rutherford, pages 20, 28, 59, 94, 108 *t*, 120; Kate Simunek, p57; Ian Fleming and Associates Limited: Terry Burton, p100; David Lewis Management: Odette Buchanan, pages 18, 45, 91, 112; Bob Harvey, pages 40, 41 *r*, 65, 69 *t*, 72, 88, 113, 121 *t*; Jon Miller, pages 10–11, 84, 121 *b*; Linda Rogers: Mike Whittlesea, pages 27, 44 *b*, 71 *l*, 82 *t*, 108 *b*, 114 *t*; Linden Artists Limited: Jon Davis, pages 30 *b*, 35, 70, 126–127; Val Sangster, pages 16, 24, 71 *r*, 96 *t*, 114 *b*.

Paul Davenport, pages 44 *t*, 52–53, 76; Paul Francis, pages 14 *b*, 15; Martin Gordon, p42; Gary Inwood, pages 41 *l*, 43, 73, 82 *b*, 123; Jane Molineaux, pages 26, 77; Chris Rawlings, pages 30 *t*, 33; Nik Spender, pages 12–13, 56, 83, 118, 132–133; Tony Streek, pages 23, 34, 54 *t*, 89, 119; Malcolm Ward, pages 19, 54 *b*, 86, 109, 111; Jack Wood, pages 51, 54 *b*, 55, 112; Mike Woodhatch, pages 106–107; John Youé & Associates.

(Abbreviations: *t*=top *b*=bottom *c*=centre *r*=right *l*=left)